The Warbler Guide

Tom Stephenson and Scott Whittle

Drawings by Catherine Hamilton

Princeton University Press
Princeton and Oxford

Requests for permission to reproduce material from this work
should be sent to Permissions, Princeton University Press
Published by Princeton University Press, 41 William Street,
Princeton, New Jersey 08540
In the United Kingdom: Princeton University Press,
6 Oxford Street, Woodstock, Oxfordshire OX20 1TW
press.princeton.edu
Cover photograph Northern Parula © Robert Royse
ISBN (pbk.) 978-0-691-15482-4
Library of Congress Control Number: 2012950887
British Library Cataloging-in-Publication Data is available
This book has been composed in Sabon LT Std and Gill Sans
Printed on acid-free paper. ∞
Printed in China
10 9 8 7 6 5 4 3 2

CONTENTS

The Warbler Guide

HOW TO USE THIS BOOK

Principal Sections of the Book

This book is designed to help you quickly and confidently identify the species and, when possible, the age and sex of any warbler you encounter in the United States and Canada. In light of this goal we have included the following sections:

Visual Finders are designed to help you quickly identify any warbler you see. These pages present the typical views you will encounter in the field: face, side, 45-degree, and underside. Each Visual Finder is organized by similar-looking plumages and some show just eastern or western birds. Since we include all similar species with each species account, it is usually necessary only to find an image close to the bird in question and then go right to that species' Species Account. Even if the initial choice turns out to be incorrect, the Comparison Species section of the Species Accounts should narrow the ID down to the correct warbler. Use the visual finders not only to identify unknown species but also to test and review your warbler identification skills.

Song and Call Finders help identify a vocalizing warbler and include songs, chip calls, and flight calls. The vocalizations are organized by similar-sounding species. Songs are further grouped using a simple and very effective "tree" system designed to narrow down the choices to one or a few species in the shortest number of steps. There is more information on how to use this section in How to Listen to Warbler Songs.

Topographic Tour and *What to Notice on a Warbler* provide guides to the key feather groups and features that are important for warbler identification. Some of the topics, such as feather contrast and understanding the undertail, are often overlooked by birders but are very valuable ID tools.

The Species Accounts include images of each species from three angles along with additional photos and notes on all similar species. This presentation should lead to the correct species even if the initial ID choice is incorrect. These pages also provide other important information including spring and fall migration paths, subspecies ranges, behavior and color impression icons, and other key ID points.

Aging and Sexing Sections in the Species Accounts help establish a bird's age and sex when possible. These sections are separate to avoid confusing the ID points for aging and sexing with the ID points needed for species identification.

Vocalization Information in the Species Accounts includes sonograms and direct comparisons with similar-sounding species. The ID points are based on a new, objective system for analyzing bird vocalizations that uses simple, easy-to-hear criteria, including a song's structure, quality, and other characteristics, and avoid traditional, often clumsy, transliterations. To take full advantage of this system, be sure to read How to Listen to Warbler Songs and Understanding Sonograms.

Quizzes offer a number of real-world ID problems to solve. Active testing greatly aids retention, so use this section to explore and reinforce your warbler ID knowledge.

Glossary. We have tried to keep all terminology as clear and jargon-free as possible. Of course technical terms are often needed for both precision and economy, and we have employed some of these as necessary. To save space, we have also had to use a few abbreviations, such as UnTC for "undertail coverts." Be sure to check the glossary for any terms you find unfamiliar. You can also use this section as a reference for the Song Analysis terminology and for abbreviations for the Aging and Sexing sections. The **Topographic Tour** is also a good resource if you are unclear about any of the terms used for feather groups or bare parts.

Other sections include *Similar Non-Warbler Species, North American Warbler Taxonomy,* and *Flight Shots.*

Alphabetical Order for the Species Accounts

To make each species fast to find, we have decided to put the Species Accounts in alphabetical order. This is a departure from the taxonomic organization of many prior field guides and deserves a note.

As shown in the **North American Warbler Taxonomy** section, the taxonomy of warblers has changed significantly in the last few years, and some species, such as Yellow-breasted Chat, are still not settled. If we were to follow current taxonomic order, we would necessarily change the prior, more familiar sequence, which would make some species more difficult to find in this book.

Also, the traditional order is actually treated very differently in many popular field guides. Species such as Cerulean, Northern Parula, and Palm Warblers are found in different locations in these books. In many previous field guides, genera were placed together so that similar-looking species could be more easily compared. *The Warbler Guide* accomplishes this by placing all similar species, including those in the same (or possibly now, new) genera, together in the Species Accounts for each relevant species.

For these reasons, we feel that placing North American warblers in alphabetical order will make all species much faster to find without sacrificing any comparative benefits.

Online Resources

At www.press.princeton.edu/titles/9968.html, we have included additional supporting materials such as quizzes, a chart of comparative song statistics, some guidelines for beginning birders, and other information.

ICONS AND KEY TERMS

To reduce the amount of text and to make the book faster to use in the field, in the Species Accounts we use various icons and codes, which are defined below.

√ Diagnostic Field Mark indicates that this field mark alone is always sufficient for a confident ID.

Shape and Color Icons It is often possible to identify or greatly narrow down an ID using just the shape and color of a bird. These can be important marks especially when a bird is seen very briefly or for picking out the rarer species in a large flock. For each species we have included shape and color icons to help sensitize your eye to these important warbler characteristics.

 Silhouettes show the shape of the species, sometimes an important aid to making a fast ID.

 Color Impression shows a generalized color diagram of the bird. It is often possible to identify or greatly narrow down an ID using just shape and color. This can be very important when a bird is seen briefly or when trying to pick out rarer species in a group of many active warblers.

 Tail Pattern shows the very important underside view from the vent to the end of the tail, including the undertail color pattern and the relative length of the tail and undertail coverts. Note we often abbreviate "undertail coverts" as "UnTC."

Quick Range Icon provides a fast way to see if the species is found in the eastern United States (east of the Rockies), western United States, the whole region, or in a very limited area (such as Big Bend, Texas).

East   **West**   **East and West**   **Southwest**   **Rare**

Preferred Habitat Icon indicates which habitat(s) the bird tends to prefer. Note that during migration many species utilize a wider range of habitats than they do on their breeding grounds.

| High Canopy | Mid-story | Under-story | Trunk and Limbs | Ground |

Behavioral Icon indicates typical behavior, an important characteristic that can often help quickly narrow an unknown bird to one or two species.

| Sally Feeding | Hover-Gleaning | Trunk Creeping | Walking on Ground | Tail Bobbing or Wagging | Tail Cocking |

Song Mnemonics present an image that can aid in memorizing the species' song. Creating an image that connects a bird's song to its name can greatly assist in remembering and recognizing the song in the field. When learning a new vocalization, it's not enough to know that you've studied a song sounding like "Please Please Please to meetcha." You also have to tie that song to the species' name. If you can visualize someone wearing a chestnut vest and a yellow cap saying this phrase, then your studies will translate better in the field.

For most species we propose an image that, for us, ties the structure of their song to their name. Since these connections are very subjective, we encourage you to use these as rough guidelines and to create your own images.

Song Analysis Symbols notate sonograms. As described in the section How to Listen to Warbler Songs, we have defined several terms that help us objectively describe the structure and quality of warbler vocalizations. Be sure to read that section to fully understand how we use these important terms. You can also find a full definition of each term in the glossary. In the sonogram layouts, we use the following symbols to highlight some of these structural characteristics and make them faster to scan and compare:

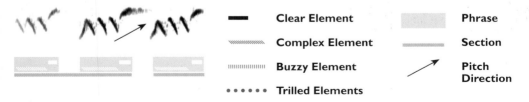

Clear Element   Phrase

Complex Element   Section

Buzzy Element   Pitch Direction

Trilled Elements

HOW TO USE THE MAPS

Migration Routes

Many warblers follow a similar route in spring and fall migration. However, some warbler species take different routes. As a result, one is unlikely to find a Connecticut Warbler in Central Park in May, but quite possibly could in late September. For this reason we are using two maps for some species, one each for its spring and fall migration paths.

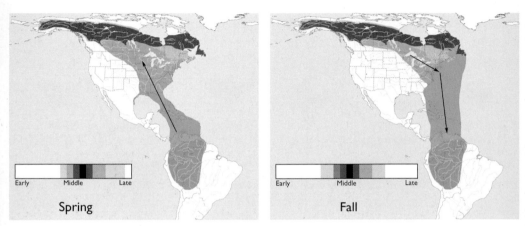

Blackpoll Warbler

Early, Middle, and Late Waves

From the arrival of the first migrant warbler to the departure of the final bird, migration lasts for a similar time span from year to year. In spring, northbound birds hit the southern edge of the United States first, and reach their northern regions about two or three weeks later. Fall migration is more drawn out than spring migration by a couple of weeks and is slightly less protracted in the northern areas, whereas spring migration is slightly shorter in the southern United States.

Rather than trying to establish precise migration dates for each species across the entire United States and Canada, we have broken both spring and fall into three equal periods, which we classify as early, middle, and late. In that way we establish a general sense of what's probable at any given time, regardless of the specific location or the vagaries of weather patterns. By using the range map and migration icon, general dates can be established for the occurrence of a species in a given location.

Time Spans

Some warbler species have an extended migration schedule, with individuals showing up over the course of many weeks, while other species seem to come all at once. The gray area in the migration icon indicates the length of migration for some species. Note that darker segments in the icon indicate a greater volume of birds.

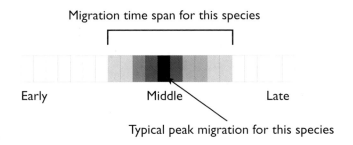

Subspecies

Several warbler species have one or more recognized subspecies (races). Some of these are difficult to separate in the field and others have recognizable plumage differences. On the maps, we show the distribution of subspecies. We also address the important field identification characteristics for each separable subspecies in the Species Accounts.

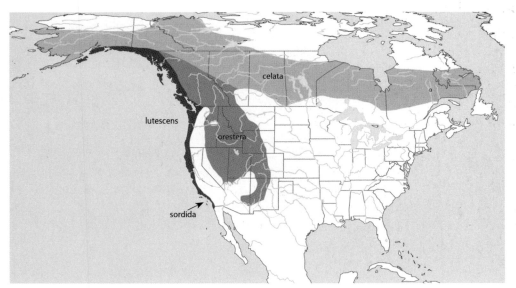

Subspecies of Orange-crowned Warbler

TOPOGRAPHIC TOUR

TERTIALS Innermost feathers of wing; when wing is folded, the top three stacked wing feathers

SECONDARIES Inner half of flight feathers; when folded, form middle layer of stacked wing feathers

PRIMARIES Outer nine flight feathers; when folded form bottom layer of stacked wing feathers and protrude beyond tertials and secondaries (this protrusion is called "primary projection")

RUMP Uppertail coverts to lower back

UPPERTAIL COVERTS Base of tail to rump

TAIL

UNDERTAIL COVERTS Legs to base of tail; cover base of tail

VENT Area betwen legs

MANTLE Central upper back

NAPE Back of neck

SHOULDER Includes scapulars and lesser coverts

THROAT Base of the bill to breast

WING BARS Formed by contrasting tips of greater and median secondary coverts

MEDIAN SECONDARY COVERTS Usually abbreviated to "median coverts"; cover base of greater coverts; when feather tips contrast feather bases, forms top line of wing bars

ALULA Covers base of primary coverts

GREATER SECONDARY COVERTS Usually abbreviated to "greater coverts"; cover bases of secondaries; when feather tips contrast with feather bases forms bottom line of wing bars

BREAST Below throat to above belly

PRIMARY COVERTS Cover bases of primaries

FLANKS Shoulder to belly next to wing

BELLY Below breast to legs

NAPE Back of neck

SHOULDER Includes scapulars and lesser coverts

MANTLE Central upper back

TERTIALS Innermost feathers of wing; when wing is folded, the top three stacked wing feathers

SECONDARIES Inner half of flight feathers; when folded, form middle layer of stacked wing feathers

PRIMARIES Outer nine flight flight feathers; when folded form bottom layer of stacked wing feathers and protrude beyond tertials and secondaries (this protrusion is called "primary projection")

RUMP Uppertail coverts to lower back

UPPERTAIL COVERTS Base of tail to rump

TAIL

THROAT Base of the bill to breast

BREAST Below throat to above belly

BELLY Below breast to legs

VENT Area betwen legs

UNDERTAIL COVERTS Legs to base of tail; cover base of tail

TAIL

SUPERCILIUM "Eyebrow"; area of contrast above eye

EYELINE Dark line that usually runs through eye; if line is only behind eye then called *post-ocular* line, if only in front of the eye then called *dark lores*

CROWN Top of head; sometimes shows central crown stripe

SUPRALORAL Above lores, in front of eye; part of a supercilium that extends in front of eye

CHEEK PATCH Below and behind eye

LORES Between eye and bill

MALAR AREA Borders the throat; can be same color as surrounding feathers, consist of contrasting colors, or just show a thin line

EYE-ARCS / EYERING Partial or complete ring around eye

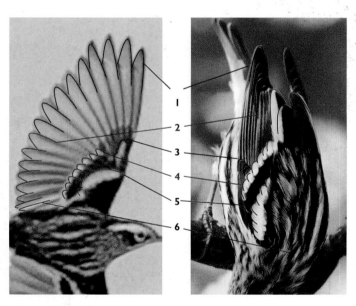

1
2
3
4
5
6

1. PRIMARIES Outer nine flight flight feathers; when folded form bottom layer of stacked wing feathers and protrude beyond tertials and secondaries (this protrusion is called "primary projection")

2. SECONDARIES Inner half of flight feathers; when folded, form middle layer of stacked wing feathers

3. PRIMARY COVERTS Cover bases of primaries

4. GREATER SECONDARY COVERTS Usually abbreviated to "greater coverts"; cover bases of secondaries; when feather tips contrast with feather bases form bottom line of wing bars

5. MEDIAN SECONDARY COVERTS Usually abbreviated to "median coverts"; cover base of greater coverts; when feather tips contrast feather bases, forms top line of wing bars

6. TERTIALS Innermost feathers of wing; when wing is folded, the top three stacked wing feathers

WHAT TO NOTICE ON A WARBLER

This section illuminates important warbler characteristics that can be used to significantly accelerate the identification process. There are five sections: Contrast and Color; Size, Shape, and Behavior; The Face; The Body; and The Undertail.

Section 1: Contrast and Color

Contrast One of the primary ways to separate warblers is by contrast. The birds in the Visual Finders are easily separated into two categories: high-contrast birds, which have bold markings and colors, and low-contrast birds, which are drab or plain. There are two basic types of contrast: tonal contrast, when adjacent areas are brighter and darker; and color contrast, where different colors intersect (for example, black and yellow are highly contrasting, while yellow and olive are not). These two types of contrast are not mutually exclusive—often a bird with high tonal contrast also has strong color contrast.

Orange-crowned Low-contrast overall; mostly the same tone and color.

American Redstart High-contrast bird in both color and tonality.

Yellow Bright-colored, low-contrast bird.

Black-and-white No color, high contrast.

The well-defined, high-contrast throat of a Common Yellowthroat is especially distinct when color contrast is removed from the equation.

Nashville Higher color contrast, but low tonal contrast in body, with contrasty eyering.

Common Yellowthroat Low color contrast, but isolated, tonally high-contrast throat.

General contrast manifests in several ways on a bird, one of which is the contrast between the lower body and the upper body and wings.

Prothonotary High contrast between the lower and upper halves of the bird.

Hooded Mid-contrast between the upper and lower body.

Yellow Low-contrast body overall.

Hooding occurs when the head color contrasts with the body color.

MacGillivray's High-contrast hood.

Orange-crowned Low-contrast hood.

Wing bars are created by white tips on the greater and median coverts and can be a striking and very important ID characteristic. There are more subtle but equally important contrasting covert patterns in the wings that are also worth noticing.

Blackpoll Strong, contrasting wing bars.

Palm Buffy edging subtly contrasts with rest of feathers, creating diagnostic pattern.

Yellow Yellow on olive is a low-contrast combination, but wing bars are still distinct.

Prairie Yellow wing bars on gray or olive makes for distinctive mid-contrast wing bars.

Facial contrast is sometimes useful in separating similar birds. Townsend's and Black-throated Green warblers are similarly shaped; both have black streaking in the sides, a black throat, and both are masked and capped. In fact, at first their faces seem very similar, but the degree of contrast becomes a key ID point.

Townsend's Auriculars and cap, high-contrast black on yellow; always dark throughout.

Black-throated Green auriculars and cap, low contrast olive on yellow; auriculars always lighter in center.

Likewise, Orange-crowned and Tennessee are similar in structure and coloration. While Tennessee has white undertail coverts and Orange-crowned has yellow undertail coverts, facial contrast can be a quicker way to separate them.

Orange-crowned Lower contrast, "even" look to facial tones, washed overall in yellow and olive.

Tennessee Higher facial contrast overall: lighter areas lighter and darker areas darker; eyeline and supercilium more pronounced.

Many warblers have bright, contrasting facial features in spring that make them easy to identify—Cape May, Blackburnian, Prairie, and Wilson's, for example. These same patterns are often present and equally diagnostic in the fall, but in a lower-contrast form.

Blackburnian, spring Shape of high-contrast cheek patch is diagnostic.

Blackburnian, fall Cheek patch pattern basically same, but lower contrast.

Color One of the delightful things about warblers is their color, which can quickly lead to an accurate identification. Note, however, that more than half of the warblers in this book lack any really distinctive colors, so it is also important to be aware of qualities like contrast and shape, and markings like wing bars and streaking.

Diagnostic colors occur on a few birds and can lead to an instant ID.

Prothonotary Distinctive golden hue, contrasting blue wings/olive back.

Blackburnian, spring Flame-orange face unmistakable.

It is often helpful to think of not one color, but rather of a combination of colors, because certain color combinations are sometimes unique to a species.

Northern Parula Powder-blue head, green back patch, yellow throat.

Cerulean Bright blue hood, white throat.

Worm-eating Brown mustard head with black stripes.

For many species it's important to notice subtle variations of color.

Yellow-throated Gray hood and back are distinctive cool, blue-gray shade, with white wing bars.

Golden-winged Gray head and body are warmer yellow tone, with yellow wing bars.

Subtle color differences can be an excellent starting point for identification. Note the different types of blue here in four species of warbler:

Northern Parula
Powder blue.

Canada
Slate blue.

Cerulean
Sky blue.

Black-throated Blue
Ocean blue.

Lighting conditions can strongly affect a bird's appearance. At sunrise or sunset, all birds seem warm, with unexpected yellow or pink tones.

Black-and-white Seen in early dawn light, looks orangey-pink; often appears bluish in flight in normal daylight.

Section 2: Size, Shape, Habitat, and Behavior

Before focusing on the specifics of plumage, it is a good practice to look at size, shape, and behavior. Like a sculptor starting with a block of marble, it is critical in identification to work on the most general characteristics first and then proceed to the fine details.

Size Size is especially useful for separating warblers from other species, such as larger orioles, tanagers, and vireos. The following silhouettes are shown in accurate proportion to each other.

Scarlet Tanager 7 in., significantly larger; also note blunter, larger bill and longer tail; more vertically perched.

Yellow Warbler 5 in., smaller; also note smaller bill and shorter tail; perches more horizontally.

Baltimore Oriole 8.75 in., significantly larger; also note long, decurved bill and longer tail; more vertically perched.

Red-eyed Vireo 6 in., larger; also note heavier, larger bill and more pronounced head.

Many warblers are of similar size: small warblers are around 4.5 in. long, average-size warblers are around 5 in., and large ones can be 5.5 in. or larger. Sometimes these size differences can help differentiate similar warbler species without one ever having to go into plumage specifics. Note that size is often noticed through a bird's movements: larger birds tend to be slower moving, while very small birds are often quick and flitting.

Louisiana Waterthrush Largest of the warblers, 6 in. and 0.74 oz. (15.2 cm, 20.9 g).

Lucy's Smallest of the warblers, 4.25 in. and 0.23 oz. (10.8 cm, 6.5 g).

Virginia's Small and active, 4.6 in. (12 cm).

Colima Similar to Virginia's but 1 in. longer at 5.7 in. (14.5 cm).

Connecticut Large, slow-moving ground dweller, 5.7 in. (14.5 cm).

Nashville Smallish, very active, 4.75 in. (12 cm).

Shape Like size, shape is most important when separating warblers from other non-warbler species. The following silhouettes are all sized the same (despite different actual sizes) to emphasize the differences in shape.

Yellow Warbler Average warbler body size and bill, shortish tail.

Kinglet Finer bill, proportionally large head.

House Sparrow Blunt, conical bill, distinct head, bulkier overall.

Gnatcatcher Very long tail, fine bill, long legs.

Differences between warbler shapes can be more subtle. Differences do exist, though, and with careful attention these can be quite useful.

Yellow-breasted Chat Large bill with curved culmen, bulky overall, head distinct.*

Yellow-rumped Large head, squarish, bulky body.

Pine More elongate, longer tail, longer bill than Blackpoll.

Blackpoll Shorter bill, deeper chest, shorter tail, plumper looking than Pine.

Similarities are also notable: many closely related warbler species are similarly shaped.

Nashville genus *Oreothlypis* Small with a fine bill.

Orange-crowned genus *Oreothlypis* Small with a fine bill.

*Yellow-breasted Chat is very likely not a warbler, based on DNA research, but is still grouped with them in some taxonomic lists.

Habitat is useful in terms of probability. A warbler high in a tree is most likely not a Common Yellowthroat (although it can occur there), and a warbler walking along a streambed is unlikely to be a Cerulean.

Waterthrush Most regularly found along bodies of water and spends much of its time on the ground.

Red-faced Usually at higher elevations and only in the southwestern United States.

Prothonotary Rarely seen outside of wet woods or swampy habitat.

Cerulean Rarely low to the ground on breeding grounds (although sometimes it is low in migration).

Behavior is an excellent starting place in identification. Non-warbler species often behave quite differently from warblers, and some warbler behavior is diagnostic.

Connecticut Regular ground dweller and walks rather than hops, unlike most other warblers.

Black-and-white Characteristically creeps along tree trunks and branches, probing with long bill for insects.

Redstart Often flashes tail and wings while feeding.

Yellow-rumped Often flocks together, especially in fall and winter.

Section 3: The Face

Almost every warbler in North America can be identified by face alone. The more sensitive your eye becomes to facial marks, the better able you will be to ID warblers, especially when only partial views are available. This section addresses *cheek patches, masks, eyerings and eye-arcs, superciliums, top-of-head markings, bills,* and *throats.*

Cheek patches, or *auriculars*, are contrastingly darker areas behind and below the eye.

Blackburnian Distinctive triangular cheek patch.

Cape May Ovoid, rufous cheek patch.

Wilson's, female Subtle but distinctive cheek patch, similar in color to nape, outlined above by pale supercilium.

Hooded, female Very faint cheek patch, dark hood, higher facial contrast than Wilson's.

Masks and other black facial marks are found on about a third of the warblers discussed in this book, often providing distinct ID points.

Golden-winged Black face patch creates a "Zorro mask" effect.

Blackburnian Dark facial marks form a triangular pattern.

Prairie These facial marks are distinct but not easily categorized.

Black-throated Blue Black face but not strongly contrasting due to dark hood and back.

These four "black-throated" warblers each have distinctive facial markings.

Black-throated Green low-contrast cheek patch and eyeline, creating faded olive facial pattern.

Hermit No facial marks, "blank-faced" look.

Townsend's Black eyeline and cheek patch create contrasty facial pattern.

Golden-cheeked Dark eyeline (mostly behind eye), no cheek patch.

Eyerings and eye-arcs are the circles or partial circles around some warbler's eyes.

Orange-crowned Thin, low-contrast, subtle eye-arcs.

Canada Bright, contrasting, wide eyering.

These three elusive, ground-dwelling warblers are separable as adults by their eyerings, eye-arcs, or lack thereof.

Connecticut, adult Pronounced eyering.

MacGillivray's, adult Thick eye-arcs.

Mourning, adult No eyering.

In each of these pairs, the eyering helps separate two similar warbler species:

Prothonotary No eyering: "beady-eyed."

Yellow Subtle yellow eyering.

Nashville Strong, contrasting, white eyering.

Common Yellowthroat Subtle, thinner, duller eyering.

In these examples, the eyering merges with the supraloral area to create a "goggled" effect.

Canada Yellow goggles.

Yellow-breasted Chat White goggles.

Eyelines are dark lines through the eye, often extending on both sides.

Yellow Plain yellow face, no eyeline.

Golden-cheeked Plain yellow face with eyeline.

Some drab fall warblers have differences in their eyelines, which contribute to different facial expressions:

Pine Faint eyeline darker in front of eyes (lores).

Bay-breasted Visible eyeline, but short and fine.

Blackpoll Longer, wider eyeline.

Lores are partial eyelines in front of the eye, and *post-ocular lines* are partial eyelines behind the eye.

American Restart Eyeline appears in front of eye: "dark lores."

Lucy's Pale lores, i.e., no dark in front of eye.

Black-and-white Eyeline is behind eye: called a post-ocular line.

The supercilium is a light contrasting area above the eye that often creates an "eye-brow" effect.

Tennessee Narrow, low-contrast supercilium.

Worm-eating Bright, contrasting supercilium.

Northern Waterthrush More even supercilium, tapering at back of head, same color as underbody.*

Louisiana Waterthrush Flared supercilium, wraps farther around back of head, white.*

Yellow-rumped "Broken" supercilium intercepted by brighter eyering.

Palm Complete, wider, more contrasty supercilium.

*Note: The shape of the supercilium is a classic mark used to separate the otherwise similar Louisiana and Northern waterthrushes. While the Northern Waterthrush generally has an even-width or rear-tapering supercilium, the Louisiana can show a "flared" supercilium, which is narrow at the lores, gets progressively wider behind the eye, then sharply tapers at the back of the head, and typically extends all the way to the intersection of the head and back. We say "generally" because the apparent shape and length of the supercilium can be tricky to see and can change with the bird's posture. There is more information on separating these birds, including marks that we like even better than the supercilium, on the waterthrush pages.

Top-of-head markings *Capped*, *hooded*, and *striped* are terms for the contrasting color area on top of some warblers' heads. *Hooded* birds have a colored head that contrasts with the body, *capped* birds have a dark upper head that contrasts with the face, and birds with *striped heads* have contrasting lines on their upper head.

Wilson's Black, beret-like cap inspires the mnemonic "Mr. Wilson is from Paris."

Wilson's, female (eastern) Faint cap still visible.

Connecticut Strongly hooded.

Hooded Hooded with a yellow face.

Ovenbird Orange and black head stripes.

Worm-eating Brown-mustard and black head stripes.

Each of these colored caps is distinctive.

Palm, spring Pronounced rufous cap.

Golden-winged Yellow cap, gray nape.

Bay-breasted, adult male Brick-red cap, diagnostic.

Chestnut-sided, fall Green upper head connects with back, so not technically "capped" but useful.

Chestnut-sided, spring Yellow cap.

Red-faced Black cap with earflaps, diagnostic.

Bills vary among warblers, especially across genera. For example, warblers in the genus *Geothlypis*, which includes Mourning, MacGillivray's, and Kentucky, all have relatively large bills. *Vermivora* and *Oreothlypis* (until 2010 considered the same genus)—Golden-winged, Blue-winged, Lucy's, Colima, Orange-crowned, Tennessee, Virginia's, and Nashville—have fine, pointed bills.

Bill shape and size have a lot to do with the feeding habits of birds. Mourning, MacGillivray's, and Kentucky feed on invertebrates on the ground and like to probe and push aside leaves, hence their heavier bills. *Vermivora* often glean insects from bark and nectar from flowers hence their fine, pointed bills.

Geothlypis **(Mourning)** Long, heavy bill.

Oreothlypis **(Nashville)** Fine, pointed bill.

Bill size can be tricky to differentiate on similar warbler species (especially in the large genus *Setophaga*), and it is often more of a supporting feature. Some species, however, have bills that are noticeably different.

Blackpoll Straight, blunt bill.

Black-and-white Longer, slightly decurved bill for probing bark.

Northern Waterthrush Wide, blunt, long bill.

Swainson's Pointed, spike-like bill, emphasized by sloped forehead.

Canada Average bill shape for a warbler.

Yellow-breasted Chat Atypical bill for a warbler; heavy with a decurved culmen (upper ridge of bill).

Bill color may vary in some warblers depending on age. In a couple of species, the bill is distinctly bicolored: black on top and pale on bottom.

Wilson's Bicolored bill (pink lower mandible).

Northern Parula Bicolored bill (orange lower mandible blends with throat).

Bill shape and size contribute to a warbler's silhouette and general appearance and provide excellent separators to differentiate a warbler from other types of birds such as vireos, flycatchers, and orioles (see the section Non-Warbler Similar Species for more details on these birds).

Red-eyed Vireo Large, hooked bill, common to many vireos.

Orchard Oriole Long, decurved bill is unlike any warbler bill.

The throat is the transitional area from below the bill to the top of the breast.

Northern Parula Strongly contrasting throat with colored bands.

Common Yellowthroat Isolated throat contrasts with both face and body.

Nashville Lower-contrast throat blends with breast.

Throat streaking can be useful in identifying Cape May and the waterthrushes.

Cape May Fine, even streaking extends from upper breast into throat.

Northern Waterthrush Usually at least some throat streaking.

Louisiana Waterthrush Usually lacks throat streaking.

Throat color is most helpful for ID purposes when it strongly contrasts with the rest of the head. For example, a strongly contrasting black throat narrows the ID choices to a small group of warblers:

Townsend's

Black-throated Green

Golden-cheeked

Hermit

Golden-winged

Lawrence's

Black-throated Gray

Hooded

The malar stripe is the contrasting line that runs from the base of the bill to the top of the shoulder along the side of the throat.

Blackpoll, spring Strong, black malar stripe.

Blackpoll, fall Faint malar stripe.

Bay-breasted No malar stripe.

Section 4: The Body

Warblers are often seen in partial view, and knowing the specifics of body topography can often be an important advantage in making an ID. To that end, this section addresses the *breast, belly, and flanks*; *the back and rump*; and *the wings*.

The breast, belly, and flanks make up the underbody of a warbler between the throat and legs. The breast is the "chest" of the bird, and the flanks are the sides below the wings and above the legs on a standing bird.

Body streaking can be important in ID.

Orange-crowned May show low contrast breast streaking.

Townsend's High contrast side streaks.

Blackpoll Always shows some degree of breast streaking.

Bay-breasted Always shows clear breast, though ruffled feathers may look mottled.

Nashville Wet or ruffled birds can show streak-like mottling.

Streaks can be closely spaced (dense) or widely spaced (sparse), and they can be evenly distributed or clumped.

Magnolia Uneven, clumped streaks.

Yellow-throated Even streaking.

Northern Waterthrush Averages denser streaking than Louisiana.

Louisiana Waterthrush Averages sparser streaking than Northern.

Only a few warbler species have colored streaking (not brown or black) on their breast, which is always diagnostic.

Yellow Red streaking contrasts with yellow body.

Palm, spring Rufous streaking.

Cerulean Blue streaking.

Necklaces are a pattern of streaking across the breast, which can be an important ID mark. Notice the full or partial necklace effect in these birds:

Canada Strong black, isolated necklace.

Magnolia Black necklace connected to side streaks.

Yellow-rumped Side-streaking can connect at throat, but not on all birds.

Prairie Partial necklace broken at the throat creates strong shoulder mark.

Cerulean Thin throat stripe.

Side stripes are a very important ID point shared by three warbler species. Such stripes consist of a single, thick band of color than runs along the side and flank.

Black-throated Blue Black sidestripe.

Chestnut-sided Wine-colored sidestripe.

Bay-breasted Rusty side stripe.

Color of breast and flanks is sometimes diagnostic.

Northern Parula Orange and/or black on yellow breast diagnostic.

Prothonotary Glowing golden-orange tone is unique.

The extent of breast color and how it blends with adjacent areas is important.

Northern Parula Strong contrast between yellow throat and white belly.

Magnolia Breast color ends abruptly.

Blackburnian Blending of breast and belly colors.

Canada Yellow throat with darker gray back; yellow of breast extends below legs.

Yellow-breasted Chat Yellow breast, darker back, yellow ends before legs.

Black-throated Green White breast, sometimes with small amount of very light yellow below the black.

Townsend's Extensive, striking yellow on breast.

Bay-breasted Rusty flank stripe extending to throat; creamy tones in breast.

Chestnut-sided Wine-colored flank stripe, with white breast and throat.

The back and rump are the upper parts of the bird. The back color can bleed into the head and rump or can stand out on its own.

Yellow Yellow head color and dusky yellow back color blend together.

Prothonotary Green back and blue wings strongly contrast with bright yellow head.

Tennessee, spring Often shows contrast between head and back.

Tennessee, fall Often does not show strong contrast between head and back.

Orange-crown, spring Often no contrast between head and back, especially on West Coast.

Orange-crown, fall May show contrast between head and back.

Back streaking occurs in many warblers.

Bay-breasted, fall Always shows back streaking.

Blackpoll, fall Shows some back streaking.

Pine No back streaks.

Blackburnian In all plumages, pair of pale lines called braces run down darker back.

Blackburnian, fall Braces, but paler.

Patches are squares of contrasting color on the center of the back found on a couple of warbler species, and can be diagnostic.

Northern Parula Olive back patch contrasts with powder blue back.

Prairie Rufous spotting creates a distinctive back patch.

The rump is the lower back, above the base of the tail. For many birds the rump is the same color as the back, but a few have a contrasting rump color.

Yellow-rumped Named for bright rump, often signals other birds with flash of yellow.

Magnolia Strong, contrasting rump color, seems to flash it less frequently than Yellow-rumped.

Lucy's Diagnostic contrasting rufous rump.

Cape May Yellow rump patch in all seasons.

Not all rump patches are created equal. While some species have small areas of strongly contrasting color, others have a more diffuse patch that extends all the way across the lower back. Diffuse patches are often overlooked but can be important ID points.

Nashville Diffuse rump patch.

Palm Diffuse brownish-yellow rump patch blends with brighter yellow undertail coverts.

Wings often have contrasting wing bars created by the contrasting tips of the greater and median coverts.

Yellow-rumped, fall Thin, but contrasting, wing bars.

Palm, fall Very low-contrast, buffy wing bars.

Yellow Low-contrast, yellow wing bars on olive-yellow wings.

Blackpoll High-contrast, wide, white wing bars.

Tennessee Faint, thin, low-contrast, yellow-olive wing bars.

It can be very useful to notice the color and contrast of the area between a bird's two wing bars.

Pine Relatively low-contrast gray between wing bars.

Bay-breasted Higher-contrast black between wing bars.

Wing panels occur when the pale covert edges are more extensive, causing the wing bars to become a solid block of color, and are found on breeding-season males in some species.

Blackburnian Wing panel with black intruding into base.

Magnolia Broad wing panel.

Cape May Narrower wing panel.

One species shows a more restricted patch, created by white bases of the primaries. Commonly referred to as a "handkerchief," it is not found on all individuals (specifically some first-year female birds), but it is diagnostic when present.

Black-throated Blue, female Shows pronounced handkerchief.

Black-throated Blue, male Extended wing shows white bases of primaries.

Flight-feather edging is a subtle but useful quality on some warbler wings and can be contrasting, colored, or both.

Yellow Yellow tertial and flight-feather edging combined with yellow in tail is diagnostic.

Nashville Intense yellow edging in flight and tail feathers, a good separator from Virginia's.

Blackpoll Strong white edging on tertials and primary tips.

Pine Lower contrast tertial edging.

Cape May Greenish edging to flight feathers (also found in Nashville).

Primary projection is how far the tips of the folded primaries extend past the tertials on the folded wing (see diagram in *Topographic Tour*). In other types of birds, such as shorebirds or flycatchers, the primary projection can be very useful for ID. On warblers, however, it is only regularly useful in a few ID problems, two of which are Blackpoll and Bay-breasted Warbler versus Pine, and Tennessee versus Orange-crowned.

Pine Shorter wings (generally short-distance migrants), short primary projection.

Blackpoll Longer wings (long-distance migrants), long primary projection.

The contrast between wing color and body color is also useful at times. One subtle example is the bluish cast of the female Wilson's warbler's wing contrasting with its body and back, unlike that of Yellow or Hooded warblers.

Wilson's Higher-contrast: bluish-cast wing with olive body.

Yellow Low-contrast: dark yellow-edged wings against lighter yellow body.

Hooded Low-contrast: olive wing with yellow body.

Section 5: The Undertail

Even from high overhead, warblers offer many important clues to their identity through the undertail. When a warbler is perched on a twig or branch, the main view offered is often from the legs back to the tail. This view shows the warbler's lower breast, vent, undertail coverts, and folded tail. In combination these areas offer important ID information that can be diagnostic or at least conclusive when combined with one or two other points such as throat color. In this section we cover what to look for in each of these areas and how to use them as a group to help identify a warbler.

A few cautionary notes about looking at warblers from below. First, be aware of lighting and shadows, because they can have a powerful effect on a bird's appearance.

Black-throated Green Backlit white tail appears dark.

Black-throated Green Better light reveals actual white tail color.

Second, birds do not always hold their tails neatly, and this can make them look very different from their "normal" pattern.

Black-throated Blue
Illustration shows idealized view.

Black-throated Blue Ruffled, odd-looking tail.

Black-throated Blue Much cleaner tail, closer to illustration.

Finally, in some situations molt can cause the tail to look odd.

Grace's Molt (especially in July and August) can make tail feathers uneven and hard to read.

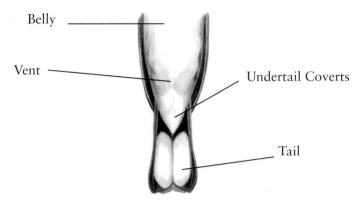

Belly

Vent

Undertail Coverts

Tail

The belly is the area just in front of the vent. We will only consider a small portion of the very bottom of the belly. Of course, the full body color offers more clues, but often this full view is not available.

Northern Parula Upper breast is yellow, but partial views only show a white belly, which can be confusing when one expects to see yellow on that species.

The vent is the small area between the legs, below the lower breast and above the undertail coverts. It often has more "texture" or fluffiness than the belly feathers or undertail coverts. In general, the color of the vent blends into the color of the belly, but there are useful exceptions.

Black-throated Green Vent has distinctively placed, unique green-yellow color.

Cape May Vent often has orangey-yellow color.

Undertail coverts are multiple rows of feathers extending from the vent: the lowermost cover the base of the tail. The length and color of these feathers is often important. The length of the undertail coverts (abbreviated "UnTC") greatly influences how we perceive the overall length of the tail from below. For tails of the same length, long undertail coverts cover more of the tail and make the tail seem shorter, while short undertail coverts cover less of the tail and make it appear longer.

Northern Parula From below, long UnTC make tail appear shorter relative to body.

Northern Parula From above, more tail visible and appears longer.

Some undertail coverts have unique patterns that are diagnostic.

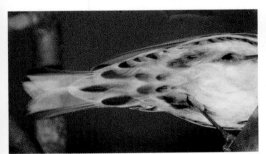

Black-and-white Large, arrow-like black spots in UnTC are diagnostic.

Worm-eating Buffy patches in UnTC unique.

Tail characteristics include length, color, width, and extension past the undertail coverts. Each of these can help distinguish among warbler species, as well as separate warblers from non-warblers.

The tail extension when seen from below is the length of the tail beyond the undertail coverts. Here, Blackpoll (and Bay-breasted) are easily differentiated from Pine by the tail extension: the long undertail coverts and long wings of the Blackpoll emphasize the short-looking tail, while Pine has a much longer tail accentuated by relatively shorter wings.

Blackpoll Short tail extension.

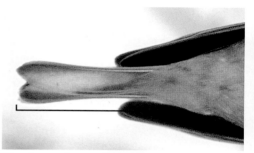

Pine Long tail extension.

Tail extension versus undertail covert length is often an important comparison.

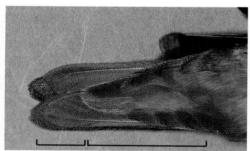

Connecticut Short tail with long UnTC.

Mourning Medium tail with longish UnTC.

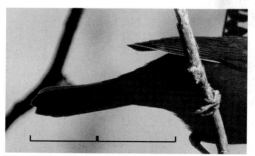

MacGillivray's Long tail with medium UnTC.

Outer tail feathers When looking at a tail from below we see the two outermost tail feathers, which are folded under the rest of the tail feathers. The apparent color of the tail, then, depends on the coloration of these outer tail feathers.

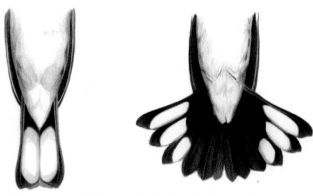

Yellow-rumped Tail shown both closed and spread open; note that location of white in tail results in black edging at tip and base.

Tail color on warblers falls into four basic categories.

All-dark tails in warblers are usually not black but, rather, some shade of gray. Depending on the light, these tails can range in appearance from near-black to light and silvery. They never look really white, unlike tails with white spots or all-white outer feathers. It's important to become sensitive to this difference, as casually identifying a silvery tail as white can lead to misidentifications.

Orange-crowned Dark tail appears silvery in direct light.

Wilson's Dark tail appears slate gray in open light.

All-white or white with dark borders occur if the outer tail feather is all white or nearly so. Some tails look completely white, but others have a black or dark edge, particularly at the tail corners. Some species, such as Hooded Warbler, flash the white of their outer tail feathers in a distinctive way.

Chestnut-sided All-white tail with dark borders.

Hooded Flashing outer white tail feathers.

Dark with white tail spots is the most common configuration. From below, the tail looks partly white, with the patches of white surrounded by dark.

Yellow-rumped Closed undertail; note the black border all the way around central white spots.

Yellow-rumped Spread tail showing white tail spots.

Palm Warbler has very little dark on the tail edges but boasts a wide, square area of black at the base of the tail. This is the nearly reverse of the Magnolia Warbler's tail pattern and is also diagnostic.

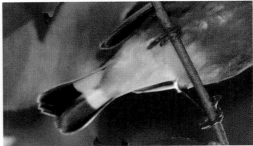

Palm Large white tail tip with large square black base.

Magnolia White tail with a wide black tip (pattern diagnostic).

When a bird is flying you can often see the limited white of tail spots or the more extensive white of mostly white tail feathers.

Magnolia From above shows white spots high on the tail, which help create its unique undertail pattern; view diagnostic from above and below.

Pine Warbler has a long, mostly white tail, with some dark visible on the outer edges and at the base of the tail extending like a "V" around the undertail coverts. This pattern of dark can separate Pine from other white-tailed warblers, like Black-throated Green and Chestnut-sided.

Pine Shows dark "V" at base of tail.

Colored Color occurs in some warbler tails and is always diagnostic.

American Redstart Tail with orange or yellow base and a wide black tip diagnostic.

Yellow Almost completely yellow tail; even drab birds show strong yellow in tail.

Color combinations and patterns Warbler undertails show many color combinations that are useful for ID. In the Undertail Finder, we group species based on the color and pattern of the undertail and indicate which combinations are diagnostic.

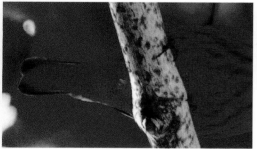

Yellow Yellow UnTC and yellow tail diagnostic.

Wilson's Gray tail contrasts with yellow UnTC.

Tennessee Contrasting white or buff UnTC an important separating mark; also note stubby tail barely projects beyond UnTC.

Orange-crowned UnTC same tone or more yellow than belly; also note longish, dark tail.

Tail movements Some warblers have characteristic tail movements that can be useful ID points. We note these in the Species Accounts, but here are some examples:

Constant, strong up-and-down tail bobbing: Palm, Waterthrushes

Often wags tail while foraging: Wilson's, Blackpoll, Pine, Nashville, Prairie, Kirtland's

Fans tail while foraging: American Redstart, Painted Redstart

Regularly flashes white in tail: Prothonotary, Hooded, Yellow-rumped

Holds tail loosely: Pine, Redstart

American Redstart Frequently fans tail, showing off distinctive pattern.

Yellow-rumped Flashing white in tail.

American Redstart Often holds tail loosely, creating clublike shape (thinner base with bulbous tip).

Pine Long tail held loosely and often appears strongly notched at tip as a result.

AGING AND SEXING WARBLERS

After identifying a warbler, there is another ID process to pursue: determining the age and sex of the bird. In the past, aging and sexing was largely relegated to banders—people who catch and tag birds for study. The excellent Pyle guide (*Identification Guide to North American Birds*, parts I and II, by Peter Pyle) is the standard handbook for this activity. Although it has useful aging and sexing information, it focuses primarily on measurements and other "in hand" criteria that often cannot be discerned with binoculars. In this book we have compiled only the characteristics we think are reasonably visible in the field using binoculars. If there are ID marks or measurements that cannot be seen with good views of the bird, we have excluded them.

The important points for this process are frequently different than those for species identification. Rather than commingle interspecies ID points with aging and sexing ID points, we are presenting the latter in a separate section within each of the Species Accounts. To avoid any confusion about what is and isn't separable, we show or note each of the possible plumage states and indicate which can and cannot be determined in the field. Crisp, high-resolution photos of a bird can be very helpful when using this section and may permit use of even some of the more subtle characteristics noted in the Pyle guide, such as feather wear.

There is a range in how possible it is to age and sex warbler species. Some, such as Black-throated Blue, can be aged and sexed reliably much of the time. Other species, such as Golden-winged, can be reliably sexed, but not as easily aged. The plumage characteristics of the different ages and sexes of some species have a smooth transition, or cline, from bright adult males to drab first-year females, with many overlapping states. Thus a drab adult male and a bright adult female can share the same colors, and for these species, only the very brightest and very drabbest individuals can be safely separated—Blue-winged is a good example. For many of these species, knowing how to appraise a bright or drab individual can also be difficult, and only birders with extensive field experience can accurately separate the ages and sexes for these difficult cases.

Finally, there are birds that usually cannot be aged or sexed at all, including the Waterthrushes, Ovenbird, and Swainson's Warbler. In all cases, when one is trying to determine the age and sex of an individual warbler, the viewing conditions, oddities of molt or feather wear, and overlap between plumages must all be taken into account, and if a bird doesn't have clear characteristics, then it is best left uncategorized.

Plumages and Molt

Molt is the process by which birds replace their worn feathers. Warblers have a fairly simple molt scheme (compared to gulls, for example), and this section provides a summary of the stages through which most species develop.

Adult Fall Plumage

All birds not hatched that summer do a complete postbreeding molt in late summer (called the prebasic molt), during which they progressively replace all of their feathers. The resulting plumage is called definitive basic and is worn by the bird as it migrates in the fall to its wintering grounds. It may seem a bit counterintuitive, but the birds with the freshest feathers are actually the fall birds, not the spring birds!

Juvenal and First-Year Fall Plumage

After hatching, young birds wear a unique juvenal plumage very briefly when they leave the nest. Soon after—well before they leave the breeding grounds and their adult attendees—they do a partial molt (called the preformative molt) to a first-year fall plumage (technically, the formative plumage). During this molt, they replace all of their body feathers, but retain their juvenal tail feathers and many wing feathers, including primaries, secondaries, alula, primary coverts, and sometimes a few greater coverts, median coverts and/or some tertials.

The retained juvenal feathers are weaker than the adult feathers and are in place until the next year's postbreeding molt, so the following summer these feathers may be over a year old. Through their first winter, and the following breeding season, these retained feathers become progressively more worn—and often duller or browner—than the replaced feathers. This difference in color of the retained alula, flight feathers, and primary coverts with that of the rest of the nearby feathers can sometimes be seen in the field or in good photos and is called molt limit. The presence of a molt limit generally indicates a first-year bird.

First-year birds molt (Preformative Molt) The areas in red indicate the feathers that are never molted by juvenal birds. These feathers will be retained for a year or longer, until the bird molts to its adult basic plumage.

The contrast between the greater coverts and the nearby alula and primary coverts can be particularly useful. If some of the greater or median coverts have been retained, then this difference is even easier to see, because fresh and worn feathers will be right next to each other and the contrast will be more evident. In the spring it can be more difficult to use these marks, because adult flight feathers will be more worn, and some species replace some of their greater coverts during a prealternate molt (see below), which will then show differences in wear even in adults.

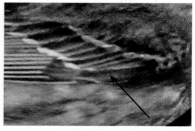

Molt Limit in Flight Feathers Notice that the alula and primary coverts are dull brown, while the greater coverts are black. This indicates two feather ages, and a first-year bird.

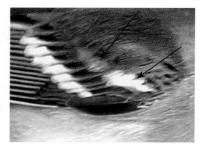

Molt Limit in Median Coverts Here there are two different ages of coverts: older, more worn and yellow coverts above; and fresher, whiter coverts below, indicating a first-year bird (sex unknown).

Another plumage difference in some warbler species is tail shape. First-year birds, especially those in the genus *Setophaga*, often have more pointed or tapered tail feathers than adults. However, since this characteristic is extremely difficult to see in the field, and requires experience to use when seen, it is beyond the scope of this book. For more information, see the Pyle guide (mentioned above).

Finally, there is a plumage characteristic present in some species that can be another useful guide to age (and sometimes sex). The feathers of the median coverts of some ages or sexes of some species have central vanes of varying darkness and thickness and therefore show black or dark streaks in the center of the covert feathers, whereas other ages or sexes do not. The shape of this streak can even be useful, and again we defer to Pyle for more complete information. We do mention this characteristic for a few species in the aging and sexing section, since it can be a useful supporting feature when visible.

Note that in most cases, subtler features, such as molt limit, tail shape, and streaks in coverts, are very difficult to see and a lot of experience and field time is necessary before they can be assessed correctly and used as reliable ID points. Consistently discerning these points requires seeing many birds in different conditions along with guidance from an experienced expert. The important thing is that knowing about molt and wear sequences for warblers will help focus your attention on these areas and add to your overall birding skills and experience.

Spring Breeding Plumage

Some warbler species conduct a partial molt, called a prealternate molt, in late winter, prior to and/or during migration to their breeding grounds. This molt includes a small selection of body feathers, particularly those parts of the head, chest, and wing that serve as species identifiers (such as the yellow crown and shoulder patches of Yellow-rumped). It never includes any flight feathers. Species that have a very different spring and fall plumage, such as Blackpoll or Bay-breasted warblers, do a prealternate body molt that is obvious. Other species may molt only a few feathers, and many species don't change any feathers at all on the wintering grounds.

Note that even if a species has not molted, its appearance can change. For example, Black-throated Green Warblers in fresh fall plumage have strong pale fringes on their throat feathers. These fringes cover the black body of the feather, making the throat look pale. During the winter, these wear away, and on the breeding grounds they look freshly black-throated, even though these feathers were not replaced in winter.

In some species the first-year birds that hatched the previous summer will molt the same feathers as the adults in the winter during their prealternate molt. In other species, such as Black-throated Green, only the first-year birds will molt and change their appearance from fall to spring plumage. Note again that this molt to spring plumage never includes the flight feathers, and the worn juvenal flight feathers mentioned above remain old and continue to wear.

Covert Streaks The black lines in the center of the median coverts on this Townsend's indicate, for this species, a first-year bird.

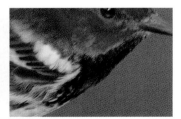

Fringing The fall bird on the left has fresh throat feathers that have pale white fringes. By spring, these fringes wear off, revealing the pure black throat on the right.

Age and Sex Codes

There are several systems for naming the molts and plumage sequences for bird species. Fortunately, warblers are a bit simpler than many species, and we have tried to keep the terminology non-technical and easy-to-use. The abbreviations we use in this book are:

AdM Sp	**Adult Male Spring**
AdM Fa	**Adult Male Fall**
AdF Sp	**Adult Female Spring**
AdF Fa	**Adult Female Fall**
1yM Fa	**First-year Male Fall**
1yM Sp	**First-year Male Spring**
1yF Fa	**First-year Female Fall**
1yF Sp	**First-year Female Spring**

Note "first-year" indicates a bird less than one year old.

AdM Sp / AdF Sp   Adult Male Spring and Adult Female Spring
This is the plumage warblers wear during spring migration and on their arrival to the breeding grounds. It can be composed of a mix of older and fresher plumage—resulting from a partial body molt on the wintering grounds or during migration—or it can be a worn version of their fall or basic plumage. Note that flight feathers are never replaced on the wintering grounds, so they will always be somewhat worn in this spring plumage.

1yM Sp / 1yF Sp   First-year Male Spring and First-year Female Spring
This is the plumage worn by birds that hatched the previous summer. It will include worn juvenal flight feathers, alula, primary coverts, and sometimes a few greater coverts, median coverts, or tertials. Some of the body feathers may be fresh in species whose first-year birds undergo a partial body molt on the wintering grounds; for most species, no feathers will have been replaced during winter.

AdM Fa / AdF Fa   Adult Male Fall and Adult Female Fall
In some species fall plumage looks drabber than spring plumage, but fall plumage is always the freshest and includes a completely new set of feathers produced during the prebasic molt. Note that for almost every warbler species, birds hatched the prior summer, now just over a year old, will also undergo this molt and will look like any other adult bird of that species.

1yM Fa / 1yF Fa   First-year Male Fall and First-year Female Fall
This plumage includes fresh feathers for most of the body. As noted above, first-year warblers retain the juvenal flight and tail feathers, alula and primary coverts. Contrast between these feathers and the newer feathers can sometimes be seen in the field.

Age and Sex Reference Strip

To help make the aging and sexing process faster, we use the following color-coded reference strip. This guide has abbreviations for all the age and sex possibilities for spring and fall.

SP: **AdM 1yM AdF 1yF**   FA: **AdM 1yM AdF 1yF**

These abbreviations are then color coded for each species depending on which ages and sexes can be reliably identified in each season.

AdM   Red indicates that the age and/or sex of that form cannot be reliably determined. In this case it is impossible to tell if a bird is an adult male. That means that adult male plumage characteristics always overlap with some other age or sex at that season.

AdM   Green indicates an age and/or sex that can always be reliably determined. In this case it is possible to identify all adult males at that season, given proper views.

AdM   Black indicates that sometimes the age or sex can be determined, but in other cases it may not be possible due to overlapping plumage characteristics with another age or sex. In this case it is sometimes possible to determine that a bird is an adult male, but other times it may not be possible. The text below will indicate what characteristics to look for and which are diagnostic, when present.

AdM   Combinations of colors are used for other possibilities. In this case it is sometimes possible to tell that a bird is a male but it is never possible to identify a bird as an adult male.

AdM 1yM   This combination indicates that it is always possible to identify a male bird, but it is impossible to age the bird, i.e., tell whether it is an adult or a 1y bird.

UNDERSTANDING SONOGRAMS

From X-rays of broken bones to CAT scans of the brain, recent technology has given us the ability to "see" into many heretofore invisible parts of the world. In a similar way, audio spectrograms (or sonograms, for short) allow birders to "see" inside bird vocalizations and provide important clues on how to differentiate similar-sounding species. Sonograms help us understand and learn warbler vocalizations by showing subtle variations in short calls or by making it easier to recognize differences in the larger patterns of complex songs. Once these differences are discerned in sonograms, they become much easier to hear in the field.

Note: please check the glossary at the end of the book for any unfamiliar terms. Also see the resources section for links to audio files for all of the vocalization examples in the book.

What Are Audio Spectrograms?

An audio spectrogram is a three-dimensional graphical representation of an audio source.
The up/down (Y) axis represents the frequency of the sound.
The right/left (X) axis represents time, or how long the sound lasts.
The lightness or darkness of the line represents the volume of the vocalization.

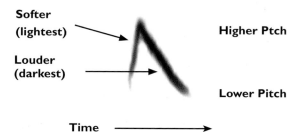

Yellow This call starts low, rises in pitch quickly, and then more slowly falls in pitch. The falling pitch is louder than the rising pitch and gets softer toward the end of the call.

If you were to do a series of short whistles, and each whistle was the same amount higher than the last, the sonogram would look like this:

Whistle One whistle every 1/10th of a second, each higher than the last.

Moving left to right in the graphic represents time from beginning to end. Pitch is represented by the vertical placement of each dot, with a higher dot representing a higher pitch. Since each whistle was made at the same volume, there is no difference in the darkness of each dot.

The highest whistle is about 17,000 hertz (17 kHz). This is very high. Middle C on the piano is about 260 cycles per second or only 0.260 kHz. Most warbler song Elements range from 3 kHz to 8 kHz.

Here is a sonogram of the song "Row, Row, Row Your Boat." Notice that a sonogram is a bit like a musical score.

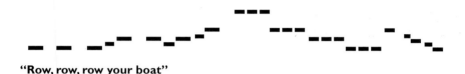

"Row, row, row your boat"

Now let us look at some examples of warbler song sonograms. Here are two smooth downslurs made by an American Redstart. They are fairly high, starting at 9.5 kHz and ending around 5.7 kHz. There is a relatively long time for this pitch change to occur, so our ears are able to hear all of the frequencies separately. As a result the slurs sound smooth and musical.

American Redstart Slow and musical downslurs.

Here's an example of a Tennessee Warbler song. Unlike the prior example, these Elements are very rapid. All of the frequencies happen in a very short period of time, and our ears can't keep up with such a fast change in frequencies. Thus they almost overwhelm our ears and sound harsh and percussive. This difference makes these sounds easily separable from the slower downslurs of the American Redstart. The sonograms of the two songs help us quickly see how they will differ in quality when we hear them in the field.

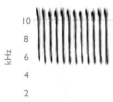

Tennessee Very fast and percussive Elements.

Trills

Trills are a rapid repetition of Elements at a speed too fast for us to count. Sonograms make it easy to see the exact shape of these Elements and how many there are per second.

Here's part of the Trill of a Worm-eating Warbler. Each Element has an Expanded (very wide) pitch range that occurs in a very short time. There is also a more complicated beginning to each Element that makes the vocalization sound more complex and emphasizes the lower frequencies of the song's range. The sonogram makes it easy to see all of this and also to determine the speed: 16 Elements per second, which is much too fast to count. (See the glossary or the section "How to Listen to Warbler Songs" for definitions of countable and uncountable speeds, as well as definitions of other terms used here.)

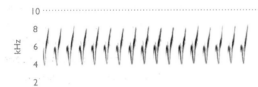

Worm-eating fast percussive trill.

Pine Warbler sings a similar Trill, but you can see obvious differences in the sonogram. The Elements are much simpler, with a lower, and more Compressed (narrow) pitch range.

The highest frequencies of the Worm-eating Warbler's song reach almost 8.5 kHz and the span of each Element ranges from 4.5 to 8.5 kHz, or about 4,000 cycles per second. It's easy to see that the Pine Warbler song, on the other hand, reaches only 5.5 kHz and spans only 2,000 cycles. The lower frequencies and smaller, Compressed range make their song sound duller and less bright than the more complicated and Expanded Elements of the Worm-eating Warbler's song.

Pine A Pine Warbler trill, duller than the Worm-eating song due to the lower and more Compressed pitch range of the Elements.

Prothonotary Warbler also repeats a slurred Element, but the sonogram reveals important differences. First, instead of 16 Elements per second, the Prothonotary sings about 5 Elements per second. This is a countable speed and will sound very different from a Trill. Also, each Element is intricate, with a short, limited up- or downslur connected to a much longer and slower upslur. Because the speed is slow, the upslurred pitch is obvious to our ear. The resulting quality is distinct from the Trilled songs in the above examples.

Prothonotary This Prothonotary Warbler song is slower than a Trill with more intricate, slowly slurred Elements.

Buzzes

Buzzy sounds also have a unique look in a sonogram. A Buzz is really an extremely fast repetition of Elements, so fast one cannot hear them as separate sounds. This high speed of repetition creates a cacophony of frequencies that our ear hears as a Buzz, or really, a kind of noise. The complex sound of a Buzz is created by the warbler's twin syrinxes, producing many very closely stacked pitches. In a sonogram Buzzes look like a wide wavy band, or sometimes, like a comb, indicating many frequencies sung at virtually the same time. Buzzes can still have pitches in that the average pitch of one Buzz can sound higher or lower than other Buzzes. However, the pitch is mostly masked by its noisy quality.

Black-throated Blue The last of these three Black-throated Blue Warbler Buzzes rises slowly in pitch.

Prairie Notice the pitches of the Buzzes of this Prairie Warbler vocalization slowly rise over the course of the song.

Complex Vocalizations

Some warbler vocalizations are very Complex and contain Elements that aren't Clear and aren't Buzzes. These Elements have many fast notes repeated in a short time but still slowly enough that we can hear articulations or a burry complexity. This is unlike Buzzes that sound like one noisy but undifferentiated sound. We explain more about these kinds of vocalizations in other sections of the book, but this is what they look like in a sonogram.

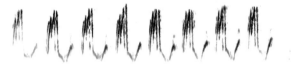

Blackburnian Notice the many lines in each Element that indicate fast, but still separately audible, repeated sounds. They sound Complex or burry to our ear, but looser and more varied than a Buzz.

Harmonics

You may have had a physics class in high school that explained the harmonics of pitched sound. When you pluck a string, there is one fundamental (or primary) pitch created by the vibration of the length of the whole string. At the same time, the string can create a "harmonic" that is twice as high as the fundamental pitch and lower in volume. There can also be additional, softer harmonics at various other multiples of the fundamental. The more harmonics in a sound, the richer it sounds to our ear, as long as the harmonics are multiples of the fundamental. Most bird vocalizations that are made up of Clear tones have harmonics that make the sound more pleasing and musical to our ears.

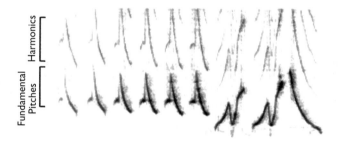

Chestnut-sided The louder, lower slurs represent the fundamental tones of this Chestnut-sided Warbler song. The quieter, higher group indicates the first harmonics, which make the song sound rich to our ears. Musical harmonics of the fundamental start with a doubling of the fundamental's frequency, and thus there is a large space between the fundamental and the first harmonic.

On the other hand, if a bird sings simultaneous pitches that are not harmonics, then the sound will become harsh or discordant. These closer frequencies compete with the fundamental, making the sound cacophonous, or less pleasant. Because birds make sound using two syrinxes, warbler vocalizations can contain a variety of simultaneous sounds. These unusual combinations of pitches are often prominent in chip and flight calls, including the "shadow" calls mentioned in the section on learning chip calls.

Mourning (left) Common Yellowthroat (right) The additional "shadow" lines in these sonograms do not represent harmonics, as they are very close in pitch to the main frequencies, and of almost equal or even greater volume (darkness in the sonogram.) These additional sounds, produced by the bird's syrinx, make the sound more complex and harsh. Sonograms show all of the components of even these short calls, and help us understand and hear how they are unique.

Using Sonograms to Understand Song Structure

Sonograms can also help us understand the structure of warbler songs, and structural differences between similar vocalization are key to understanding how to separate them in the field. We point out and discuss these differences extensively in the Species Accounts.

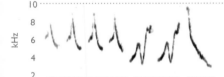

Chestnut-sided Type A Accented Song The sonogram of this song makes it very easy to see the song's structure including the 3 Sections, the number of Phrases in each Section, and how the pitch and speed of the Elements in each Section change. This is very important information for separating similar-sounding species.

Summary

Sonograms are important and useful tools that can help us understand the individual Elements of a vocalization as well as its overall structure. They can help us learn how to differentiate similar-sounding vocalizations and to train our ear to hear these vocalizations more clearly. We will provide many more examples of how sonograms can help us identify songs in the "How to Listen to Warbler Songs" section and in the Species Accounts. Rest assured that, as you read and study the text and explore the sonograms for the songs and calls in the book, they will become easier to interpret and hear and will help you identify more birds in the field.

HOW TO LISTEN TO WARBLER SONGS

One of the joys of spring is hearing the vast profusion of warbler songs as these beautiful birds come north to breed. It is very satisfying to be able to recognize each species by ear, and then set off to find the birds you most want to see.

Current field guides try to help readers recognize songs by transliterating them from warbler "speak" to vowels and consonants. These authors hope the descriptions will resemble the sounds closely enough to be useful aids to recognition. Although sometimes helpful, this process is very subjective. What sounds "sweet" or "musical" to one person might not help another person recognize a song in the field. One person's "tseet tseeo tseet" might sound like something completely different to a second birder. There is no better evidence of this problem than the wide variety of descriptions found in different field guides for the songs of the same species.

In this book we use a different system based on objective, structural criteria. By understanding the basic structure of a vocalization, it is possible to hear more clearly what makes that species' song unique. In addition, objective criteria are easier to remember in the field and to use with new or unknown species.

Our system is fairly simple, and we explain it in the following sections:

Sonograms describes the benefits of using sonograms to visualize vocalizations.
Song Structure defines the three key organizational terms we use to describe songs: Elements, Phrases, and Sections.
Element Qualities explores specific characteristics of Elements that are important in song analysis.
Song Qualities defines the more general characteristics of songs that are also important to note.
Notational Symbols explains the system we use to help one quickly scan and compare songs.
Song Finder Categories goes over the six qualities used to organize songs in the Song Finders.
Summary Chart collects all the terms defined in this section for review.

With careful study, this system of analyzing songs and calls will lead to more confident identification of songs in the field.

Sonograms

To help in understanding a song's structure, and also as a visual aid to memory, we use graphical representations of songs called audio spectrograms (or "sonograms," for short.) As familiarity increases, sonograms become faster to "read," and they reveal important aspects of both individual song Elements, such as subtle pitch and tonal changes, and of larger, overall structural trends of warbler vocalizations. Once noticed, these more subtle vocalization features become easier to hear in the field and will help to quickly and confidently identify a singing or calling warbler.

If sonograms are unfamiliar, be sure to read the section, "Understanding Sonograms," and also check the glossary for any unfamiliar terms.

Sonograms can rapidly reveal important differences in structure. The following two songs sound similar and are often confused. However the Bay-breasted Warbler Elements are of a more even length and pitch, and the first is a downslur (a smoothly sung note descending in pitch.) Black-and-white Warblers have a much longer, rising first Element followed by a higher, much shorter second Element, creating a rising but uneven quality. Seeing these structural characteristics in a sonogram makes it much easier to hear these differences in the field.

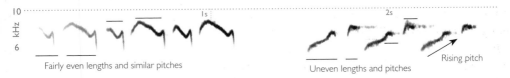

Bay-breasted and Black-and-white Structural differences are often much easier to compare using sonograms, and can lead to effective ways of differentiating similar-sounding species.

Understanding Song Structure

To describe the structure of a song, we use three simple terms. It may take some time for this terminology to become second nature, but the benefits are worth the effort. As the annotated sonograms in the species accounts are studied, this system should quickly become a natural way of understanding and then hearing both the internal and overall structure of warbler vocalizations.

We have purposely used words not typically found in the context of musical analysis. By doing this we hope to avoid any preconceptions or confusions based on past usage. There are a couple of reasons we created this terminology. The most important is to streamline the discussion of the structure and quality of warbler songs, because we needed efficient ways of comparing songs that, on the surface, may appear to be similar. We are confident that as these terms become familiar, analysis of songs and calls will become more precise and differences that were once subtle will become more obvious.

A download of a playlist of all of the audio for this section and the rest of the book is available on the Princeton University Press website (press.princeton.edu/titles/9968 .html). Listening to these examples as you read the text will make it much easier and faster to understand the terminology. These playlists will also assist in following the Species Account analyses of each species' vocalizations.

Structural Organization: Elements, Phrases, and Sections

All warbler songs consist of combined patterns of unique sounds, repetitions of the same sound, or a series of two or three different sounds repeated a few times as a group. To make it possible to discuss the way one species organizes its song using an exclusive combination of repeated and unique sounds, we use the terms Elements, Phrases, and Sections. Here are a couple of simple examples.

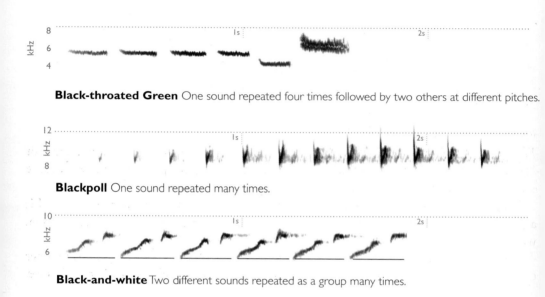

Black-throated Green One sound repeated four times followed by two others at different pitches.

Blackpoll One sound repeated many times.

Black-and-white Two different sounds repeated as a group many times.

Elements

Every separate sound you hear when listening to a song is an Element. An Element can be a single long note, a short note, or even a long Buzz. Elements are the building blocks of songs. If it sounds like one smoothly continuous sound to our ears, it's an Element.

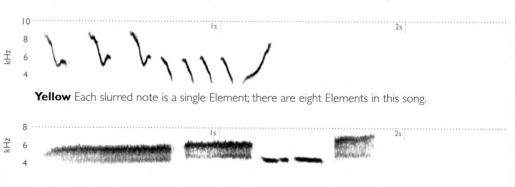

Yellow Each slurred note is a single Element; there are eight Elements in this song.

Black-throated Green Each sound is an Element, some at the same pitch, others at different pitches; there are five Elements in this song, three are Buzzes.

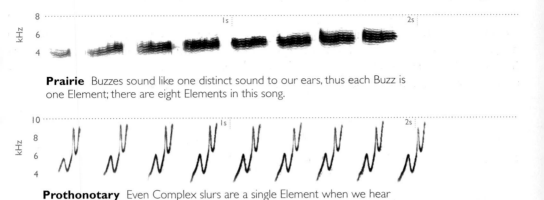

Prairie Buzzes sound like one distinct sound to our ears, thus each Buzz is one Element; there are eight Elements in this song.

Prothonotary Even Complex slurs are a single Element when we hear them as one Clear, smooth sound; there are nine Elements in this song.

Phrases

The next term, Phrases, allows us to point out patterns of single Elements or groups of Elements. We use "Phrase" to indicate a single Element or a group of two, three, or more different Elements that are repeated 2 or more times without change.

When a Phrase is made up of two different Elements repeated several times, we call it a 2-Element Phrase. When it is made up of three different Elements repeated as a group, we call it a 3-Element Phrase.

When one Element is unique and not repeated, or is repeated without variation a number of times, then the Phrase and the Element are the same, and are called a 1-Element Phrase.

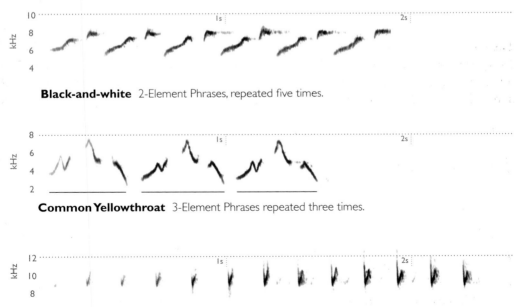

Black-and-white 2-Element Phrases, repeated five times.

Common Yellowthroat 3-Element Phrases repeated three times.

Blackpoll All Elements are the same, thus these are 1-Element Phrases, repeated thirteen times.

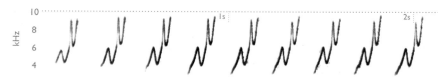

Prothonotary These are also 1-Element Phrases, because we hear the Elements as one continuous slur and not as two separate sounds.

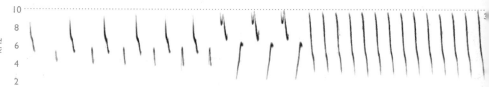

Tennessee This is a more Complex song, beginning with 2-Element Phrases, which are followed by different 2-Element Phrases, and then by many 1-Element Phrases. This structure is an important ID point for this species.

Sections

There is one more essential term we need to define: Sections. Sections are simply groups of similar Phrases, and are very important structures to recognize when listening to warblers. How a song's Sections are organized, and how many there are, is key to identifying many warbler songs.

A Section is a collection of the same-sounding Phrases. When the pitch, speed, or Phrase type changes significantly or abruptly, the song enters a new Section. A Section could simply be a single, 1-Element Phrase that is not repeated, or a Section could contain several 1-, or 2-Element Phrases that are repeated more than once.

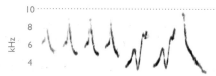

Chestnut-sided A 3-Section song, the first Section has four slurred, repeated 1-Element Phrases, the second has two slurred, 1-Element Phrases; and the third one slurred, very Expanded (wide pitch range) Phrase.

Black-throated Green This song has three Sections, the first a 1-Element Phrase repeated four times, while the second and third are each 1-Element Phrases that aren't repeated and have obviously different pitches.

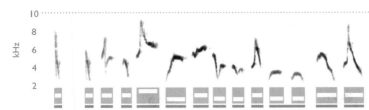

Canada There are only two repeated Phrases in this whole song; all other Phrases represent separate Sections, because each Phrase is very different. Among eastern warblers, a short song with so many unique Sections is a diagnostic ID point for Canada Warbler.

Trills Are Sections

Trills (see below under "Element Qualities" for a definition) are considered one Section, since they consist of the same Phrase repeated many times without any obvious or drastic changes in pitch or speed.

Pine This song is a 1-Section Trill with many Phrases repeated too quickly to count. Note that small fluctuations of pitch don't sound different enough to break the song into different Sections.

Pitch and Speed Changes

If a Phrase changes pitch or speed in a very obvious and dramatic way, then it signals a change in Sections.

Black-throated Green This song is a 4-Section song of mostly Buzzy Phrases. The third Section has a Clear 1-Element Phrase sung twice. The Sections are demarcated by obvious changes in pitch.

If changes in speed or pitch are only gradual, then the song will sound smoothly continuous and we consider these Phrases to be in the same Section.

Prairie This is a 1-Section song of Buzzy, 1-Element Phrases repeated eight times, with a gradual change in pitch. Although the pitch rises and the Elements get a bit buzzier, the changes sound gradual and none is abrupt enough to signal a new Section.

Understanding and hearing song Sections is one of the most helpful techniques for learning to identify warbler songs. We discuss Sections extensively in each Species Account.

Summary

Element: Each simple, separate "event" or sound you hear in a song

Phrase: A single Element or two, three or more different Elements that are repeated as a group

Section: Group of similar, repeated Phrases, differentiated by an abrupt change in Phrase pitch, speed or type

Element Qualities

To help us discuss how Elements are different from species to species, we will use three terms that define the quality of an Element: Clear, Buzzy, and Complex.

Clear Elements

Many warbler songs consist of only Clear Elements. These can be described as simple, pure notes or smooth slurs. They are easy to reproduce by whistling. On a sonogram they look like simple lines.

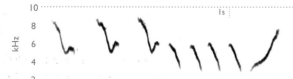

Yellow Songs always consist of Clear Elements, usually up or down slurs. The Prothonotary, Black-and-white, Blackpoll, Tennessee, and Common Yellowthroat song examples above consist of only Clear Elements.

Buzzy Elements

As mentioned above, a single Buzz is also an Element, because, to our ears, it sounds like one continuous sonic event. Buzzes are actually Elements repeated so quickly that they are no longer heard by humans as separate sounds. The resulting quality is a Buzz, like a bee, or like an Element in a Black-throated Blue Warbler song. Buzzes consist of many frequencies sung at the same time, sounding to our ears more like noise than the musical slur of a slowly repeated Clear Element. We consider a single Buzz a 1-Element Phrase, since our ears cannot differentiate the very rapid individual notes that make up the sound.

A Buzzy Element is indicated on a sonogram by a very wide band, with many densely packed repeated lines, and looks a bit like a comb. If a Buzz is slowed down enough, one can actually hear the individual Elements, but since to our ear a Buzz sounds like one event, we will call individual Buzzes one Element, or 1-Element Phrases.

Black-throated Blue Four Buzzy, 1-Element Phrases, the last much longer than the first.

Golden-winged Three Buzzy 1-Element Phrases.

Phrases can be a combination of a Buzz with another sound, often a downslur. We still consider these Phrases as 1-Element Buzzes unless they sound like two very distinct Elements. We will discuss them with each species in which they occur.

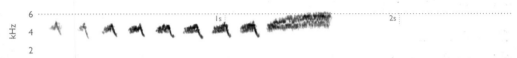

Black-throated Blue These are nine 1-Element Buzzy Phrases, each sounding like a single sound.

Complex Elements

Both Clear slurs and single Buzzes are considered Elements because each type sounds like one event to our ears. There is one last kind of Element we need to define that is easily distinguishable from a Clear tone and a Buzz, but still sounds like one note or event—it is called a Complex Element.

Like a Buzz, a Complex Element consists of many notes sung in a short time; however, they are not nearly as rapidly or densely repeated as in a Buzz. As with a Buzz, we hear the collection of these sounds as one Element or event; they're too quickly repeated to sound like separate Elements. But, unlike a Buzz, we also hear the individual components of the Element fairly distinctly, giving the Element a Complex, loosely articulated, rough or burry quality.

Although Clear Elements and Buzzy Elements are fairly consistent and easy to identify, Complex Elements take more varied forms. The key point is that Complex Elements sound, to our ears, as if there is a lot going on in the Element, creating a Complex or burry quality. We can reproduce a Clear Element by whistling, and we could even make a Buzzy sound fairly easily, but Complex sounds are more difficult to describe and probably not possible to reproduce using our limited vocal chords. With familiarity and practice, Elements with this quality can be differentiated fairly easily, and noticing them is very useful in identifying the species that sing Complex Elements.

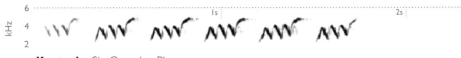

Kentucky Six Complex Phrases.

This song is a good example of Complex Phrases. Note the easily audible articulations that sound burry or rough. The pitch changes are too slow to make the Phrases sound like Buzzes but are too quickly repeated and complicated to sound like separate, individual, clear tones.

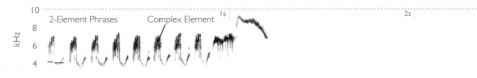

Blackburnian The first Section contains eight 2-Element Complex Phrases.

The first Elements of these 2-Element Phrases are not slurs, and they are not really Buzzes. They are Complex Elements that sound burry, or even like very short, loosely articulated Trills.

Since there is also a lower, Clear Element heard as a separate sound from the first Complex Element, we call these 2-Element Phrases.

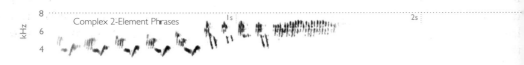

Cerulean This song also begins with Complex, 2-Element Phrases.

Pitch Span and Length

Close examination of the precise shape of Elements is very often the key to hearing the characteristics that make one song different from a similar-sounding species. For warblers, this is particularly true for Clear 1-Element Phrases. To differentiate similar-sounding Clear Elements, it is helpful to carefully study the length of the Element and its pitch span (see definition below.) The relationship of these two parameters determines how our ears hear the Element. These criteria are also critical in hearing and differentiating warbler calls, which we discuss in a later section. The following are a few terms that we use to focus on these important characteristics.

Slurs, Downslurs, Upslurs, Up/down Slurs

For our purposes, a slur is a smoothly sung note that covers a range of pitches without an obvious break. Downslurs fall in pitch, upslurs rise. The last Phrase in the Chestnut-sided

Warbler example, on page 72, is a long downslur. The ending Element in the Yellow Warbler examples is an upslur. Up/down slurs combine the rising of an upslur with the falling of a downslur without any space or break between the slurs. Up/down slurs are found in several warbler chip calls.

Pitch Span
One of the most important characteristics of an Element is how Expanded or Compressed a pitch range it spans. This has nothing to do with the height of the pitch but is instead a measurement of how many frequencies are covered during the singing of the Element. Usually these terms are used to compare two different vocalizations and are therefore relative.

Expanded An Element with an Expanded or wide pitch range means an Element that covers a relatively large number of frequencies when it is sung. For example, a note that spans 3 kHz to 8 kHz would be considered an Element with an Expanded pitch range. The pitch span would be 5 kHz.*

Compressed
An Element with a Compressed pitch span would cover a narrower frequency range—for example, 3 kHz–4kHz, a span of only 1kHz.

Element Length
In addition to its pitch span, the length of time it takes to sing the Element is another very important characteristic that shapes how we hear the sound. Both pitch span and Element length are important, interactive, and relative parameters that often help us compare and then differentiate two similar vocalizations.

Long
A "long" time is a relative term and usually means only 150 or 200 ms.** This brief time, however, is still enough for our ear to clearly hear all of the pitches of the Element.

Short
A "short" Element lasts about 50 or 60 ms. During a short Expanded Element with a wide pitch range, our ear cannot hear all of the pitches individually, but instead is assaulted by a large number of frequencies sung during a very brief time. These short Expanded Elements sound very forceful, emphatic, or even harsh; our ears can't process so many frequencies so quickly.

On the other hand, short, Compressed Elements can sound like a brief "seet" or "tick,"

---

* kHz = 1,000 cycles/sec. Middle C on the piano is about 262 cycles/sec or 0.262 kHz. Most warbler vocalizations range from 3 kHz to 8 kHz.

** Note that a millisecond is 1/1000 of a second (abbreviated "ms"); 1/10 of a second is 100 ms. Some nonwarbler species have much longer Elements.

without much pitch, depending on their frequency. Both Expanded and Compressed short Elements sound obviously different than similarly pitched long Elements, and this distinction is very important in distinguishing warbler vocalizations. We discuss these differences at length below and in the Species Accounts.

Let us look at some examples and explain how these parameters affect how we hear Elements of different types.

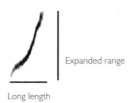

Expanded range

Long length

Yellow   Long, Expanded Element.

This Element from a Yellow Warbler song's last Section is an Expanded, long upslur lasting about 160 ms. The pitch span is from 3 kHz to 8 kHz. Our ears clearly hear all of the pitches, from low to high, and it sounds rich, bright, and pleasing.

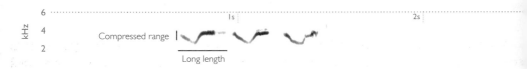

Hooded   Long, Compressed Elements.

This song starts with three 1-Element Phrases that are long (about 200 ms or 0.2 sec.) and very Compressed slurs with a narrow pitch range. The Elements span only some 1.3 kHz (2.5 kHz to about 3.8 kHz). To use more subjective language, they sound darker, smoother, and lazier, or less energetic, than does the previous Yellow Warbler Element.

Recognizing these kinds of differences in pitch spans makes separating songs such as those of Yellow Warbler and Hooded Warbler much easier.

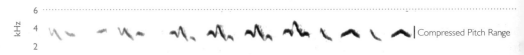

Painted Redstart   Long, Compressed Elements.

These Elements are somewhat long but are very Compressed, spanning only 1 kHz or so. The quality is dull, lacking the energy provided by more Expanded Elements.

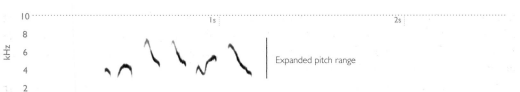

Red-faced Several long, Expanded Elements.

This song is somewhat similar in structure to that of the Painted Redstart song, and the two species occur together. Note that these Elements are also long but that the pitch range is Expanded, with some Elements spanning 3.7 kHz. This added pitch range gives the song a very different, richer, brighter quality that makes it easy to differentiate from the Painted Redstart song. The song also sounds higher, due to the Expanded ranges, even though the lowest notes are very similar in pitch to those of the Painted Redstart's notes. Notice that the first Elements are more Compressed and this combination of Expanded and Compressed Elements can also be an important ID point.

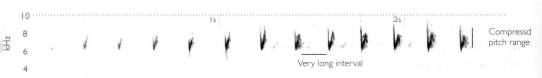

Blackpoll Very short, Compressed Elements. with very long Intervals

Composed of Compressed and very short Elements, about 24 ms long, this song sounds staccato and thin, almost the opposite of the Hooded example, which was Compressed but with much Longer and lower-pitched Elements. The very long Interval (see below for definition) creates the distinct and staccato quality of this song.

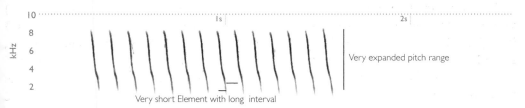

Tennessee Short, extremely Expanded Elements with long Intervals.

This example shows several Expanded but extremely short notes. The pitch range is from 3.2 kHz to 10 kHz, a very Expanded range. The length, however, is only 60 ms. The speed of this pitch change, then, is so fast that our ears don't distinguish the pitches but rather, hear them as bright, emphatic, percussive notes, due to all of those frequencies happening at nearly the same time. Although the pitch range is similar, the quality is very different from the much slower Yellow Warbler slur above.

This emphatic quality is enhanced by the relatively long Interval between Elements, increasing the staccato or accented quality of the song.

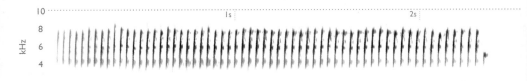

Worm-eating Another song with Expanded Phrases (4–7.5kHz) and relatively long Intervals creating a bright and emphatic song.

Compare this song with that of Pine Warbler. The very Expanded pitch range of the Worm-eating Warbler's Elements give the song bright and emphatic qualities. Pine Warbler's Elements have a much more Compressed pitch range (3.5–5kHz) and are noticeably lower. This creates a darker and more slurred, less emphatic quality that helps separate these two similar-sounding species.

Pine The more Compressed Elements give the song a darker, more muted sound.

Element Intervals
As seen above, the length of an Element is very important in how we hear it. Just as important is the Interval, or length of silence between each Element or Phrase. Intervals can be either long or short. The terms "long" or "short" are based on comparing the length of the Element itself to the length of Interval.

This interaction of the Element's length and the Interval length affects the quality of the song. Short Elements with long Intervals sound staccato. Long Elements with long Intervals sound distinct. Relatively short Intervals create a slurred or rushed quality.

In the Blackpoll and Tennessee warbler examples above, the Intervals are much longer than the Elements in their songs. This makes each Element remain very distinct and contributes to a staccato sound. The emphatic quality of the Tennessee Warbler song above is also enhanced by the relatively long Intervals.

Following are two species that sing fairly similar 2-Element Phrases. One key difference is the relative duration of the Phrase lengths and Intervals. The American Redstart song has very short Intervals and sounds more run on and smoothly slurred, whereas that of the Cape May has relatively longer Intervals, making the Elements sound more emphatic and rhythmic.

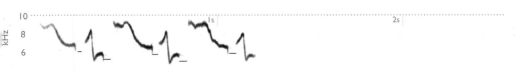

American Redstart Relatively short Intervals create a smoother, more slurred quality.

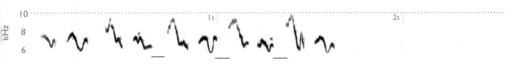

Cape May Much longer Intervals give the Elements a more rhythmic, distinct, and emphatic quality.

Example of the Importance of Pitch Range, Length and Interval

Let us now revisit the first comparison we used in this section, complete with our newly defined terms. In this Black-and-white Warbler song, the first Element of the 2-Element Phrase is a relatively long, Expanded upslur, rising in pitch. The second Element is higher, short, and has a very Compressed pitch range, contrasting with the first Element. The combination of these two uneven Elements makes the song sound choppy. The Interval is relatively short, and the Phrases sound slurred together. The Phrase has an overall rising pitch profile.

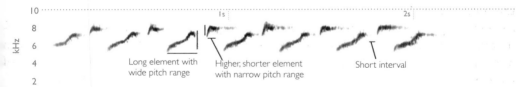

Black-and-white Contrasting Elements, one long, Expanded; the other short, Compressed; the two-Element phrase has a rising pitch profile and uneven rhythm.

Bay-breasted Warbler's Elements have a more Compressed pitch range and the lengths and pitches are more similar to each other. The first Element becomes a downslur, and the Interval is a bit longer. The sound of this song is more even and the Elements are more distinct, with a slightly falling pitch profile.

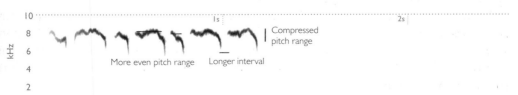

Bay-breasted Compressed Elements of more even length and pitch.

Focusing on these structure qualities makes it easier to hear the difference between the choppier, obviously upwardly accented Black-and-white song and the smoother, more even Bay-breasted Warbler song that has a slightly downslurred Phrase pitch profile.

Elements and Speed

"Countability" Another important ID point is the speed at which a warbler sings its Elements and Phrases. Since it is difficult in the field to judge the exact speed of an isolated song, we categorize speeds primarily on what we call "countability."

If one can count the number of Phrases as they are sung, either out loud or silently, we call that speed "countable." We consider a song's Phrases countable up to speeds of about nine Phrases per second. At that speed, even though it might be difficult to speak the numbers, one can still count them silently. For example, it is very easy to count the number of 2-Element Phrases in the Bay-breasted and Black-and-white songs cited above.

Trills Songs sung at faster speeds are called Trills. Trills are Phrases repeated too quickly to count but still slowly enough that the individual Phrases are heard as separate, distinct sounds. Although a bit arbitrary, we feel this distinction, between countable and uncountable Phrase speeds, is easy to learn and is very often a useful and important song differentiator.

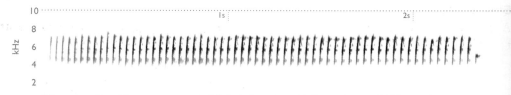

Worm-eating Phrases sung at a definitely "uncountable" speed, over 26 Phrases/sec.

In many ways, Trills are similar to Complex Elements and Buzzes, the difference being length and speed. Buzzes are sounds that are much more rapidly repeated and are denser; the notes are impossible for us to hear as distinct.

Complex Elements are more similar to Trills, because they contain rapidly repeated but distinctly audible, separate notes. For this reason we further define Trills as having a longer length than a Complex Element. Typically a Complex Element lasts only a very short time, similar to the Phrase length of the Kentucky Warbler example above, 150–200 ms. Trills are more sustained, and last from 0.3 sec (300 ms) to more than 3.0 sec.

The separation of Trilled and Complex Elements may seem subtle, but in fact it serves an important role in separating similar-sounding species and is fairly easy to learn. The same is true for countable and Trill-speed songs. For example, Virginia's and Nashville warbler songs can be similar. However, whereas Nashville's 2nd Section can be a Trill, Virginia's never has any Phrases sung at Trill speed. We note song speed in the Species Accounts and indicate when it is important for identification.

Song Qualities

Here are some simple qualities that are useful when describing the differences between songs. We will use these in the Species Accounts.

Pitch refers to the frequency (kHz) of a sound.

Rising Pitch

A song has a Rising pitch trend or pitch profile when Phrases of more than half of the song slowly rise in pitch, as in the Prairie Warbler example on page 73.

Falling Pitch

A song has a Falling pitch trend when the first or second half of a song contains several Phrases that slowly fall in pitch from one to the next, or when there is a downward pitch trend from Section to Section.

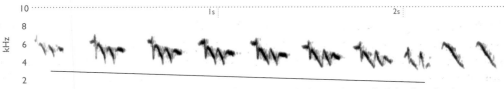

Yellow-throated This song falls in pitch from the beginning to the end of the first Section.

Steady Pitch

A song has a Steady Pitch when the Phrases of a song do not change in pitch throughout the song.

Blackpoll The 13 1-Element Phrases of this song have the same pitch. Although they gradually get louder in the first half of the song, the change is not abrupt, thus the song has only one Section.

We consider a song with a repeated, multiple-Element Phrase to be a Steady Pitch song. Even though the Elements within the Phrase may have different pitches, the Phrases themselves do not change, and thus they maintain a Steady Pitch profile.

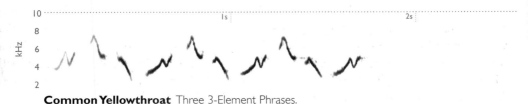

Common Yellowthroat Three 3-Element Phrases.

The pitches of the Elements in these 3-Element Phrases are different from each other. However the Phrase itself is repeated several times with no variation or pitch change from Phrase to Phrase; we consider this song as having a steady pitch.

Variable Pitch

A song with several Sections without any consistent pattern of rising or falling pitch from Section to Section is considered a song with a variable pitch profile.

Rising Volume

Many warbler songs start softly and then quickly, over one or two Phrases, reach full volume. Some songs, however, fade in slowly from a soft level to a much louder volume reached a third or more into the song. These songs we say have a Rising volume. The most common examples are Ovenbird and Blackpoll Warbler (shown above.) This characteristic is often diagnostic when combined with Phrase type or pitch profile.

Rhythm

Rhythm describes the timing of Elements and Intervals, varying from very steady, evenly repeated Elements to uneven, irregular patterns.

Steady Rhythm

Some warbler songs have a very steady, even pace from start to finish, with no slowing down or speeding up, as in the Blackpoll Warbler song (shown above.)

Slowing Rhythm

Some songs slow down, usually in the last third or so of the song, either gradually or in a separate Section. In order to qualify as a song that slows down, it must have at least five Phrases that gradually and evenly slow down or are in a markedly slower Section at the end of the song. It is usually fairly obvious which songs have just a couple of slower Elements and which have an overall slowing trend, and, when relevant, we make a note of this in the Species Accounts.

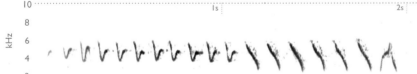

Grace's The 1-Element Phrases in the second Section of this song are obviously slower than those of the first, and thus the song has an overall slowing rhythm.

Accelerating Rhythm

Some songs speed up toward the end. Often this acceleration is in a separate Section of more quickly repeated Phrases. In order to qualify as a song that speeds up, it must have at least five Phrases that either gradually and steadily speed up or are in a final Section with Phrases repeated much faster than in the preceding Section. Again, it should be very clear when a song has an accelerating profile.

Phrase Speed versus Element Speed

When we characterize songs as speeding up or slowing down, we use the Phrase speed as the benchmark, so it is important to distinguish between Element speed and Phrase speed in some songs. For example, Nashville Warbler songs usually have 2-Element Phrases in the first Section and 1-Element Phrases in the second. The second Section Phrases are usually repeated at a faster speed, often twice as fast as the first. However, if you were only paying attention to Elements and not their organization, you might think the song speed remained the same.

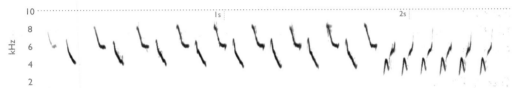

Nashville The 1-Element Phrases in the 2nd Section are twice as fast as the 2-Element Phrases in the 1st, but the Element speed remains about the same.

Variable Rhythms

The Phrases in many songs have a Variable rhythm. Unless the song obviously has one of the above rhythmic trends, then we consider the rhythm Variable.

Song Section Count

Most species' songs have a set number of Sections for each type of their song. This can be an important ID characteristic and we refer to these songs as 1-Section Songs, 2-Section Songs, and so on. Prairie Warbler songs, as in the above example, are always 1-Section songs. Black-throated Blue Warblers, with a similar Buzzy quality, have at least two Sections, and never just one.

Song Length

While most warbler songs average 1.7 sec or less in length, some songs are unusually short or unusually long, and for these species song length can be used as an ID point. For example, although both songs are Buzzy or Partly Buzzy, the Black-throated Blue Warbler's song is fairly short, well under 2 sec (avg. 1.5 sec.), while Prairie Warbler's song is almost always over 2 sec long (avg. 2.2 sec.). This difference in length can be a good ID point. The section on our website "Song Statistics" presents averages and ranges of song lengths for all of the warblers covered in the Species Accounts.

Sonogram Notation Symbols

To supplement the sonograms, we have designed a set of symbols to make it faster and easier to see some of the important structural components of each song. They can be particularly useful when scanning and comparing several similar species. The symbols also indicate the overall pitch trend of a Phrase or Song and can be used to quickly see Element length and Interval.

Here is a key to these symbols, which includes Element, Phrase, and Sectional organization, and Element quality.

Phrases are represented by a gray rectangle.

Clear Elements are represented by a white bar, indicating both the length of the Element and its quality. The basic pitch profile is indicated by the height of each Element.

    A 1-Element Clear Phrase.

    A 2-Element Clear Phrase with a falling pitch profile.

Complex Elements are represented by many slanted lines.

    A 1-Element Complex Phrase.

Buzzy Elements are represented by many straight lines.

    A 1-Element Buzzy Phrase.

Trills are represented by many dots.

Sections are represented by a darker, thin bar underlining all of the Phrases in one Section.

Purple Arrows indicate important Element or Phrase pitch trends.

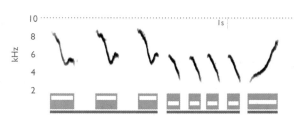

Yellow Three Sections, all with Clear Elements. The height of the Elements indicates the pitch falls from the first to the second Section. The last Section is a 1-Element Clear, Expanded upslur.

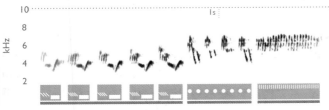

Cerulean Three Sections.
The first has five 2-Element Phrases. The first Element is Complex, the second is lower and Clear.
The second Section is a higher Trill. The third Section is an even higher Buzz.

Song Finder Categories

The Element qualities and song structures discussed above can help one quickly identify a vocalizing warbler. To aid in this process we have designed the Song Finder which provides a fast way to narrow down the identity of an unknown singing warbler in just a few steps. Once the field has been narrowed, the vocal comparisons in the Species Account for the most likely candidate should allow a confident ID.

Following are descriptions of the categories used in the Song Finder:

Trilled Song

A song has a Trilled quality when all or almost all of the song is a Trill, for example, the Worm-eating Warbler song (p. 82).

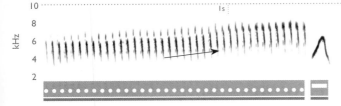

Northern Parula This 2-Section song has a Trilled Phrase followed by a very short 1-Element Phrase, a Clear, Up/Down slur, and is in the Trilled song category.

Partly Trilled Songs Songs that contain some Trills as well as untrilled Sections we consider Partly Trilled.

Wilson's The first Section of this song has eight Elements sung at a countable speed; the 2nd Section is a faster Trill. This song is Partly Trilled.

Buzzy Song A song has a Buzzy quality when all of the Phrases of the song are Buzzes.

Partly Buzzy Some songs, like those of Black-throated Green Warbler, have a combination of Buzzy and Clear Phrases. We call these songs Partly Buzzy.

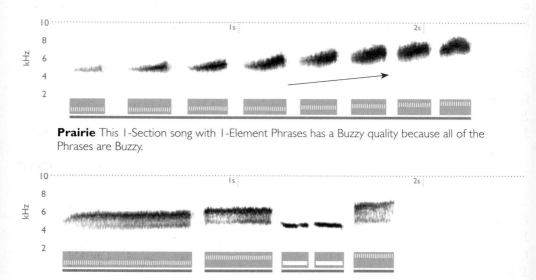

Prairie This 1-Section song with 1-Element Phrases has a Buzzy quality because all of the Phrases are Buzzy.

Black-throated Green This song has three Buzzy Phrases and one repeated Clear Phrase; a Partly Buzzy song.

Complex Some songs have Complex Phrases that, as defined above, sound burry or rough. We categorize these songs as Complex. If there are some Complex and some Buzzy or Clear tones, we always put the song into both categories in the Song Finder, to avoid any possible confusion.

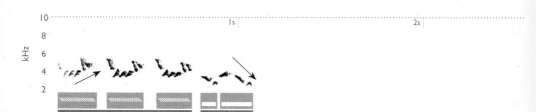

Mourning This song has three Complex Phrases followed by two Clear Phrases. It would be considered a Complex song.

Clear All songs that have simple, smooth slurs or don't contain predominantly Complex, Buzzy, or Trilled Elements we call "Clear." This is the largest warbler song category.

Conclusion

By studying the sonograms and the accompanying notes in the Species Accounts, we are confident that this simple analytic system of Elements, Phrases, and Sections will become very easy to understand and, more important, to hear. We also believe that it will become a valuable tool to use in the field, helping in the identification of most of the warbler songs heard, no matter how difficult they may have been to separate in the past.

Summary

Structure

Element Every individual sound that is heard as one event

Phrase A single Element or two, three, or more different Elements that are repeated as a group

Section Grouping of similar Phrases; large changes in pitch, speed, or Phrase type signal a change in Sections

Element Analysis

Expanded Element with a large pitch range, for example, from 3 kHz to 8 kHz

Compressed Element with narrow pitch range, for example, from 3 kHz to 4 kHz

Short Rapidly sung Element, often shorter than 60 ms

Long Longer Element, lasting 120 ms or longer; our ears hear all of the Element's pitch range

Interval The length of the space between Elements

Element, Phrase, and Song Qualities

Clear Simple slurs or notes; easy to whistle

Trilled Phrases repeated too quickly to count; we can still hear that there are many individual Elements; a song that contains only Trilled Sections

Partly Trilled At least one Section of the song is Trilled

Complex An Element that has several rapid pitch changes giving it a burry or rough quality. Short enough (<0.3 sec) to not sound like a Trill; a song that contains Complex Phrases

Buzzy Very rapid repetition of pitches so dense that separate notes cannot be heard; a song with all or almost all Buzzy Phrases

Partly Buzzy A song with some Buzzy Phrases

Falling Pitch A song with the first or second half containing several Phrases falling in pitch from one to the next, or with a downward pitch trend from Section to Section

Steady Pitch A song without any pitch changes from Phrase to Phrase or Section to Section

Rising Pitch A song with Phrases in more than half of the song that slowly rise in pitch within a Section or rise obviously from Section to Section

LEARNING CHIP AND FLIGHT CALLS

Overview of Warbler Vocalizations

There are three basic kinds of warbler vocalizations: Songs, Chip Calls, and Flight Calls. A few species also sing other, less-often-heard vocalizations including night songs; whisper, or "sotto voce," songs; and flight or display songs.

Songs The most "popular" warbler vocalizations are, of course, the songs. Warbler males sing their songs on their breeding grounds to attract mates and to define and defend their territory. They also often sing during spring migration. Studies have shown that many warbler species have two general types of songs: accented and unaccented. Much research is still ongoing about how often, when, and why birds sing, and we have cited some of this research in the "Resources" section.

Chestnut-sided Warbler, for example, sings an accented song that is very familiar to many birders, often transliterated as "Pleased, Pleased, Pleased Pleased to ME EEET CHA"; the ending is accented and the song is fairly short. They also sing unaccented songs, which are usually longer, sound more rambling, and don't end with emphatic or accented Elements. Sometimes these songs have Elements similar to the endings of the accented songs embedded within them. Both types of songs can be given during migration.

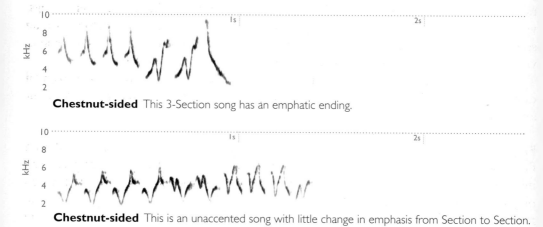

Chestnut-sided This 3-Section song has an emphatic ending.

Chestnut-sided This is an unaccented song with little change in emphasis from Section to Section.

Studies on the use of these two types of songs have shown that songs with accented endings are usually sung to attract mates, and unaccented songs, to defend territories. Time of day also may influence which songs are sung, especially on breeding grounds, with unaccented songs more frequently sung at dusk or dawn and accented songs sung during the day. Once a territory has been established, the percentage of unaccented songs usually increases, and if a female is removed from a territory, the male then returns to favoring accented songs to attract another mate. There is often a lot of variability in the unaccented songs. This may be to help neighboring males, who are all singing unaccented songs "at" each other, maintain their own unique sound. Other theories suggest that it may be to fool the neighbor into thinking there are several males nearby, all ready to defend against any intruders!

It is important to know and study unaccented songs as well as the easier-to-identify accented ones. Knowing only the accented "Please to meet cha" song of the Chestnut-sided Warbler may lead to confusing the unaccented songs with those of other species or to missing them entirely. There is more variation in the unaccented songs than in accented songs, making them a bit harder to identify, but they are almost always distinct and recognizable after a little study.

In each Species Account we discuss how many types of songs the species has, including accented and unaccented songs where relevant, and how to separate the species' songs from similar-sounding species. Some warblers have fairly consistent song types, and we define these groups whenever we can, using the terms Type A, Type B, etc. The songs for other species are more variable, and we note this as well in the Species Accounts.

Chip Calls During the day, warblers make short vocalizations we refer to as chip calls. (These are sometimes also known as "contact" or "alarm" calls.) Only rarely have females of a species been documented singing songs, but chip calls are produced by both males and females. Calls are usually more obvious during fall migration and on the wintering grounds, when males aren't singing as often. Some species call often, while other species rarely call. A few species, like Black-throated Green Warbler, mix calls between songs, which can be a useful ID characteristic. For example, Cerulean Warbler, which has a song somewhat similar to Blackburnian Warbler, rarely if ever calls during a singing session, whereas Blackburnian often calls multiple times prior to singing a song.

Chip calls are more difficult to learn than songs because of their brevity, and we will discuss this below. The typical calls for each species are presented in its Species Account and in the Chip Call Finder.

Flight Calls Warblers have another very short vocalization that is used most often during flight. Warbler flight calls are given especially during night migration, presumably to keep migrating flocks together or to help maintain spacing between individuals. There is much ongoing research about flight calls. Stations that record night-flight calls are being set up to monitor migrating birds, and there are efforts to correlate these data (which identify the species) with radar data (which show numbers and flying heights) to learn more about migration routes. This area of research will undoubtedly uncover a lot of valuable information about migration patterns and timing, and may even help birders predict the best times to visit their local parks to witness a particularly good migration day.

Flight calls are made all night during migration but are given most often when it's foggy or right before dawn, as birds end their flight and land for the day. It's a fascinating and challenging experience to listen to, and try to identify, flocks of warblers and other species calling overhead during an active migration event.

Flight calls are also given during the day, when birds are flying between trees, or sometimes just when they are foraging. Increased sensitivity to flight calls can be very exciting, because it leads to noticing more and more warblers using these vocalizations. Flight calls are also a bit more challenging to learn than songs, but it's well worth the effort. They are presented in the Species Account and in the Flight Call Finder.

American Redstart Chip call (left) and flight call (right).

Understanding Call Structure

Becoming sensitive to warbler calls can vastly improve one's ability to detect and identify warblers. However, unlike the luxuriously long and distinctive warbler songs, chip and flight calls are very short and many sound extremely similar.

It is possible to learn many warbler songs or calls over the course of a few days, with proper study, testing, and review; however, learning chip and flight calls takes more time. As part of the process, one needs to become sensitive to the small pitch changes in these very short vocalizations. This can be a bit daunting at first, but the more one works on it, the easier it becomes.

The first step in identifying a call during the day is determining whether it is a flight call or a chip call. With just a little study they should become fairly easy to distinguish. As a general rule, flight calls tend to be higher-pitched, longer, thinner, and more modulated, features that can also make them harder for our ears to localize.

For calls in particular, sonograms are especially valuable tools for seeing and, in turn, hearing the complexities of these short vocalizations. Sonograms also assist in the memorization process. In addition, using slow-speed playback is an effective way to learn to hear the very fast pitch changes of these vocalizations.

We recommend not thinking of calls as "chips," because once a vocalization is named with a nonspecific term, as in "that's just a chip," there is a good chance that one will stop really listening to it. It's much more productive to listen to each sound as intensely as possible while carefully describing the call: Does it rise or fall in pitch, or is it hard to tell if there is any pitch movement? Is it Clear or Complex and modulated? Does it sound low or high? These questions combined with the Call Finders and the sonograms in the Species Accounts, should greatly help in learning to ID these important vocalizations.

A set of vocalizations for this book is available as a download on Princeton's website, press.princeton.edu/titles/9968.html. These files contain all the vocalization examples for the book, including chip and flight calls, and also have slow-speed versions that facilitate hearing the more subtle, but important, characteristics of each vocalization.

Pitch Direction We find that listening to the pitch direction of a call can be an effective first step in learning to separate different species. We use pitch to separate calls into falling, rising, flat, and up/down pitch groups. Here are examples of each type. If possible, listen to the calls in the examples below and try to assess the pitch directions of each. Calls are very short, so it can be challenging at first to hear these pitch movements, but with practice most of them should become clear.

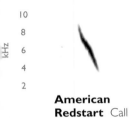

American Redstart Call with falling pitch.

Northern Waterthrush Call with rising pitch.

Louisiana Waterthrush Flat call with little pitch change.

Chestnut-sided Call with up-down pitch profile.

Pitch Range and Speed and How They Affect Songs and Calls Each call or song Element is a sound that starts at one frequency and ends on another in a short period of time. Some calls have very Expanded (wide) frequency ranges, and others, fairly Compressed (narrow) ranges. Calls also vary in length from extremely short to just very short.

The relationship between time and change in frequency determines how the vocalizations sound to our ears. The more time spent listening to these differences, the easier it will be to distinguish vocalizations that, on the surface, sound very similar. We covered this topic in the section "How to Listen to Warbler Songs." Please review this section for a more in-depth explanation of how frequency range and time spans interact.

Long Expanded Calls Some song Elements and calls are made up of simple, Expanded frequency sweeps that slowly rise or fall in pitch. Because these are sung relatively slowly, our ears hear all of the frequencies separately, and this sounds "pleasant" or "rich."

Yellow At 40 ms this is a very long call. Note the fast rise and slow fall of the pitches.

Short Expanded Calls As discussed above, wide frequency sweeps, sung very quickly, can become too fast for our ear to hear as separate frequencies. Hit with many frequencies in a very sort time, our ear hears these sounds as more percussive or harsh.

Palm and Black-and-white Fast, but Expanded slurs sound chip-like or percussive.

Beginning or Ending Attacks Very fast and Expanded frequency sweeps can occur at the beginning or end of a call that is otherwise mostly a slur. We call such percussive sounds an "attack," sharply emphasizing the start or ending of a vocalization. Calls with attacks are fairly easy to separate from calls that are just simple slurs. The very short and Expanded pitch change at the beginning of this Canada Warbler chip call gives it a percussive attack. The more prolonged lower frequencies give the call a distinctive low sound.

Canada

Small Frequency Ranges Some calls have an extremely Compressed frequency range. When sung over a very short time, they sound like a "tick" or a "tink," depending on the height of the pitch. This Magnolia call has a very Compressed frequency range and is high, thus sounding like a "tink" or a pencil hitting a crystal glass. This MacGillivray's call also has a Compressed pitch range that is much lower than the prior call, sounding darker. It is also much more Complex.

Magnolia

MacGillivray's

Complex and Shadow Calls Birds create their vocalizations using two syrinxes that are capable of acting independently. The resulting sounds can be very complex, unlike anything we could imitate with our own single voice boxes. Even simple slurs can have complex up/down/up pitch movements in very short time spans. These complexities can add either "richness" to a smooth tone or "roughness" and an accented quality to other sounds.

Sometimes these complexities produce a softer echo or shadow of the louder Elements of the main call. These "shadow" vocalizations can add rhythmic complexity, accented beginnings (or attacks), or nonharmonic complexity to a simpler, louder Element. We call these additional vocalization parts Shadow Calls.

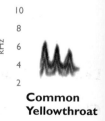

Common Yellowthroat

The Shadow Calls in these vocalizations double the main call Elements, adding complexity and emphasizing their fast rhythmic attacks.

Mourning

Shadow Calls also add multipitch complexity and a roughness to this rising call. This very Expanded, short "Shadow" slur gives the beginning of this vocalization a sharp attack or percussive edge, a very different sound than a simpler call like that of the Yellow Warbler above.

Swainson's

Call Volume Distribution A warbler's call can span an Expanded frequency range, often very quickly, as seen above. Each frequency produced during a call, however, does not always have the same volume or energy. Very often there is an emphasis of volume in the upper, middle, or lower ranges of the sweep that contribute to the call sounding high or low, bright or breathy. The softer part of the vocalization usually adds either a percussive edge or a breathiness to the whole call, making it sound more complex than if the emphasized frequencies had been vocalized alone.

The downslurred portion of this call has a fairly even distribution of volume across all frequencies. To our ears this sounds like a smooth, rich, and pleasing vocalization.

Yellow Note the Expanded pitch range and even volume throughout the downward slur of this call.

Here's an example of a call that emphasizes the higher parts of the frequency sweep. This call will sound thinner than a more full-range call, but very different than a more Compressed "tink" that lacks the "tail" of this call.

Northern Parula

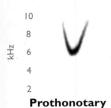

This last call example has almost all of its volume or energy in the lowest, and center, section of the call. The "wings" of the call, the beginning high downslur and the ending Expanded and fast upslur, add an almost wispy or breathy complexity to what would otherwise sound like a much simpler "chink." The softer slurs make the call sound somewhat hollow.

Prothonotary

Learning Chip Calls

Chip Call Finder Organization

We have organized calls in the Call Finder into six different groups, based on the pitch direction and speed of the calls. We have further arranged them according to the height of their pitch (high to lower) and the complexity of their structure.

One way to start learning them is to take one call from each group and test to see if you can differentiate the calls by their group pitch profile. Using the vocalizations downloaded from the Princeton website press.princeton.edu/titles/9968.html create a small playlist of a few select calls to aid in this process.

It can also help to learn a few of the most common calls, such as those of Yellow-rumped Warbler, Common Yellowthroat, and Yellow Warbler. These can then become "anchor" calls to be used as comparisons for shape and speed when listening to other species. Here are some chip call examples from each of the six groups.

Calls That Fall in Pitch

American Redstart

American Redstart This species calls frequently and has a simple, downslurred call that is representative of the largest group of calls, those that clearly fall in pitch over a relatively long time period.

Two things to notice about this call that affect how it sounds are the Expanded frequency range (from well over 9,000 cycles to about 3,000 cycles) and the fairly long length, which allows our ears to hear all of the frequencies of the smooth downslur.

This call also lacks the complexity added by any shadow calls. It has a fairly even distribution of volume over the whole call but is a bit softer in the lower frequencies, adding a slight breathiness. Overall it has a clear and clean quality.

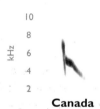

Canada

Canada Warbler Here's another call from the falling pitch group, though one very different from the American Redstart call. First, there is a very fast, Expanded sound at the beginning of the call that is so fast that, to our ears, it sounds like all the frequencies occur at once. As mentioned above, this sounds like noise or a percussive, explosive chip-like attack. This attack is followed by a slower, longer downslur that does not have an Expanded frequency range and that starts at a low pitch. Note that using half-speed vocalizations downloaded from our website can make it easier to hear the pitch profile and quality of each call.

This call sounds like a fairly pure, low downslur with an initial percussive, complex attack. The pitch range and explosive edge make it easy to separate from the American Redstart's higher downslurred call above.

Short Calls That Fall in Pitch Very Quickly

The calls in this second group also fall in pitch but do so rapidly enough to be, with some practice, differentiated from the first group.

Northern Parula The calls of this species, like those of American Redstart, span a wide frequency range and are pure, without any additional complicating sounds.

The length of the call is, however, much shorter, 13 ms vs 38 ms for the American Redstart. This speed is still slow enough that we can

Northern Parula

hear the frequency sweep of the call. It is also noticeably faster and shorter than that of American Redstart, which, in comparison, has a luxuriously long time to present all of its frequencies. Northern Parula's frequency sweep doesn't go as low as American Redstart's, and concentrates more volume in the highest parts of the call, causing it to sound even shorter, thinner, and higher than the American Redstart call. It can be difficult to hear the pitch direction of such short calls.

Calls without Pitch Change

Some chip calls have little pitch change. Depending on their length they can sound like dense "blobs," "cheks," or high-frequency "tinks" or "seets."

Common Yellowthroat This is one of the most complex warbler chip calls. In a very short period of time there are three, sharp up/down "peaks," all produced at the same low pitch. The call is fast, but it is still slow enough for our ear to detect each peak as a separate, albeit very brief, sound, such that the vocalization sounds like a dark, low, grainy rattle. The graininess is reinforced by the very strong shadow call, doubling the main Element.

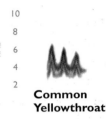

Common Yellowthroat

Compare that call to another very high call with minimal pitch change. This call sounds like a very short "tink," or the plink of a string.

Magnolia

Calls That Rise in Pitch

A number of warbler chip calls rise in pitch and are separated here into two groups: those with longer lengths and those with shorter ones. There aren't as many warblers in these two groups, and most of these calls are very complex. It is interesting that there are not any smoothly upslurred warbler chip calls given by the warblers in the United States and Canada. It's almost as if warblers find it is easy to vocalize calls that fall in pitch, but it is lots of work for them to produce rising calls.

This Mourning Warbler call has a very dense, complex, rising quality.

This sonogram reveals several Elements that rapidly rise in pitch, one after the other. The call is fairly long, and the resulting sound is of a complex, dense rising chord: a unique sound.

Mourning

Short Rising Calls

The calls in this second group with rising pitches are vocalized very quickly. This Nashville call starts with a very fast, Expanded sound that is so fast there is barely time for our ear to hear any of its pitches, although there is still a sense of a rising quality. After this initial "attack" (forceful or percussive noise at the beginning of the call), the

Nashville

call then has a very fast but narrow upslur vocalized within a very small, high pitch range. The result sounds like an explosive, high, and very fast rising slur.

Up/down The final group of calls combines qualities of both the rising and falling groups: an upward slur followed by a downward slur. The speed of this kind of vocalization determines whether it sounds like a rich, pleasing call or more like a lip-smacking call without an obvious, clear pitch. In other words (and these transliterations are only vague references to be replaced by your own listening experience), when very fast, the up-and-down pitch movements serve to make the call sound thicker and richer than a very fast simple upslur or downslur. Most of these calls have faster, shorter upslurs followed by longer downslurs. The fast upslur tends to emphasize, or accent, the beginning of the call, giving it a slightly more explosive start. These calls can sometimes sound a little "nagging."

Yellow Warbler The initial upslur of this call is fast, whereas the following downslur takes a much longer time over a wider frequency. Thus the call has a bit of an initial accent or attack followed by a more prominent, longer falling pitch. The initial upward part makes the call sound considerably different than the calls in the downslur group, and, while providing an opening accent, is still slow enough to be heard as an upslur, and thus the whole call has an up/down pitch profile.

Yellow

A good starting point for learning chip calls is to learn to separate the calls into their various groups, then explore how each group member is different. The results are worth the effort. Even a modest amount of initial study will undoubtedly increase awareness of warbler calls in the field.

Learning Flight Calls

Of all of a warbler's characteristics, flight calls are probably the least well known. There are, however, many benefits to learning to recognize these vocalizations, the primary one being that they can assist in locating and identifying previously undetected warblers. They also make it possible to identify many warblers when they are migrating at night.

In addition to their chip calls, many species of warblers give flight calls during the day while flying from tree to tree or even when feeding. Many species, like Connecticut, Blackpoll, and Worm-eating warblers, give flight calls more often than chip calls. Listening for flight calls may lead to discovering a warbler that may not have been seen or to finding a different species among a group of more common birds.

Flight calls are primarily given by warblers and other species while they are migrating at night. If you have a chance, find a quiet spot, like a rooftop or open parking lot, and listen to the warblers, thrushes, buntings, and other species flying over your area during spring or fall migration. It can be an exhilarating experience.

There has been much work done in the last few years collecting recordings of migrat-

ing birds to help understand flight patterns and migration timing. Researchers ha
correlating the night-flight data from these recording stations with radar data to
predict where migrating birds will be the next day. Pioneers in this field include Micha
O'Brien, Bill Evans, Andy Farnsworth, Mike Lanzone, David LaPuma, J. Alan Clark, Cornell University, and the Cape May Bird Observatory's morning flight program.

Compared to chip calls, flight calls are usually higher, thinner, less emphatic, and lack
the short, Expanded slurs that give an accented attack to many chip calls. While the majority of chip calls are falling (25 of our examples versus 13 rising), most flight calls have
a rising pitch profile (25 rising versus 7 falling.)

Flight Call Pitch Groups

The process outlined above on learning chip calls will work for flight calls as well. To assist in the process, we have outlined three main categories based on the pitch trend of the
call: rising, falling and steady. Of course, many species' calls are variable, but we feel these
examples represent a solid reference that can then be augmented by time in the field.

Both chip and flight calls are very short, so the first step in learning them is to practice
hearing their pitch contours. After learning these differences, listen for other characteristics of these vocalizations. Qualities to listen for include the length of the call; whether
the call is Clear, Buzzy, or Complex; and whether the pitch of the call is high or low. Also,
some flight calls have a very consistent quality throughout, while others have a quality
change within the call, for example, from thin to dense.

Final Tip

When hearing a warbler call, do not try to identify the bird immediately, but first note the
call's qualities: Is the pitch profile rising, falling, steady, or up/down? Is the quality Clear,
modulated or Buzzy? Does it sound very short or fairly long? Asking these questions will
focus the ear on hearing the call more carefully and provide more information for an
eventual ID, if not to a species, then to a group of similar-sounding warblers.

Not everyone finds it is easy to learn warbler chip and flight calls; it often takes time
and a lot of concentration. There is a link to our article on "How to Learn Warbler Vocalizations" on the Princeton University Press website, press.princeton.edu/titles/9968.html
where we outline an efficient approach to this task.

The benefits from starting this process begin long before one can identify many of the
warblers heard. Even a limited amount of study will increase awareness of these subtle
vocalizations in the field. Careful study and focused listening will also aid in learning the
longer warbler songs and, indeed, all bird vocalizations.

We want to greatly thank Mike Lanzone and Andrew Farnsworth for their help with
our flight call samples. For more information and examples we recommend the excellent
Flight Calls of Migratory Birds, by Bill Evans and Michael O'Brien.

Red-faced, p. 422

American Redstart, p. 138

Painted Redstart, p. 390

Black-throated Blue, p. 186

Audubon's, p. 476

Canada, p. 216

Grace's, p. 286

Yellow-throated, p. 492

Cerulean, p. 232

Kirtland's, p. 312

Magnolia, p. 340

Blackburnian, p. 166

Prothonotary, p. 416

Yellow, p. 466

Pine, p. 402

Blue-winged, p. 208

Wilson's, p. 452

Common Yellowthroat, p. 254

Hooded, p. 300

Hooded, p. 300

Hermit, p. 294

Canada, p. 216

Common Yellowthroat, p. 260

Canada, p. 216

Myrtle, p. 480

Mourning, p. 350

MacGillivray's, p. 330

Connecticut, p. 264

Virginia's, p. 446

Blackpoll, p. 176

MacGillivray's, p. 336

Mourning, p. 356

Pine, p. 402

American Redstart, p. 146

Palm, p. 396

Palm, p. 396

Swainson's, p. 428

L. Waterthrush, p. 318

N. Waterthrush, p. 372

Worm-eating, p. 460

Ovenbird, p. 384

Blackburnian, p. 172

FACE QUICK FINDER

Bay-breasted, p. 150

Blackpoll, p. 176

Black-throated Gray, p. 196

Black-and-white, p. 160

Northern Parula, p. 366

Brewster's, p. 214

Golden-winged, p. 280

Chestnut-sided, p. 238

Myrtle, p. 476

Cape May, p. 222

Lawrence's, p. 214

Prairie, p. 410

Townsend's, p. 440

Black-throated Green, p. 202

Kentucky, p. 306

Golden-cheeked, p. 274

Black-throated Green, p. 202

Townsend's, p. 440

Hermit, p. 294

Audubon's, p. 480

Bay-breasted, p. 150

Bay-breasted, p. 156

Chestnut-sided, p. 244

Prairie, p. 410

Tennessee, p. 434

Orange-crowned, p. 378

Colima, p. 248

Nashville, p. 360

Magnolia, p. 346

Cape May, p. 228

Lucy's, p. 324

Tennessee, p. 434

Blackpoll, p. 182

Orange-crowned, p. 378

Connecticut, p. 270

Cerulean, p. 232

Black-throated Blue, p. 192

Mourning, p. 356

Yellow, p. 466

Black-throated Gray, p. 196

Black-throated Gray, p. 196

Blackpoll, p. 176

Black-and-white, p. 160

Blackpoll, p. 176

Connecticut, p. 264

Black-throated Blue, p. 192

Cerulean, p. 232

Cerulean, p. 232

Black-throated Blue, p. 18

Mourning, p. 350

MacGillivray's, p. 330

Kentucky, p. 306

Hooded, p. 300

Common Yellowthroat, p. 25

Golden-winged, p. 280

Brewster's, p. 214

Audubon's, p. 476

Myrtle, p. 476

Yellow-throated, p. 492

Magnolia, p. 340

Townsend's, p. 440

Black-throated Green, p. 202

Golden-cheeked, p. 274

Hermit, p. 294

Connecticut, p. 270

Orange-crowned, p. 378

Tennessee, p. 434

Canada, p. 216

Kirtland's, p. 312

Tennessee, p. 434

Orange-crowned, p. 378

Hooded, p. 300

Wilson's, p. 452

Pine, p. 402

Chestnut-sided, p. 244

American Redstart, p. 146

Bay-breasted, p. 156

Bay-breasted, p. 150

Palm, p. 396

Virginia's, p. 446

Colima, p. 248

Lucy's, p. 324

SIDE QUICK FINDER

N. Waterthrush, p. 372

L. Waterthrush, p. 318

Swainson's, p. 428

Worm-eating, p. 460

Ovenbird, p. 384

Painted Redstart, p. 390

American Redstart, p. 138

Bay-breasted, p. 150

Chestnut-sided, p. 238

Red-faced, p. 422

Blackburnian, p. 166

Prothonotary, p. 416

Prairie, p. 410

Yellow, p. 466

Cape May, p. 222

Grace's, p. 286

Northern Parula, p. 366

Canada, p. 216

Blue-winged, p. 208

Lawrence's, p. 214

Golden-cheeked, p. 274

Black-throated Green, p. 202

Townsend's, p. 440

Mourning, p. 356

MacGillivray's, p. 336

Hermit, p. 294

Magnolia, p. 346

Prairie, p. 410

Nashville, p. 360

Canada, p. 216

Yellow, p. 466

Mourning, p. 356

Common Yellowthroat, p. 260

Audubon's, p. 480

Myrtle, p. 480

Blackburnian, p. 172

Palm, p. 396

Blackpoll, p. 182

Pine, p. 402

Cape May, p. 228

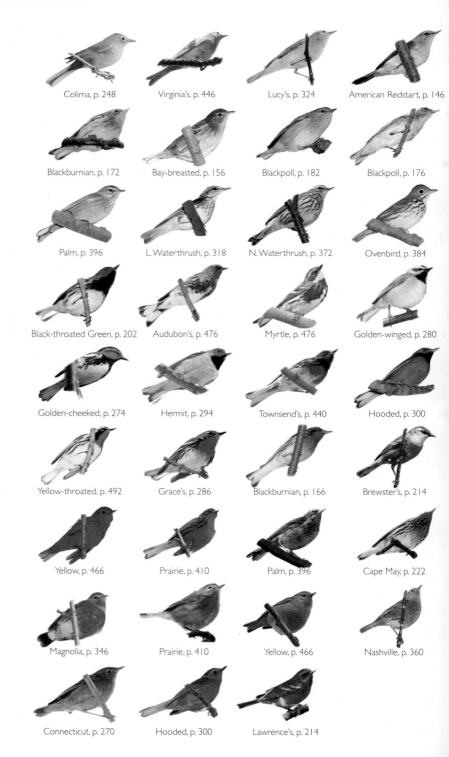

Colima, p. 248

Virginia's, p. 446

Lucy's, p. 324

American Redstart, p. 146

Blackburnian, p. 172

Bay-breasted, p. 156

Blackpoll, p. 182

Blackpoll, p. 176

Palm, p. 396

L. Waterthrush, p. 318

N. Waterthrush, p. 372

Ovenbird, p. 384

Black-throated Green, p. 202

Audubon's, p. 476

Myrtle, p. 476

Golden-winged, p. 280

Golden-cheeked, p. 274

Hermit, p. 294

Townsend's, p. 440

Hooded, p. 300

Yellow-throated, p. 492

Grace's, p. 286

Blackburnian, p. 166

Brewster's, p. 214

Yellow, p. 466

Prairie, p. 410

Palm, p. 396

Cape May, p. 222

Magnolia, p. 346

Prairie, p. 410

Yellow, p. 466

Nashville, p. 360

Connecticut, p. 270

Hooded, p. 300

Lawrence's, p. 214

45° VIEW QUICK FINDER

Chestnut-sided, p. 244   Pine, p. 402   Black-throated Blue, p. 192   Tennessee, p. 434   Orange-crowned, p. 378

Cape May, p. 228   Audubon's, p. 480   Myrtle, p. 480   Worm-eating, p. 460   Swainson's, p. 428

Red-faced, p. 422   Painted Redstart, p. 390   Bay-breasted, p. 150   American Redstart, p. 138   Chestnut-sided, p. 238

Black-throated Gray, p. 196   Blackpoll, p. 176   Black-and-white, p. 160   Cerulean, p. 232   Black-throated Blue, p. 186

Kentucky, p. 306   Common Yellowthroat, p. 254   Hermit, p. 294   Townsend's, p. 440   Black-throated Green, p. 202

Mourning, p. 350   MacGillivray's, p. 330   Connecticut, p. 264   Mourning, p. 356   MacGillivray's, p. 336

Magnolia, p. 340   Kirtland's, p. 312   Canada, p. 216   Northern Parula, p. 366   Canada, p. 216

Prothonotary, p. 416   Wilson's, p. 452   Blue-winged, p. 208   Pine, p. 402   Common Yellowthroat, p. 260

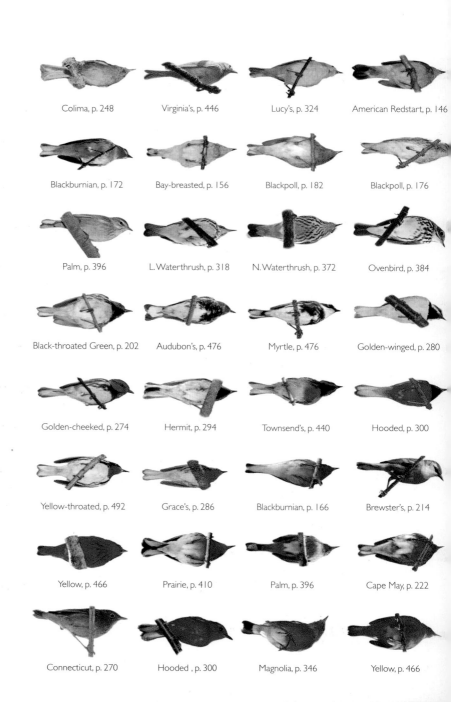

Colima, p. 248   Virginia's, p. 446   Lucy's, p. 324   American Redstart, p. 146

Blackburnian, p. 172   Bay-breasted, p. 156   Blackpoll, p. 182   Blackpoll, p. 176

Palm, p. 396   L. Waterthrush, p. 318   N. Waterthrush, p. 372   Ovenbird, p. 384

Black-throated Green, p. 202   Audubon's, p. 476   Myrtle, p. 476   Golden-winged, p. 280

Golden-cheeked, p. 274   Hermit, p. 294   Townsend's, p. 440   Hooded, p. 300

Yellow-throated, p. 492   Grace's, p. 286   Blackburnian, p. 166   Brewster's, p. 214

Yellow, p. 466   Prairie, p. 410   Palm, p. 396   Cape May, p. 222

Connecticut, p. 270   Hooded , p. 300   Magnolia, p. 346   Yellow, p. 466

UNDERVIEW QUICK FINDER

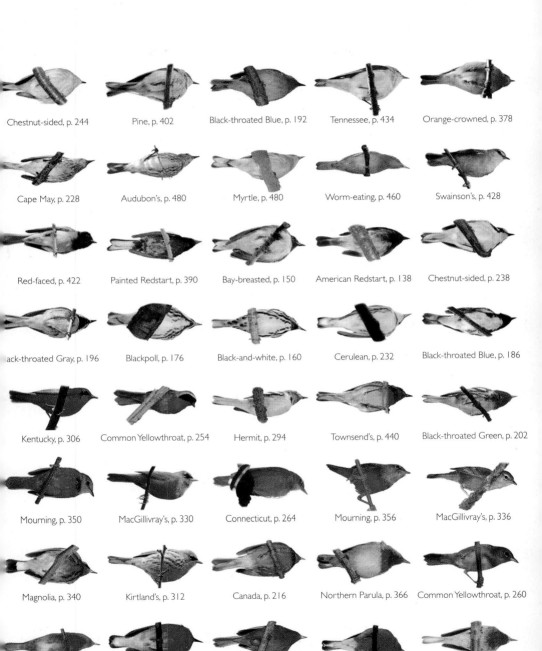

Chestnut-sided, p. 244

Pine, p. 402

Black-throated Blue, p. 192

Tennessee, p. 434

Orange-crowned, p. 378

Cape May, p. 228

Audubon's, p. 480

Myrtle, p. 480

Worm-eating, p. 460

Swainson's, p. 428

Red-faced, p. 422

Painted Redstart, p. 390

Bay-breasted, p. 150

American Redstart, p. 138

Chestnut-sided, p. 238

ack-throated Gray, p. 196

Blackpoll, p. 176

Black-and-white, p. 160

Cerulean, p. 232

Black-throated Blue, p. 186

Kentucky, p. 306

Common Yellowthroat, p. 254

Hermit, p. 294

Townsend's, p. 440

Black-throated Green, p. 202

Mourning, p. 350

MacGillivray's, p. 330

Connecticut, p. 264

Mourning, p. 356

MacGillivray's, p. 336

Magnolia, p. 340

Kirtland's, p. 312

Canada, p. 216

Northern Parula, p. 366

Common Yellowthroat, p. 260

Nashville, p. 360

Prothonotary, p. 416

Wilson's, p. 452

Blue-winged, p. 208

Pine, p. 402

American Redstart, p. 138

Black-throated Blue, p. 186

Cerulean, p. 232

Northern Parula, p. 366

Kirtland's, p. 312

Magnolia, p. 340

Canada, p. 216

Mourning, p. 350

Brewster's, p. 214

Golden-winged, p. 280

Myrtle, p. 476

Yellow-throated, p. 492

Wilson's, p. 452

Prairie, p. 410

Yellow, p. 466

Prothonotary, p. 416

Blue-winged, p. 208

Pine, p. 402

Hooded, p. 300

Yellow, p. 466

Black-and-white, p. 160

Ovenbird, p. 384

L. Waterthrush, p. 318

N. Waterthrush, p. 372

Blackpoll, p. 176

Bay-breasted, p. 150

Chestnut-sided, p. 238

EAST SPRING QUICK FINDER

Cerulean, p. 232

Black-throated Blue, p. 192

MacGillivray's, p. 336

Mourning, p. 356

Connecticut, p. 264

Nashville, p. 360

Orange-crowned, p. 378

Tennessee, p. 434

Lawrence's, p. 214

Golden-cheeked, p. 274

Black-throated Green, p. 202

Kentucky, p. 306

Cape May, p. 222

Blackburnian, p. 166

Common Yellowthroat, p. 254

Hooded, p. 300

Palm, p. 396

Common Yellowthroat, p. 260

Tennessee, p. 434

Orange-crowned, p. 378

Swainson's, p. 428

Worm-eating, p. 460

Pine, p. 402

American Redstart, p. 146

American Redstart, p. 138

Black-throated Blue, p. 186

Cerulean, p. 232

Northern Parula, p. 366

Blue-winged, p. 208

Palm, p. 396

Prairie, p. 410

Kentucky, p. 306

Canada, p. 216

Hooded, p. 300

Pine, p. 402

Prothonotary, p. 416

Yellow, p. 466

Mourning, p. 350

Connecticut, p. 264

Mourning, p. 356

Common Yellowthroat, p. 260

Connecticut, p. 270

Black-throated Blue, p. 192

Cerulean, p. 232

Orange-crowned, p. 378

Orange-crowned, p. 378

Tennessee, p. 434

Blackburnian, p. 172

Tennessee, p. 434

Prairie, p. 410

Swainson's, p. 428

Worm-eating, p. 460

EAST FALL QUICK FINDER

Yellow-throated, p. 492

Golden-winged, p. 280

Brewster's, p. 214

Black-throated Green, p. 202

Common Yellowthroat, p. 254

Hooded, p. 300

Golden-cheeked, p. 274

Black-throated Green, p. 202

Yellow, p. 466

Lawrence's, p. 214

Wilson's, p. 452

Canada, p. 216

Nashville, p. 360

Canada, p. 216

Magnolia, p. 346

Kirtland's, p. 312

Chestnut-sided, p. 244

American Redstart, p. 146

Pine, p. 402

Myrtle, p. 480

Blackpoll, p. 182

Bay-breasted, p. 156

Cape May, p. 228

Palm, p. 396

Ovenbird, p. 384

N. Waterthrush, p. 372

L. Waterthrush, p. 318

Black-and-white, p. 160

American Redstart, p. 138

Painted Redstart, p. 390

Red-faced, p. 422

American Redstart, p. 146

Black-throated Gray, p. 196

Myrtle, p. 476

Audubon's, p. 480

Myrtle, p. 480

Lucy's, p. 324

Hermit, p. 294

MacGillivray's, p. 330

Northern Parula, p. 366

Common Yellowthroat, p. 260

Common Yellowthroat, p. 254

Wilson's, p. 452

WEST QUICK FINDER

Hermit, p. 294

Golden-cheeked, p. 274

Townsend's, p. 440

Townsend's, p. 440

Grace's, p. 286

Audubon's, p. 476

Virginia's, p. 446

Colima, p. 248

Orange-crowned, p. 378

Nashville, p. 360

Ovenbird, p. 384

MacGillivray's, p. 336

Yellow, p. 466

Yellow, p. 466

Orange-crowned, p. 378

EASTERN UNDERTAILS

Dark Tail, Yellow Undertail Coverts

Spotted UnTC

| Wilson's | Common Yellowthroat | Orange-crowned | Black-throated Blue, Female | Nashville | Mourning | Connecticut | Kentucky | ✓Black-and-white | ✓Worm-ea... |

Dark Tail, Non-yellow UnTC

Colored and Patterned

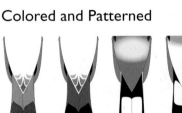

| Swainson's | ✓Canada | Tennessee | Louisiana Waterthrush | Northern Waterthrush | Ovenbird | ✓American Redstart, Female | ✓American Redstart, Male | ✓Palm | ✓Magnol... |

Dark Tail Base, White UnTC

Black Edging White UnTC

| Yellow-throated | Northern Parula | Blackpoll | Myrtle | Cerulean | Black-throated Blue, Male | Pine | Tennessee | Golden-winged | Chestnut-... |

White Tail Spots, Yellow Body or Vent

Yellow Ta... and UnT...

| Hooded | Prairie | Blue-winged | Black-throated Green | Prothonotary | Blackburnian | Cape May | Bay-breasted | ✓Yellow |

WESTERN UNDERTAILS

Dark Tail, Yellow UnTC

Dark Tail Base, White UnTC

Yellow Tail and UnTC

Wilson's   MacGillivray's   Common Yel-lowthroat   Orange-crowned   Nashville   Virginia's   Audubon's   Tennessee   ✓ Yellow

Dark Tail, White UnTC

Black Edging, White UnTC

Red-faced   Tennessee   Lucy's   Louisiana Waterthrush   Northern Waterthrush   Ovenbird   Hermit   Black-throated Gray   Grace's

Spotted UnTC

Rare Birds

Townsend's   ✓ Painted Redstart   ✓ Colima   Kirtland's   Tropical Parula   Golden-cheeked

✓ = Diagnostic Pattern

Note: Black edging and black at the base of the tail can be difficult to see and can vary depending on how an individual bird is holding its feathers.

Non-Warblers

Chipping Sparrow   Olive Warbler   Yellow-throated Vireo   Red-eyed Vireo   Scarlet Tanager   Baltimore Oriole   Yellow-breasted Chat

BUZZY

Rising Pitch
1 Section   *2 Sections*

10
kHz
2

Prairie Usually long; distinct, 1-Element Phrases; even rhythm; initial Phrases can be Clear

Black-throated Blue Short; 1-Element Phrases; last Section 1 rising, longer Phrase

Northern Parula Trill, could be heard as Buzz; diagnostic fast up/down ending; 1 very long rising Buzzy or Trilled Phrase

Falling Pitch
2 Sections

Steady Pitch
1 Section

10
kHz
2

Golden-winged 1-Element Phrases; 2nd Section usually 3 lower Phrases; tight, high Buzzes; all Phrases same quality

Blue-winged 2 1-Element Phrases, the 2nd usually lower; Sections of different quality: one Buzz, one Trill

Palm Trill speed, but could sound like Buzz due to very coarse, rough Phrase quality; very even speed/pitch

Palm 7–12 1-Element, Complex Phrases with Buzzy/Clear quality; distinct Phrases with unique down/up shape, steady delivery

PARTLY BUZZY

Rising Pitch
1 Section   *2 Sections*   *3 Sections*

10
kHz
2

Prairie Usually distinct, long, 1-Element Phrases; even rhythm; initial Phrases can be Clear

Black-throated Blue Short; 1-Element Phrases; 1st Section can have Clear Phrases; last Section 1 longer, rising Buzzy Phrase

Cerulean 1st Section Complex, 2-Element Phrases; ending higher, steady Trill or loose Buzz

Cerulean Each Section higher, faster; 1st Complex 2-Element Phrases; ending steady Trill or loose Buzz

Variable Pitch
3 Sections

10
kHz
2

Black-throated Green Always some Clear Elements; pitch shape consistent, diagnostic in East, easy-to-learn

Golden-winged Starts like Blue-winged; extra Section Buzzes higher, tighter; could be hybrid

Blue-winged Type A song with added Section(s); first two 1-Phrase Sections usually distinctive; loose, lower Buzzes than Golden-winged; check for hybrids

TRILLED

Rising Pitch
1 Section   *2 Sections*   *3 Sections*

10
kHz
2

Prairie Usually long; 1-Element Phrases; even rhythm; initial Phrases can be Clear; becoming Buzzy; some variations are Trills

Northern Parula Trill, could be heard as Buzz; diagnostic fast up/down end; 1 very long, rising Buzzy or Trilled Phrase

Northern Parula Long Section of rising, fast modulated Trill/Buzz distinctive; usually diagnostic fast up/down ending

Steady Pitch
1 Section

10
kHz
2

Pine A 1-Section Trill; lower; Compressed, slower, simpler slurred Phrases than Worm-eating or Chipping Sparrow

Pine B Faster song types; still lower, more Compressed than Worm-eating

Worm-eating A 1-Section Trill; Expanded Phrases, staccato, bright; less tinkling and/or Buzzy than Chipping Sparrow; ending usually less abrupt

3 Sections

Black-throated Blue Short
song; 1-Element Phrases; last 2
Sections 1 longer, rising Phrase each

Northern Parula
Fast, rising, modulated Trills
or Buzzes; diagnostic fast
up/down ending

Variable Pitch
3+ Sections

Blue-winged Type A song
with added Section(s); first two
1-Phrase Sections distinctive;
loose, lower Buzzes than
Golden-winged; check for hybrids

Golden-winged Variable; can
sound like Blue-winged but Buzzes
usually tighter, higher, often shorter;
check for hybrids

Falling Pitch
2 Sections

Steady Pitch

Northern Parula
Long Section of rising, fast
modulated Trill/Buzz
distinctive; usually diagnostic
fast up/down ending

Blue-winged 2
1-Element Phrases, the 2nd
usually lower; Sections of
different quality one Buzz, one
Trill

Palm 7–12 1-Element, Complex
Phrases with Buzzy/Clear quality;
distinct Phrases with unique down/
up shape, steady delivery

4 Sections

American Redstart High; 4–7
1-Element slurs in 1st; subsequent Sections
only 1 Phrase each; often alternates with
1-Section song; sometimes last Phrase is Buzz

Black-throated Green
Always 2 Clear Elements in 3rd
Section; pitch shape consistent,
diagnostic in East, easy to learn

Falling Pitch
1 Section

2 Sections

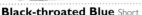

Orange-crowned Always
Trill speed; pitch and/or speed
often wanders during song, often
falling at end

Orange-crowned Both
Sections Trills; pitch and/or speed
often wanders; 2nd Section lower,
different speed

Worm-eating B Faster, still
Expanded Phrases, dry, staccato;
higher than Pine

Blackpoll Very high, very
Compressed, 1-Element
Phrases; thin, simple, staccato

Orange-crowned
Usually obvious wavering of
pitch and/or speed; more
slurred, rich than others

Palm Very buzzy, harsh quality;
steady, shorter, with fewer
Phrases than Pine, Worm-eating,
or Orange-crowned

PARTLY TRILLED

Rising Pitch
2 Sections   *3 Sections*

Cerulean Each Section higher, faster; 1st Complex 2–5, 2-Element Phrases; ending steady Trill or loose Buzz

Northern Parula Trill, could be heard as Buzz; 1 very long, rising Buzzy or Trilled Phrase; diagnostic fast up/down ending

Yellow-rumped M 1–2 Sections of loosely Complex, Compressed Phrases with slurred, warbly quality; 1st Section never Trill; ending often falls in volume

Cerulean Each Section higher, faster; 1st Complex 2–5, 2-Element Phrases; 2nd Section slow Trill; ending steady Trill or loose Buzz

Falling Pitch
2 Sections

Blue-winged 2 1-Element Phrases, the 2nd usually lower; Sections of different quality one Buzz, one Trill

Nashville 6–9 usually 2-Element Clear Phrases; followed by lower, faster Section, often Trill; fairly emphatic, staccato

Wilson's 1–2 Sections; 1-Element, emphatic Phrases, usually falling in pitch; 2nd Section often Trill; 1st never Trill

Yellow-rumped M 1–2 Sections of loosely Complex, Compressed Phrases with slurred, warbly quality; 1st Section never Trill; ending often falls in volume

COMPLEX

Rising Pitch
2 Sections

Cerulean Each Section higher, faster; 1st 2–5, Complex, falling 2-Element Phrases; ending steady Trill or loose Buzz

Blackburnian Complex, falling 2-Element Phrases; strong contrast between Elements; last Section very high slur

Mourning Low, burry, Complex, 2-Element Phrases; 1st Section rising pitch profile; 2nd often falling profile and Clearer

Yellow-rumped M 1–2 Sections of loosely Complex, Compressed Phrases with slurred, warbly quality; ending often falls in volume

Falling Pitch
2 Sections   *2+ Sections*

Blackburnian Very high 1st Section of long, Compressed Phrases; 2nd Section Complex, lower 2-Element Phrases

Mourning Low, burry, Complex, 2-Element Phrases; 1st Section rising pitch profile; 2nd often falling profile and Clearer

Yellow-rumped M 1–2 Sections of loosely Complex, Compressed Phrases with slurred, warbly quality; ending often falls in volume

Yellow-throated Long song; long 1st Section with 6–8 1-Element Phrases falling pitch profile; variable, short ending usually upslur. Clear Phrases but some variations might be heard as Complex

Steady Pitch
1 Section

Kentucky Fairly low, chanting, burry; 5–8 2-Element Phrases with rising Phrase pitch profile; even, distinct; always 1 Section

Ovenbird Very long song; starts softly, grows very emphatic; Expanded, short downslurs; falling 2-Element Phrase pitch profile

Mourning Low, burry, 2-Element Phrases; dense, Complex; lower than Kentucky and coarser, more loosely Complex

Palm 7–12 1-Element, Complex Phrases with Buzzy/Clear quality; distinct Phrases with unique down/up shape, steady delivery; higher, denser, faster Phrases than Kentucky/Mourning closer to Buzz than Complex

Blackburnian Wide
pitch range; Complex
2-Element Phrases to
extremely high, Clear slurred
ending; 2nd Section can be Trill

Northern Parula
Long Section of rising, fast
modulated Trill/Buzz
distinctive; usually has
diagnostic fast up/down
ending

Northern Parula
Buzzier, Complex version
with Trill-speed Phrases;
ending diagnostic

Variable Pitch
3 Sections

  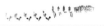  

Tennessee Very long song; 3 Sections of
Expanded, emphatic Phrases; speed/pitch vary
Section–Section; 1, sometimes 2 Sections often
Trills; 1st Section never

Golden-winged Starts
like Blue-winged; extra Section
Buzzes higher, tighter; could be
hybrid

Blue-winged Type A song with
added Section(s); first two 1-Phrase
Sections usually distinctive; loose,
lower Buzzes than Golden-winged;
check for hybrids

3 Sections

Northern Parula
Long, rising Section; could
sound like Trill, Buzz or
Complex Phrases; usually has
diagnostic fast up/down ending

Cerulean Each
Section higher, faster; 1st
Complex 2–5, 2-Element
Phrases; 2nd Section slow
Trill; ending steady Trill or
loose Buzz

Blackburnian Wide pitch
range from beginning to end; 1st
Section 7–8, Complex, 2-Element
Phrases; ending extremely high,
Clear slur

Northern Parula More
complicated version with
Complex, Trill-like Phrases
followed by longer rising
Section and up/down ending

Variable Pitch
2+ Sections

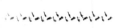

Yellow-rumped M
9–12 loosely Complex,
Compressed slurs; short
Interval, so slurred together;
often fades out at end

Blackburnian 2-Element
Phrase; 1st Element very
Compressed, long, high Clear slur;
2nd much lower, short, dense,
Complex

Mourning Low, burry, Complex,
2-Element Phrases; 1st Section rising
pitch profile; 2nd often lower, with
falling profile; more likely to have
Clear Section than MacGillivray's

CLEAR

Rising Pitch
2 Sections

10
kHz
2

Magnolia Very short; high, Clear; 2–3 usually 2-Element Phrases; next Sections only 1 Phrase each; ending a bit higher

American Redstart High; uncommon form; 4–7 1-Element slurs in 1st; 2nd Section higher; 3–4 similar Phrases; often alternates with 1-Section songs

Yellow-rumped M 1–2 Sections of loosely Complex (but can sound Clear), Compressed Phrases with slurred, warbly quality; 2nd Section avg. 4 Phrases; ending often falls in volume

Blackburnian Complex, falling 2-Element Phrases; strong contrast between Elements; last Section very high slur

Falling Pitch (cont.)
2 Sections

10
kHz
2

American Redstart High; 4–7 1-Element slurs in 1st; 2nd Section only 1 Phrase; often alternates with 1-Section songs

Yellow Expanded, long, high slurs; less common, unaccented 2-Section songs; often lower 2nd Section; always 1-Element Phrases in 1st Section; variable, usually more Sections

Yellow-throated Long song; long 1st Section with 6–8 1-Element Phrases, falling pitch profile; variable, short ending, usually upslur

Yellow-rumped M 1–2 Sections of loosely Complex (but can sound Clear), Compressed Phrases with slurred, warbly quality; 2nd Section avg. 4 Phrases; ending often falls in volume

Falling Pitch (cont.)
3–4 Sections

10
kHz
2

Northern Waterthrush Expanded, emphatic Phrases; pitch of Section steady; pitch drops Section to Section; speed increases; usually 3–4 Sections

Yellow-throated Long song; long 1st Section with 6–8 1-Element Phrases, falling pitch within Section; variable, short ending, usually upslur

Louisiana Waterthrush 1st Section 2–4 long downslurs, falling pitch within Section; intricate diagnostic Sections follow

Swainson's 3–5 1-Element, long Compressed slurred Phrases in 1st Section; ending Sections long Expanded slurs; simpler than Louisiana's diagnostic Sections

Steady Pitch
1 Section 1-Element Phrases

10
kHz
2

Cape May Very high, thin, short; 3–8 long, distinct, Compressed 1-Element upslurred Phrases; 1 Section

American Redstart High; short song; 4–7 simple Phrases, usually downslurs; often alternates with longer accented songs

Nashville Usually 6–9, fairly Expanded 2-Element Phrases; 1 Section only first half of main song; usually sings full song eventually

Pine Usually Trill; rarely slow enough to be countable; low, somewhat Expanded; Elements long enough to sound slurred and not strongly emphatic

Steady Pitch (cont.)
1 Section 2-Element Phrases

10
kHz
2

Bay-breasted Short; very high, thin; 3–6 fairly Compressed downslurs; short Interval so slurred; Element pitches even; lengths can vary so rhythm a little erratic

Black-and-white Long song; high, thin; uneven Phrases with rising pitch profile; usually longer, upslurred 1st Element

American Redstart Short; fairly high; 2 uneven Elements: usually long downslur then lower, short, more Expanded Element; often alternates with longer accented songs

Cape May Short, 4 Phrases; evenly pitched, spaced; long Interval so distinct Phrases; often alternates with simpler 1-Element Phrase song

Steady Pitch (cont.)
1 Section 2-Element (cont.)   *1 Section 3-Element Phrases*

10
kHz
2

Kentucky Complex but sometimes could be heard as Clear; low, chanting, burry; 5–8 2-Element Phrases with rising pitch profile; even, distinct; always 1 Section

Ovenbird Rare form; quality same as common form: fades in, emphatic, short Elements, falling Phrase pitch profile

Common Yellowthroat Slurred, variable-length/pitch Elements; usually up/down pitch profile within Phrase; often loud

Falling Pitch

East

1 Section | 2 Sections

Wilson's 1-Element Phrases repeated 8–12 times; fairly Expanded, emphatic; often grows louder/falls in pitch

Wilson's 1–2 Sections; 1-Element, emphatic Phrases, usually falling in pitch; 2nd Section often Trill; 1st never Trill

Nashville 6–9 usually 2-Element Clear Phrases; followed by lower, faster Section, often Trill; fairly emphatic, staccato

Black-and-white Very high; long songs; 2-Element Phrases; uncommon 2-Section song; 2nd Section always lower; similar Phrases

3 Sections

Mourning Low, burry, Complex but could sound Clear from distance; rising 2-Element Phrases in 1st Section; more likely to have Clear Elements than MacGillivray's

Yellow Less common, falling 3-Section song; fairly long, Expanded slurs; 1st Section 3–4 1-Element Phrases; always 2+ Phrases in 2nd Section; pitch steady within Sections

Yellow-throated Long song; long 1st Section with 6–8 1-Element Phrases, falling pitch profile; variable, short ending, usually upslur

Wilson's Uncommon short 3rd Section; 1-Element, short, emphatic Phrases, usually falling in pitch; 2nd Section often Trill; 1st never Trill; always 1-Element Phrases; usually fairly consistent Phrase quality

4 Sections (cont.) | 5+ Sections | Many

Northern Waterthrush Expanded, emphatic Phrases; pitch 1st Section steady; pitch drops Section to Section; speed increases; usually 3–4 Sections

Louisiana Waterthrush 1st Section 2–4 long downslurs, falling pitch within Section; intricate diagnostic Sections follow

Swainson's 3–5 1-Element, long Compressed slurred Phrases in 1st Section; ending Sections longer, Expanded slurs; simpler than Louisiana's diagnostic Sections

Louisiana Waterthrush Very long, Type B songs have wide variety of short, Expanded "chips" and longer slurs; usually fades out gradually; beginning same as shorter songs

Prothonotary 6–10 Expanded, long, distinct upslurs; even, bright, rich

Wilson's 8–12 1-Element Phrases; fairly Expanded, emphatic; often grows louder/falls in pitch; never Trill in 1st Section

Blackpoll Long song; very high, Compressed, 1-Element Phrases; staccato; starts soft and slowly fades in

1 Section 2-Element Phrases (cont.)

Nashville 6–9, fairly Expanded Phrases; 1st part of main, 2-Section song which usually is eventually sung

Blackburnian Expanded pitch range; Elements very different length, quality; long, Compressed slur then short, much lower, Complex Element

Yellow-rumped M 9–12 loosely Complex (but could be heard as Clear), Compressed 2-Element Phrases with short Intervals; very smooth, slurred; often weakly sung, fading out at end

Ovenbird Very long song; starts softly, grows very emphatic; Expanded, short downslurs; falling 2-Element Phrase pitch profile

1 Section 4+ Element Phrases

Connecticut Irregular, jerky rhythm; Expanded, short, emphatic Elements, long Intervals; often speeds up/gets louder

Common Yellowthroat Slurred, variable-length/pitch Elements; usually up/down pitch profile within Phrase; often loud

Connecticut Irregular, jerky rhythm, Expanded, short, emphatic Elements, long Intervals; often speeds up/gets louder

Variable Pitch
3 Sections

10
kHz
2

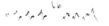

American Redstart
High, thin; 4–7 1-Element slurs in 1st; subsequent Sections only 1 Phrase each; ending usually higher, faster; often alternates with 1-Section song

Magnolia High; very short songs; 1st Section 2–4 1- or 2-Element Phrases; all subsequent only 1 Phrase each; accented ending similar speed, pitch

Hooded Low, rich, short songs; very Compressed, long Phrases; ending slightly rushed; only 1 Phrase per Section after 1st

Yellow Expanded, long, usually 1-Element Phrases; large pitch/Phrase change Section–Section; 2nd Section 2+ Phrases; song speeds up; last Section usually upslur; variable

10
kHz
2

Hooded Low, rich; short songs; very Compressed, long Phrases; only 1 Phrase per Section after 1st

Yellow Expanded, long, usually 1-Element Phrases; large pitch/Phrase change Section–Section; 2nd Section 2+ Phrases; song speeds up; last Section usually upslur; variable

Chestnut-sided 4–6 Phrases in 1st Section; slow Expanded slurs; 2nd, (often 3rd) Sections 2+ Phrases; ending usually Expanded downslur

Swainson's 3–5 1-Element, long Compressed slurred Phrases in 1st Section; ending Sections longer, Expanded slurs; simpler than Louisiana's diagnostic Sections

BUZZY

Rising Pitch
3+ Sections

Variable Pitch
2+ Sections

10
kHz
2

Golden-cheeked
Dense, Buzzy Phrases, usually Clear, emphatic, downslurred ending

Golden-cheeked
Dense, Buzzy Phrases, usually Clear, emphatic, downslurred ending; wide pitch changes between Sections

Golden-cheeked
Another form with Trill-speed Sections

Rising Pitch
3+ Sections

Variable Pitch
3+ Sections

10
kHz
2

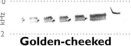

Golden-cheeked
Virens-like Buzzy/Clear Elements; (others not in range); dense, Buzzy Phrases, usually Clear, emphatic, downslurred ending

Kirtland's Short, low, Compressed; loud, almost explosively sung; usually increases in speed/volume/pitch; Complex Phrases could be heard as Buzzy

Kirtland's Short, low, Compressed, Complex; loud, almost explosively sung; usually increases in speed/volume/pitch

Golden-cheeked Dense Buzzy Phrases, usually Clear, emphatic, downslurred ending; wide pitch changes between Sections

Rising Pitch
2 Sections   *3+ Sections*

Variable Pitch
3 Sections   *5 Sections*

10
kHz
2

Kirtland's Complex, rough, low, short, Compressed Phrases with long Intervals; speeding up for most of song; loud

Kirtland's Starts with Complex, Compressed Phrases; subsequent become more Expanded and Clearer; long Intervals; rarely fully rising pitch profile in whole song

Kirtland's Short, low, Compressed, Complex; loud, almost explosively sung; usually increases in speed/volume/pitch

Kirtland's Compressed short Phrases with long Intervals; rhythm uneven; rough, almost liquid quality; loud

East

3 Sections (cont.)

Chestnut-sided 4–6 Phrases in 1st Section; slow Expanded slurs; 2nd, (often 3rd) Sections 2+ Phrases; ending usually Expanded downslur

Black-and-white Very high; long songs; 2-Element Phrases; uncommon 3-Section form; 2nd Section always lower; usually 2-Element Phrases throughout

4 Sections

Tennessee Very long song; 3 Sections of Expanded, emphatic Phrases; speed/pitch vary Section–Section; 1, sometimes 2 Sections often Trills

Magnolia High; very short songs; 1st Section 2–4 1- or 2-Element Phrases; all subsequent only 1 Phrase each

5 Sections

Hooded Low, rich; short songs; very Compressed, long Phrases; only 1 Phrase per Section after 1st

Yellow Expanded, long, usually 1-Element Phrases; large pitch/Phrase change Section–Section; 2nd Section 2+ Phrases; song speeds up; last Section usually upslur; variable

6+ Sections

Chestnut-sided 4–6 Phrases in 1st Section; slow Expanded slurs; 2nd, (often 3rd) Sections 2+ Phrases; ending usually Expanded downslur or up/down slur

Canada Many Sections, avg. 10; usually 1 Phrase per Section; variable slurs, Compressed and Expanded, varying pitches; often starts with short, Expanded "chip"

Local

Falling Pitch
2 Sections

Colima 1 or 2 Sections; 1st always Trill; 2nd (rarely 3rd) short; pitch wanders some; slower than Orange-crowned, 2nd Section shorter

Steady Pitch
1 Section

Colima Pitch often varies or wanders some throughout song; slower than Orange-crowned

Variable Pitch
3 Sections

Colima 1st always Trill; 2nd (rarely 3rd) short; pitch often wanders some; slower than Orange-crowned, 2nd Section shorter; Orange-crowned never has 3rd Section

Falling Pitch
2 Sections

Colima 1 or 2 Sections; 1st always Trill; 2nd (rarely 3rd) short; pitch often wanders some; slower than Orange-crowned, 2nd Section shorter

Variable
3+ Sections

Golden-cheeked Common song form with 1 or 2 Trilled Sections; other Sections dense Buzzy or hybrid Buzzy Phrases

Colima 1st Section always Trill; 2nd–3rd Sections always short (1–3 Phrases) and can be slower; pitch/speed can waver throughout; Orange-crowned never has 3rd Section

Rising Pitch
2 Sections

Kirtland's Complex (could be heard as Clear), rough, low, short, Compressed Phrases with long Intervals; speeding up for most of song; loud

3+ Sections

Kirtland's Starts with Complex, rough Phrases; subsequent become more Expanded and Clearer; long Intervals; rarely fully rising pitch profile in whole song; loud

Variable Pitch
3 Sections

Kirtland's Starts with Complex, rough Phrases; subsequent become more Expanded and Clearer; long Intervals; rarely fully rising pitch profile in whole song; loud

5 Sections

Kirtland's Compressed, short Phrases with long Interval; rhythm uneven; rough, almost liquid quality; loud

BUZZY

Rising Pitch

1 Section   *3+ Sections*

10

kHz

2

Black-throated Gray Only all-Buzzy western species; Compressed, low, 2-Element Phrases with uneven rhythm; overall slurred, run-on quality

Black-throated Gray Variable; slurred, run-on, Buzzy quality; 1st Section Compressed, low, 2-Element Phrases of uneven length; ending short, Clearer up/down Phrases

Townsend's Never totally Buzzy, except possibly from distance; 3–9 1-Element Phrases in 1st Section; ending usually Buzzy + Clear Elements

Rising Pitch

1 Section   *2 Sections*   *3+ Sections*

10

kHz

2

Black-throated Gray 1st Section low, Compressed, 2-Element Phrases with uneven rhythm; this form lacks Clear tones but can sound partly Complex, partly Buzzy

Hermit Variable; mixture of Clear and Buzzy Phrases; often 2-Element, Expanded Phrases; Buzzes usually less dense than Townsend's; higher, more Expanded than Black-throated Gray

Townsend's Variable; very similar to Hermit; sometimes Buzzes lower, simpler, denser; only 1-Element Phrases in 1st Section; Phrases often more Compressed

Black-throated Gray Variable; slurred, run-on, Buzzy quality; 1st Section low, Compressed, 2-Element Phrases of uneven length; ending short, Clearer up/down Phrases

PARTLY BUZZY

Steady Pitch

1 Section   *2+ Sections*

10

kHz

2

Black-throated Gray Low, Compressed 2-Element Phrases with uneven rhythm; overall slurred, run-on quality; Buzzy/Complex; rarely Clear except for short endings

Olive Unique Clear slurs; sometimes 2nd Element Buzzy

Black-throated Gray Variable; slurred, run-on, Buzzy quality; 1st Section low, Compressed 2-Element Phrases of uneven length; ending short, Clearer up/down Phrase

Olive Unique quality, strong Clear slurs with Complex/Buzzy Elements

Variable Pitch

2 Sections   *3 Sections*

10

kHz

2

Hermit Simple song; 2-Element Phrases in 1st Section; could be heard as all Clear but sometimes this form has Buzzy Elements

Black-throated Gray Low, Compressed 2-Element Phrases with uneven rhythm; often ends with higher up/down Section; usually only 1 Phrase in last Sections

Hermit Many more Clear Elements than Black-throated Gray; often thinner, more Complex than Townsend's

Hermit Combination of Buzz and Clear Elements; more Expanded than Black-throated Gray; 2-Element Phrases in 1st Section, unlike Townsend's

TRILLED

Rising Pitch

1 Section   *2 Sections*

Falling Pitch

1 Section   *2 Sections*

10

kHz

2

Grace's 13–20 distinct downslurs; usually getting louder, higher; somewhat Complex quality; almost always just slower than Trill

Grace's 1st Section 13–20 distinct downslurs; usually getting louder, higher; somewhat Complex quality; 2nd Section almost always higher; rarely a Trill

Orange-crowned Always Trill speed; pitch and/ or speed often wanders during song; often falling at end; faster than Grace's

Orange-crowned Both Sections Trills; pitch and/or speed often wanders 2nd Section lower pitch, different speed

West

Steady Pitch
1 Section

Black-throated Gray
Only all-Buzzy western species; low, Compressed, 2-Element Phrases with uneven rhythm; overall slurred, run-on quality

Variable Pitch
2+ Sections

Black-throated Gray
Variable; slurred, run-on, Buzzy quality; 1st Section Compressed, low, 2-Element Phrases of uneven length; ending Clearer up/down Phrases

Hermit Ending often Clear; variable; mixture of Clear and Buzzy Phrases; often 2-Element, Expanded Phrases; more Expanded than Black-throated Gray; Buzzes usually less dense than Townsend's

Townsend's Variable; very similar to Hermit; sometimes Buzzes lower, simpler, denser; only 1-Element Phrases in 1st Section; Phrases often more Compressed

4 Sections

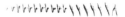

Black-throated Gray
Variable; slurred, run-on, Buzzy quality; 1st Section low, Compressed 2-Element Phrases of uneven length; ending short, Clearer up/down Phrase

5 Sections

Townsend's
Uncommon form, many pitch changes; Clear and Buzzy Elements

Steady Pitch
1 Section

3 Sections

Grace's Slower speed than Orange-crowned; pitch doesn't wander; more emphatic; only very rarely falling

Grace's Slower speed than Orange-crowned; pitch doesn't wander; more emphatic; only very rarely falling; rarely has 3rd, short Section

Grace's Almost always rising but could be heard as steady; 13–20 distinct downslurs; usually getting louder, higher; somewhat Complex quality; almost always just slower than Trill

Orange-crowned
Uncommon variation; speed/pitch usually wanders, often falling at end; always Trill speed, faster than Grace's

PARTLY TRILLED

Rising Pitch
2 Sections

Grace's 1st Section 13–20 distinct downslurs; usually getting louder, higher; somewhat Complex quality; 2nd Section almost always higher; rarely a Trill

Lucy's Fairly Compressed, usually 1-Element Phrases; often 3+ Sections; usually small pitch changes Section–Section; only 1 Trilled Section

Variable Pitch
4+ Sections

Lucy's Fairly Compressed, usually 1-Element Phrases; often 3+ Sections; usually small pitch changes Section–Section; only 1 Trilled Section

Falling Pitch
2 Sections

Nashville 6–9 usually 2-Element Clear Phrases; fairly emphatic, staccato; 2nd Section lower, faster, often Trill (less likely in western birds)

Wilson's 1–2 Sections; 1-Element, emphatic Phrases, usually falling in pitch; 2nd Section often Trill; 1st never Trill

Lucy's Fairly Compressed, usually 1-Element Phrases; often 3+ Sections; usually small pitch changes Section–Section; only 1 Trilled Section

Orange-crowned Always Trill speed; pitch and/or speed often wanders during song; oft falling at end; rarely 2nd Section can be short and countable speed

COMPLEX

Rising Pitch
1 Section   *2 Sections*   *3+ Sections*

Black-throated Gray 1st Section low, 2-Element Compressed Phrases with uneven rhythm; overall slurred, run-on quality; can sound Buzzy or Complex

MacGillivray's Complex, low, burry Phrases in 2–3 Sections; harsh, Expanded, loosely Complex 2-Element Phrases; rising pitch profile in 1st Section, usually falling in 2nd Section

Yellow-rumped A Loosely Complex, Compressed Phrases in 2–3 Sections; warbly, slurred quality; 1st Section 2-Element Phrases; last Sections short; not Buzzy like Black-throated Gray

Hermit Variable; mixtur of Clear and Buzzy/Comple Phrases; often 2-Element, Expanded Phrases; Buzzes usually less dense than Townsend's; higher, more Expanded than Black-throated Gray

Steady Pitch
1 Section   *2 Sections*

Black-throated Gray 1st Section 2-Element Compressed Phrases with uneven rhythm; overall slurred, run-on quality; can sound Buzzy or Complex

MacGillivray's Complex, low, burry Phrases; harsh, Expanded, loosely Complex 2-Element Phrases (rarely only 1 Section)

Olive Unique, whistled tone; Expanded Phrases, loosely Complex

Olive Loosely Complex, almost whistled quality; end whistle unlike any warbler

Variable Pitch
3+ Sections

Black-throated Gray Variable; slurred, run-on, Buzzy quality; 1st Section low, Compressed, 2-Element Phrases of uneven length; ending short, Clearer up/down Phrase

Hermit Variable; mixture of Clear and Buzzy/Complex Phrases; often 2-Element, Expanded Phrases; Buzzes usually less dense than Townsend's; higher, more Expanded than Black-throated Gray

MacGillivray's Complex, low, burry Phrases in 2–3 Sections; harsh, Expanded, loosely Complex 2-Element Phrases; rising pitch profile in 1st Section, usually falling in faster 2nd Section

Black-throated G Variable; slurred, run-on, Buzzy quality; 1st Section low, Compressed, 2-Element Phrases of uneven length; ending short, Clearer up/c Phrase; this example slightly more Expanded and loose Complex than usual

3+ Sections

Grace's Uncommon 3-Section songs can rarely reach Trill speed; also only rarely falling

Lucy's Fairly Compressed, usually 1-Element Phrases; often 3+ Sections; usually small pitch changes Section– Section; only 1 Trilled Section

Falling Pitch
2 Sections

Townsend's Variable; very similar to Hermit; sometimes Buzzes lower, simpler, denser; only 1-Element Phrases in 1st Section; Phrases often more Compressed

Yellow-rumped A Loosely Complex, Compressed Phrases in 2–3 Sections; warbly, slurred quality; 1st Section 2-Element Phrases; last Sections short; not Buzzy like Black-throated Gray

MacGillivray's Complex, low, burry Phrases in 2–3 Sections; harsh, Expanded, loosely Complex 2-Element Phrases; rising pitch profile in 1st Section, usually falling in faster 2nd Section

Yellow-rumped A Loosely Complex, Compressed Phrases in 2–3 Sections; warbly, slurred quality; 1st Section 2-Element Phrases; last Sections short; not Buzzy like Black-throated Gray

Yellow-rumped A Loosely Complex, Compressed Phrase in 2–3 Sections; warbly, slurred quality; 1st Section 2-Element Phrases; last Sections short; not Buzzy like Black-throated Gray

CLEAR

Rising Pitch
1 Section

Grace's 13–20 distinct downslurs; usually getting louder, higher; somewhat Complex quality; almost always just slower than Trill

2 Sections

Grace's 1st Section 13–20 distinct downslurs; usually getting louder, higher; 2nd Section almost always higher; both usually just below Trill speed

Falling Pitc[h]
1 Section

Yellow-rumped A Loosely Complex, Compressed Phrases in 2–3 Sections; warbly, slurred quality; 1st Section 2-Element Phrases; last Sections short, often fade out

Wilson's 8–12 1-Element Phrases; fair[ly] Expanded, emphatic; often grows louder/fall[s] in pitch

Falling Pitch (cont.)
2 Sections (cont.)

Yellow Expanded, long, high slurs; uncommon, unaccented 2-Section songs; 2nd Section lower; always 1-Element Phrases in 1st Section; variable, usually more Sections

Yellow-rumped A Loosely Complex, Compressed Phrase in 2–3 Sections; warbly, slurred quality; 1st Section 2-Element Phrases; last Sections short; often fade out

Painted Redstart Low, long, Compressed Phrases with short Intervals so slurred together; little pitch change throughout; rhythm often uneven; 1st Section often long 2-Element Phrases

3+ Sections

Virginia's Slow, usuall[y] 2-Element Phrases in 1st Section; subsequent Secti[ons] longer Phrases, less emphatic; Nashville never has 3+ Sections; slower, more Expanded than Luc[y's]

Steady Pitch
1 Section

Nashville Usually 6–9, fairly Expanded 2-Element Phrases; 1 Section actually first half of main song; usually sings full song eventually

Wilson's 8–12 1-Element Phrases; fairly Expanded, emphatic; often grows louder/falls in pitch; never Trill in 1st (or single) Section

Grace's 13–20 1-Element Phrases; downslurs; more Complex so rougher, less emphatic than Wilson's; usually some rising pitch profile; almost always just below Trill speed

Olive Unique whistle[d] quality, unlike any other warbler; slow 2-Element Phrases

Variable Pitch (cont.)
3 Sections

Virginia's Slow, usually 2-Element Phrases in 1st Section; subsequent Sections longer Phrases, less emphatic; Nashville never sings 3-Section songs; overall slower than Lucy's

Lucy's Fairly Compressed, usually 1-Element Phrases; usually small pitch changes Section–Section; 2nd Section 3–8 Phrases; partly Trilled as almost always 1 Trill Section; slowest variations could be heard as Clear

Yellow Expanded, long, usually 1-Element Phrases; large pitch/Phrase change Section–Section; 2nd Section 2–4 Phrases; song speeds up; last Section usually emphatic upslur; variable

Yellow-rumped Loosely Complex, Compressed Phrase in Sections; warbly, slurred quality; 1st Section 2-Element Phrases; last Sections short; often fa[de] out

Variable Pitch (cont.)
4 Sections (cont.)

Red-faced Many Sections of usually 1 (1–3) Clear Phrases; Elements long but variable; some Expanded, others Compressed, so lacks repetitive rhythm

5 Sections

Yellow Expanded, long, usually 1-Element Phrases; large pitch/Phrase change Section–Section; 2nd Section 2–4 Phrases; song speeds up; last Section usually upslur; variable

Painted Redstart Low, long, Compressed Phrases with short Intervals so slurred together; little pitch change throughout; rhythm often uneven; 1st Section often long 2-Element Phrases

Lucy's Fairly Compressed, usually 1-Element Phrases; usually small pitch changes Section–Section; 2nd Section 3–8 Phrases; partly Trilled as almost always 1 Trill Section; slowest variations could be heard as Clear

2 Sections

Virginia's Similar to Nashville; usually longer, more slurred Elements; 2nd Section never Trill, usually less Emphatic than 1st (and than Nashville); usually small pitch/speed changes Section–Section; often 3+ Sections

Nashville 6–9 usually 2-Element Clear Phrases; fairly emphatic, staccato; 2nd Section lower, faster, often Trill (less likely in western birds); never 3+ Sections

Wilson's Always 1-Element Phrases; 2nd Section usually Trill; short Phrases, long Intervals so distinct, emphatic; usually fairly consistent Phrase quality

Lucy's Fairly Compressed, usually 1-Element Phrases; usually small pitch changes Section–Section; partly Trilled as almost always 1 Trill Section; slowest variations could be heard as Clear; generally faster than Virginia's

Lucy's Fairly Compressed, usually 1-Element Phrases; usually small pitch changes Section–Section; 2nd Section 3–8 Phrases; partly Trilled as almost always 1 Trill Section; slowest variations could be heard as Clear

Yellow Less common, falling 3-Section song; fairly long, Expanded slurs; always 2–3 Phrases in 2nd Section; 1st Section always 1-Element Phrases

Grace's 1st Section 13–20 distinct downslurs; usually getting louder, higher; 2nd Section almost always higher (this example uncommon); speed usually just below Trill

Wilson's Uncommon short 3rd Section; 1-Element, short, emphatic Phrases, usually falling in pitch; 2nd Section often Trill; 1st never Trill; usually fairly consistent Phrase quality

Variable Pitch

2 Sections

2 Sections

Painted Redstart Low, long, Compressed Phrases, short Intervals so slurred; little pitch change throughout; rhythm often uneven

Painted Redstart Low, long, Compressed Phrases with short Intervals so slurred together; little pitch change throughout; rhythm often uneven; 1st Section often long 2-Element Phrases

Hermit Almost always Clear + Buzzy quality, but could be heard as Clear; Expanded, fairly high; usually hybrid Buzzy tones will be heard eventually

4 Sections

Painted Redstart Low, long, Compressed Phrases with short Intervals so slurred together; little pitch change throughout; rhythm often uneven; 1st Section often long 2-Element Phrases

Virginia's Slow, usually 2-Element Phrases in 1st Section; subsequent Sections longer Phrases, less emphatic; usually small pitch/speed changes Section–Section; Nashville never sings 3 or more Section songs

Lucy's Fairly Compressed, usually 1-Element Phrases; usually small pitch changes Section–Section; 2nd Section 3–8 Phrases; partly Trilled as almost always 1 Trill Section; slowest variations could be heard as Clear

Yellow Expanded, long, usually 1-Element Phrases; large pitch/Phrase change Section–Section; 2nd Section 2–4 Phrases; song speeds up; last Section usually upslur; variable

6+ Sections

Red-faced Many Sections of usually 1 (1–3) Clear Phrases; Elements long but variable; some Expanded, others Compressed, so lacks repetitive rhythm

Red-faced Many Sections of usually 1 (1–3) Clear Phrases; Elements long but variable; some Expanded, others Compressed, so lacks repetitive rhythm

Red-faced Many Sections of usually 1 (1–3) Clear Phrases; Elements long but variable; some Expanded, others Compressed, so lacks repetitive rhythm

Falling Pitch (Longer)
High Pitch

Pine	Am. Redstart	Cerulean	Bay-breasted	Blackpoll

kHz — 10, 8, 6, 4, 2

Clear, energetic downslur; even energy throughout

Smooth and rich; thinner end, slightly hissing; lacks complexity of Yellow and up/down group; commonly heard in fall

Doesn't call often; distinctive, long, loosely modulated; not as Clear as others in group

More likely to use flight call; rich, falling; shorter ending, more complex beginning that Am. Redstart; not as long as Yellow

More likely to use flight call; very similar to Bay-breasted and can have similar slightly Complex beginning

Falling Pitch (Shorter)
High Pitch

N. Parula	Tennessee	Blue-winged	Golden-winged	Orange-crowned	Hooded

kHz — 10, 8, 6, 4, 2

Fast, short, Clear, high; similar to Pine, Am. Redstart, but usually clearly shorter; sometimes hard to hear pitch fall, so sounds flat

Fairly high, fast; similar to N. Parula but bit longer, more Expanded range, not quite as Clear

High, fast, fairly rich, pure call; identical to Golden-winged

Identical to Blue-winged

Short, high, unique call; fast slide into metallic, Complex ending; fairly flat without much pitch drop; calls often

Explosive, short, somewhat hollow Clear, unique; without any Complex qualities higher than Kentucky

Steady Pitch
Very High, Thin

Black-throated Blue	Magnolia	Black-throated Gray	Blackburnian	Hermit

kHz — 10, 8, 6, 4, 2

Very high, short

High, short, flat call unlike main "chiff" call

Very high, short; as other virens, often gives a few high calls between songs

Given between songs, often with lower, richer Up/Down call (see below); calling between songs good ID point

High range of call, similar to other virens inter-song calls; this example somewhat rising, breathy

Falling Pitch (Longer)

Lower, More Complex

Grace's

Fairly fast, a bit lower than Pine; similar to Yellow-throated but less powerful, more falling, lacks bulk of up/down form

Prairie

Dense, fairly Complex and fast; like Palm but more consistently Complex

Palm

Explosive, fairly dense beginning then falling Clear tone; fairly low; lower, darker than Am. Redstart

Lower and Denser

Canada

Low, dense, falling; fast falling attack so percussive beginning; body very low, flatter

Kentucky

Dark, fairly low, Clear slur; useful for locating this skulker

Kirtland's

Short, low; ending emphatic; a bit shorter, slightly more Complex or abrupt than Kentucky

Lower, Complex

Black-and-white

Short, falling, Expanded; dense, less pitched than similar species; sounds Complex; variable, see "Up/Down" Section

Worm-eating

More likely to give flight call; simple, short downslur with Complex "shadow" quality

Black-throated Blue

Unique, abrupt "lip smack" with chiff-like beginning, Complex, abrupt ending; given often in fall

Lowest, Most Complex

Red-faced

Complex, rich, Compressed; similar to Black-throated Gray but more strongly falling profile

Wilson's

Dark, Compressed, Complex with slightly falling profile; breathier, not as low, coarsely modulated or even as Common Yellowthroat

Ovenbird

Very low, short; Complex and dense; variable, see "Up/Down" Section

Medium Pitch

Black-throated Green

High inter-song call; similar to main call but much higher, shorter

Townsend's

High, short version of call given mainly between songs, as do other virens

Prothonotary

High, short version of main call; slightly rough quality

Cape May

Very short, high, often falling a bit in pitch

Golden-cheeked

Very high, fast inter-song call; similar to other virens; too fast, high, to have much pitch shape

Prothonotary

Short, flat, high, somewhat hollow; can be fairly loud, emphatic; "wings" give hollow or breathy quality

Steady Pitch (cont.)
Low Pitch and Denser

MacGillivray's	Louisiana Waterthrush	Yellow-rumped Myrtle	Common Yellowthroat

kHz — 10 8 6 4 2

Dark, Complex, compact; calls best way to separate from Mourning, which is lower, more rising, more loosely Complex

Calls often; loud, emphatic, Complex, metallic; usually flatter, lower than Northern Waterthrush, without any rising profile

Calls very often, good to learn; flatter, more Compressed, duller than Audubon's; pitch can vary

Very rough, low, dense; modulations easy to hear; quality like two stones being hit together

Rising Pitch (Long)
High Pitch

Magnolia	Colima

Unique, breathy, Complex, long, upslurred "chiff"

Clearly rising with percussive ending; similar to Virginia's/Nashville/Lucy's but longer, more coarsely modulated

Rising Pitch (Short)
High Thin Pitch

Nashville	Lucy's	Nashville

kHz — 10 8 6 4 2

Very high, short inter-song version of main call; too short to have much pitch shape, but somewhat rising

Short, high version; a bit Complex or rough

Higher version of next call; a bit simpler; with less rise

Lower Pitch

Nashville	Virginia's	Lucy's	Virginia's

Fast rise to dense, flat body; similar to but maybe bit simpler than Virginia's/Lucy's

Similar in shape, quality to Nashville/Lucy's

Clearly rising with percussive end; bit lower, denser than Nashville; bit more compact than Virginia's

Lower, more rising call; somewhat dense, rough; on lower end of Lucy's/Nashville group

Up/Down Pitch (cont.)
Lower Pitch

Townsend's	Golden-cheeked	Black-and-white	Blackburnian	Yellow	Swainson's	Yellow-throated

kHz — 10 8 6 4 2

Short *virens* shape; lowest for species, still higher than Black-throated Gray; faster, brighter than many Black-throated Green

Short, compact, similar to *virens*; higher than Black-throated Gray; often lower, denser, less bright than rest of western group

Complex, a bit harsh, lacking Clear tones; variable, see "Falling" section

Rich, with short rising, longer falling profile; often combines with shorter, higher call during singing bouts

Long, strong, rich, "nagging"; when agitated can simplify or get higher; similar to Chestnut-sided but often higher

Emphatic, strong attack, loud, Clear; sometimes simpler with less "up" quality at beginning

Simple, Clear; mostly falling profile; similar to Grace's and Pine but richer, more Complex

Lower, Shorter, Denser

Unique

Connecticut	Northern Waterthrush	Northern Waterthrush	Mourning	Yellow-rumped Audubon's	Olive

More likely to give flight call in migration; doesn't call often, unlike Mourning/ MacGillivray's; not as Complex, rough | Calls often; rising, loud, fairly long, sharp; usually more rising, a bit higher than Louisiana's flatter call | Lower version | Dense, Complex; calls useful for separating from MacGillivray's; Mourning longer; more rising pitch profile | More rising, loosely Complex than Myrtle; sim. form to Mourning but not as low or percussive, with narrower pitch range | Dense, short, rising, rough "chup" call; unique

Up/Down Pitch
High Thin Pitch

Blackburnian	Townsend's	Hermit	Black-throated Green	Yellow	Palm

Higher, inter-song call; faster, bit more falling than typical, lower Up/ Down call | Usually higher, shorter, sharper than other virens except Hermit; all have variable pitches | Virens shape; similar to Townsend's; higher than lowest versions of other virens | Virens Up/Down shape; variable pitch; often given during singing bouts, sometimes doubled | Higher, faster version of typical call; often given when agitated | Higher, more Complex version of call, which can vary greatly in pitch

Unique

Chestnut-sided	Black-throated Green	Black-throated Gray	Chestnut-sided	Ovenbird	Olive	Painted Redstart

      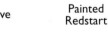

Shorter, higher version, showing range of possible calls | Lower version of typical Up/Down call; longer, higher than Black-throated Gray; longer, lower than Townsend's | Usually lowest of virens, with same fast Up/ Down or Up shape; short, dense | Strong, almost "naggy" quality; similar to Yellow, but averaging lower | Dense, Complex, low call, without any really Clear tones | Sonogram length compressed by 50%. Very slow, unique, falling, mournful call | Sonogram length compressed by 70%. Long, slurred call, unlike any other North Am. warbler

Rising Pitch
Highest, Thinnest

					Unique
Swainson's	Prothonotary	Colima	American Redstart	Ovenbird	Black-throated Blue

Clear; very long, thin, smooth, sibilant, piercing

Clear to Complex; Long, slow rise, sometimes initial downslur

Clear; long, smooth, thin, slightly modulated, piercing

Clear to Complex; Falls at beginning, like "hitch" or lack of continuity; distinctive

Clear; long, high, a bit shrill; more Complex toward end; distinctive

Clear; simple, unmodulated, shor[t], unique, very chip-l[ike]

Rising Pitch
Lower (cont.)   *Lower, Buzzy*   *Lower, Complex*

Virginia's	Golden-cheeked	Black-and-White	Blue-winged	Golden-winged	Northern Waterthrush

Complex; dense due to equal volume shadow call; fairly even in volume, quality

Complex; short, dense, brighter attack, then trails off in volume

Buzzy; dense; initial downslur keeps from having smooth profile; gives this call during day; distinctive

Buzzy; Thin, tightly modulated, sibilant upslur; not much rise; similar to Golden-winged

Buzzy; Thin, tightly modulated, sibilant upslur; similar to Blue-winged

Complex; Very long, obviously rising, coarsely modulated; distinctive "zeep"

Shorter, More Evenly Modulated

Nashville	Orange-crowned	Tennessee	Black-throated Green
Clear; Short but fairly full or dense	**Clear**; Denser, more Complex ending abrupt	**Complex**; Large rise; equally loud shadow call so dense, Complex; trails off in hiss	**Clear**; Short with modulated shadow that adds sibilance

Lower

Townsend's	Black-throated Gray	Hermit
Clear; Short, thin, slightly modulated	**Clear**; Short, slightly arched	**Clear**; Short, thin, slightly modulated, arched; maybe bit lower, more Complex than other *virens*

Mourning	Yellow-rumped
Complex; Low, dense, strongly rising	**Clear to Complex**; Starts thin, sibilant; becomes buzzier; fairly long, low, hollow due to shadow call; often mixes chip call with flight call

Lower, Clearer

Wilson's	Canada
Clear; Dense; similar to Canada but slower; less explosive	**Clear**; Compressed, explosive, almost liquid; low

Lowest, Densest

Kentucky	MacGillivray's	Painted Redstart
Complex; Coarsely modulated, long, rough; "zeep"	**Complex**; Initially small rise, slight hissing; very low, dense, heavily modulated	**Complex**; Very long, low, dense; unique

Falling Pitch
Highest, Thinnest

Cape May	Pine	Yellow-throated

Complex; Thin, very high, sharp, almost squeaky; slight fall; distinctive

Clear; Short; fairly simple; ending a bit more modulated; amount of drop variable

Clear; Short, pure tone

Steady or Fast Up/Down Pitch
Highest, Thinnest   ### Denser, Buzzier

Worm-eating	Magnolia	Connecticut	Blackburnian	Yellow

Complex; Coarsely modulated, dense, high; often doubled; given during day; "zeep"

Complex; High, long; starts thin, gets thicker, then thinner; light, breathy; distinctive "zeep"

Complex; Short, rich, modulated; given during day in migration; "zeep"

Complex/Buzzy; Fairly high, densely Complex; high shadow creates bright shrillness; distinctive "zeep"

Complex/Buzzy; Fairly long, richly modulated; often given during day; distinctive "zeep"

Steady or Fast Up/Down Pitch (cont.)
Lowest, Densest

Chestnut-sided	Kirtland's	Lucy's	Cerulean	Red-faced

Buzzy; Long, dense, sometimes falling slightly; distinctive

Complex; Short, slightly falling, dense, low, almost liquid; "zeep"

Clear/Complex; Fairly short; grows more Complex toward end

Complex/Buzzy; loose, well-articulated modulations; "zeep"

Complex; Coarsely modulated; breathy; slight rise at start

Lowest, Densest

Northern Parula	Grace's	Prairie	Palm

Clear; Long, obviously falling, slightly rough; distinctive

Clear; Fairly long, slightly rough, arched but overall falling

Clear; Arched but usually falling; somewhat sibilant

Clear; Long, arched; slightly shrill due to higher shadow; more modulated towards emphatic ending; distinctive

Medium Pitch

Louisiana Waterthrush	Blackpoll	Bay-breasted

Complex; Long, dense, flat, somewhat sibilant; sometimes slightly rising; "zeep"

Complex; Loosely modulated, somewhat whistled tone; often given during day, especially in fall; "zeep"

Complex; Short, Complex; modulations far apart so not fully buzzy; sim. to Blackpoll; given during day; "zeep"

Hooded	Common Yellowthroat

Complex/Buzzy; Fairly long, coarsely modulated; "zeep"

Complex/Buzzy; Fairly long, lazy; very widely modulated; some shrillness from shadow; distinctive

AMERICAN REDSTART

Setophaga ruticilla   Adult Male - All Seasons

- Black head and throat
- ✓ Orange sides of breast, base of wings and base of tail
- Flashes and droops wings, fans tail and holds open
- Sallies frequently
- Often vocal

- ✓ Black throat and breast with orange shoulders and tail base
- White belly contrasting with black throat and upper breast
- Broad-based bill
- Rictal bristles often conspicuous

- ✓ Black terminal band, orange base
- Undertail coverts white with black smudgy tips
- ✓ Long tail, narrow base creates unique wedge or clublike shape
- General elongated shape

Distinctive Views

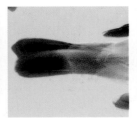

Additional Photos

Note distinct rictal bristles (hair-like feathers) around the broad-based bill

Often holds tail loosely, creating a clublike appearance

Some birds have extensive orange wash on the breast and underside

Often fans tail and droops wings, spinning 180 degrees back and forth to pick up insects

Note distinct pattern even in flight

Orange-based tail/flight feathers unique; visible above/below; only Blackburnian shares orange/black plumage

Amount and pattern of black extending into breast can vary

Frequent tail fanning and sallying are typical behaviors

Redstarts are often inquisitive and responsive to pishing

Some past nicknames have been Halloween Warbler and Red-tailed Motheater

Some birds may show orange fringing on edges of back feathers, especially in fresh fall plumage

Black head and throat
Orange shoulders, wing patch
Long, club-shaped tail
Orange tail base
Actively fans tail

Comparison Species

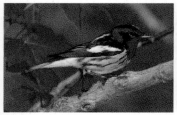

Blackburnian Only other U.S./ Canada warbler with black and orange plumage; orange on face, throat, and breast (vs. black); black, triangular face marking (vs. solid black); streaking; white undertail (vs. orange/black); white back braces

Black-throated Blue Dark head and body but blue upper body (vs. black); no orange anywhere; different tail pattern

Painted Redstart Striking red belly (vs. orange); white wing patch (vs. none); eye-arc (vs. none); longer, white tail (vs. black/orange); range rarely overlaps

Aging and Sexing

Spring AdM 1yM AdF 1yF **Fall** AdM 1yM AdF 1yF

Races: 1 Summary *Spring:* AdM separable, 1yM sometimes separable, females sometimes separable but not ageable   *Fall:* AdM separable, AdF, 1yM, 1yF sometimes separable   **What to Notice** *Spring:* Black/orange plumage, black flecks in breast/head, contrast of head and back, orange vs. yellow shoulder patches, uppertail covert color   *Fall:* Contrast in head and back, intensity of yellow patches, presence of orange in patches, uppertail covert color

AdM Sp/Fa *Diagnostic:* black and orange pattern year-round.

1yM Sp Dark lores, gray head often shows more contrast with back; *Diagnostic when present:* black flecks in head/breast, deep orange shoulders, all black uppertail coverts; *May overlap female:* yellowish shoulders, darkish uppertail coverts.

AdF/1yF Sp 1yF not separable from AdF *May overlap 1yM:* yellow shoulder patches range from yellow to yellow-orangey; *Diagnostic when present:* pale lores indicate female (some AdF have dark lores).

1yM Fa Same as 1yM Sp, but no black spots in face or breast, no dark in lores; *Diagnostic when present:* deep orange shoulder patches, black uppertail coverts; *overlaps female:* yellow shoulder patches, pale lores, no black in face.

AdF/1yM Fa *Diagnostic when present:* pale or olive uppertail coverts indicate female; *Overlaps 1yM Fall:* shoulder patches range from yellow to yellowy-orange, pale lores.

1yF Fa Often paler than AdF/1yM *Diagnostic when present:* little or no yellow on shoulders (never orangey); *Overlaps AdF:* yellow shoulders, pale lores, pale uppertail coverts (many birds not separable).

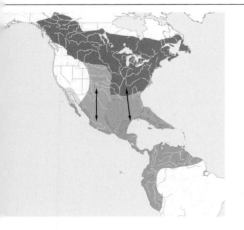

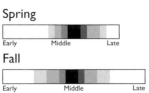

Spring

Early   Middle   Late

Fall

Early   Middle   Late

American Redstart
American red team starts with 4 running steps, then jumps up/down for success

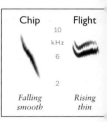

Chip	Flight
Falling smooth	Rising thin

Summary Highly *variable*; *higher, thinner* than many similar species; 1st Section many (4–7) Compressed, 1-Element Phrases. Short, even-tempo songs with slightly faster ending. Often sings throughout day, even when other birds are silent. **3 Types: A,** 1st Section *always 4 or more Elements,* followed by 1 or 2 single-Element Sections; endings accented; **B,** Only 1 Section, short; 1- or 2-Element Phrases. *Often alternated with A or C (good ID point);* **C,** unaccented, 2 Sections, 2nd higher; a bit longer than Type A or B; usually repeated Phrases similar to those found in A/B type songs.

Type A1 Many Phrases in 1st Section (4–7) (important for all Type A songs).

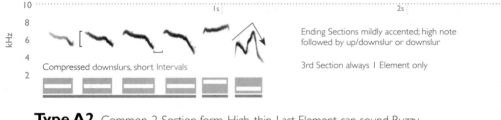

Ending Sections mildly accented; high note followed by up/downslur or downslur

Compressed downslurs, short Intervals

3rd Section always 1 Element only

Type A2 Common, 2-Section form. High, thin. Last Element can sound Buzzy.

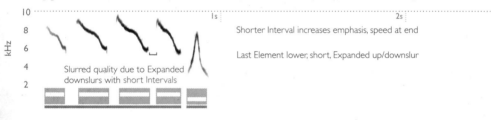

Shorter Interval increases emphasis, speed at end

Last Element lower, short, Expanded up/downslur

Slurred quality due to Expanded downslurs with short Intervals

Type A3 Less common, longer song with very high accented ending. Could be confused with Blackburnian, **but** simple, slurred Phrases lack Blackburnian's Complexity and last Element is a lower, longer downslur.

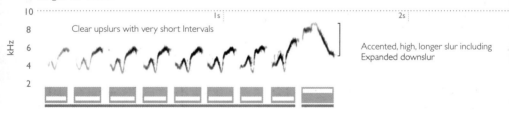

Clear upslurs with very short Intervals

Accented, high, longer slur including Expanded downslur

Type B1 Very short song with even tempo and easily countable speed. Rhythm clearer and more regular than Bay-breasted.

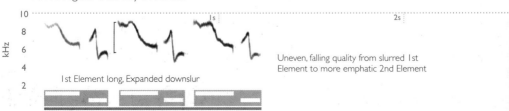

1st Element long, Expanded downslur

Uneven, falling quality from slurred 1st Element to more emphatic 2nd Element

Type B2 Short, thin and high; 1- or 2-Element Phrases, short Intervals.

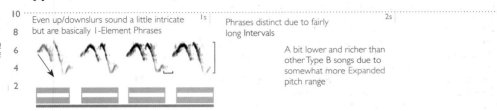

Even up/downslurs sound a little intricate but are basically 1-Element Phrases

Phrases distinct due to fairly long Intervals

A bit lower and richer than other Type B songs due to somewhat more Expanded pitch range

Type C1 2nd Section similar to Type B songs, with either 1- or 2-Element Phrases; slurred quality of 1st Section contrasts more emphatic 2nd.

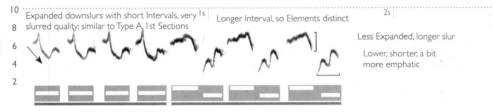

Expanded downslurs with short Intervals, very slurred quality; similar to Type A 1st Sections

Longer Interval, so Elements distinct

Less Expanded, longer slur

Lower, shorter, a bit more emphatic

Type C2 Slightly more emphatic with high, thin ending.

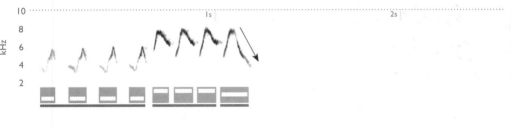

Magnolia Warbler (2 songs) Very similar, variable; can be hard to differentiate. Usually sounds richer, lower. Never 1-Section song (common in Am. Redstart). Rarely 4 (never more), Phrases in 1st Section; Am. Redstart always 4 or more. Over half of songs 3 Sections, often 4 Sections; Am. Redstart rarely 3 Sections (~17%), never 4 Sections.

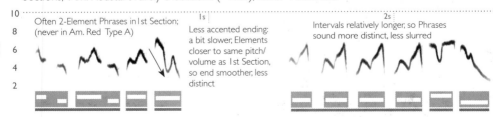

Often 2-Element Phrases in 1st Section; (never in Am. Red Type A)

Less accented ending: a bit slower, Elements closer to same pitch/ volume as 1st Section, so end smoother, less distinct

Intervals relatively longer, so Phrases sound more distinct, less slurred

American Redstart (cont.)

Yellow vs. A
Richer, with more high and low pitches; always 3 or 4 Sections (eliminates Type B/C); each Section at least 2 Phrases, vs. Type A 2nd/3rd Section with only 1 Phrase.

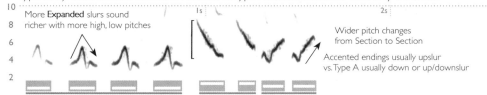

More **Expanded** slurs sound richer with more high, low pitches

Wider pitch changes from Section to Section

Accented endings usually upslur vs. Type A usually down or up/downslur

Chestnut-sided vs. A
Usually obviously lower pitched; never sings 1 or 2-Section songs (eliminates Types B/C); often 4+ Sections (vs. Type A max 3 Sections); always 2 or more Phrases in 2nd Section (vs. Type A with only 1 Phrase in 2nd/3rd Sections).

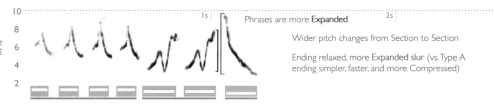

Phrases are more **Expanded**

Wider pitch changes from Section to Section

Ending relaxed, more **Expanded** slur (vs. Type A ending simpler, faster, and more Compressed)

Hooded vs. A
Lower, richer sound; always at least 3 Sections (eliminates B/C); Fewer Phrases 1st Section (avg. 2.4 vs. Type A avg. 5); never alternates with 1-Section songs like Am. Redstart.

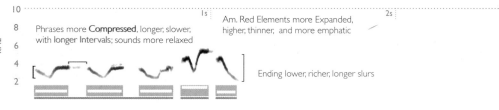

Phrases more **Compressed**, longer, slower, with **longer Intervals**; sounds more relaxed

Am. Red Elements more Expanded, higher, thinner, and more emphatic

Ending lower, richer, longer slurs

Blackburnian vs. A
Similar to some Type A accented songs, **but** much longer (avg. 1.9 sec. vs. Am. Redstart 1.2 sec.).

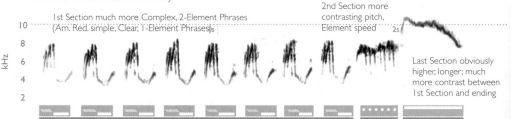

1st Section much more Complex, 2-Element Phrases (Am. Red. simple, Clear, 1-Element Phrases)

2nd Section more contrasting pitch, Element speed

Last Section obviously higher, longer; much more contrast between 1st Section and ending

Black-and-white vs. B

I-Section songs with 2-Element Phrases, similar to some Type B songs; never I-Element Phrases as in some Type B; Phrases have rising pitch and uneven rhythm vs. Am. Redstart even rhythm and falling pitch; full songs always longer (avg. 2.1 sec. vs. 1.2 sec.).

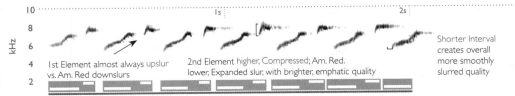

1st Element almost always upslur vs. Am. Red downslurs

2nd Element higher, Compressed; Am. Red. lower, Expanded slur, with brighter, emphatic quality

Shorter Interval creates overall more smoothly slurred quality

Bay-breasted / Cape May (excerpts) vs. B

Both species higher, thinner, slower; Type B Elements have different qualities and lengths that sound much different than either. **Bay-breasted** doesn't sing nearly as often during migration; Elements often less regular, so can sound clumsy or uneven vs. Type B more even, active rhythm.

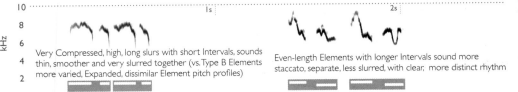

Very Compressed, high, long slurs with short Intervals, sounds thin, smoother and very slurred together (vs. Type B Elements more varied, Expanded, dissimilar Element pitch profiles)

Even-length Elements with longer Intervals sound more staccato, separate, less slurred, with clear, more distinct rhythm

Nashville / Blackburnian vs. B (excerpts)

Nashville longer with more Phrases (avg. 9 vs. Type B 5); 2 Sections, with strong pitch and speed difference (easily separable); sometimes sings only 1st Section of song (similar sounding to Type B), but usually will eventually sing full 2-Section song.

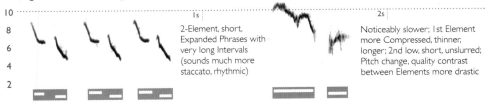

2-Element, short, Expanded Phrases with very long Intervals (sounds much more staccato, rhythmic)

Noticeably slower; 1st Element more Compressed, thinner, longer; 2nd low, short, unslurred; Pitch change, quality contrast between Elements more drastic

Prothonotary / Yellow-rumped vs. B (excerpts)

Both songs longer, more Phrases (Prothonotary avg. 8, Yellow-rumped avg. 10 vs. Am. Redstart avg. 4.6).

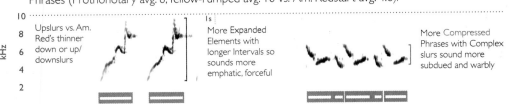

Upslurs vs. Am. Red's thinner down or up/ downslurs

More Expanded Elements with longer Intervals so sounds more emphatic, forceful

More Compressed Phrases with Complex slurs sound more subdued and warbly

AMERICAN REDSTART

Setophaga ruticilla   Female/1Y Male - All Seasons

- Overall gray head, throat, and underparts with plain, olive-toned wings and upperparts

✓ Yellow or apricot shoulder patches, base of flight feathers, and base to tail

- Thin white, slightly broken eyering; darker lores; usually lighter supraloral

- No wing bars or streaking

- Flashes and droops wings; fans, holds open, and cocks tail; flits out and back acrobatically

- Yellow and gray color pattern

✓ Yellow or apricot shoulder patches and base of flight feathers

✓ Dark terminal tail band with yellow tail base

- Undertail coverts whitish

- Long tail with unique wedge or club shape even in silhouette

- Broad-based bill with often conspicuous rictal bristles

Distinctive Views

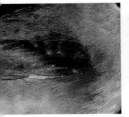

Additional Photos

Elongated rictal bristles (hair-like feathers at the bill base) and broad-based bill facilitate fly catching

Long tail held loosely forms clublike shape, visible even in silhouette

Curious and active, Redstarts often flit and sally for insects and are responsive to pishing

Frequently fans tail and droops wings along side, probably to kick up insects; orangey patches and black uppertail coverts indicate this is a first-year male

May flit along tree trunks as well as branches and undergrowth

Yellow side patches may extend across breast

First spring males are similar to females but often show black flecks in head and/or breast, black in lores

Singing is a sure sign that the bird is a male

Black lores may be accented by a whitish supraloral mark

Young males may show black on uppertail coverts

Females show olive uppertail coverts

Note the gray hood contrasting with olive back

Plain gray head
Darker lores, light supraloral
Basically plain gray with yellow
shoulder patches
Long clublike tail/yellow base
Actively fans tail

Comparison Species

Black-throated Blue F Blue-gray above, buffy below (vs. greenish/gray); dark cheek, thin pale eyebrow (vs. plain); no yellow; often shows white handkerchief; plumper shape; shorter dark tail (vs. yellow base)

Yellow-rumped Myrtle Side and breast streaking/faint wing bars (vs. none); gray/brown upperparts (vs. olive); supercilium, more contrasting throat; lacks black/yellow tail

Palm Black tail base (vs. tip); yellow UnTC (vs. whitish); rufous streaking in breast (vs. plain); constant tail pumping (vs. flashing)

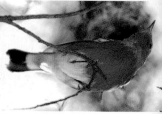

Tennessee Greener back and wings; lacks any yellow; stronger eyeline and supercilium; smaller with finer, pointy bill; shorter, thinner, plain tail (vs. yellow/black)

Orange-crowned Overall lower contrast; yellowish UnTC; lacks yellow tail base, shoulders; finer, pointy bill; shorter, thin, plain gray tail (vs. black/yellow)

Magnolia Extensive yellow in underparts (vs. gray); side streaking (vs. none); pale throat band; shares black terminal tail band but base of tail is white

Lucy's More uniform pale gray; lacks yellow; pale lores (vs. darker); chestnut uppertail coverts; shorter, white tail; smaller, with fine bill

Virginia's Isolated yellow in breast, UnTC, uppertail coverts (vs. shoulders/tail); contrasting eyering without light supraloral; gray back and underparts (vs. olive); rufous crown patch (not always visible); all-gray tail (vs. yellow/black); finer bill

BAY-BREASTED

Setophaga castanea   Bright Birds

- ✓ Black face with chestnut crown, throat, and flanks
- Large buffy neck patch
- Strong white wing bars contrast with dark upperparts
- Black-streaked gray back
- ✓ Extensive chestnut and lack of yellow

- ✓ Extensive chestnut and lack of yellow
- Chestnut throat and sides with buffy or whitish belly
- Bulky body, short tail
- Sluggish in movements and feeding
- Large with long primary projection

- Short tail with white tail spots
- Chestnut throat and buffy or off-white belly
- Boat-shaped bulky body
- Large bill

Distinctive Views

Additional Photos

Rump feathers show strong black centers

Dark legs

Note the buffy tones in the undertail which are present to some degree in all plumages (may be very faint)

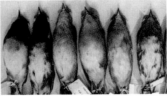

Strong rusty side stripe shared only by Chestnut-sided

Amount of rust is variable

Note black face, rusty breast and throat, and striking pale neck patches

Probably a young male, showing less rufous in cap, overall lower contrast

Strong black between wing bars good ID point in most plumages

Heavy streaking in back, rusty cap and contrasting black head; notice pale sides of neck

This bird has caught a large insect; Bay-breasted are also budworm specialists

Spring females much less contrasty and lack strong black in the face and head; note pale sides of neck

Spring female from below, with pale wash of rust

Black face/rust-colored throat
Rusty side stripe
Short tail with white tail spots
Contrasting buff collar
Chestnut crown
Contrasting white wing bars

Comparison Species

Chestnut-sided Yellow wing bars and crown (vs. white); white collar (vs. buff); black facial marks (vs. solid black); white throat/underparts (vs. rusty/buffier); longer, all-white tail; chestnut is a stripe, not a full flank wash, and is a different tone

Blackpoll No chestnut; black cap with white cheeks and black malar (vs. black face); heavier black streaks on back; orange/yellow feet and often legs (vs. dark)

Aging and Sexing

Spring AdM 1yM AdF 1yF **Fall** AdM 1yM AdF 1yF

Races: 1 Summary *Spring:* Adult females not separable, others sometimes separable *Fall:* Females ageable/sexable, males difficult to age **What to Notice** *Spring/Fall:* Chestnut on sides, crown and rump, black in face, eye arcs, lores

AdM Sp Black face, lores and crown; *Diagnostic when present:* no eye-arcs, unstreaked chestnut cap, extensive chestnut in flanks, breast, and throat.

AdF/1yM/1yF Sp Duller than AdM, less chestnut below (or only buffy wash), only faint chestnut in crown, buffy eye-arcs.

1yM Sp Extreme *Diagnostic:* buffy lores and noticably duller than AdM combined with clear chestnut in crown and eye-arcs.

1yF Sp Extreme As AdF/1yF but very dull, little or no chestnut; *Diagnostic when present:* no chestnut on bird.

AdM/1yM Fa Reduced chestnut in sides (vs. spring), gray lores, gray rump with little or no green; *Diagnostic from female:* some chestnut in crown.

AdF Fa No chestnut in crown, AdF may show some chestnut in flanks and gray in rump.

1yF Fa *May overlap AdF:* no chestnut or buff in flanks; *Diagnostic from AdF:* obvious green in rump.

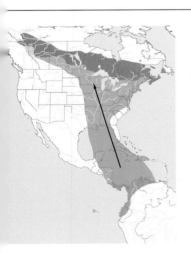  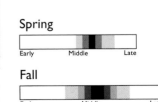

Spring

Early		Middle		Late

Fall

Early		Middle		Late

Bay-breasted
Short, monotonous vacation by the bay with waves rolling back and forth

Summary *Very high-pitched*, thin, *short* and *slow* (only 3 or 4 Phrases). Compressed, evenly slurred Elements; inconsistent shapes create an unstable rhythm. Sings less often than many species. **I Type:** 1 Section of 2-Element Phrases (note: rarely can sing 1-Element slurred Phrases).

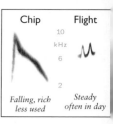

Chip	Flight
Falling, rich less used	Steady often in day

Type A1 Slow, short, high, smoothly slurred song. Distinct, 2-Element Phrases.

Very **Compressed**, subtly downslurred Elements sound thin

Uneven shape and length of Elements create unstable rhythmic quality

Type A2 Smooth, slurred with clearly 2-Element Phrases; long Elements separated by fairly long Intervals.

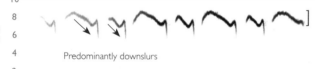

Predominantly downslurs

Consistently **Compressed** pitch range sounds smooth and slurred (vs. percussive or accented)

Type A3 Short, high, thin song with 3 Phrases; clearly 2-Element Phrases.

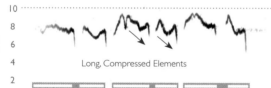

Long, Compressed Elements

Uneven shape and length of Elements create unstable rhythmic quality

Clearly 2-Element Phrases with long Intervals.

Black-and-white A 1-Section songs with slurred 2-Element Phrases; most easily confused with Bay-breasted, **but** usually more Phrases (avg. 6 vs. 4), longer (avg. over 2 sec. vs. 1.2).

Expanded, rising, long upslurred 1st Element (vs. Compressed downslurs)

2nd Element higher, much shorter

Song more uneven, syncopated rhythm and rising Phrase pitch profiles; (vs. flatter, less pitch change, more even-length Elements)

Cape May B
Type A songs very simple, 1-Element upslurred Phrases (vs. 2-Element downslurred, less regular Phrases); Type B, 2-Element variation could be confused (similar high, thin quality).

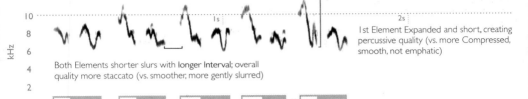

1st Element Expanded and short, creating percussive quality (vs. more Compressed, smooth, not emphatic)

Both Elements shorter slurs with longer Interval; overall quality more staccato (vs. smoother, more gently slurred)

American Redstart A
Am. Redstart A/C songs 2 or 3 Sections (vs. Bay-breasted 1 Section); Type B songs often noticeably lower 1-Element Phrases (vs. 2); more frequent singers, and often alternate 1-Section songs with 3-Section accented songs.

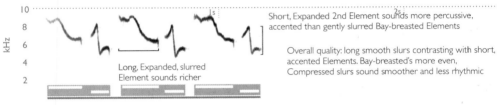

Short, Expanded 2nd Element sounds more percussive, accented than gently slurred Bay-breasted Elements

Overall quality: long smooth slurs contrasting with short, accented Elements. Bay-breasted's more even, Compressed slurs sound smoother and less rhythmic

Long, Expanded, slurred Element sounds richer

Yellow-rumped (Myrtle)
Usually 2 Sections (vs. 1 Section Bay-breasted); noticeably lower.

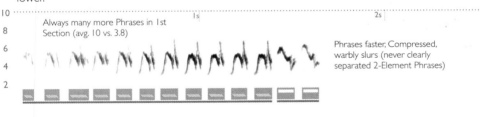

Always many more Phrases in 1st Section (avg. 10 vs. 3.8)

Phrases faster, Compressed, warbly slurs (never clearly separated 2-Element Phrases)

Blackpoll A
High, repeated Phrases like Bay-breasted, **but** easy to separate; longer, with many more Phrases (avg. 17 vs. 3.8), much faster (avg. 8 Phrases/sec. vs. 3).

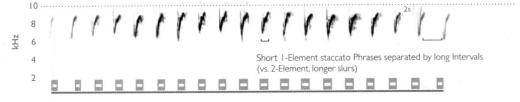

Short 1-Element staccato Phrases separated by long Intervals (vs. 2-Element, longer slurs)

BAY-BREASTED

Setophaga castanea　　Drab Birds

- Large, bulky, with long primary projection, short tail
- Often some chestnut on flanks
- Yellow-green with light back streaking; paler neck patch
- Two strong wing bars with high-contrast black in between
- Broad white edges to tertials, white tips to primaries

- Often some buff in underside and undertail coverts, so underparts low contrast overall
- Unstreaked breast
- Often some chestnut in flanks
- Large, sluggish warbler

- Short tail with white tail spots
- Buffy or off-white belly and undertail coverts; low contrast overall
- Often some chestnut in flanks
- Boat-shaped, bulky body
- Large bill
- Dark legs and feet

Distinctive Views

Additional Photos

...usty stripe may vary from some ...

...to a little ...

... to virtually none

...ote strong black contrasty area be-
...veen wing bars; this area more con-
...asty than Blackpoll or Pine

Many birds show black streaking in the back, but others show little to none

Note relatively plain face; tail projection past UnTC is shorter than in Pine

...sually buffy wash along the flanks
...ather than pure white), eyeline usually
...ss prominent than Blackpoll

Underparts unstreaked, but be careful not to mistake faint feather tract lines for streaking

Legs generally dark; feet always dark

...en birds lacking chestnut usually
...ow buffy tint to rear flanks and vent,
...ut...

...beware of using buffy UnTC as a diagnostic mark: almost no buff in UnTC
in this individual

Most birds show dark cap connected to dusky auricular patch, with eyering and faint eyeline, and buffy neck patch

Short tail with white tail spots
Buffy/pale undertail coverts
Contrasting white wing bars
Unstreaked below
Short eyeline/faint supercilium
Pale, light-green neck patch

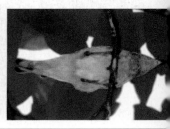

Comparison Species

Blackpoll Yellow-olive wash on sides and flanks (vs. buffy, often with some rufous); duller yellowy upperparts; more distinct eyeline with eye-arcs, so more contrasty face; streaking in breast and flanks; more contrast between yellow underparts and white UnTC (vs. buffy UnTC, lower contrast in underparts); yellow/orange feet, often legs (vs. dark)

Chestnut-sided Distinct eyering or gray face; greener upperparts and cleaner whitish underparts; longer, whit tail; yellowish wing bars (vs. white)

Pine Longer tail showing much more extension beyond UnTC; white tail spots look elongate (vs. round spots in Bay-breasted); less contrasty wing bars; lacks distinct white tertial/primary edging; unstreaked back; yellow in body is usually stronger in breast, which often shows some streaking

Blackburnian Small with finer bill; distinctive triangular cheek patch, wide supercilium; pale braces on back; variable orange wash across face into breast; usually some streaking; longer all-white tail

Cape May Duller, thinner wing bars; smaller, with finer bill; even, fine streaking across breast and into throat; yellow-green rump; usually some patchy yellow in breast

BLACK-AND-WHITE

Mniotilta varia   Male/Female - All Seasons

- Distinctive creeping behavior along trunks and branches
- ✓ Black-and-white-striped crown and back diagnostic in all plumages
- Long slightly curved bill
- ✓ Contrasty white wing bars join wide white tertial edgings
- Very broad white supercilium

- Long slightly curved bill
- Extensive, wide, black side streaks
- ✓ Large black arrowheads on white undertail coverts diagnostic

- ✓ Black arrowheads on white undertail coverts
- Medium-long tail with white tail spots
- Long, thin, curved bill

Distinctive Views

Additional Photos

old white wing bars with bottom bar connecting to wide white tertial edging l plumages

Short tail, deep chest, long decurved bill and pointed head make the shape distinctive

Black-and-white crown stripes are diagnostic

emales show pale lores; many have xtensive buff throughout flanks and ce, especially younger birds

Creeping on trunks and limbs (including creeping downward, head first) is typical and distinctive

Often uninterested in observers; Black-and-whites probe for insects in tree bark

rong black spotting in UnTC sepa-tes this Black-and-white from all her warblers, including this Black-roated Blue

Often curious and investigates pishing

Black-and-white pattern is striking, even in flight

nother view of the striking back pat-rn; in shade, Black-and-whites look rprisingly blue!

Upside-down, trunk-creeping bird with spotted UnTC can only be a Black-and-white

Black-and-white is the longest-lived warbler on record, at eleven years

Black-and-white only
White supercilium, crown stripe
Black spots on UnTC
Wing bars touch tertial edgings
Long, curved bill
Creeps along branches, trunks

Comparison Species

Blackpoll Lacks crown stripes; white cheeks (vs. often black); lacks supercilium; olive tones in back and wings (vs. black and white); fainter side streaking and wing bars; often shows orange legs or feet; much less creeping behavior; UnTC unmarked (vs. spotted)

Yellow-throated Also creeps alon branches, but yellow throat (vs. white); streaking on sides only; all-white tail an UnTC (vs. spotted)

Black-throated Gray Much less streaked overall; plain gray back (vs. black/white); diagnostic yellow supraloral spot; lacks central crown stripe; lacks spotted UnTC

White-breasted Nuthatch Routinely creeps along branches, but thicker, wedge-shaped bill; blue, plain back; unstreaked; plain white face; shorter tail

Black-throated Green Less streaking; yellow in vent (vs. spotted UnTC); yellow face

Aging and Sexing

Spring AdM 1yM AdF 1yF **Fall** AdM 1yM AdF 1yF

Races: 1 Summary *Spring:* Sexable, not ageable except 1yM sometimes separable
Fall: AdM and some 1yM and 1yF separable **What to Notice** *Spring/Fall:* Black in throat, cheek, and lores, white mottling in throat and cheek, black spots in a white throat, buffy wash on underparts and face, intensity of streaking on underparts

AdM/1yM Sp Heavy black streaking on underparts; *Diagnostic:* black cheeks, throat, and lores, may show a little white at base of bill; 1yM may show white mottling in throat and cheek patch (diagnostic for age).

AdF/1yF Sp Streaking grayer and less contrasty than males; *Diagnostic for sex:* grayish auriculars variably mottled white, white throat, grayish lores; sometimes buffy wash on underparts.

AdM Fa Similar to spring male, but white edging on throat feathers may diminish or conceal black; *Diagnostic:* black cheeks and heavily streaked underparts.

AdF/1yM Fa Similar to spring female with white throat, grayish lores, and often buff-washed underparts; streaking duller and less bold than AdM; *Diagnostic when present 1yM:* may show some black spots in throat.

1yF Fa Duller than all adults and more buffy wash, especially on face, than AdF; streaking dull gray; birds showing extremes of these characteristics safely ageable, but otherwise not always separable from AdF/1yM.

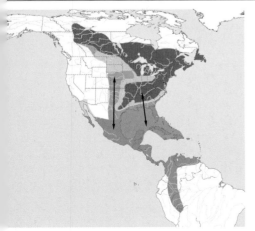

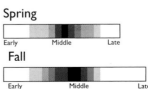

Spring

Early   Middle   Late

Fall

Early   Middle   Late

Black-and-white

Parade of 7 or 8 black-and-white carts, all with uneven squeaky wheels

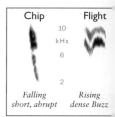

	Chip	Flight
		10 kHz
		6
		2
	Falling short, abrupt	*Rising dense Buzz*

Summary *High, piercing,* long; always starts with repeated 2-Element Phrases; Elements vary in length/pitch, *rising pitch in each Phrase;* **2 Types: A,** Most common, 1 Section with repeated 2-Element Phrases, rising Phrase pitch profile, uneven rhythm; **B,** Less common, 3+ Sections (never 2) slightly varying in pitch and speed; 2nd section almost always lower; 2-Element Phrases similar to A.

Type A1
High, long, 1-Section song. Long, Expanded 1st Element gives song a slurred, not strongly emphatic, quality.

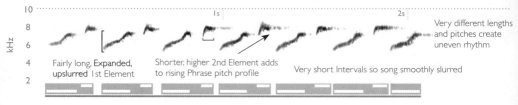

Very different lengths and pitches create uneven rhythm

Fairly long, **Expanded,** upslurred 1st Element

Shorter, higher 2nd Element adds to rising Phrase pitch profile

Very short Intervals so song smoothly slurred

Type A2
Less common variation with Elements more evenly balanced in length. Retains rising Phrase profile with higher, shorter 2nd Element.

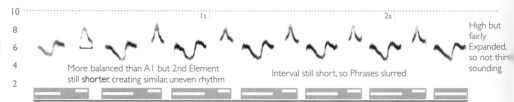

High but fairly **Expanded,** so not thin sounding

More balanced than A1 but 2nd Element still **shorter,** creating similar, uneven rhythm

Interval still short, so Phrases slurred

Type B1
Less common form; 3 Sections at different pitches, speeds; 2-Element Phrases are faster, more slurred so 2-Element division not as well defined. 2nd Section almost always lower than 1st. Rarely ending is unstructured warbling.

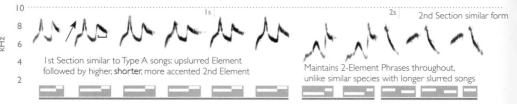

2nd Section similar form

1st Section similar to Type A songs: upslurred Element followed by higher, **shorter,** more accented 2nd Element

Maintains 2-Element Phrases throughout, unlike similar species with longer slurred songs

Bay-breasted A2
High, thin, 1-Section songs with 2-Element, slurred Phrases; most easily confused with Black-and-white. Shorter (avg. 1.2 sec. vs. 2.1).

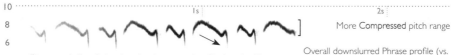

More **Compressed** pitch range

Elements similar pitches, lengths, thus smoother; Black-and-white Elements more varied, with active, more uneven rhythm

Overall downslurred Phrase profile (vs. Black-and-white rising Phrase profile)

American Redstart B1
Only 1-Section, 2-Element Phrase songs similar; Black-and-white never has 1-Element Phrases. Shorter (avg. 1.2 sec. vs. 2.1), regularly alternates 1-Section songs with 2- or 3-Section accented songs.

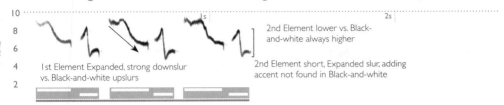

2nd Element lower vs. Black-and-white always higher

1st Element Expanded, strong downslur vs. Black-and-white upslurs

2nd Element short, Expanded slur, adding accent not found in Black-and-white

Cape May B1
Most songs easy to separate (simple 1-Element, slurred Phrases); 2-Element variation could be confused. Songs almost always shorter (avg. 1.3 sec. vs. 2.1); less uneven rhythm.

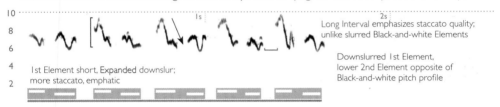

Long Interval emphasizes staccato quality; unlike slurred Black-and-white Elements

1st Element short, Expanded downslur; more staccato, emphatic

Downslurred 1st Element, lower 2nd Element opposite of Black-and-white pitch profile

Nashville
Main songs easy to separate, **but** partial 1st Section of song could be confused. Noticeably lower pitch; usually sings full song eventually.

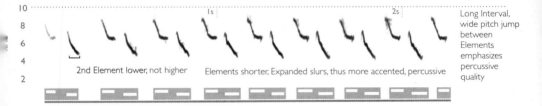

2nd Element lower, not higher

Elements shorter, Expanded slurs, thus more accented, percussive

Long Interval, wide pitch jump between Elements emphasizes percussive quality

Blackburnian
Slower, with fewer Phrases; much different, obviously falling Phrase pitch profile; much more contrast between Elements; less smoothly slurred; often calls before song.

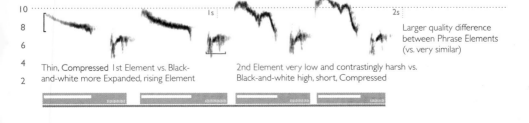

Larger quality difference between Phrase Elements (vs. very similar)

Thin, Compressed 1st Element vs. Black-and-white more Expanded, rising Element

2nd Element very low and contrastingly harsh vs. Black-and-white high, short, Compressed

BLACKBURNIAN

Setophaga fusca   Bright Birds

- ✓ Auricular patch has distinctive triangular shape, pointed at rear and bottom
- ✓ Fiery orange throat, face, supercilium, crown patch, and under-eye arc
- • Broad white wing patch
- • Relatively long, streamlined body
- ✓ Two pale braces on back unique among warblers

- • White tail and UnTC
- • Vent area usually yellowy-orange
- • Flanks streaked
- ✓ Fiery orange throat, face, and under-eye arc

- • Long tailed, but attenuated body and long UnTC can make the tail look shorter
- • Thick neck creates a pointed front end
- ✓ Fiery orange throat
- • Often high in trees
- • May show yellow wash in body and vent

Distinctive Views

Additional Photos

All Blackburnians show orange or yellow under-eye crescent and forehead stripe

Note white back braces and yellow head stripe on this adult male

Especially in a dim forest, the bright flash of a Blackburnian can be startling as they sally for insects

Color and contrasty black pattern are a giveaway for this bird, even head-on

Blackburnians nest and are often found high in trees, but color often makes them quickly identifiable

Adult females in spring not as bright orange as males, less contrasty overall; note distinctive cheek-patch shape

Note white wing patch, and triangular black facial marking; present to one degree or another on all birds

Note range of orange on different birds (includes spring and fall and both sexes)

Bright fall bird in flight; note broad supercilium and triangular cheek patch

This spring female shows streaking rather than solid black back and wing bars instead of wing patch

Female might be mistaken for Yellow-throated warbler, but Blackburnian much more orangey than yellow, and triangular face patch is different

These are long-distant migrants, with relatively long wings

Fiery orange throat and head
Triangular cheek patch
Broad white wing patch
Fairly long white tail
White back braces

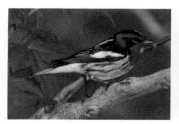

Comparison Species

Yellow-throated Plain gray upperparts (vs. black); white neck patch (vs. orange); white ground to face with black mask (vs. orange); sharply delineated bright yellow throat (vs. more diffuse orange); heavier side streaking; longer bill; more white in tail

American Redstart M Black throat/breast (vs. orange); orange shoulders, base of primaries and base of tail (vs. throat/breast); club-shaped tail; active fly catching and sallying; much longer tail with orange base and black tip

Aging and Sexing

Spring AdM 1yM AdF 1yF   **Fall** AdM 1yM AdF 1yF

Races: 1 **Summary** *Spring:* Sexable, 1yM may be separable   *Fall:* Extreme AdM and some 1yF, 1yM separable   **What to Notice** *Spring:* Wing panel, back color and intensity, throat color and intensity, color of face masking   *Fall:* Intensity of orange and of streaking, black eyeline over brown ear patch, overall contrast

AdM/1yM Sp *Diagnostic for male:* wing panel, white braces on black back; *Diagnostic when present 1yM:* black back combined with incomplete wing panel or two wing bars, black may be less intense due to feather edging.

AdF/1yF Sp *Diagnostic female:* olive upperparts with pale streaks, face similar to male but more olive tones, less intense orange; 1yF similar to adult.

AdM Fa Duller than spring AdM, wing panel usually reduced to wing bars, often shows yellow wash on underparts; *Diagnostic when present:* partial wing panel.

AdF/1yM Fa AdF lighter orange and streaking less diffuse than spring AdF; 1yM similar but usually shows black in auriculars, and more yellow than orange tones.

1yM Fa Cheek patch *Diagnostic when present:* often shows some black in auriculars vs none in females (subtle).

Note Bill color is not a good separator for sex in fall: bills often appear light in females and winter males.

1yF Fa Very dull, low contrast; light buffy tones in face and breast; *Diagnostic when present:* some individuals whitish; very diffuse, brownish side streaking/smudging (can be hard to detect) vs. gray streaking in 1yM Fa.

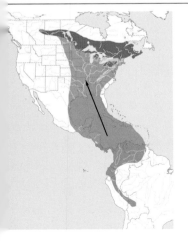

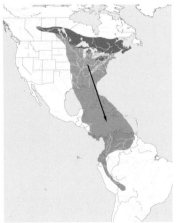

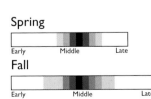

Spring

Early   Middle   Late

Fall

Early   Middle   Late

Blackburnian

Sunburned, blackened swimmers try diving board, 3 or 4 jumps, then very high

Summary *Very wide pitch range* for song; *very high* Elements; Complex Elements contrast with Clear Elements; can be easy to miss if you only know 1 Type; often alternates Types. Regularly calls 2 or 3 times right before song (unlike similar-sounding Am. Redstart or Cerulean). **3 Types: A,** 3 Sections, rising pitch trend, ends very high; **B,** 2 Sections, first higher; **C,** 1 Section, large pitch/quality contrast between Elements.

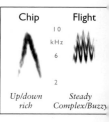

Chip	Flight
	10 kHz 6 2
Up/down rich	*Steady Complex/Buzzy*

Type A
3-Sections, rising pitch trend, very high ending slur. Complex quality of 1st Section similar to other Types. No other warbler species has such low beginning to such high ending.

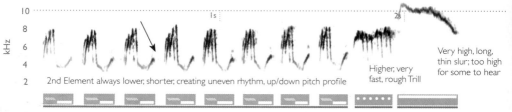

2nd Element always lower, shorter, creating uneven rhythm, up/down pitch profile

Higher, very fast, rough Trill

Very high, long, thin slur; too high for some to hear

Type B
2 Sections, highest notes in 1st Section; usually not as high as Type A ending. Obvious contrast between Clear first Section and Complex 2nd.

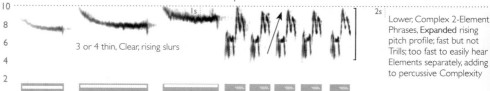

3 or 4 thin, Clear, rising slurs

Lower, Complex 2-Element Phrases, Expanded rising pitch profile; fast but not Trills; too fast to easily hear Elements separately, adding to percussive Complexity

Type C1
1 Section of 2-Element Phrases. 1st Element very high. Large pitch/quality contrast between Elements, unlike other species with 2-Element Phrases (e.g., Black-and-white).

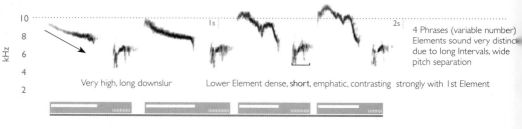

Very high, long downslur

Lower Element dense, short, emphatic, contrasting strongly with 1st Element

4 Phrases (variable number) Elements sound very distinct due to long Intervals, wide pitch separation

Type C2
Fairly common hybrid of Type C and A. Very high ending; lacks high, Trilled 2nd Section of Type A; long Intervals and long 1st Elements, so Phrases sound distinct, separate.

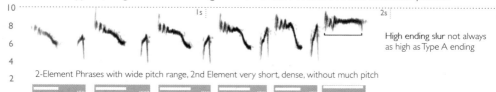

2-Element Phrases with wide pitch range, 2nd Element very short, dense, without much pitch

High ending slur not always as high as Type A ending

Cerulean A

Cerulean A 3 Sections, similar quality of 1st Section and rise between Sections, **but** overall lower, denser, with very different, fast Trilled or Buzzed ending. 1st Section more Compressed, less bright; subsequent Sections not as high.

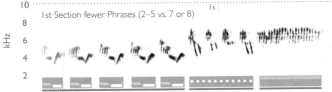

1st Section fewer Phrases (2–5 vs. 7 or 8)

2nd Section denser, slower, amost countable speed (vs. higher, thinner, uncountable or rough, fast slur)

Last Section long, steady, fast Trill or slow Buzz (vs. Clear, slurred ending)

American Redstart A

American Redstart A Some Type A accented songs similar shape, ending with very high slur. Overall song quality simpler, more slurred, lacking Complex Elements. 2- and 3-Section songs much shorter (avg. 1.2 sec. vs. 1.9), and often alternated with simpler 1-Section song.

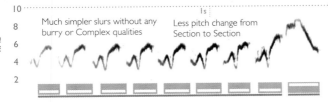

Much simpler slurs without any burry or Complex qualities

Less pitch change from Section to Section

High ending notes not as high or as long, often falling more in pitch

Always missing faster, Trilled 2nd Section that builds to high slur in Blackburnian songs

Northern Parula B

Northern Parula B Songs with Complex, separate Trills similar. Most songs end in an abrupt up/down diagnostic slur (western N. Parula Buzzier, upslurred endings also different).

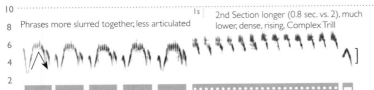

Phrases more slurred together, less articulated

2nd Section longer (0.8 sec. vs. 2), much lower, dense, rising, Complex Trill

Diagnostic: much lower, fast up/down-slur (vs. higher, thinner, longer upslur)

American Redstart/Cape May/Black-and-white/Nashville/ (Kinglets)

American Redstart/Cape May/Black-and-white/Nashville/ (Kinglets) Nashville only confusing when sings just 1st Section. **Kinglets** very high-pitched, simple slurs, followed by low, Complex Phrases (compare Blackburnian Type B), **but** 1st Section higher, thinner, less even, with following Sections fast, thinner, and more varied chatter.

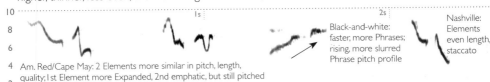

Black-and-white: faster, more Phrases; rising, more slurred Phrase pitch profile

Nashville: Elements even length, staccato

Am. Red/Cape May: 2 Elements more similar in pitch, length, quality; 1st Element more Expanded, 2nd emphatic, but still pitched

BLACKBURNIAN

Setophaga fusca   Drab Birds

- Variable pale peachy/buffy throat
- ✓ Pale braces on back
- ✓ Dark-olive ear coverts are distinctive triangular shape: pointed at rear and bottom; bordered by wide supercilium and pale neck patch
- Yellowish stripe on forehead distinctive
- White wing bars

- Variable pale peachy/buffy throat
- Wide streaks on sides and shoulders but not throat
- White tail

- Pale peachy/buffy throat
- Thick neck helps give it a pointed front end
- Variable amount of yellow/orange below
- Medium-long white tail

Distinctive Views

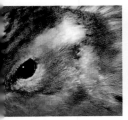  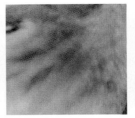 

Additional Photos

Drab birds usually still show orangey wash

Note variation of orange wash in these specimens

All plumages show pale median forehead stripe

  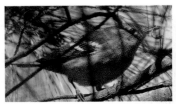

ide streaking may be very limited but always present

Fall males show duller orange in face than spring males but maintain moderate contrast

Fall females can be very drab with almost whitish appearance

Note lack of streaking in throat or center of breast

ointed edge of cheek patch and buff wash both useful marks

Drab birds show the same triangular cheek patch that bright birds do

Wide, buffy supercilium
Triangular cheek patch
Fairly long, white tail
Pale back braces
Diffuse streaking with variable
buffy orange wash below

Comparison Species

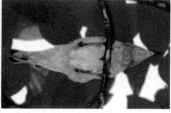

Bay-breasted Lacks wide supercilium, auricular patch, pale back braces; may bob tail; usually some chestnut wash in flanks (vs. none); shorter tail with white spots only; lacks underpart streaking; more even buffy wash underneath (vs. orangey)

Palm Constant, exaggerated tail-pumping; brown-toned back/rufous crown (vs. dark); streaking in center of breast; fainter, buffy wing bars; wide black tail base; yellow undertail coverts (vs. whitish/buff)

Blackpoll Lacks wide supercilium, pale mantle streaks, auricular patch; buffy green wash overall (vs. orangey); may bob tail; shorter tail with only white spots; streaking more focused on upper breast; always white UnTC (vs. whitish/buff)

Cerulean Blue back tones and streaking (vs. orangey); often shows blu collar; whiter underparts with yellowish wash in fresh fall plumage (vs. more orangey); lacks triangular face patch; shorter tail

Cape May Greenish-yellow rump; fainter wing bars; little or no supercilium; finer, even streaking in throat and body; finer, pointy bill; varying wash of yellow in throat and breast (may be patchy)

BLACKPOLL

Setophaga striata   Spring Birds

- ✓ Unique black cap with white cheeks
- Bold streaks on upperparts and underparts
- White wing bars
- Large, long-winged, with short tail
- Distinct black malar stripe on white throat

- Distinct black malar stripe on white throat
- Basically black and white
- ✓ Usually bright orangish legs and feet
- Side streaking
- Long and pointy wings; long primary projection

- Long white UnTC and short tail
- Relatively large
- Short tail and boat-shaped body create a distinct profile (similar to Bay-breasted)

Distinctive Views

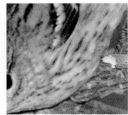

Additional Photos

Note orange legs, strong streaking and black cap; streaking not as evenly distributed as in Black-and-white Warbler

Periodically pumps tail

Hindneck is often narrow collar of black and white streaks; strong black cap in male is distinctive

Short tail with long undertail coverts, which makes the tail appear even shorter

Females often show finer, broken streaking; less contrasty overall; note malar stripe defined by denser streaking

Females also lack black cap; note broken eyering and eyestripe, and spotty streaking above and below

Long wings indicate a long-distance migrant: up to 7,000 miles each way (more than any other warbler)

Overall large and stocky, with proportions similar to Bay-breasted

Black streaking in throat varies; note strong malar stripe

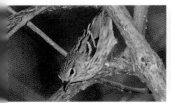

Females show olive or gray tones; pattern is a fainter version of the male

Noticeable eyestripe and broken eyering present in all plumages except adult spring male

Females often difficult to see in spring as they remain high in trees and are generally silent and slow moving

Black cap, white cheek (male)
Short tail
White tail spots/UnTC
Monochromatic
Black malar stripe/white throat
Heavy streaking on back/flanks
Often orange legs/feet

Comparison Species

Black-and-white White striped crown (vs. black cap); black cheek patch (vs. white); white supercilium (vs. none); creeping behavior; spotting in UnTC (vs. none); longer, decurved bill; longer tail extension

Black-throated Gray Diagnostic yellow supraloral spot; plainer gray back (vs. streaked); black mask and throat (vs. white); smaller; shorter side streaks; slimmer profile; longer, all-white tail

White-breasted Nuthatch Thicker, wedge-shaped bill; blue, plain back (vs. streaked/dark); lacks streaks; plain white face; creeps on trunks

Chickadee Plumper; shorter billed; very active and often vocal; lacks streaking; solid black throat (vs. white); longer gray tail

Aging and Sexing

Spring AdM 1yM AdF 1yF   **Fall** AdM 1yM AdF 1yF

Races: 1 Summary *Spring:* Sexable; 1yM, 1yF may be separable with difficulty in some cases   *Fall:* Not sexable, first-year birds sometimes ageable   **What to Notice** *Spring:* Black in cap, throat, cheeks and lores; black and white tones vs. olive and white/buffy; white mottling in throat and cheek; buffy wash on underparts and face; intensity of streaking on underparts   *Fall:* Overall contrast, quality of streaking; amount of yellow wash

AdM/1yM Sp High-contrast streaking; *Diagnostic:* dark black cap.

1yM Sp Extreme *Diagnostic when present:* may be lower contrast than AdM, grayer cap; brown flight feathers contrast with greater coverts (may be difficult to see).

AdF/1yF Sp *Diagnostic female:* no black cap, olive tones overall (vs. males); *Diagnostic 1yF when present:* brown flight feathers and primary coverts contrast surrounding blackish feathers (may be difficult to see).

1yF/1yM Fa Extreme Duller with fainter, blurrier streaking above and below, less gray and more yellow, and lower contrast overall; only the most extreme examples of these characteristics should be considered separable.

AdM/AdF Fa Adults generally not sexable, although females usually show fainter streaking, lighter green rump and uppertail coverts, and darker legs (these points are subtle and there is significant overlap with AdM).

AdM/AdF Fa Extreme example of adult with unusually heavy marking.

Note Spring birds' legs are usually orange; fall birds may have darker legs, back of legs orange, or only feet (or just bottoms of feet) are orange.

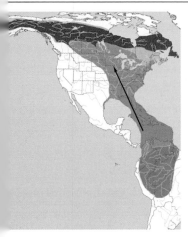

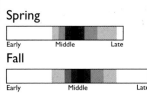

Spring

Early	Middle	Late

Fall

Early	Middle	Late

Blackpoll

Pollsters, in black of night, knock softly, steadily, but have to get louder, louder

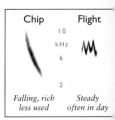

Chip | Flight
10
kHz
6

2

Falling, rich | *Steady*
less used | *often in day*

Summary *Extremely high* (hard to hear for many). Very short, steadily repeated 1-Element Phrases; relatively long Intervals enhance *staccato*, clipped effect. Starts softly, slowly grows in volume over 1/3 or 1/2 of song, fades at end. *Extremely high staccato notes combined with slow fade-in diagnostic.* Long songs. **2 Types: A,** Most common; slower, countable speeds; **B,** Uncountable Trill speed.

Type A1 Most common type; slower, countable speeds.

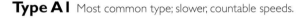

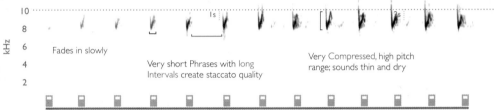

kHz
10
8
6
4
2

Fades in slowly

Very short Phrases with long Intervals create staccato quality

Very Compressed, high pitch range; sounds thin and dry

1 s

Type A2 Long (avg. 2 sec.), with steady, even rhythm; fades in and out, loudest in middle.

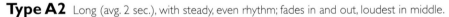

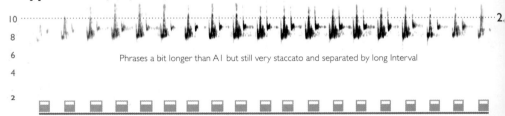

kHz
10
8
6
4

2

Phrases a bit longer than A1 but still very staccato and separated by long Interval

2

Type B Similar to Type A **but** uncountable Trill speed. Very high, thin (hard for many to hear).

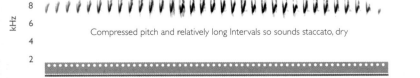

kHz
10
8
6
4
2

1 s   2s

Fades in and out

Compressed pitch and relatively long Intervals so sounds staccato, dry

Cape May A
Also very high pitched, thin, 1-Section song with simple Phrases, **but** much shorter, (avg. 4–6 Phrases vs. 17).

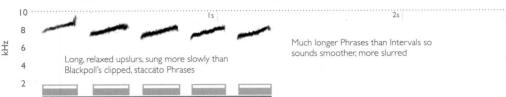

Long, relaxed upslurs, sung more slowly than Blackpoll's clipped, staccato Phrases

Much longer Phrases than Intervals so sounds smoother, more slurred

Pine
Only confusable with Type B; much lower pitch.

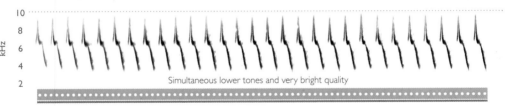

Doesn't fade in over long time like Blackpoll

Short Phrases, but much more Expanded pitch range: sounds richer, lower, more slurred, less dry and thin.

Chipping Sparrow
Only confusable with Type B; much more Expanded pitch range and more complicated Elements sounds richer, more slurred.

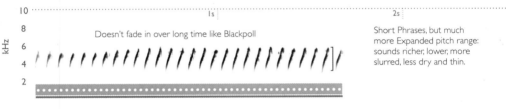

Simultaneous lower tones and very bright quality

Worm-eating
Only confusable with Type B; much more Expanded pitch range and more complicated Elements, especially in low frequencies. Quality very different: fuller, with lower, darker tones as well as brighter quality.

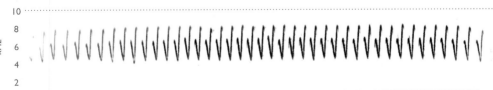

2.9s

BLACKPOLL
Setophaga striata   Fall Birds

- Green-yellowish above
- Yellowish throat/breast contrasts with white on lower belly and UnTC
- White edges to tertials
- Distinct eyeline
- Streaked back and body
- Bold white wing bars
- Long wings and primary projection

- Faintly streaked sides of breast
- Legs orangish in spring, darker in fall but still orange/yellow on soles of feet
- Contrast between yellowish breast and white lower breast and UnTC
- Short tail with long UnTC
- Wings quite long with considerable primary projection

- Contrast between yellowish breast and white lower breast and UnTC
- Short tail with long UnTC
- Faintly streaked sides of breast

Distinctive Views

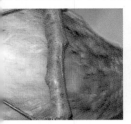

Additional Photos

Note short tail with long UnTC; yellow body wash contrasting with white UnTC and tail; long wings

Distinct eyeline with broken eyering in all plumages except adult male breeding

Legs often orange, but even when dark, soles of the feet are always orange

Contrasting tertial edging, flight feathers white-edged on tips

Note streaking, dark eyeline, and yellowy wash

Contrast between olive back/yellow underparts and between variably yellow breast/white UnTC

Streaking in sides and back is always present even when faint

Note orange toes, white UnTC and short tail/long UnTC

Long wings indicate a long-distance migrant: up to 7,000 miles each way (more than any other warbler)

Variable diffuse streaking below
Varying yellow wash in breast
Pure white vent/UnTC
Short tail with white tail spots
Contrasting white wing bars
Orange feet, often legs
Short eyeline/supercilium

Comparison Species

Bay-breasted Similar shape; face pattern plainer with shorter, less distinct eyeline and less contrasting eye-arcs; wide contrasting collar on nape; brighter green on upperparts; wing bars often thicker with black between them (vs. olive); often shows chestnut in flanks; lacks distinct streaking below (sometimes appears vaguely streaked); UnTC buffy or duller, so less contrast with undersides (vs. whiter/more contrast); legs and soles of feet dark (never orange)

Cerulean 1yF Smaller; bluer tones/ streaking (vs. buff/olive); more contrast in face and body; often shows wider supercilium; white or slightly buffy underparts (vs. yellow and white)

Pine Unstreaked upperparts; larger bill; less supercilium; lighter eyering/ supraloral; females browner above; lacks bright tertial/primary edging; black between wing bars less contrasty; varying yellow in breast, but often concentrated below throat; legs and soles of feet dark (not orange); longer tail with more white, often appears more deeply notched

Cape May Finer even streaking in throat, upper breast, sides; varying patchier wash of yellow in throat and breast; greenish-yellow rump; fainter wing bars; little or no supercilium; finer, pointy bill

Blackburnian Triangular face patch; wider supercilium; pale back braces (vs. none); orange wash across face into breast (vs. yellowy); smaller with finer bill; longer, all-white tail

Yellow-rumped Myrtle Browner upperparts; totally white throat (vs. yellow); lacks eyeline; longer tail with more prominent black border

Palm Browner upperparts; large, obvious supercilium; constant, exaggerated tail-pumping; tail longer with large black base; yellow UnTC (vs. white); brown/rufous streaking in breast (vs. black); brown/rufous cap

BLACK-THROATED BLUE

Setophaga caerulescens   Male - All Seasons

✓ Plain blue back and all black face and throat

• Plump shape

✓ White "handkerchief" at base of primaries

✓ Strong black side stripe

• Black throat and bright white undersides

✓ White unstreaked breast bordered by black throat and side stripe

• Medium-long tail with large white tail spots bordered by black at base

Distinctive Views

Additional Photos

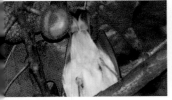

Note the warm wash in vent, seen on some birds

From beneath might be confused with Cerulean; note the black throat and sides; longer tail

Very strong black face with blue hood is unique and diagnostic; bill is an average weight *Setophaga* bill

On some birds UnTC cover black base of the tail, but on others it shows clearly ... when the tail is spread the black is clear on all birds

White wing stripe becomes the "handkerchief" on the folded wing

Even at this angle there are two good marks: white "handkerchief" and the angle black side stripe

This shade of blue is unique; also note handkerchief, lack of back streaking, and prominent black face

Green fringing on back feathers indicates a first-year bird

Black stripe, white handkerchief, and black mask are all identifiers

Black-throated Blue male and female together. These warblers are not timid and are often in the understory at eye level or below

Plain blue back
All black face and throat
White handkerchief
Black side stripe
No yellow

Comparison Species

American Redstart Male Black back (vs. blue); orange markings; more extensive black across breast; club-shaped, orange/black, frequently fanned tail

Northern Parula White eye-arcs (vs. none); lacks black face; yellow breast (vs. white); different color blue; wing bars (vs. handkerchief)

Black-and-White Black and white streaking throughout; creeps habitually on branches; side streaking (vs. stripes); spotting in UnTC (vs. none); longer bill and overall shape.

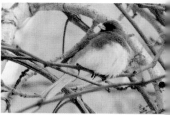

Cerulean Blue side-streaking (vs. black stripes); lacks black in head; wing bars (vs. handkerchief); different tone of blue; shorter tail; often shows neck band (vs. black throat); more likely in tree tops

All other Black-throated Some yellow (vs. none); lacks blue in backs or heads; lacks side stripes; Black-throated Green shows yellow in vent (vs. white/buff)

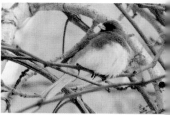

Golden-winged Gray back (vs. blue); yellow wing bars and cap (vs. no yellow); smaller, with finer bill; white in face (vs. none); lacks side stripes; tail proportionally longer and whiter

Chickadee Gray back (vs. blue); no side stripe; pale cheeks; buffy flanks and underside; plumper bodied; very long, gray tail; often in groups and vocal

Dark-eyed Junco Paler bill; rarely overlaps seasonally; often in flocks; gray back, sides, and throat (vs. blue/black); plumper shape; longer, all-white tail

Aging and Sexing

Spring AdM 1yM AdF 1yF   **Fall** AdM 1yM AdF 1yF

Races: 1 (possibly 2—see below) **Summary** *Spring/Fall:* Sexable, often ageable   **What to Notice** *Males Spring/Fall:* Greenish edging on back and white edging in black areas, especially throat; extent of handkerchief *Females Spring/Fall:* Blue vs. green tones in head and back, presence/extent of handkerchief

AdM Sp/Fa Averages bolder handkerchief than 1yM; *Diagnostic from 1yM:* no greenish tones in back and no white fringing in black areas.

AdF Sp/Fa May show blue tones in the head and back; limited or complete handkerchief.

Appalachian Race The sometimes recognized Appalachian mountain region race, *cairnsi,* is generally darker and more contrasty, and males show more extensive black in back that tends to be spots, longer white handkerchief; this difference is clinal and may not be reliably separable.

1yM Sp/Fa Often more limited handkerchief than AdM; *Diagnostic when present:* may show greenish tones in back, white fringing on black areas (especially throat), and greenish edges to primary coverts (subtle).

1yF Sp/Fa *Diagnostic when present:* lacking a handkerchief (some have limited handkerchief); flight feathers, alula and primary coverts more worn and brownish (subtle).

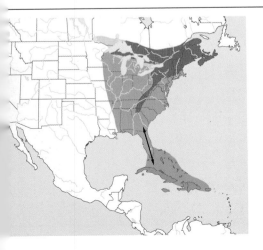

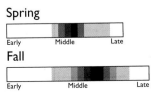

Spring

Early   Middle   Late

Fall

Early   Middle   Late

Black-throated Blue

Very laaaaaazzzzzzzzy and spoiled, in blue smoking jacket, black ascot

Summary *Overall Buzzy, slow-paced, few Sections and Phrases; 1st Section Buzzes or semi-Buzzes, sometimes with Clear Phrases (rarely all Clear); 2nd Section almost always longer, Buzzy, rising single Phrase*
2 Types: A, 2 Sections, variable number of Clear/Buzzy Phrases followed by longer, rising Buzz; **B,** 3 Sections, similar to Type A.

Chip	Flight
10 kHz	
6	
2	
Falling, short "lip smack"	*Rising Clear*

Type A1 2 Sections, variable number of Phrases in 1st, longer, rising Phrase in 2nd; very slow.

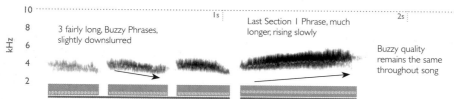

3 fairly long, Buzzy Phrases, slightly downslurred

Last Section 1 Phrase, much longer, rising slowly

Buzzy quality remains the same throughout song

Type A2 Typical simple, short, slow song. This variation has Clearer Phrases in 1st Section.

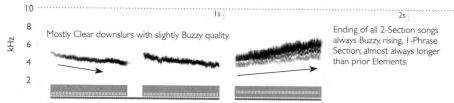

Mostly Clear downslurs with slightly Buzzy quality

Ending of all 2-Section songs always Buzzy, rising, 1-Phrase Section; almost always longer than prior Elements.

Type A3 1st Section Phrases have Clear/Buzzy sound typical of many Type A songs; number of 1st Section Phrases and speed varies between individuals.

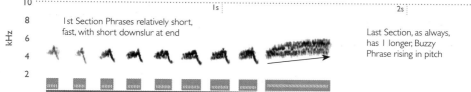

1st Section Phrases relatively short, fast, with short downslur at end

Last Section, as always, has 1 longer, Buzzy Phrase rising in pitch

Type B Less common, 3 Sections; still very simple, slow, and Buzzy, with few Phrases.

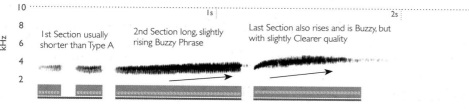

1st Section usually shorter than Type A

2nd Section long, slightly rising Buzzy Phrase

Last Section also rises and is Buzzy, but with slightly Clearer quality

Cerulean B
Usually 3 very different Sections, each with different Phrase qualities, speeds. Black-throated Blue songs simpler, slower, more consistent. This 2-Section version more similar. Less common to mistake Cerulean for Black-throated Blue than the reverse.

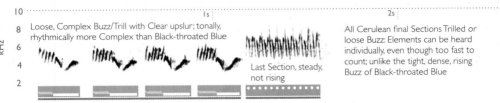

Loose, Complex Buzz/Trill with Clear upslur; tonally, rhythmically more Complex than Black-throated Blue

Last Section, steady, not rising

All Cerulean final Sections Trilled or loose Buzz: Elements can be heard individually, even though too fast to count; unlike the tight, dense, rising Buzz of Black-throated Blue

Prairie A
Similar Buzzy quality, **but** only 1-Section songs (vs. 2- or 3-) and almost always much longer, with more and consistently faster Phrases (avg. 18 Phrases vs. 4 in 1st Section). Rising pitch from Phrase to Phrase vs. 1st Section usually steady pitch.

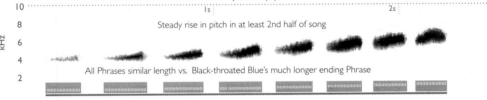

Steady rise in pitch in at least 2nd half of song

All Phrases similar length vs. Black-throated Blue's much longer ending Phrase

Black-throated Green B
Similar quality, speed, and few Phrases, **but** all Phrases have steady pitch vs. rising pitch in final Black-throated Blue Section. Always 3 or 4 Sections; Black-throated Blue usually 2 Sections, never 4.

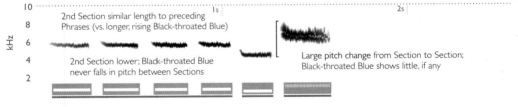

2nd Section similar length to preceding Phrases (vs. longer, rising Black-throated Blue)

2nd Section lower; Black-throated Blue never falls in pitch between Sections

Large pitch change from Section to Section; Black-throated Blue shows little, if any

Northern Parula
Usually easy to separate: 1 long rising Section, followed by accented, fast, up/downslur. This version is a bit more similar to Black-throated Blue.

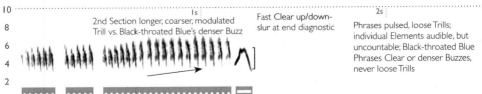

2nd Section longer, coarser, modulated Trill vs. Black-throated Blue's denser Buzz

Fast Clear up/down-slur at end diagnostic

Phrases pulsed, loose Trills; individual Elements audible, but uncountable; Black-throated Blue Phrases Clear or denser Buzzes, never loose Trills

BLACK-THROATED BLUE

Setophaga caerulescens   Female - All Seasons

- Blue-green back and buffy undersides create a relatively low-contrast appearance
- Long, thin supercilium
- Under-eye arc
- Darker cheek creates faintly masked appearance
- ✓ White "handkerchief" on most birds

- Buffy, unstreaked underparts and throat
- Dark grayish tail
- Plump shape
- Under-eye arc and faint mask

- Buffy, unstreaked underparts
- Dark grayish tail
- Plump shape

Distinctive Views

Additional Photos

From some angles, the mask can be very prominent

White handkerchief mark is created by white coloration at the base of the outer primaries

Some first-year birds don't show any white handkerchief

In flight, handkerchief is still often visible, and white mark can also be seen on the open wing

Buffy underside is a distinctive feature

Trunk creeping not an uncommon behavior for this species

Also may forage on the ground, especially in the fall

Black-throated Blue is an active, understory forager, often seen near eye level. They frequently make a loud, dry, "kissy" chip call while foraging in the fall

Black-throated Blue is a good example of sexual dimorphism: the male and female are very different in color, although their body structure is the same

Thin, long supercilium
White handkerchief
Under-eye arc
Buffy undersides
Dark grayish tail

Comparison Species

Cerulean Female Aqua blue tones (vs. greenish/buff); wing bars (vs. sometime handkerchief); side streaks (vs. none); wide supercilium (vs. thin); white tail (vs. dark)

Pine Drab Larger, more elongated; longer tail with white spots (vs. dark); wing bars (vs. sometime handkerchief); overall gray tones/yellow breast (vs. green/buff); larger bill.

Yellow-rumped Myrtle 1yF Fa Side streaking (vs. plain); gray/brown upperparts (vs. greenish); faint wing bar (vs. sometime handkerchief); wider supercilium; usually yellow shoulders; yellow rump; black-and-white tail (vs. dark)

Common Yellowthroat Drab Eyering (vs. eye-arc, supercilium); brown and buffy olive tones (vs. greenish); isolated, contrasting throat; all grayish flanks in East (vs. paler breast); contrasting yellow UnTC

American Redstart Drab Yellow in shoulders and tail; eye-arcs (vs. under-eye arc) and lacks supercilium; gray undersides (vs. buff); often flashes black and yellow tail

Bay-breasted Fall Often shows chestnut in flanks; greener in back and head; pale collar; wing bars (vs. sometime handkerchief); white in tail (vs. dark); larger, more sluggish

Blackburnian Fall Different face pattern with triangular face mask, wider orange supercilium; side streaking (vs. none); wing bars (vs. sometime handkerchief); white tail (vs. dark); more orangey, less uniform coloration

Orange-crowned Finer bill; lacks distinct supercilium; indistinct eye-arcs and eyeline (vs. eye-arc/none); lower contrast overall

Cape May Fine, even streaking in breast and throat (vs. none); lacks pronounced supercilium; finer bill; ofte shows some patchy yellow in breast (v plain buff); white tail (vs. dark)

BLACK-THROATED GRAY

Setophaga nigrescens   Male/Female - All Seasons

- Black-and-white face contrasts with gray back
- White wing bars
- Bold white supercilium
- ✓ All black and white with yellow spot above lores

- White underparts
- Sides streaked with black
- Black throat in male, variable black in others

- Long white tail, with white UnTC
- All black or partial black in throat
- Side streaks

Distinctive Views

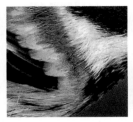

Additional Photos

Note dark smudge on sides of breast, yellow supraloral mark

Long, all-white tail

Note diagnostic yellow supraloral mark, gray back with streaking, and black-and-white face

High contrast, streaking, and yellow supraloral mark often noticeable even in brief views

Shares overall pattern with Townsend's warbler

Adult females have white chins with variably mottled black throats and black upper breast band

Some fine back streaking

Adults maintain basically the same plumage year round

Found in all kinds of woodland and scrub during migration

Relatively frequent vagrants, this bird was seen in Central Park, New York City, fall 2008

Diagnostic face pattern including yellow supraloral mark

Note streaking on flanks only (not center of breast)

Wide white supercilium
Black mask
Diagnostic yellow supraloral
Fairly long all-white tail
Contrasting white wing bars
Black side streaks

Comparison Species

Black-and-white Rarely overlaps range; white median crown stripe (vs. none); white streaking on back (vs. dark); lacks yellow in lores; creeps along branches; spotting in undertail (vs. none); longer bill; denser streaking on flanks; stronger white tertial edgings

Chestnut-backed Chickadee Lacks wing bars, side streaks; chestnut/gray flanks (vs. streaked); vocal and often in flocks; longer, gray tail; white cheeks with black cap; shorter, conical bill

Blackpoll Only overlaps range in winter; lacks black auriculars; more back streaking; larger; often with orange legs (vs. dark); shorter tail, longer UnTC; white throat without breast band (vs. all black or mottled with band)

Bridled Titmouse Larger; blunter bill; more upright; black crest; black eyeline (vs. mask); longer tail; lacks wing bars

All other Black-throated (*virens*) In this example, Townsend's (left) and Hermit (right); yellow on bird (vs. only supralorals); olive upperparts (vs. gray)

Golden-winged No range overlap; yellow wing-bars and crown, finer bill, no streaking

Aging and Sexing

Spring AdM 1yM AdF 1yF   **Fall** AdM 1yM AdF 1yF

Races: Possibly 2, not separable in field   **Summary** *Spring:* Sexable, 1yM sometimes ageable   *Fall:* Extreme adult males and 1y females separable, other first-year birds sometimes ageable   **What to Notice** *Spring:* Extent of black in throat, streaking on back, intensity of side streaking, darkness of cheeks and crown   *Fall:* Extent of black in throat, streaking on back, intensity and quality of side streaking, smudgy markings by shoulder, darkness of cheeks and crown

AdM/1yM Sp Black throat, black streaks or spots in back; only some 1yM separable by white in chin.

1yM Sp Extreme Duller back streaks than AdM; *Diagnostic when present:* some 1yM show white in chin.

AdF/1yF Sp Whitish chins, cheeks grayer, streaks less contrasting and crown grayer in center and blacker on sides than AdM/1yM; *Diagnostic for female:* white throat sometimes mottled black.

1yF Fa White throat, sometimes with black flecks; crown and cheek gray, streaking fine and pale, back streaking absent or faint and brownish; *Diagnostic when present:* all-white throat, molt limit in greater coverts, black streaking by shoulder smudgy.

AdF/1yM Fa Similar to AdF spring; 1yM may show less side streaking and more white fringing in throat, but not safely separable; *Diagnostic when present for 1yM:* molt limit in greater coverts.

AdM Fa Extreme Black throat may show some white edging, black streaks, or spots in back; *Diagnostic when present:* all-black throat.

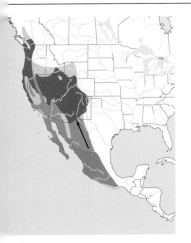

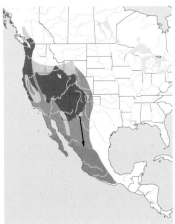

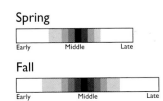

Spring

Early   Middle   Late

Fall

Early   Middle   Late

Black-throated Gray

Flies buzz around the old gray mare with the black throat and smooth gait

Summary Variable even within one singing session; overall *dense Buzzes with slurred, run-on quality*; 1- to 4-Section songs; *1st Section most often 2-Element Phrases of uneven-length Buzzes*, which increase in length, volume through Section. Ending usually accented, slightly Clearer up/down tones. **Types:** variable.

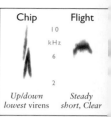

Chip   Flight

Up/down   Steady
lowest virens   short, Clear

Black-throated Gray
Buzzy/loosely Trilled Elements slurred together; small pitch changes from Section to Section. Many variations have "stuck in mud" quality.

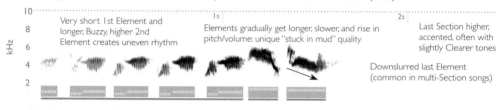

Very short 1st Element and longer, Buzzy, higher 2nd Element creates uneven rhythm

Elements gradually get longer, slower, and rise in pitch/volume: unique "stuck in mud" quality

Last Section higher, accented, often with slightly Clearer tones

Downslurred last Element (common in multi-Section songs)

Black-throated Gray
Generally Buzzy quality with slightly Clearer ending.

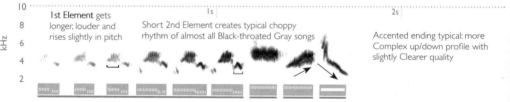

1st Element gets longer, louder and rises slightly in pitch

Short 2nd Element creates typical choppy rhythm of almost all Black-throated Gray songs

Accented ending typical: more Complex up/down profile with slightly Clearer quality

Black-throated Gray
Unaccented, 1-Section variation: more loosely Complex. As usual, Elements run smoothly into next creating an overall slurred quality; speed of Phrases also slows down some throughout song.

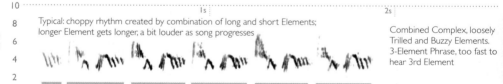

Typical: choppy rhythm created by combination of long and short Elements; longer Element gets longer, a bit louder as song progresses

Combined Complex, loosely Trilled and Buzzy Elements. 3-Element Phrase, too fast to hear 3rd Element

Black-throated Gray
More Complex version without strongly accented ending. As other songs, combination of Complex, loosely Trilled and Buzzy Elements. Elements slurred, smeared together; so Complex it is difficult to read sonogram.

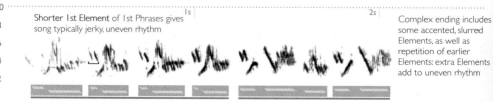

Shorter 1st Element of 1st Phrases gives song typically jerky, uneven rhythm

Complex ending includes some accented, slurred Elements, as well as repetition of earlier Elements: extra Elements add to uneven rhythm

Hermit
Higher, thinner overall; most have some Clear Elements, larger pitch differences (vs. narrower pitch changes, Compressed); longer 2nd, 3rd Sections, more varied structures.

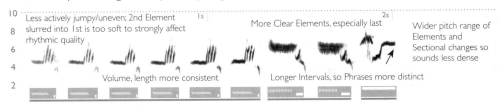

Less actively jumpy/uneven; 2nd Element slurred into 1st is too soft to strongly affect rhythmic quality

More Clear Elements, especially last

Wider pitch range of Elements and Sectional changes so sounds less dense

Volume, length more consistent

Longer Intervals, so Phrases more distinct

Townsend's
Usually easy to separate: most songs are higher, thinner and have Clearer or brighter Elements. 1st Section always 1-Element Phrases (vs. always 2-Element Phrases). Some, as below, are more similar, with Buzzy Phrases that get longer, higher, louder, slower; and an accented, high-to-low ending.

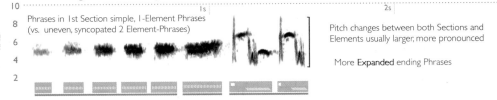

Phrases in 1st Section simple, 1-Element Phrases (vs. uneven, syncopated 2 Element-Phrases)

Pitch changes between both Sections and Elements usually larger, more pronounced

More **Expanded** ending Phrases

MacGillivray's
Structurally very similar, with similarly Complex Phrases, **but** rhythm less tightly syncopated; Phrases more distinct, less slurred. Elements have looser quality, more Trill-like than Buzzy timbre. Most songs have 2nd Section with 2–4 Elements. Black-throated Gray almost always has long 1st Section followed by very short, 1-Phrase ending Sections.

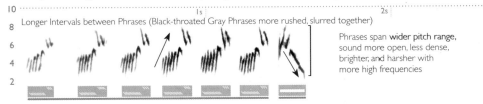

Longer Intervals between Phrases (Black-throated Gray Phrases more rushed, slurred together)

Phrases span **wider pitch range**, sound more open, less dense, brighter, and harsher with more high frequencies

Yellow-rumped (Audubon's)
Often similar structurally. Sounds smoother, duller, less rhythmically complex; not as Buzzy or energetic.

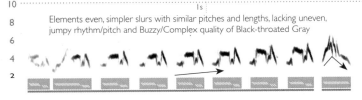

Elements even, simpler slurs with similar pitches and lengths, lacking uneven, jumpy rhythm/pitch and Buzzy/Complex quality of Black-throated Gray

BLACK-THROATED GREEN
Setophaga virens   Male/Female - All Seasons

- Olive auriculars with a light center
- Bright yellow face
- Bright olive-green back with little or no streaking, contrasts with dark wings
- Two strong wing bars
- Variably black throat and upper breast (some birds show pale throats)
- Variable black streaks on sides, flanks

- Black throat and upper breast
- Bold black streaks on sides, flanks; white-throated birds usually show smudgy black in shoulders and grayer streaking
- Underparts whitish with very little yellow wash below

- Yellow wash across vent distinctive
- Long white tail with short white UnTC
- Underparts whitish
- Faint yellow wash may be present in breast

Distinctive Views

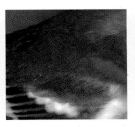

Additional Photos

Amount of black in throat is variable and can be extensive

Some white flecking may be present in throat in fall

There may be some yellow wash on lower breast but never as extensive as Townsend's

Some birds show faint black streaks on back

Throat may have limited or no black; side streaking and olive auriculars on a yellow face are constant

Often sings throughout the day during spring

Yellow wash around vent / base of legs shared only with Cape May (and contrasts more than in Cape May)

Olive auriculars are lighter in the center; they vary in darkness but are never black

Note strong contrast between greenish back and flight feathers (diagnostic within *virens* group)

Streaking may be clean stripes, or, as in this case, more chaotic

Black throat, white breast, yellow face: in the East, very likely a Black-throated Green

Migration is prolonged in the fall, and Black-throated Green often lingers later than many other warblers

Light-centered olive auriculars
Variably black throat
Side streaking
Bright olive-green back
Strong wing bars
Yellow in vent
Long white tail and UnTC

Bright

Drab

Comparison Species

Golden-cheeked Very restricted range; lacks auricular patch; stronger eyeline; lacks yellow in vent; duller back with black streaks; darker crown

Blackburnian Fall Triangular cheek patch; pale braces on darker back (vs. none); orange wash across face into breast (vs. yellow/black); usually paler bill

Black-throated Gray Black in throat variable; rarely overlaps range; lacks yellow in vent; no yellow in face except supraloral mark; black-and-white face (vs. olive/yellow); gray back (vs. olive)

Townsend's Rarely overlaps range; more contrasty overall; black or solid olive auricular patch (vs. paler, lighter centered); stronger yellow extends further into breast; darker olive above; lacks yellow in vent

Black-and-white Overall strongly streaked black and white (no yellow); black marks in undertail coverts; creeps along branches

Hermit Rarely overlaps range; yellow on crown (vs. olive); plain face lacks eye stripe and more defined auriculars; gray/black in back (vs. olive); lacks side streaking; lacks yellow in vent

Chickadee Lacks yellow in face and vent; long gray tail (vs. white); lacks side streaks; flittier; often in pairs or small flocks; often vocal (very different vocalizations)

Aging and Sexing

Spring AdM 1yM AdF 1yF **Fall** AdM 1yM AdF 1yF

Races: 2 (*S.v. waynei* breeds in coastal N. and S. Carolina, averages duller, with less black and smaller bill) **Summary** *Spring:* Sexable, first-year birds sometimes ageable *Fall:* Extreme adult males and 1y females separable; other first-year birds sometimes ageable **What to Notice** *Spring:* Extent of black in throat, mottling in upper breast, back streaking *Fall:* Extent of black in throat, overall contrast, quality and extent of side streaking

AdM/1yM Sp Black throat, bold side streaks, some back streaking.

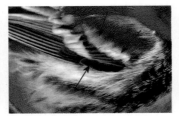

1y Spring Extreme *Diagnostic when present:* worn dull-black flight feathers and primary coverts, median covert molt limit.

AdF/1yF Sp Upper breast black with mottling, which bleeds into side streaks; little or no back streaking; *Diagnostic female:* varying white or pale yellow in throat with black flecking.

1yF Fa Very dull, little or no black on throat or breast, light streaking or grayish smudging on sides, overall lower contrast; *Diagnostic vs. Townsend's:* olive auriculars lighter centered, yellow wash in vent; *Diagnostic when present 1yF:* may be separable as above in 1yM Spring Extreme, no black in throat.

AdM/1yM/AdF Fa Varying amounts of black in throat, dark sides streaks, dark mottling in throat and chest; *Diagnostic 1y:* may be separable as above in 1yM Spring Extreme.

AdM Fa Extreme *Diagnostic when present:* dark black throat, dark black side streaking; only very contrasty birds should be separated.

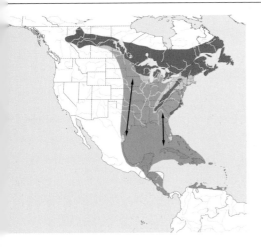

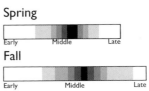

Spring

Early	Middle	Late

Fall

Early	Middle	Late

Black-throated Green

Suzy at the zoo, see: she's in her green outfit with a black scarf

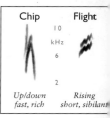

Chip	Flight
	10
	kHz
	6
	2
Up/down fast, rich	Rising short, sibilant

Summary Little variation. Buzzy Phrases with at least 1 or 2 Clear Elements; *2 consistent, fixed, wide, obvious pitch patterns* easy to learn and diagnostic in the East. **2 Types: A,** 4 Sections, unvaried structure; 1st Phrase longest, large pitch changes (low, high, low low, high); **B,** 3 Sections, mostly Clear Phrases with accented Buzzy ending.

Type A
4 Sections, always same number of Phrases; 1st Phrase longer than 2nd. Large, fixed pitch changes: low, high, low, low, high; diagnostic in East.

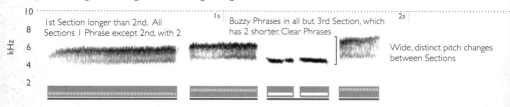

1st Section longer than 2nd. All Sections 1 Phrase except 2nd, with 2

Buzzy Phrases in all but 3rd Section, which has 2 shorter, Clear Phrases

Wide, distinct pitch changes between Sections

Type B
3 Sections, accented ending; quality and pitch profile diagnostic in East. All Phrases except last mostly Clear with slight rough Buzzy quality (as all *virens* superspecies); never as Clear as Hooded or Yellow Warbler, for example.

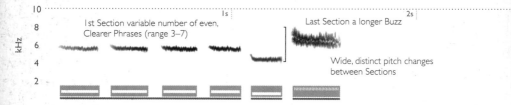

1st Section variable number of even, Clearer Phrases (range 3–7)

Last Section a longer Buzz

Wide, distinct pitch changes between Sections

Black-throated Blue
Usually 2 Sections (unlike any Black-throated Green); pitch never falls between Sections; Black-throated Green always 1 lower Section (either 2nd or 3rd).

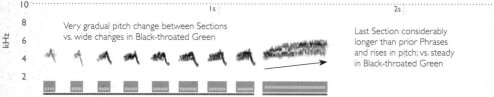

Very gradual pitch change between Sections vs. wide changes in Black-throated Green

Last Section considerably longer than prior Phrases and rises in pitch; vs. steady in Black-throated Green

Townsend's
Hermit and Townsend's are out of range, **but** have a similar quality; differences similar for both. Most have different structure and lack Black-throated Green's exact pitch profiles.

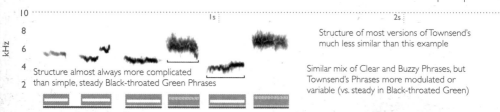

Structure almost always more complicated than simple, steady Black-throated Green Phrases

Structure of most versions of Townsend's much less similar than this example

Similar mix of Clear and Buzzy Phrases, but Townsend's Phrases more modulated or variable (vs. steady in Black-throated Green)

BLUE-WINGED

Vermivora cyanoptera   Male/Female - All Seasons

- Small and bright yellow, with blue-gray wings
- Sharp bill
- Blackish eyeline strongest in lores
- Narrow white or yellowish wing bars
- Greenish back

- Bright yellow below with white undertail coverts
- Small, with sharp bill
- Black eyeline

- Bright yellow below with white undertail coverts
- Sharp bill
- White tail with large dark tips look like white arrow pointing to tail tip; good ID point

Distinctive Views

Additional Photos

...ay flick open tail to flash white

There is a seasonal change in bill color: paler in fall and darker in spring

Insects and caterpillars are a common source of food

...dult males show broad white wing ...rs

Black bill and eyestripe form a unique, thin black "zorro mask" that wraps around the front of the face

This female has a dusky olive wash to the head and faint wing bars

...et warblers can hard to identify by ...ape, but the mask, color, and pointy ...ack bill are all good clues

Olive back, yellow head, and a fine, pointy bill

Strong contrast between white UnTC/ tail and the yellow body plus very fine bill is diagnostic combination

...eeding birds like transitional habitat ...e power-line cuts and have increased ...amatically since the early 1900s

Agile and often seen hanging upside down from branches to probe leaves and crevices

Often seen low to ground

Black eyeline on yellow head
White wing bars
Blue-gray wings
Contrasting white UnTC, tail
Fine, pointy bill
Greenish back and nape

Comparison Species

Prothonotary Lacks eyeline, wing bars; larger; longer, thicker bill; prefers different habitats; more orangey-gold color; shorter tail with different pattern: less black at tips so white area more blunt, less pointed

Brewster's Gray body (vs. olive/yellow); isolated yellow cap (vs. none)

Orange-crowned Much duller olive color and lower contrast overall; faint eyeline at best (vs. strong); lacks wing bars; UnTC yellowish; tail all dark (vs. some white)

Lawrence's Bright yellow wing bars (vs. white/slightly yellow); gray back/undersides (vs. olive/yellow); mask (vs. eyeline)

Yellow Olive/yellow wings and back (vs. green); lower contrast overall; lacks eyeline; yellow wing edging (vs. white wing bars); may show red breast streaks (vs. unstreaked); different yellow tone; yellow UnTC and tail (vs. white); blunter bill

Golden-winged Whitish to yellowish wing bars; gray body (vs. yellow); black mask/throat (vs. none)

Aging and Sexing

Spring AdM 1yM AdF 1yF Fall AdM 1yM AdF 1yF

Races: 1 Summary *Spring/Fall:* Only extreme AdM and 1yF separable **What to Notice** *Spring/Fall:* Brightness of head and contrast with nape, intensity of eyeline, width and intensity of wing bars

AdM Sp/Fa Extreme *Diagnostic when present:* strong contrast between head and nape, strong black eyeline, wide white wing bars; only extreme examples should be separated.

AdM/AdF/1yM/1yF Sp/Fa Clinal qualities from AdM to 1yF, from higher contrast, wider wing bars, and brighter colors in AdM to lower contrast, thinner wing bars, and duller colors in 1yF, but overlapping qualities prevents separation in all but extreme AdM and 1yF.

1yF Sp/Fa Extreme *Diagnostic when present:* dullest 1yF shows uniform olive-green head and back, dull eyeline, and dull, thin wing bars.

Note Some birds, especially in fall, may show a pale yellow tint to the wing bars. Birds with strong, all-yellow wing bars are very likely Golden-wing hybrids, but no hard data are currently available.

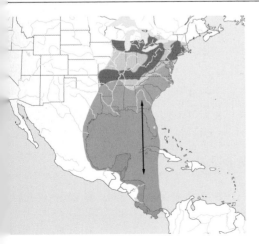

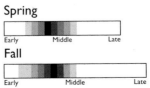

Spring

Early Middle Late

Fall

Early Middle Late

Blue-winged

When you're out of breath and wheezing, even your wings turn blue

Chip	Flight
Falling *Short, pure*	*Rising* *Buzzy, thin*

Summary Usually very short, 2-Section songs with *1 Phrase in each Section* (*diagnostic*). Sectional contrast a good ID point from other Buzzy-sounding species. Hybrids can sing both Types, so visual ID often critical. **2 Types: A,** 2 contrasting Sections, 1 Phrase each, Buzz, then longer, lower (hard to see in sonogram) Buzz or loose Trill; **B,** 3 Sections, Type A plus added Phrases in 3rd Section.

Type A1 2 Sections, a Buzz and a lower Trill; sounds like inhale then wheezy exhale.

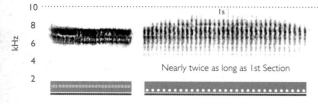

Nearly twice as long as 1st Section

Type A2 Type A song with Sections reversed, **but** still a 2-Section song with 1 Buzzy Phrase and 1 Trilled Phrase.

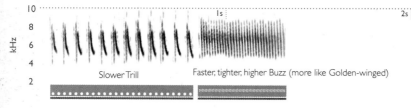

Slower Trill

Faster, tighter, higher Buzz (more like Golden-winged)

Type B 3 Sections (Type A first then added Phrases).

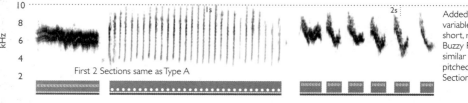

First 2 Sections same as Type A

Added Section: variable number of short, repeated Buzzy Phrases; similar or higher pitched than 1st Section

Golden-winged A Often found near, and hybridizes with, Blue-winged. 2 Sections with Buzzy quality. Phrases usually similar to each other, lacking contrasting quality found in Blue-winged songs. There are records of these species singing the song of the other.

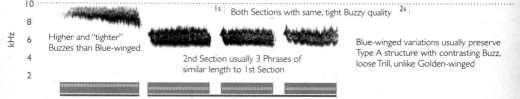

Both Sections with same, tight Buzzy quality

Higher and "tighter" Buzzes than Blue-winged

2nd Section usually 3 Phrases of similar length to 1st Section

Blue-winged variations usually preserve Type A structure with contrasting Buzz, loose Trill, unlike Golden-winged

BREWSTER'S/LAWRENCE'S

Vermivora cyanoptera x V. chrysoptera   Male/Female-All Seasons

Golden-winged and Blue-winged Warblers are frequently found in similar breeding habitats, and when they hybridize they produce Brewster's and Lawrence's Warblers. There are two basic versions of these hybrids, shown below, as well as a number of additional plumage variations caused by further hybridizations. It is not possible to determine the exact parentage of a hybrid in the field: even "classic" Brewster's and Lawrence's are not necessarily the result of a given hybridization. All birds share the same basic structural qualities of Blue-winged/Golden-winged, and can sing either Blue-winged or Golden-winged type songs.

Brewster's Warbler

- Typically a Blue-winged x Golden-winged hybrid

- Note eyeline with yellow crown and breast, white face

- Plumage is variable

Lawrence's Warbler

- Typically a Golden-winged x Brewster's hybrid

- All-yellow body with black mask and throat.

- Plumage is variable

Distinctive Views

Golden-winged (left) compared with **Brewster's**: note black eyeline and pale throat on hybrid

Brewster's: examples of plumage variations

Brewster's variation: gray body with yellow cap and black eyeline

Lawrence's: examples of plumage variations

Lawrence's: yellow face and body with black mask and throat, yellow wing bars

Hybrid properties: note the strongly yellow wing bars, which probably indicates hybridization. Pale yellow fringing in wing bars may be normal for pure Blue-winged

CANADA

Cardellina canadensis Male/Female - All Seasons

- Plain blue-gray upperside and plain yellow underparts
- Bold black or faint gray necklace
- Black lores and throat border
- Whitish eyering and yellow supraloral in all plumages (spectacles)
- ✓ Bicolored eyering (white rear, yellow front) diagnostic when present
- Lacks wing bars

- Bold black or faint gray necklace
- Yellow breast with white UnTC and long dark tail
- Flips tails or holds at odd angles, often drooping wings
- Pinkish legs

- Bold black or faint gray necklace
- Yellow breast with contrasting white UnTC
- Long dark tail (no white)
- Flips tails conspicuously when foraging
- Pinkish legs
- ✓ Dark tail with white UnTC and yellow body diagnostic

Distinctive Views

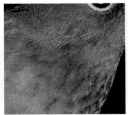

Additional Photos

Bill is dark gray with fleshy base on the lower mandible; also note the wide base to bill

Totally plain, bluish-slate upperparts are unique among warblers

Plain bluish-slate back and yellow underparts are distinct from many angles

Extent of necklacing is variable but always present

Note streaking in the cap, dark necklace, white eyering, and black throat border

Black streaking in cap, contrasting blue upperparts with yellow underparts

White UnTC contrast with yellow lower body and long dark tail—a diagnostic combination

Often forages in shady, low canopy, actively gleaning and fly catching

Often cocks tail and droops wings

all birds may be bright

May skulk in undergrowth: behavior and habitat can suggest Wilson's

Pink legs, long tail

Plain slate-blue upperparts
Goggles
Yellow throat, breast
Black necklace
White UnTC; long dark tail

Comparison Species

Kirtland's Larger; streaked back (vs. plain); no necklace; no yellow supraloral; frequently pumps tail (vs. infrequent flips); streaked flanks (vs. plain); white in tail (vs. dark); thin wing bars (vs. none); eye-arcs (no eyering)

Magnolia Bright More black in cheeks; white supercilium (vs. none); white wing patch, black side and back streaks (vs. plain); white lower belly (vs. yellow); white base of tail with broad black tip (vs. all dark)

Yellow All-yellow undersides (vs. necklace/dark tail); diagnostic yellow in tail with yellow UnTC; breast streaking is red if present (vs. black necklace)

Kentucky Larger; no black necklace; ground-walking bird (vs. low canopy); no complete eyering; olive back (vs. blue-gray); yellow UnTC (vs. whitish)

Magnolia Drab Thin wing bars (vs. none); yellow rump patch; pale neck band (vs. streaky necklace); often shows flank streaking (vs. none); white base of tail with broad black tip (vs. all dark)

Wilson's Olive upperparts (vs. blue-gray); black cap (vs. blue head); plainer face; no black necklace; yellow UnTC (vs. white)

Yellow-breasted Chat Larger, much larger bill; white goggles (vs. eyering); back olive (vs. bluish); yellow stops higher on breast/more white below; longer tail

Nashville Olive back contrasting blue-gray head (vs. same color); no necklace; smaller with finer bill; yellow UnTC (vs. white)

Prairie White in tail (vs. dark); shoulder marks (not full necklace); black side streaks (vs. plain); different face pattern; olive back with red patch; yellow wing bars (vs. none)

Aging and Sexing

Spring AdM 1yM AdF 1yF **Fall** AdM 1yM AdF 1yF

Races: 1 Summary *Spring:* Male and female separable, ages not *Fall:* Adult male, 1yF
separable, all others not **What to Notice** *Spring:* Intensity of necklace, black in face,
gray in upperparts *Fall:* Intensity of necklace, black in face, olive cast to plumage

AdM/1yM Sp *Diagnostic male:*
slate-blue back, well-defined black
necklace, extensive black in
forehead, face, lores, and more
toward back of eye than female;
some 1yM average reduced
necklace, but not separable.

AdF/1yF Sp *Diagnostic female:*
duller, with grayer upperparts,
reduced black in face (often just in
lores), gray forehead and faint
necklace (older females may show
more black in head).

AdM Fa *Diagnostic:* similar to spring
male, but sometimes slightly duller
with fringing on crown.

AdF/1yM Fa *Diagnostic from AdM:*
similar to spring female; 1yM may
have more contrasty necklace and
black in face but generally not
separable.

1yF Fa Duller than AdF/1yM
Diagnostic: olive cast to upperparts
and no black in plumage.

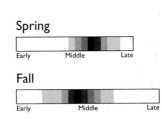

Spring

Early				Middle				Late

Fall

Early				Middle				Late

Canada
Each Canadian is very different; but the first one has a chip on his shoulder

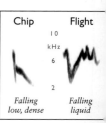

Chip | Flight

Falling low, dense | *Falling liquid*

Summary *Many Sections* (avg. 11), comparable only to L. Waterthrush and Red-faced; *variable collection of fast musical slurs of uneven lengths and erratic rhythms, not repetitive; usually starts with 1 or 2 Expanded "chips,"* but no "chips" within song. Avg. 11 Sections; most only 1 Phrase, so no repetition. Ends abruptly, usually on downslur or up/downslur. Individuals often sing multiple song variations in one session. **Types:** variable.

Type A1 Typical: many Sections, almost all 1 Phrase; fast, so hard to hear or remember individual Elements (a good ID point).

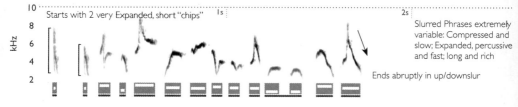

Starts with 2 very Expanded, short "chips"

Slurred Phrases extremely variable: Compressed and slow; Expanded, percussive and fast; long and rich

Ends abruptly in up/downslur

Type A2 Shorter variation; rhythm and pitch erratic and hard to remember.

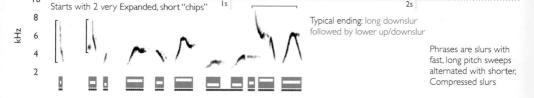

Starts with 2 very Expanded, short "chips"

Typical ending: long downslur followed by lower up/downslur

Phrases are slurs with fast, long pitch sweeps alternated with shorter, Compressed slurs

Type A3 Another shorter example, without "chips" at start.

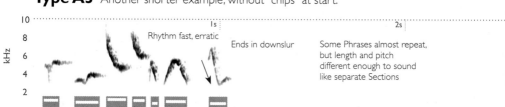

Rhythm fast, erratic

Ends in downslur

Some Phrases almost repeat, but length and pitch different enough to sound like separate Sections

Connecticut

Connecticut Shares habitat. Rather erratic rhythms, and some songs begin in unorganized manner with isolated Phrases, **but** Phrases almost always repeated later, so basically 1-Section song with a few, similar, repeated Elements. Slower, so Elements easier to hear.

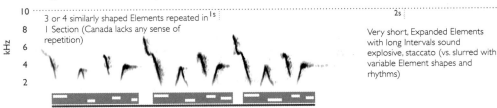

3 or 4 similarly shaped Elements repeated in 1 Section (Canada lacks any sense of repetition)

Very short, Expanded Elements with long Intervals sound explosive, staccato (vs. slurred with variable Element shapes and rhythms)

Common Yellowthroat

Common Yellowthroat Shares habitat, **but** only 1 Section, and always very steady rhythm throughout, vs. Canada's erratic rhythm and unrepeated Phrases.

Expanded, slowly slurred Elements

Only 1 Section with 3 or more repeated Elements, creating strong sense of repetition

Magnolia A1

Magnolia A1 Similar Element quality **but** short (2–4 Sections vs. avg. 11); easily separable.

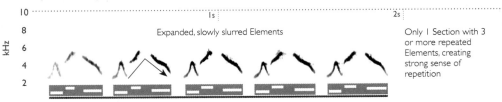

Elements slower and much easier to remember

Consistent and organized (regular rhythm, repeated Phrases of similarly shaped and pitched Elements); Canada unorganized, fast jumble

Louisiana Waterthrush B1

Louisiana Waterthrush B1 Ending similar in structure/quality with many 1- or 2-Phrase Sections in succession, **but** much longer, thinner, and fades out. Many "chips" (not slurred, musical). Canada shorter with consistently emphatic volume; ends abruptly.

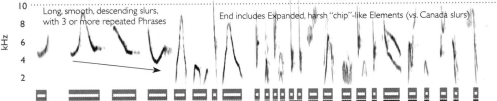

Long, smooth, descending slurs, with 3 or more repeated Phrases

End includes Expanded, harsh "chip"-like Elements (vs. Canada slurs)

CAPE MAY
Setophaga tigrina   Bright Birds

- ✓ Strong chestnut cheek patch surrounded by yellow
- Even, black streaking in breast
- Black eyeline
- Greenish-yellow rump
- Yellow collar
- White wing patch
- Greenish edging to flight feathers

- Underparts bright yellow, becoming whitish on belly and UnTC
- Even streaking across breast
- Fine, slightly decurved bill

- White tail spots
- Even streaking in upper breast
- Variable yellow breast usually fading to white UnTC
- Fine, slightly decurved bill

Distinctive Views

Additional Photos

Often forages methodically, high in the canopy

Small and chunky, with fine, slightly downcurved bill and medium-short tail

The "Tiger of the Woods," Cape May can be pugnacious and vigorously defend a food source

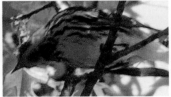

...treaking in cap, and red forehead ...tripe

Black streaking and yellow body wash are variable—here the throat streaking is so dense as to appear black-throated

Streaking, tail spots, yellow wash, and rufous auriculars may all be apparent in flight

...all birds may maintain a considerable ...ellow wash

Yellow nape contrasts with black back streaking

Rufous auriculars are unique

...uter three tail feathers have large ...hite spots

Long flight feathers

Flight feathers always have some greenish edging

Fine streaking in breast/throat
Yellow below
White UnTC, tail
Rufous cheek patch
Strong yellow supercilium
White wing patch

Comparison Species

Blackburnian Distinctive triangular face patch, lacks rufous facial patch; stronger orangey color; black back with white braces (vs. olive); no streaking in middle of breast; longer, all-white tail

Magnolia Black mask (vs. rufous); white supercilium (vs. yellow); streaking thicker, less even, and forms black necklace; more black in back; diagnostic white base of tail/large black tip; more lemon tone

Pine Breast streaking diffuse and less contrasty; plain face (no rufous or contrasting cap); wing bars (not a patch); more lemony yellow; longer, white tail; lacks yellow flight feather edging; longer, thicker bill; larger

Yellow-rumped Myrtle White throat and supercilium (vs. yellow); larger tail with strong black borders; mostly white and black below with yellow only on sides

Palm Brown back (vs. olive); face lacks rufous except in cap; rufous breast streaking (vs. black); continuous tail-pumping distinctive; UnTC bright yellow (vs. white); longer bill; longer tail with wide black base

Aging and Sexing

Spring AdM 1yM AdF 1yF   **Fall** AdM 1yM AdF 1yF

Races: 1 Summary *Spring:* Males and females separable, ages are not   *Fall:* Adult and 1y males separable from females; 1y females often separable   **What to Notice** *Spring:* Cheek patch, black crown, wing bars, back streaks   *Females:* Chestnut in cheek patch, quality of wing bar, back streaking, amount of yellow, intensity of underpart streaking

AdM/1yM Sp *Diagnostic male:* chestnut cheek patch, black crown, bright wing panel (averages larger in AdM than 1yM), streaked, dark back.

AdF/1yF Sp Less streaking in back than male, 1yF often duller with less yellow than AdF but much overlap; *Diagnostic female:* olive crown with black streaks, single thin wing bar; lacks strong chestnut cheek patch.

AdM Fa Similar to spring but less chestnut in cheek, smaller wing panel and lighter crown; *Diagnostic AdM:* chestnut in cheek, wing panel, dark crown.

1yM Fa Less back streaking than AdM, blackish side streaks; some features overlap with AdF: no chestnut in cheek, usually one wing bar, some yellow on underparts.

AdF Fa Similar to spring AdF but duller with a reduced wing bar, blurrier, duller streaking, no back streaking; some features overlap 1yM: usually some yellow, no chestnut in cheek.

1yF Fa Dullest plumage, little or no yellow, thin streaking, little or no wing bar; *Diagnostic 1yF when present:* no yellow and no wing bar.

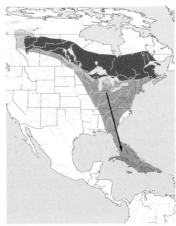

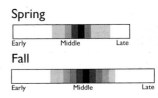

Spring

Early   Middle   Late

Fall

Early   Middle   Late

Cape May
Birding at Cape May is steady, short streams of birds: see see see see

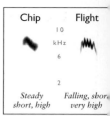

Chip	Flight
	Steady short, high	Falling, short very high

Summary *Very high, thin, 1-Section* songs. Types often alternated.
2 Types: A, 4 to 8 long 1-Element Phrases (flat or slight upslurs) with short Intervals; very simple, short, slow, even, with smooth, slurred quality; very Compressed pitch range, so thin; **B,** More Expanded, 2-Element Phrases with longer Intervals; pitch falls within each Phrase; Elements heard as more distinct, somewhat emphatic slurs.

Type A Very high, thin. 1 Section, avg. 5 flat, or slightly upslurred, Phrases.

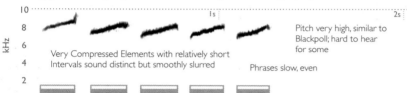

Very Compressed Elements with relatively short Intervals sound distinct but smoothly slurred

Phrases slow, even

Pitch very high, similar to Blackpoll; hard to hear for some

Type B Lower song with wider pitch range. Falling-pitch Phrases of 2 Elements; slow, distinct, somewhat emphatic; often alternated with Type A.

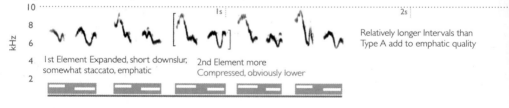

1st Element Expanded, short downslur, somewhat staccato, emphatic

2nd Element more Compressed, obviously lower

Relatively longer Intervals than Type A add to emphatic quality

Kinglet vs. A Both Kinglets start their songs with very high, repeated simple slurs; easily confused with Cape May, **but** separable by speed increase and jumbled ending. Sometimes sings first Section only, **but** usually some obvious variation in slurs, or some hint of jumble at end.

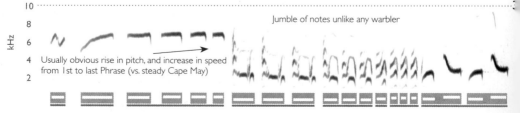

Usually obvious rise in pitch, and increase in speed from 1st to last Phrase (vs. steady Cape May)

Jumble of notes unlike any warbler

Bay-breasted vs. B Very high, 2-Element Phrases, **but** Elements more similar to each other and are more Compressed in pitch, so lack staccato, emphatic quality.

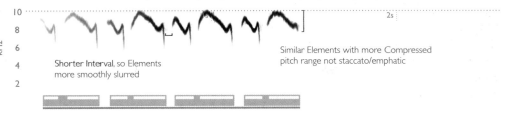

Shorter Interval, so Elements more smoothly slurred

Similar Elements with more Compressed pitch range not staccato/emphatic

Black-and-white vs. B High, 2-Element Phrases, **but** song considerably longer (avg. 2 sec. vs. 1.2) with uneven rhythm and less emphatic, accented quality.

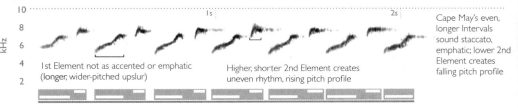

1st Element not as accented or emphatic (longer, wider-pitched upslur)

Higher, shorter 2nd Element creates uneven rhythm, rising pitch profile

Cape May's even, longer Intervals sound staccato, emphatic; lower 2nd Element creates falling pitch profile

American Redstart vs. B Am. Redstart 2-Element Type B can be very similar **but** often lower or richer and usually faster, shorter (avg. 1.2 sec. vs. 1.5); Am. Redstart usually alternates with accented ending songs (A/C) that are obviously different from Cape May.

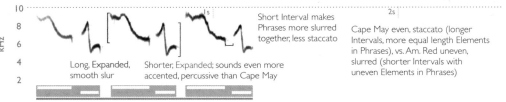

Long, Expanded, smooth slur

Shorter, Expanded; sounds even more accented, percussive than Cape May

Short Interval makes Phrases more slurred together, less staccato

Cape May even, staccato (longer Intervals, more equal length Elements in Phrases), vs. Am. Red uneven, slurred (shorter Intervals with uneven Elements in Phrases)

Prothonotary vs. A 1 Section of repeated 1-Element slurs, **but** longer with more Elements (9–12 vs. 5–6), and noticeably lower, richer, more emphatic.

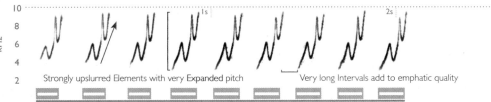

Strongly upslurred Elements with very Expanded pitch

Very long Intervals add to emphatic quality

CAPE MAY

Setophaga tigrina   Drab Birds

- Even streaking across breast and into throat
- Sharp, dark bill
- Eyeline and eye-arcs
- Greenish-yellow rump and flight feather edging
- Most show at least hint of yellow around auriculars

- Extensively, evenly streaked below, especially in upper breast/throat
- Even dullest immatures usually show traces of pale yellow
- Yellow often patchy
- Fine, slightly decurved bill

- Extensively streaked below, including throat and middle of breast
- Fine, slightly decurved bill
- White tail spots

Distinctive Views

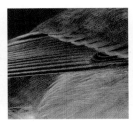

Additional Photos

Bill fine and slightly decurved; body chunky, and head small, as is tail

All birds show greenish-yellow rump, an especially useful mark on otherwise drab birds

Back may show some limited streaking; note hint of yellow rump and fine, decurved bill

Fall birds range from relatively bright with extensive yellow . . .

. . . to totally drab; all birds have fine, even chest streaking extending into throat

Facial pattern on drab females may be quite indistinct compared to adult males; note faint yellow breast wash

This bird shows an intermediate amount of yellow and a more distinct facial pattern

This bird has limited yellow but a defined facial pattern

This bird shows more defined streaking and some yellow but a very plain facial pattern

Insectivore in migration; Cape May has a unique tubular tongue that helps it feed on berries/nectar in the winter

Note faint wing bars, yellow rump, and even streaking; there is also a hint of a yellow neck patch

Fine, even streaking with a yellow wash in breast and a "pointy-headed" look

Fine streaking in breast/throat
Patchy yellow focused in breast
Pale sides of neck
Short tail, white tail spots
Thin, low-contrast wing bars
Greenish flight feather edging

Comparison Species

Bay-breasted Larger; frequently shows rufous on sides (vs. none); bolder wing bars; greener, streaked upperparts; unstreaked underparts

Blackburnian Orangey face and breast, fading into body (vs. yellowy, patchier); triangular ear patch; striking, wide supercilium (vs. faint); bolder wing bars; no streaking in center of breast and throat

Blackpoll Bolder wing bars; streaked upperparts (vs. plain); streaking not as even across breast; larger with larger bill; shorter tail with long UnTC

Palm Larger; often in flocks; often on ground; constant tail pumping; more distinct eyeline and supercilium; rufous streaking in chest; yellow UnTC (vs. pale); longer white tail/large black base

Pine Brighter wing bars but otherwise lower contrast overall; lacks yellowish wing edgings, greenish rump; larger, with larger bill and longer tail; more diffuse streaking, never in throat

Orange-crowned Duller olive color; overall less contrasty; streaking more diffuse and not concentrated in throat; yellow UnTC (vs. pale), all-dark tail (vs. some white)

Yellow All yellow, with olive back; plainer face; streaking is red if present (vs. gray); yellow UnTC and tail (vs. pale)

Tennessee Greener back (not grayish); lacks pale neck sides; unstreaked below; shorter, darker tail

Yellow-rumped Myrtle Bright yellow rump patch (vs. greenish); heavier bill; browner upperparts (vs. gray); lacks yellow in face; coarser side streaking; unstreaked throat; usually yellow shoulder patches (vs. none); longer tail with large black border; chip call distinctive

CERULEAN

Setophaga cerulea   Male/Female - All Seasons

- ✓ Blue breast band and flank streaks
- • White throat
- • Bold white wing bars
- • Unique shade of blue (cerulean for male, aquamarine for female)
- • Small

- • Very short tailed, short legged, and stout billed with very pointed wings
- ✓ Blue breast band and flank streaks (more prominent in males)
- • Often hover-gleans, showing white tail spots

- • Very short tailed, short legged and stout billed with very pointed wings
- • White tail spots
- ✓ Blue breast band and flank streaks diagnostic when present

Distinctive Views

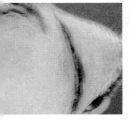

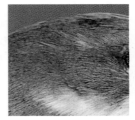

Additional Photos

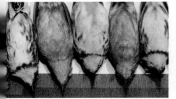

Significant variation in color between male and female; males brighter blue; females show yellow-green wash and can look quite yellowish

Narrow breast band ranges from blue to black and is often veiled with white

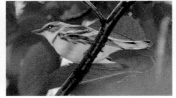

Blue to black back streaking found in males only

Long-winged, long-distance migrant

Male on the left, female on the right

Small, thick bill, wide supercilium

Often high in the canopy, so knowing the song is very useful; note very short tail

Females may not show a breast band and can be very drab

Uncommon and shows highest rate of decline of any U.S. warbler

Note brighter blue and smaller size of Cerulean (vs. Yellow-rumped); Cerulean is the smallest *Setophaga*

White supercilium on cerulean-blue bird indicative of a first-year male

Short tail with white spots
Variable blue streaking below
Overall bluish tones above
Wide white wing bars
Often wide supercilium
Often thin blue collar

Comparison Species

Black-throated Blue Black side stripe (vs. blue streaking); black throat and face (vs. white/blue); different shade of blue; white handkerchief (vs. none); larger tail; no blue in undersides (vs. blue streaking)

Blackpoll Olive above (vs. blue); buffy wash in throat (vs. white); stronger back streaks; eye-arcs and eyeline (vs. under-eye arc); orange feet and often legs (vs. black); larger and stockier

Blackburnian Triangular cheek patch; buffy orange color (not yellow washed); pale orange supercilium joins neck patch; pale braces and dark streaking on back; longer, all-white tail

Pine Larger, with longer tail and larger bill; variable yellow in head and when present, concentrated in upper breast (vs. white or aqua tones on head; light yellow-green wash below)

Tennessee White UnTC with dark tail (vs. white tail); no breast streaking (vs. blue); finer bill; green back contrasts with bluish head (vs. same color); lacks strong wing bars; lacks wide supercilium

Black-throated Gray Rarely in the same range; wider, more well-defined cheek patch; gray (not blue or aqua) upperparts; diagnostic yellow loral spot; longer, all-white tail; black side steaks (not blue); may show band across throat, but wider, black and less defined

Chestnut-sided Eyering on gray face; green upperparts and gray underparts (vs. blue/aqua and white); yellowish wing bars (vs. white); all white underneath (vs. streaks); longer, all-white tail

Aging and Sexing

Races: 1 Summary *Spring:* Male and female separable, 1yM may be separable   *Fall:* AdM separable, all others generally not   **What to Notice** *Spring/Fall:* Supercilium, chest band, streaking in back, yellow wash on underparts, greenish wash on upperparts

dM/1yM Sp Full blue head, dark lores, black streaking in back, strongly streaked flanks; *Diagnostic male:* no supercilium, complete breastband.

1yM Sp Extreme *Diagnostic when present:* as AdM, but whitish supercilium behind eye, slight yellow wash on underparts, finer streaking.

AdF/1yF Sp *Diagnostic female:* greenish wash to upperparts, no back streaking or chest band, wide supercilium, often yellow or greenish wash to underparts; 1yF may be duller with more yellow wash below and aqua-green wash above, flight feathers may show wear (lack blue edging), but generally not separable.

dM Fa Similar to spring male, but with some white supercilium behind eye; *Diagnostic:* weak breast band.

AdF/1yM1yF Fa No breast band, strong white supercilium; 1yM usually has some back streaking and less yellow wash but not safely separable from AdF; 1yF duller with no blue tones, no back or crown streaks, fainter breast streaking and more yellow wash, but not necessarily separable from 1yM.

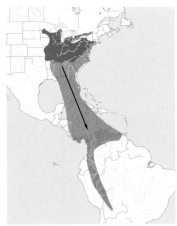

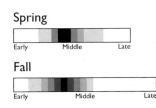

Spring

Early   Middle   Late

Fall

Early   Middle   Late

Cerulean

After I climb the steps to the fashion show my cerulean suit creates a buzz

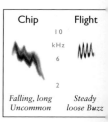

Chip	Flight
	10
	kHz
	6
	2
Falling, long	Steady
Uncommon	loose Buzz

Summary Usually *3 Sections, each higher than previous*; 1st Section 2–5 Complex 2-Element Phrases that fall within each Phrase; 2nd Section obviously faster, 4 or 5 Complex, almost whistled, Trilled Phrases; *ending Section 1 steady Trill or Loose Buzz*; obvious *difference in quality between 2nd and 3rd Section* useful for separating similar species; **1 Type.**

Type A1
Typical 3-Section song; speed, pitch increase between Sections; obvious difference in quality between 2nd and 3rd Section (vs. Black-throated Blue, Northern Parula).

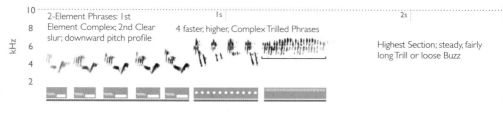

2-Element Phrases: 1st Element Complex; 2nd Clear slur; downward pitch profile

4 faster, higher, Complex Trilled Phrases

Highest Section; steady, fairly long Trill or loose Buzz

Type A2
2-Section version, missing 2nd Section of A1, otherwise the same.

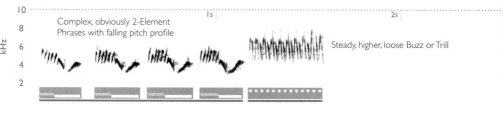

Complex, obviously 2-Element Phrases with falling pitch profile

Steady, higher, loose Buzz or Trill

Type A3
Fewer Phrases in 1st Section; usually slower than A1, otherwise similar.

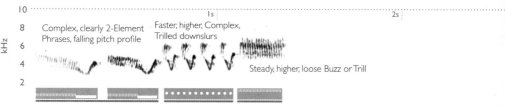

Complex, clearly 2-Element Phrases, falling pitch profile

Faster, higher, Complex, Trilled downslurs

Steady, higher, loose Buzz or Trill

Black-throated Blue A3
Can be surprisingly confusing: Cerulean rarely confused for Black-throated Blue, but Black-throated Blue often confused with Cerulean; Cerulean has more Complex Elements, more varied quality and speed between Sections; different, steady ending.

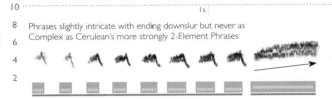

Phrases slightly intricate with ending downslur but never as Complex as Cerulean's more strongly 2-Element Phrases

Dense long Buzz always rising, usually slowly (more subtle in shorter versions)

Cerulean last Section shorter (avg. 0.2 sec vs. 0.5), steady Trill or looser Buzz

Northern Parula B1
2-Section songs easily separable (long ascending Trill, short up/down accent). 3-Section songs more similar, with rising pitch Section to Section, **but** Cerulean has 3 unique, steady-pitched Sections, while N. Parula Sections are similar in quality to each other, with pitch rising within each Section, and much longer 2nd Section with usually more Elements.

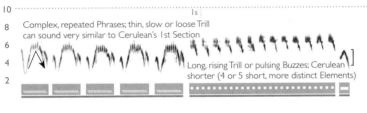

Complex, repeated Phrases; thin, slow or loose Trill can sound very similar to Cerulean's 1st Section

Long, rising Trill or pulsing Buzzes; Cerulean shorter (4 or 5 short, more distinct Elements)

Lacks Cerulean's ending: short, steady Trill or loose Buzz

Usually fast up/downslurred note (never in Cerulean)

Blackburnian A1
Similar form: 3 Sections, each higher, faster than previous and last Section high, single Phrase; 1st Section similar quality **but** more Phrases (7–9 vs. 2–5); last 2 Sections much higher, thinner; Cerulean Phrases more Complex, dense, with narrower overall pitch range.

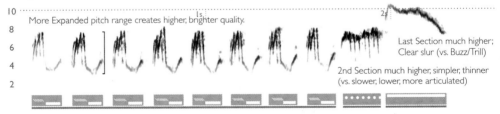

More Expanded pitch range creates higher, brighter quality.

Last Section much higher; Clear slur (vs. Buzz/Trill)

2nd Section much higher, simpler, thinner (vs. slower, lower, more articulated)

CHESTNUT-SIDED

Setophaga pensylvanica   Bright Birds

- ✓ Chestnut side stripe and yellow wing patch and crown
- • Stout bill
- • Black eye stripe and malar stripe

- ✓ Chestnut side stripe and yellow wing patch and crown
- • Black malar stripe
- • White throat, undersides
- • Medium-long, all-white tail and UnTC
- • Stout bill

- • All white below including throat, tail, and UnTC
- • Chestnut side stripe
- • Black malar stripe
- • Stout bill
- • Medium-long, all-white tail and UnTC

Distinctive Views

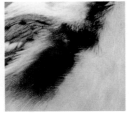
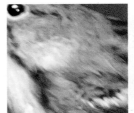

Additional Photos

Habitually cocks tail

Length of chestnut side stripe varies among individuals

hick back streaking

Bright yellow-green cap and chestnut stripes are visible even from the front

One of few warblers benefiting from forest clearing, since it uses scrub and secondary growth

often gleans at low to medium levels f the canopy

First-year males may show minimal black in face and limited chestnut

Long-distance migrant: note the longish wings

tensity of chestnut flanks and facial marking may vary among individuals and ges

Yellow crown, wing bars, and chestnut stripes all visible even from the back

Yellow wing bars or patch
White cheek, yellow cap
White collar
White below
Chestnut side stripe
Long, all-white tail

Comparison Species

Bay-breasted Darker overall, with all-dark face; buffy collar (vs. white); wing bars about equal size (vs. uneven); rufous in throat (vs. white); shorter tail with dark edges (vs. white); buff in UnTC (vs. white)

Blackpoll Black cap (vs. mask); all-white cheeks (vs. black markings); larger; often with orange legs or feet (vs. grayer); black streaking on sides (vs. chestnut stripe); shorter tail

Aging and Sexing

Spring AdM 1yM AdF 1yF **Fall** AdM 1yM AdF 1yF

Races: 1 Summary *Spring:* Sexable, not ageable except extreme 1yF *Fall:* Only AdM separable, first-year birds sometimes ageable but not sexable **What to Notice** *Spring:* Length of chestnut stripe, crown color and streaking, back streaking, black in face *Fall:* Back streaking, presence and extent of chestnut stripe

AdM/1yM Sp Heavily streaked black-and-yellow back, strong eyeline, lores, and malar stripe; *Diagnostic male:* bright, unstreaked yellow crown, long chestnut side stripe.

AdF/1yF Sp Paler lores, duller black in face, less back streaking (less yellow) than male; *Diagnostic female:* dull green yellow cap, short side stripe.

1yF Sp Extreme *Diagnostic when present:* some show no chestnut, and may be separable, all others not.

AdM Fa *Diagnostic:* strong back streaking, long chestnut side stripe.

AdF/1yM/1yF Fa Little or no chestnut, back may show some streaking; 1yF similar to 1yM with no chestnut, no back streaking, yellowish wing bars; *Diagnostic when present for 1y:* may be separated by molt limit in coverts (see note).

Note Differences in covert age indicate a 1y bird: here the yellow, older median coverts contrast with the whiter, newer median coverts (molt limit), so this is a first-year bird (sex unknown).

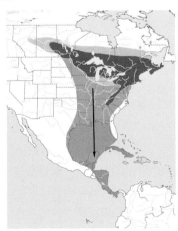

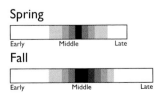

Spring

Early Middle Late

Fall

Early Middle Late

Chestnut-sided

With your chestnut vest and yellow cap, we're "Pleased, Pleased to Meet cha"

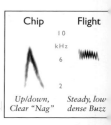

Chip	Flight
Up/down, Clear "Nag"	Steady, low dense Buzz

Summary Most *start with 4–6 Clear slurred Phrases*, more than some similar species. Long, Expanded Slurs, especially in ending Sections; *almost always ends in downslur*; **2 Types: A,** 3+ Sections, the 2nd always with 2+ Phrases; ends with accented, Expanded, slow downslur, often preceded by 2 upslurs; **B,** Usually longer, more rambling; less emphatic last Section; harder to separate from similar species.

Type A1 Familiar, accented song: "Please please please please TOOO MEEET CHA."

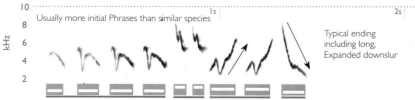

4 Phrases in 1st Section

Long, slow, Expanded slurs in last Sections, typically 2 upslurs then a downslur

Type A2 More elaborate, 2-Section intro than A1, followed by typical accented ending (2 upslurs and very Expanded downslur).

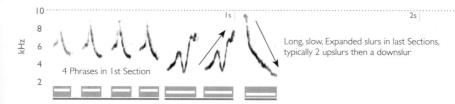

Usually more initial Phrases than similar species

Typical ending including long, Expanded downslur

Type B1 Unaccented song; important to learn these longer, more amorphous songs. Typically more Phrases in 1st Section than similar species; pitch usually lower, but not completely diagnostic. Some very similar to Yellow Warbler.

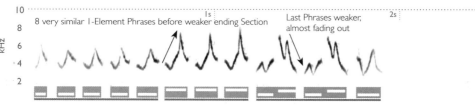

8 very similar 1-Element Phrases before weaker ending Section

Last Phrases weaker, almost fading out

Type B2 Unaccented song; 4 Phrases in 1st Section, and similar Phrases in following Section, which can be helpful ID point.

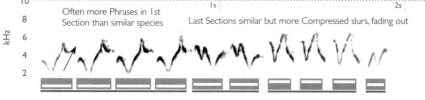

Often more Phrases in 1st Section than similar species

Last Sections similar but more Compressed slurs, fading out

Yellow A1 vs. A

Usually accented songs easily separable: simpler with fewer slurs in 1st Section, upslurred ending. Rarely, sings much more similar song, **but** usually still has fewer Phrases in 1st Section, ending less emphatic.

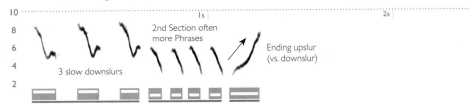

3 slow downslurs

2nd Section often more Phrases

Ending upslur (vs. downslur)

Yellow B3 vs. B

Unaccented songs can be very similar, **but** usually fewer Elements in 1st Section, often ends on upslur, and usually higher (avg. 6–9 kHz vs. 5–8 kHz); may be hard to separate with isolated bird.

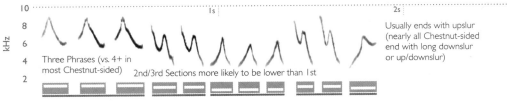

Three Phrases (vs. 4+ in most Chestnut-sided)

2nd/3rd Sections more likely to be lower than 1st

Usually ends with upslur (nearly all Chestnut-sided end with long downslur or up/downslur)

American Redstart A1 vs. A

Similar repeated slurs with accented up/down ending, **but** usually obviously higher pitched; only 1 or 2 (max. 3) Sections, and unaccented songs only 2 Sections vs. Chestnut-sided 3 or often 4+ Sections. Am. Redstart 2nd/3rd Section only 1 Phrase each in accented songs (vs. 2–4).

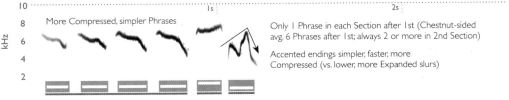

More Compressed, simpler Phrases

Only 1 Phrase in each Section after 1st (Chestnut-sided avg. 6 Phrases after 1st; always 2 or more in 2nd Section)

Accented endings simpler, faster, more Compressed (vs. lower, more Expanded slurs)

Hooded A1 / Magnolia A1 vs. A

Forms similar: opening slurs, accented, downslurred ending, **but** Magnolia length noticeably shorter (avg 0.9 sec. vs. Type A 1.5).

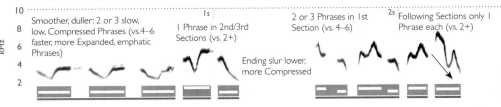

Smoother, duller: 2 or 3 slow, low, Compressed Phrases (vs. 4–6 faster, more Expanded, emphatic Phrases)

1 Phrase in 2nd/3rd Sections (vs. 2+)

Ending slur lower, more Compressed

2 or 3 Phrases in 1st Section (vs. 4–6)

Following Sections only 1 Phrase each (vs. 2+)

CHESTNUT-SIDED

Setophaga pensylvanica   Drab Birds

- Yellowish wing bars
- ✓ Striking, white eyering, plain face, lime-green cap
- ✓ Upperparts lime green
- Underparts plain gray
- Habitually cocks tail

- Clean whitish below
- Plain face with white eyering
- ✓ Lime-green crown and back
- Long, all-white tail and undertail coverts

- Clean whitish below
- Often cocks tail
- Long, all-white tail

Distinctive Views

Additional Photos

Very white underside with variable amount of chestnut in flanks

Almost no chestnut in this bird; note the white throat, body, and tail

Lime-green back may show streaking

Conspicuous eyering, even in flight; striking yellow wing bars

Very plain face with striking eyering and green crown

Low- and medium-story gleaners

Often droops wings and cocks tail

Bright lime-green upperparts diagnostic

Plain white underside with only a little black visible in tail, depending on how the bird is holding it

Wide yellowish wing bars
Fairly long, thin white tail
Plain white below
Striking lime-green above
Bold white eyering

Comparison Species

Bay-breasted White wing bars (vs. yellow); darker upperparts; larger, more sluggish; faint eye-arcs/eyeline (vs. bold eyering); shorter tail with less white

Blackpoll White wing bars (vs. yellow); duller olive upperparts; eye-arcs with black eyeline (vs. bold eyering); streaking in underparts (vs. plain); larger; shorter tailed

Blue-gray Gnatcatcher Blue back (vs. green); long, thinner tail; longer finer bill; smaller and more active

Ruby-crowned Kinglet White wing bar (vs. yellow); gray back (vs. green); smaller and more energetic; plumper, neckless shape; tinier bill; longer, gray tail

Golden-winged F Gray back (vs. green); brighter wing patches; bright yellow crown (vs. none); gray mask and throat (vs. plain with eyering); doesn't cock tail; generally grayer below (vs. pure white)

Tennessee Lacks strong eyering; finer, pointier bill; shorter, darker tail; duller olive upperparts

Yellow 1yF Yellow tail and UnTC (vs. white); overall lower contrast; plain face (vs. strong eyering, green cap)

Cerulean F Aqua blue tones (vs. green/gray); side streaks (vs. none); shorter tail; finer bill; wide supercilium (vs. plain face/eyering)

COLIMA
Oreothlypis crissalis   Male/Female - All Seasons

- Brownish-gray uppers and flanks, paler gray below
- Greenish-yellow rump
- Thin white eyering
- Always lacks yellow in breast
- Long bill, thick at base
- Rufous crown patch, often hidden

- Bright golden to orangey UnTC
- Always lacks yellow in breast
- Extremely limited range

- Bright golden UnTC
- Long dark tail
- Long bill thick at base
- Large
- Keeps tail still

Distinctive Views

Additional Photos

Gleans at low levels, usually in undergrowth, with slow, rather deliberate movements; preferred habitat usually includes scrub grass and leaf litter

Larger and browner than Virginia's; no sharp contrast between upperparts and underparts

Limited range in U.S.; found in high Chisos Mountains, TX (up to 300 pairs in Big Bend) at 1800 to 3000 m; although not declared endangered, probably the rarest breeding warbler in the U.S./Canada

Colima does not normally wag or bob tail, as do Virginia's and Nashville warblers

Brownish-gray uppers, flanks
Clear, thin, white eyering
Never yellow breast
Orangey/golden UnTC
Large, with long, dark tail
Greenish-yellow rump

Comparison Species

Virginia Scarce in Chisos Mountains; smaller; shorter bill; usually yellow in breast (vs. none); deeper rufous crown patch; grayer tones above and below (vs. brownish); yellow UnTC (vs. orangey-golden); wags tail more

Orange-crowned Some yellow wash and diffuse streaking below (vs. grayish); more complex facial pattern with eyeline and supercilium; overall yellowy olive (vs. brownish); thinner bill; yellowish UnTC (vs. orangey)

Lucy's Smaller; rufous rump (vs. yellow); finer bill; gray tones to undersides and back (vs. brownish); white UnTC (vs. orangey-golden)

American Redstart F Yellow in shoulders and tail (vs. none); gray undersides (vs. buffy/brown); more active; black-and-yellow tail (vs. plain); shorter, stout bill with pronounced rictal bristles

Aging and Sexing

Races: 1 Summary *Spring/Fall:* Not sexable or ageable. Wintering birds usually more washed with brown on back, head, and sometimes below. Flight feathers, primary coverts, rectrices probably browner due to wear in first-year birds. Rufous in crown probably more restricted in adult female and especially first-year female. However, species not well studied and plumage differences not clearly documented.

All Birds Not easily ageable or sexable: see Summary.

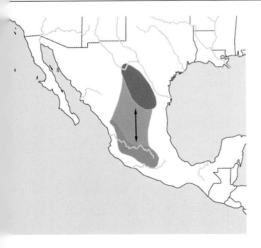

Migration Generally arrives on breeding grounds in early April through May, and departs breeding grounds by early September.

Colima
A colander of lima beans, dripping quickly and evenly, then dumped out

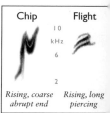

Chip   Flight

Rising, coarse   Rising, long
abrupt end   piercing

Summary Usually 1 or 2 Sections (rarely 3), *1st a long slow simple Trill,* 2nd/3rd very short (1–3 Phrases); *pitch, speed often wander slowly,* but not enough to indicate new Section; slow, Expanded Slurs in ending Sections; always Compressed, medium pitch 1-Element Phrases that don't sound forceful or accented. **2 Types: A,** 1 Section, Trill; **B,** 2 (rarely 3) Sections, Trill followed by lower 1-3 Element Section.

Type A Typical 1-Section song; uncountable Trill, **but** distinctly heard as separate sounds.

Small pitch and speed fluctuations, with fading speed and volume at end

Compressed pitch range, medium frequency, so sounds dull and unemphatic

Type B1 Lower 2nd Section. Similar to Orange-crowned, **but** faster than Virginia's or 1st Section of Nashville.

Pitch, speed can be fairly steady or wander slightly

Very short 2nd Section slower, lower in pitch

Type B2 Some Type B songs have 2nd or 3rd Section with longer, accented slur, often separated by a pause from the main Trill.

Typical fluctuations of speed and pitch

Separated, long, Expanded slur

Nashville A3 Nashville usually easy to separate (2 very distinct, rhythmic Sections), **but** sometimes sings only 1 Section, or one with very short 2nd Section, like this one.

Slurred, 2-Element Phrases at slow, countable speed (vs. 1-Element Trilled Phrases)

Expanded Elements with long Intervals, sound bright, emphatic (vs. muted, less emphatic)

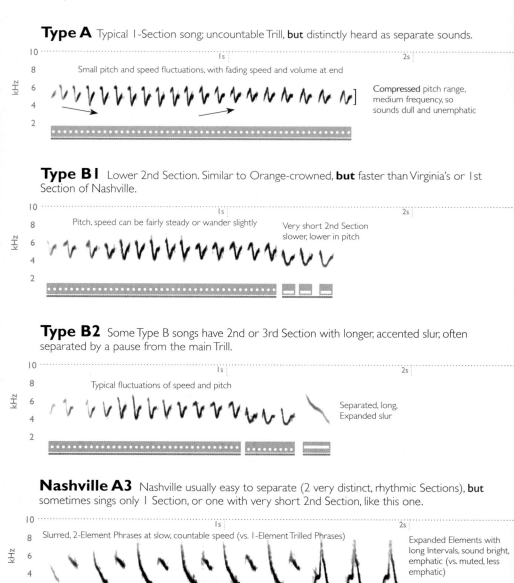

Orange-crowned B1 Trill with fluctuating pitch, **but** faster (21 Phrase/sec. vs. 12), and more Phrases in 2nd Section (avg. 8 vs. 1.7).

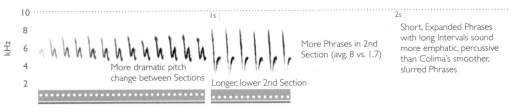

More dramatic pitch change between Sections

More Phrases in 2nd Section (avg. 8 vs. 1.7)

Longer, lower 2nd Section

Short, Expanded Phrases with long Intervals sound more emphatic, percussive than Colima's smoother, slurred Phrases

Orange-crowned Abrupt speed or pitch changes and many Phrases in the ending Section, unlike Colima's slight pitch, speed changes, and 1–3 Elements at end.

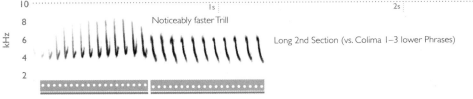

Noticeably faster Trill

Long 2nd Section (vs. Colima 1–3 lower Phrases)

Orange-crowned Similar speed and structure and could be hard to separate; Elements more Expanded and thus somewhat more emphatic and percussive.

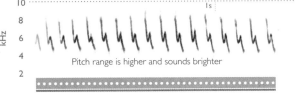

Pitch range is higher and sounds brighter

Virginia's A1 Easy to separate: Phrases easily countable (vs. uncountable Trill).

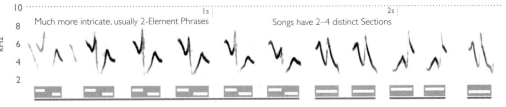

Much more intricate, usually 2-Element Phrases

Songs have 2–4 distinct Sections

COMMON YELLOWTHROAT

Geothlypis trichas   Adult Male - All Seasons

- ✓ Broad black mask across forehead and face, with paler border above
- • Olive back
- • Wren-like and skulking, often cocks tail
- • Yellow throat and UnTC
- • Variable yellow/pale/brownish buff in rest of underparts

- • Wren-like and skulking, often cocks tail
- • Yellow throat and UnTC
- • Variable yellow/pale/brownish buff in rest of underparts
- ✓ Unique black mask
- • Long, dark tail
- • Short, rounded wings

Distinctive Views

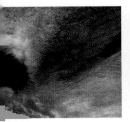

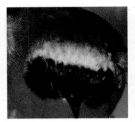

Additional Photos

One of our most widespread warblers; wren-like and skulking, often in marsh or low brush near water

The gray-brown flanks of this eastern race bird are a good separator from Mourning and other confusion species

Hops when on the ground; frequently seen at or below eye level

Young males show dark face as they transition toward bright adult male plumage

Small-billed, with short neck and plump appearance

Bright yellow UnTC; tail frequently twitched

Short, rounded wings and cocked tail in flight; generally a weak flier

Note white border above the black mask—unique among warblers

Bright males are relatively easy to ID if you see their facial pattern

These are the only U.S. and Canada warblers to nest in open marshes

A rare underside view shows the white belly and yellow UnTC of a worn eastern race bird

When disturbed, often pops up quickly, and then dives back down into cover

Black mask
Yellow throat, UnTC
Long, dark tail
Plain olive-brown above
Often skulky

Comparison Species

Canada Necklace (vs. none); bright eyering, bright goggles (vs. black face); white UnTC (vs. yellow); more evenly yellow below including lower breast, belly

Yellow-breasted Chat Much larger; much heavier bill; undereye arc, white supercilium (vs. mask); more extensive yellow in breast; longer tail; white UnTC (vs. yellow)

Kentucky Different facial pattern; often on ground (vs. low brush); yellow above and around eye (vs. none); all yellow below (vs. uneven); shorter tail; brighter greenish above

Gray-crowned Yellowthroat Heavier, bicolored bill; gray or brownish crown; eye-arc (vs. none); usually in dry grassy scrub (vs. often near water); black lores (vs. mask)

Aging and Sexing

Spring AdM 1yM AdF 1yF   **Fall** AdM 1yM AdF 1yF

Races: 13+, including *G.t. trichas* (east, most photos below) and *G.t. chryseola* (south-west U.S.); races vary in mask border color and extent of yellow on underparts, many not separable in field   **Summary** *Spring:* Sexable, some 1yM ageable;   *Fall:* Adults sexable, first year not sexable except for 1yMs with black in face   **What to Notice** *Spring/Fall:* Black in face, overall contrast, brightness, and contrast of throat

AdM Sp/Fa,1yM Sp *Diagnostic male:* black mask with paler border; *diagnostic when present 1yM:* may show buffy eyering (often partial).

AdF/1yF Sp *Diagnostic female:* no black in face; age not determinable.

AdF Fa Similar to spring AdF; *Diagnostic:* brighter yellow throat and upper chest (which contrasts with underparts) than 1yF/1yM.

1yM Fa *Diagnostic when present:* molting birds show some black feathers in mask area, buffy eyering and faint supercilium (facial molt may start as late as October), otherwise not separable from 1yF.

1yF Fa Duller, paler, and less contrasty than AdF; flanks brownish, little or no yellow on throat; never definitively separable, since some 1yM without black in face appear identical.

G.t. chryseola Southwest, U.S., Yellowest race in U.S./Canada, yellow-tinged border to mask and extensive yellow underparts.

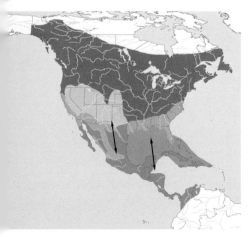

Spring East

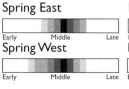

Early   Middle   Late

Spring West

Early   Middle   Late

Fall East

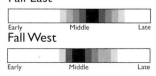

Early   Middle   Late

Fall West

Early   Middle   Late

Common Yellowthroat
Only in Wichita do common folk wear yellow bow ties on their throats

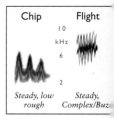

Chip | Flight

Steady, low rough | Steady, Complex/Buzz

Summary *1 Section of steadily repeated 3- to 6-Element Phrases* (uncommonly 2). Loud, consistent, emphatic rhythm; fairly long, varied, slurred Elements of differing pitches; Phrases usually have up/down pitch shape, and complex rhythm. Also sings flight song of Phrases from main song with "sputtered" shorter notes; **I Type.**

Type A I
Common 3-Element Phrases: "Witch it tahh, witch it tahh, witch it tahh, witch"; often with 1 or 2 extra but similar Elements sung at beginning or end.

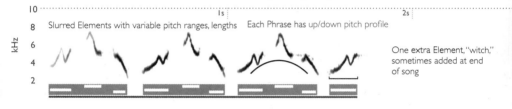

Slurred Elements with variable pitch ranges, lengths   Each Phrase has up/down pitch profile

One extra Element, "witch," sometimes added at end of song

Type A2
I Section with 3 Phrases made up of 5 varied, repeated Elements.

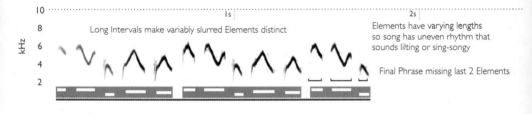

Long Intervals make variably slurred Elements distinct

Elements have varying lengths so song has uneven rhythm that sounds lilting or sing-songy

Final Phrase missing last 2 Elements

Type A3
6-Element version; 3 "extra" Elements at beginning (identical to other Elements repeated in Phrases, so not considered a separate Section).

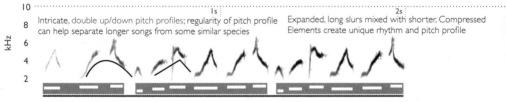

Intricate, double up/down pitch profiles; regularity of pitch profile can help separate longer songs from some similar species

Expanded, long slurs mixed with shorter, Compressed Elements create unique rhythm and pitch profile

Type A4
4-Element version with long, varied slurs and intricate rhythm created by Elements with different lengths and pitches.

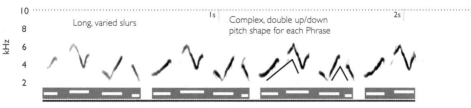

Long, varied slurs

Complex, double up/down pitch shape for each Phrase

Carolina Wren (excerpts)
Shares habitat, **but** 1-Section songs with 6 or 7 Phrases (vs. usually 3 or 4; some overlap). Phrase speed often much faster (avg. 4 Phrases/sec. vs. 1.8).

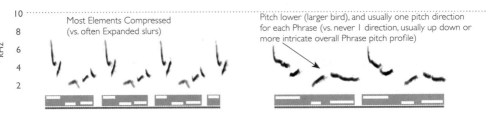

Most Elements Compressed (vs. often Expanded slurs)

Pitch lower (larger bird), and usually one pitch direction for each Phrase (vs. never 1 direction, usually up down or more intricate overall Phrase pitch profile)

Kentucky A1
Similar habitats and 1-Section songs, **but** 5–8 repeated Phrases (vs. 3 or 4, max 5). 2-Element Phrases (vs. 3+).

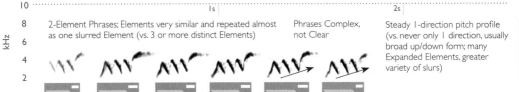

2-Element Phrases; Elements very similar and repeated almost as one slurred Element (vs. 3 or more distinct Elements)

Phrases Complex, not Clear

Steady 1-direction pitch profile (vs. never only 1 direction, usually broad up/down form; many Expanded Elements, greater variety of slurs)

Mourning B1
Similar habitats, **but** almost always 2 or more Sections (vs. 1), so easily separable. This less common version has only 1 Section, **but** Phrases more Complex and with fewer Elements (1 or 2 vs. 3+).

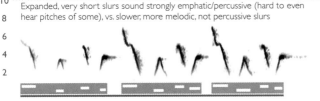

Very Complex, short Phrases, almost loose Trills (vs. Clear slurs with variety of shapes)

Phrases only 1 or 2 Elements (vs. 3+)

Connecticut A2
Similar habitats, 1-Section with 3- or 4-Element Phrases, **but** easily separable by Elements almost always speeding up as song begins, emphasizing uneven quality; Common Yellowthroat songs smoother, with more consistent rhythm.

Expanded, very short slurs sound strongly emphatic/percussive (hard to even hear pitches of some), vs. slower, more melodic, not percussive slurs

Irregular Rhythm combined with very Short Elements and Long Intervals sounds uniquely jerky (vs. similarly uneven Elements but with slower slurs and shorter Intervals that blend together more smoothly)

COMMON YELLOWTHROAT

Geothlypis trichas Female/1y Male - All Seasons

- Sharp contrast between darker face and paler throat
- Faint but complete eyering
- Brown/olive back
- Yellow throat and UnTC
- Variable yellow/pale/brownish buff in rest of underparts
- Some show black in auriculars

- Lighter throat contrasting with body and head
- Buffy gray underparts
- Dark, long tail
- Wren-like and skulking, often cocks tail
- ✓ Distinctive call, useful for separating from MacGillivray's/ Mourning

- Lighter throat contrasting with body and head
- Yellow throat and UnTC
- Variable yellow/pale/brownish buff in rest of underparts
- Almost all races have pale area in lower belly, brownish on flanks
- Long, dark tail

Distinctive Views

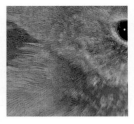

Additional Photos

Veak, reluctant fliers: have short,
bunded wings and often fly with tail
anging down

Sometimes nondescript plumage; note
plump, neckless outline, brownish flanks,
malar contrast, wren-like behavior

Even drab birds usually show yellow
UnTC

dult females have brighter throats and
nTC; richer and more contrasty
verall

Yellowthroats are much smaller and
more active than Mourning or
MacGillivray's

This is the only U.S. warbler to nest in
open marshes

ung males show at least hint of blue-
ay mask and often have brighter yel-
w throat

Unlike Nashville, yellow limited to
throat and contrasts with the body and
head; also note the olive-brown tones

Yellowthroats are frequently seen
below eye level and prefer brushy,
dense growth to skulk in

me birds may show drab undertail
verts; note pale vent and drab flanks,
ntrasting yellow throat

Plump shape, gray-brown flanks, and
restricted, contrasty throat

Pale birds still show some contrast in
the throat

Contrasty yellow throat, UnTC
Brownish-gray flanks
Dark cheek, thin eyering
Long dark tail
Plain olive-brown above
Often skulky

Comparison Species

Black-throated Blue Cooler blue-gray above (vs. gray olive); thin pale supercilium and under-eye arc (vs. plain face, faint eyering); often shows white handkerchief (vs. never); plumper shape; whitish UnTC (vs. yellow); shorter tail; lacks strong yellow anywhere

Nashville Blue-gray head contrasts green upperparts (vs. blending); throat blends into breast (vs. contrasting); distinct white eyering (vs. paler, buffy); yellower flanks; finer bill; thinner tail; smaller and flittier

Connecticut More striking eyering; larger, chunkier, longer wings; larger bill; shorter tail; pale throat less yellow; walks on ground (vs. wren-like); belly can be pale, but more uniform yellowish

MacGillivray's Hooded (vs. contrasting throat); bolder white eye-arcs; longer wings; brighter yellow below (vs. pale in belly and buffy flanks)

Mourning F Brighter, uniform yellow below; shorter tail; pink-based bill (vs. gray); longer wings; brighter greenish above; brownish hood or breast band; no white in belly

Wilson's Brighter yellow overall; higher contrast olive back and all-yellow underparts (vs. grayish olive/buffy); many show a black cap (vs. never); lacks eyering; longer, thinner, gray tail

Hooded Yellow face with contrasting olive or black hood (vs. plainer face/back); uniform yellow below (vs. buffier, uneven); white tail often flashed (vs. dark tail)

Canada Striking yellow supraloral (vs. none); brighter eyering; black or gray necklace (vs. none); gray back (vs. gray olive); brighter, more uniform yellow below; white UnTC (vs. yellow)

CONNECTICUT

Oporornis agilis   Bright Birds

- Large and usually ground dwelling, walks deliberately on ground
- ✓ Slaty-gray hood and complete white or buffy eyering
- Lores same color as hood
- Olive back and yellow underparts
- Long, pinkish legs

- ✓ Slaty-gray hood and complete white or buffy eyering
- Yellow never as bright as some similar species

- UnTC reaching more than halfway to tip of tail, creating rather short-tailed appearance
- Long, bicolored bill
- Long, pinkish legs

Distinctive Views

Additional Photos

Walks rather than hops; only other warblers to do so are Ovenbird and Waterthrushes

Hood is paler in adult female

Very long wings and short tail accentuate the large bulky body

In flight may give the impression of a thrush

Often skulks in dense cover, making it very difficult to detect in migration

When flushed off the ground may sit motionless on a branch for long periods

Among our most southerly wintering warblers, probably in Amazonia

Compared to Macgillivray's (top), shows complete eyering, lacks dark lores, and is bulkier with a shorter tail

Large, walks on ground
Striking eyering
Full gray hood
Uniform yellowish below
Plain olive-brown back
Short tail, long UnTC

Comparison Species

Nashville Smaller and more active; much finer bill; hood broken by yellow throat (vs. hooded, never yellow in throat); pale vent area (vs. yellow); longer, thinner tail projects farther beyond UnTC

MacGillivray's Rarely overlaps range; broken eyering (vs. complete); hops more than walks; black in throat and lores (vs. none); typically calls more; brighter colors; longer tail, shorter UnTC

Mourning Hops more than walks; earlier migrant, but some overlap; brighter colors; fainter eyering, if any; black in throat (vs. never); calls more often; somewhat longer tail, shorter UnTC

Aging and Sexing

Spring AdM 1yM AdF 1yF **Fall** AdM 1yM AdF 1yF

Races: 1 Summary *Spring:* Sexable, some 1yM may be separable from AdM, AdF/1yF not separable *Fall:* Not reliably ageable/sexable **What to Notice** *Spring:* Intensity and contrast of hood, brownish tones and contrast overall *Fall:* Contrasting hood, brownish tones, eyering completeness, throat contrast and tone

AdM/1yM Sp Strong hood with gray tones.

1yM Sp *Diagnostic when present:* may be separable from AdM when duller and browner above.

AdF/1yF Sp Duller overall with paler throat, hood browner, less contrasty.

AdM/1yM

1yM/AdF/1yF

Probable 1y

Note Fall birds show a clinal overlap that makes definitively aging or sexing impossible without bird in hand (and often not even then): AdM Fa duller than AdM spring; some 1yM have complete hoods and are inseparable from AdM; AdF similar to spring female; many 1yM more buffy eyering, undersides paler, flanks washed browner, chin and throat paler brown or even white compared to AdF, but these differences are average and clinal; 1yF similar to 1yM but average duller, fewer gray tones, browner face and hood blending with back, eyering is buffy but complete or slightly broken at rear, paler throat, often slightly buffy; differences between 1yM and 1yF are still average and clinal, so definitive separation not possible.

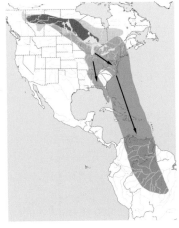

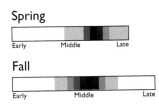

Spring

Early   Middle   Late

Fall

Early   Middle   Late

Connecticut

Con nec ti cut; 4 quirky syllables; try repeating those 3 times!

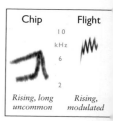

Chip | Flight

Rising, long uncommon | *Rising, modulated*

Summary *1 Section of 3- or 4-Element Phrases repeated 3 or 4 times* (only shared with Common Yellowthroat); *irregular, jerky, percussive* rhythm due to very short, Expanded Elements and long, varying Intervals; staccato, emphatic quality; *often starts softly and slowly, gaining speed, volume;* **I Type.**

Type A1 One 3-Element Phrase repeated 3 times.

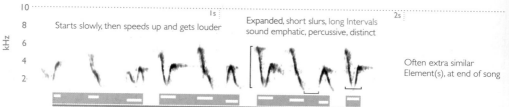

Starts slowly, then speeds up and gets louder

Expanded, short slurs, long Intervals sound emphatic, percussive, distinct

Often extra similar Element(s), at end of song

Type A2 One 4-Element Phrase repeated 3 times.

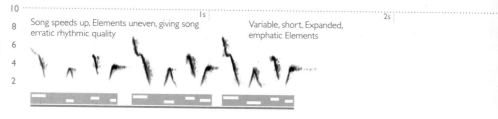

Song speeds up, Elements uneven, giving song erratic rhythmic quality

Variable, short, Expanded, emphatic Elements

Type A3 3 Elements, but the 3rd is very soft, so can sound like 2-Element Phrases from distance.

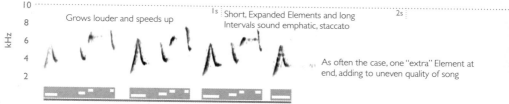

Grows louder and speeds up

Short, Expanded Elements and long Intervals sound emphatic, staccato

As often the case, one "extra" Element at end, adding to uneven quality of song

Canada A1
Similar habitats and rather erratic rhythm, **but** many more Sections, and usually only one, 1-Element Phrase/Section. Faster (Elements harder to hear) and not repetitive.

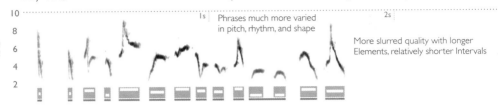

Phrases much more varied in pitch, rhythm, and shape

More slurred quality with longer Elements, relatively shorter Intervals

Common Yellowthroat A4
Similar habitat and song structure: 1 Section of 3- or 4-Element Phrases, **but** steadier, smoother rhythm (vs. erratic, jerky quality); noticeably higher.

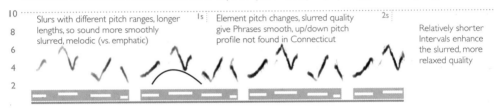

Slurs with different pitch ranges, longer lengths, so sound more smoothly slurred, melodic (vs. emphatic)

Element pitch changes, slurred quality give Phrases smooth, up/down pitch profile not found in Connecticut

Relatively shorter Intervals enhance the slurred, more relaxed quality

Northern Waterthrush
Similar habitats, walks on ground, similarly emphatic, **but** multiple Sections (3+) vs. 1, and Phrases repeated with steady rhythm (vs. uneven, jerky rhythm).

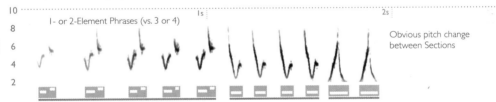

1- or 2-Element Phrases (vs. 3 or 4)

Obvious pitch change between Sections

Ovenbird A1
Similar habitat, walks on ground, and 1-Section song starts softly and grows louder, **but** does not noticeably speed up, is longer (avg. 2.7 sec. vs. 1.6), and has many more Phrases, (avg. 10 vs. 3); also very steady rhythm, consistent 2-Element Phrases (vs. more erratic rhythm and 3+ Elements per Phrase).

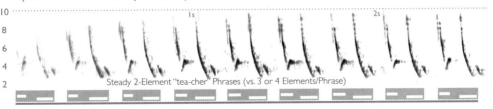

Steady 2-Element "tea-cher" Phrases (vs. 3 or 4 Elements/Phrase)

CONNECTICUT

Oporornis agilis Drab Birds

- All plumages have complete white or buffy white eyering
- Large, ground dwelling, and walks on ground
- Brownish hood
- Pale or buffy throat, but not yellow
- No supraloral line

- Pale greenish-yellow underside
- Pale throat
- UnTC reaching more than halfway to tip of tail, creating short-tailed appearance
- Long, bicolored bill

Distinctive Views

Additional Photos

yering is thick and complete, even in
his extremely drab individual

Skulkiness and affinity for dense cover
in shrubby habitats make it one of the
least-seen birds in migration

Bulky in appearance; our largest warbler besides Yellow-breasted Chat

arge, ambling bird, with short tail and long wings

Duller above and paler below than
Mourning or MacGillivray's

/hen flushed, may perch for several
inutes on a branch

Mostly walks (vs. hops) on the ground, somewhat like Ovenbird, but more
ambling and less chicken-like

Complete white/buffy eyering
Large, walks on ground
Short tail, long UnTC
Uniform pale yellow below
Some hooding
Throat never yellow

Comparison Species

Common Yellowthroat Smaller, slimmer; contrasting yellow throat (vs. hooded); contrasting UnTC (vs. blends with body); less uniform below with pale or buffy flanks/belly; hops (vs. walks); longer tail

Nashville F Yellow throat (vs. hooded or pale); much smaller; finer bi more active, hover-gleans (vs. walks); longer tail with shorter UnTC; contrast ing white vent, lower belly (vs. uniform)

MacGillivray's Range rarely overlaps; broken eyering (vs. solid); longer tail, shorter UnTC; brighter above and below; paler birds more complex facial pattern with hint of eyeline or darker lores and paler supraloral (vs. very plain face)

Yellow Yellower upperparts; plain fac (vs. hooded); yellow fringing on wings (vs. none); almost always yellow or yel lowish throat but can be pale (vs. pale/ hooded); yellow tail (vs. dark)

Mourning Very thin eyering, almost always incomplete (vs. thicker, complete); pale supraloral (vs. uniform face); somewhat longer tail, shorter UnTC; usually throat has yellow tones of breast (vs. complete breast band or hooded look, whitish or buffy throat)

Ovenbird Orange crown with black stripe (vs. plain); white below with blac streaking (vs. yellow/buff); pronounced head-bobbing "chicken walk" (vs. head more still); rounder and fatter

GOLDEN-CHEEKED

Setophaga chrysoparia   Bright/Drab - All Seasons

- Extremely restricted range
- Yellow face
- Simple, dark eyeline
- Lacks dark ear coverts
- Variably black in throat
- Crown and back olive with black streaks or all black

- Variably black throat
- White breast
- ✓ Isolated yellow face with long, black eyeline
- Varying amount of black side streaking, heaviest at shoulders
- Strong white wing bars

- Variably black throat
- White below with variable black side streaking
- Long, all-white tail
- White UnTC with some black flecking

Distinctive Views

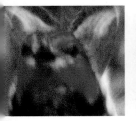

276 • GOLDEN-CHEEKED

Restricted range
Yellow face with black eyelin...
Contrasting white win...
No yellow bel...
Black f...

Additional Photos

Forages by gleaning foliage and branches, especially in oaks

Black eyeline divides yellow face into two unequal parts (1/3 and 2/3)

Note back streaking

Some black streaking in UnTC

Amount of yellow in male is variable

...ar more flexible in wintering ground ...abitat than in breeding grounds

...edian yellow crown stripe may be ...sible in adult males

Breeds only on Edwards Plateau in central Texas: along with Kirtland's, our most endangered warbler

bars
w throat
ank streaking
Dark back

Comparison Species

Black-throated Green Rarely occurs in same range; complex olive cheek patch below pale olive eyeline (vs. just black eyeline); lighter olive back, usually unstreaked except adult males (vs. darker back with streaks); diagnostic yellow in vent (vs. white)

Hermit Rarely occurs in same range; unstreaked below (vs. side streaking); plain face with pale lores (vs. dark eyeline)

Townsend's Dark cheek patch (vs. eyeline only); finer streaking below; yellow on upper breast (vs. white)

Aging and Sexing

Spring AdM 1yM AdF 1yF   **Fall** AdM 1yM AdF 1yF

Races: 1 Summary *Spring:* Sexable, 1yM sometimes separable   *Fall:* AdM and extreme 1yF separable, others not   **What to Notice** *Spring/Fall:* Black in throat, intensity of side streaks, olive or gray in back

AdM/1yM Sp *Diagnostic:* back and throat completely black, bold flank streaking.

1yM Sp Extreme *Diagnostic when present:* similar to AdM with less black and some olive in back.

AdF/1yF Sp Streaking below and eyeline duller than male; *Diagnostic female:* streaked, gray/olive back, upper chest black but upper throat mottled black fading to yellowish at chin; 1yF may show less streaking on back and below and paler throat and chin, but not generally separable.

AdM Fa Similar to spring AdM but with some olive in back.

1yF Fa Duller than AdF/1yM, with little or no back streaking, underpart streaking diffuse and concentrated in upper breast, pale yellowish throat with little or no black; upper wing-bar feathers may show black central streaks (birds strongly showing all qualities may be separated).

AdF/1yM Fa Similar to spring female but chin may be lighter, mottled white or yellowish.

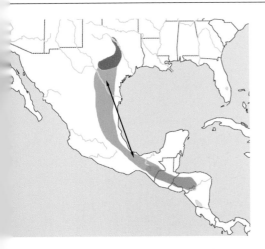

Migration Rarely seen in migration. Generally arrives on breeding grounds between March 10-15, and departs breeding grounds by the first week of August.

Golden-cheeked
When your cheeks are full of gold, of course you're Buzzy, uneven, not Clear

Summary *Dense, very Buzzy Phrases*, and usually Clear, emphatic, downslurred ending; *often calls* a few times just before singing. **2 Types:** A, 5 (rarely 6) Sections; one 1-Element Phrase/Section; each different pitch, often length, 3rd usually notably shorter; **B,** 3 Sections, rising pitch, 1st Section 4 or 5 Buzzy Phrases, others 1 Phrase, ending similar to A.

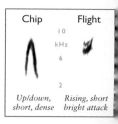

	Chip	Flight

Up/down, short, dense   Rising, short bright attack

Type A1
Dense, fairly low Buzzes until last Phrase. 2nd Section usually significantly higher or lower than 1st; 3rd Phrase usually notably shorter.

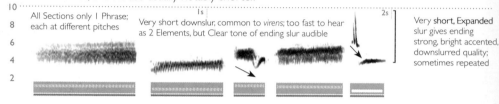

All Sections only 1 Phrase; each at different pitches

Very short downslur, common to *virens*; too fast to hear as 2 Elements, but Clear tone of ending slur audible

Very short, Expanded slur gives ending strong, bright accented, downslurred quality; sometimes repeated

Type A2
Less common, beginning with several fast, Trilled Phrases. Can also end in fast, short Trill, as in this example.

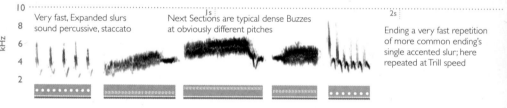

Very fast, Expanded slurs sound percussive, staccato

Next Sections are typical dense Buzzes at obviously different pitches

Ending a very fast repetition of more common ending's single accented slur; here repeated at Trill speed

Type B
3 Sections with rising pitch profile; 1st Section 4 or 5 Buzzy 1-Element Phrases; the rest 1 Phrase each. 2nd Section similar, longer, rising Phrase. Ending similar to Type A.

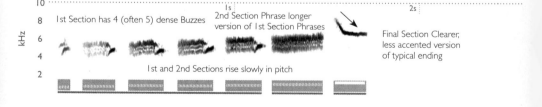

1st Section has 4 (often 5) dense Buzzes

2nd Section Phrase longer version of 1st Section Phrases

Final Section Clearer, less accented version of typical ending

1st and 2nd Sections rise slowly in pitch

Townsend's A1 vs. B
Many similarities, including Buzzy Phrases, downslurred endings **but** in general Buzzes a bit higher, less rich or dense; endings more intricate, although some overlap in structure. Unlikely to be found in same range.

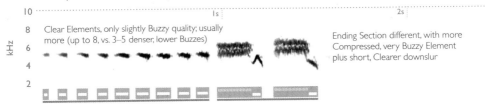

Clear Elements, only slightly Buzzy quality; usually more (up to 8, vs. 3–5 denser, lower Buzzes)

Ending Section different, with more Compressed, very Buzzy Element plus short, Clearer downslur

Townsend's A3 vs. A
Sections that vary greatly in pitch, **but** usually don't have accented, downslurred ending or short Trilled ending.

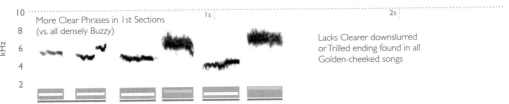

More Clear Phrases in 1st Sections (vs. all densely Buzzy)

Lacks Clearer downslurred or Trilled ending found in all Golden-cheeked songs

Black-throated Gray A1 vs. B
Never like Type A songs, with wide pitch changes from Section to Section; unlikely to be found in same area.

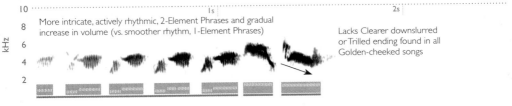

More intricate, actively rhythmic, 2-Element Phrases and gradual increase in volume (vs. smoother rhythm, 1-Element Phrases)

Lacks Clearer downslurred or Trilled ending found in all Golden-cheeked songs

Black-throated Green A1 vs. A
Very unlikely to be confused, or for birds to be found in same area. Unique, fixed pitch profile not matched by Golden-cheeked.

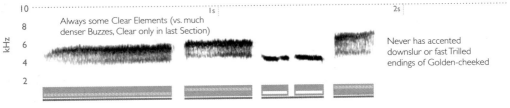

Always some Clear Elements (vs. much denser Buzzes, Clear only in last Section)

Never has accented downslur or fast Trilled endings of Golden-cheeked

GOLDEN-WINGED

Vermivora chrysoptera   Male/Female - All Seasons

- Pearl-gray above and paler below
- Golden yellow patches on crown and wing
- Black or gray throat and mask
- Transitional habitat specialist
- Long, spike-like bill
- ✓ Bright yellow crown and wing patches on gray body

- Black or gray throat and mask
- Yellow crown and wing patch
- Pale gray/whitish underside
- All-white tail and white UnTC

- Pale gray/whitish undersides
- All-white tail and white UnTC
- Black or gray throat
- Long, spike-like bill
- Wide white malar area

Distinctive Views

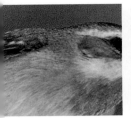

Additional Photos

Prefers open woodland, forest clearings, and other disturbed habitat

Frequently hybridizes with Blue-wing, creating Brewster's and Lawrence's (shown here)

Acrobatic, often hanging upside down to probe for insects

Gray, yellow, white, and black color combination is striking and diagnostic

Usually feeds at low to middle levels of vegetation

Small, active bird

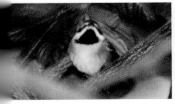

May prefer more specialized habitat than Blue-winged

All light gray underneath with a black throat

Golden wing bars
Gray above and below
Black or gray throat and mask
Long white tail
Fine, pointy bill

Comparison Species

Chestnut-sided Eyering on gray face (vs. none); lime-green upperparts; paler yellow wing bars; all-white underparts (vs. grayish, with black or darker gray throat)

Blue-winged Bright yellow below (vs. whitish); thin black eyeline (vs. mask); white wing bars (vs. bright yellow); olive back (vs. gray)

Chickadee Black cap (vs. yellow); white cheek (vs. black/gray); lacks wing bars; buffy flanks (vs. whitish); plumper; often in flocks; long, thin, dark tail (vs. white); conical bill (vs. pointed)

Brewster's Often white wing bars (vs. yellow); lacks mask; overall lower contrast except for yellow cap

Black-throated Gray Rarely overlap range; black streaking on sides (vs. none); no yellow except in supraloral spot; larger supercilium; white wing bar (vs. yellow); darker gray upperparts

Lawrence's Yellow below and usually yellow malar region; wing bars often whitish

Aging and Sexing

Races: 1 Summary *Spring/Fall:* Sexable, not ageable   **What to Notice** *Spring:* Black vs. gray in throat and face mask, extent of yellow in wing panel   *Fall:* Black vs. gray in throat and face mask, extent of yellow in wing panel, yellow edging on tertials and secondaries, yellow wash below

AdM/1yM Sp *Diagnostic male:* black throat, strong contrasting black mask.

AdF/1yF Sp *Diagnostic female:* gray mask and throat, less and duller yellow on head than males, and reduced wing panel (sometimes to wing bars).

AdM/1yM Fa Similar to spring males; 1yM may show stronger yellow edges to tertial and secondaries and yellow wash on undersides, but not reliably separable.

AdF/1yF Fa Similar to spring female; 1yF may show stronger yellow edges to tertials and secondaries, reduced yellow in crown, and be paler overall but not reliably separable.

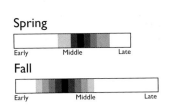

Spring

Early   Middle   Late

Fall

Early   Middle   Late

Golden-winged
Golden wings are all the Buzz, but soon fall from favor

Summary *Short, Buzzy 2 or 3 Sections; high, tight Buzzes*, usually of similar length/quality. Longer songs can contain Elements of Blue-winged and may indicate hybrids. **2 Types: A,** 2-Section song; long Buzz followed by 3 shorter, lower Buzzes; Buzzes thinner, "tighter," higher-pitched and more insect-like than Blue-winged; **B,** Variable, usually 3 Sections; Buzzes like A but different pitches, sometimes with looser Buzzes or Trills.

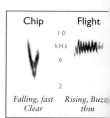

Chip   Flight

Falling, fast Clear   *Rising, Buzz thin*

Type A 2 Sections; very even, slow pace. Buzzes very fast, bright, high.

1st Section a tight, Buzzy Phrase

2nd Section has 3 usually shorter, lower but very similar Buzzes

Type B1 Shares some similarities with Blue-winged Type B: visually check for hybrids.

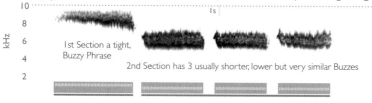

1st 2 Sections very similar to dense Buzz, lower, loose Trill of Blue-winged Type A

Last Section's Phrases not found in Blue-winged Type A song, but Type B songs can be similar; Golden-winged often higher, tighter Buzzes

Type B2 Uncommon version of song, with greater number of shorter Phrases in 1st 2 Sections. Buzzes and Trills high-pitched.

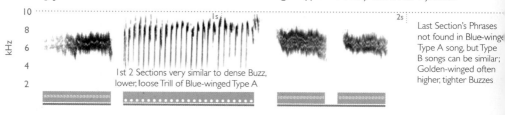

High pitch, very thin quality vs. Blue-winged

Lower Buzz, tighter than loose Trill or Buzz of Blue-wing

Blue-winged B1 Added Buzzes after 2nd Section confusable with Type B; Type A songs usually separable with only 2 Sections, the 2nd a slow Trill; 2-Section Golden-winged songs don't include a Trill, and Buzzes are higher, tighter.

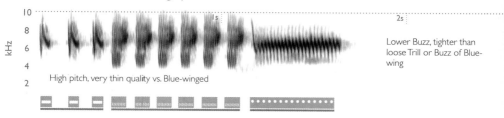

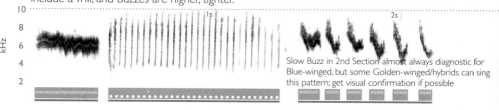

Slow Buzz in 2nd Section almost always diagnostic for Blue-winged, but some Golden-winged/hybrids can sing this pattern; get visual confirmation if possible

Prairie A1
Shares breeding habitat, and similarly Buzzy Elements, **but** usually longer (avg. 2.2 sec. vs. 1.4) and many more Phrases (avg. 18 vs. 4).

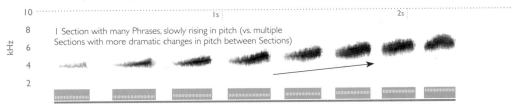

1 Section with many Phrases, slowly rising in pitch (vs. multiple Sections with more dramatic changes in pitch between Sections)

Black-throated Green B1
Buzzy Phrases, **but** structure different.

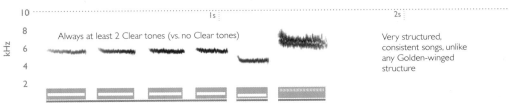

Always at least 2 Clear tones (vs. no Clear tones)

Very structured, consistent songs, unlike any Golden-winged structure

Black-throated Green A1
Similarly separable as Type B above; this Type has fairly wide, fixed pitch changes between Sections, unlike Golden-winged.

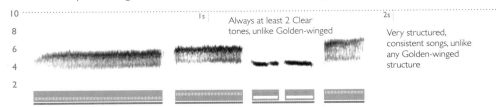

Always at least 2 Clear tones, unlike Golden-winged

Very structured, consistent songs, unlike any Golden-winged structure

Northern Parula B2 vs. B
Parula Type A easily separable by long, loose, rising Trill and accented up/downslur, **but** Parula Type B similar with many Trilled Phrases in 2 or 3 Sections. Always lacks tight, high Buzzes found in all Golden-winged songs; noticeably lower pitch.

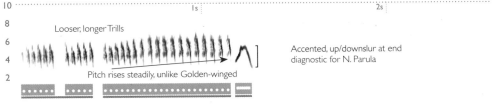

Looser, longer Trills

Pitch rises steadily, unlike Golden-winged

Accented, up/downslur at end diagnostic for N. Parula

GRACE'S

Setophaga graciae Male/Female - All Seasons

- Yellow throat, under-eye arc, and supercilium, white behind eye
- Gray back with some black streaking
- Black side streaking
- White wing bars

- Yellow throat, under-eye arc, and supercilium bordered by black
- Black side streaking
- White belly
- All-white tail and UnTC

- Yellow throat with black border
- White belly, UnTC, and tail
- Black side streaking
- Small with small bill

Distinctive Views

Additional Photos

Closely related to Yellow-throated but found only in West

Plainer-faced than Yellow-throated, with much less black

Bright yellow throat sharply cut off by white belly

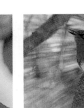

Yellow throat more extensive than Audubon's (Yellow-rumped)

Shows a strong preference for pines throughout the year and breeds in pine oak forests

Often found high in trees

Often creeps along branches, exploring pine clusters for insects

Thin black border to yellow throat

Sometimes sallies for insects

Only western warbler with underparts 1/2 yellow, 1/2 white

Overall long-bodied; though head seems small, tail is long

Wide yellow supraloral
Strong yellow throat/breast
Restricted black throat border
Black flank streaking
Long white tail
Contrasting white wing bars

Comparison Species

Yellow-rumped (Audubon's) Yellow rump and crown patch (vs. none); yellow in throat more restricted; no yellow above eye; black "U" or overall black streaking on upper breast (vs. plain yellow); tail spot pattern distinctive; isolated yellow shoulder patches

Hermit Yellow forehead (vs. black/gray); lacks contrasting cheek and supraloral; plain white undersides (vs. streaks); often black or mottled black throat (vs. never); yellow never below throat

Townsend's Isolated black cheek patch (vs. none); much longer supercilium; more yellow/no white in face; olive back (vs. gray); usually some black in throat (vs. never); first-year birds from below can be confusing, but paler yellow may continue further below on sides and streaking more diffuse

Pine No range overlap; lacks gray in face; longer tail; less, more-diffuse side streaking; yellow less restricted

Yellow-throated Rarely overlaps range; black-and-white facial pattern with long white supercilium; white patch behind ear; more contrast between black face and yellow throat; no streaking in back; larger; longer bill; heavier streaking, especially higher on breast

Blackburnian Dull Only range overlap outside U.S./Canada; different facial markings; orange (vs. yellow) throat more diffuse and extensive; lower contrast side streaks

Aging and Sexing

Races: 4, only one north of Mexico **Summary** *Spring:* Sexable, not ageable *Fall:* AdM and extreme 1yF separable, others not **What to Notice** *Spring:* Streaking in cap, streaking on back, intensity of yellow, intensity of lores/side streaking *Fall:* Color of mask, intensity of streaking above and below, color of yellow, brownish cast to back

AdM/1yM Sp Heavily streaked forehead, upperparts heavily streaked black, black auriculars.

AdF/1yF Sp Duller than males, less streaking on head, flanks, and back, somewhat paler yellow in throat, lores paler, gray auriculars.

AdM/1yM Fa Similar to spring males.

AdF/1yM Fa Duller than AdM Fa, with fainter streaking, and possibly a light brownish wash on upperparts.

1yF Fa Extreme Dullest birds show little or no streaking on upperparts, reduced streaking below, paler yellow in head and throat.

Migration Generally arrives on breeding grounds in early April, and departs breeding grounds by late September.

Grace's

You can always count on Grace to go on and on, and get more emphatic

Summary Fairly *long, with distinct downslurs evenly repeated 13-20 times,* usually getting louder and higher toward the end. Slightly intricate, 1-Element downslurred Phrases; "shadow" Elements add Complexity. Rhythmic, but slow enough and Phrases long enough so *not strongly percussive or emphatic.* **2 Types:** A, 1-Section, usually just under Trill speed; B, 2-Sections, very similar Elements, one Section often slow Trill.

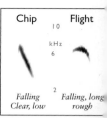

Chip	Flight
Falling Clear, low	*Falling, long rough*

Type A Speed countable, always just slower than Trill.

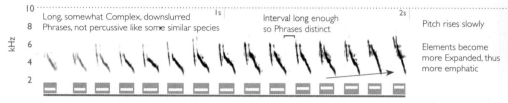

Long, somewhat Complex, downslurred Phrases, not percussive like some similar species

Interval long enough so Phrases distinct

Pitch rises slowly

Elements become more Expanded, thus more emphatic

Type B1 2nd Section, if present, almost always a little faster, but never large jumps in speed; Elements similar, speed still countable, one Section sometimes slowly Trilled.

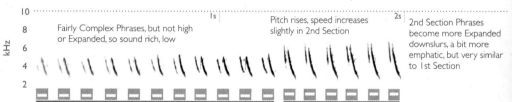

Fairly Complex Phrases, but not high or Expanded, so sound rich, low

Pitch rises, speed increases slightly in 2nd Section

2nd Section Phrases become more Expanded downslurs, a bit more emphatic, but very similar to 1st Section

Type B2 Fewer Phrases in 1st Section and more contrasting 2nd Section than B1.

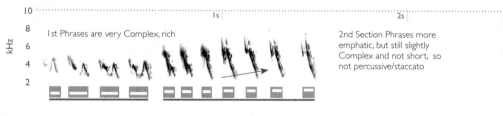

1st Phrases are very Complex, rich

2nd Section Phrases more emphatic, but still slightly Complex and not short, so not percussive/staccato

Type B3 Rare form with falling pitch profile (vs. other Types rising); slower, lower 2nd Section.

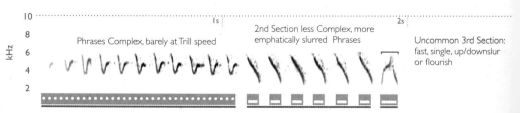

Phrases Complex, barely at Trill speed

2nd Section less Complex, more emphatically slurred Phrases

Uncommon 3rd Section: fast, single, up/downslur or flourish

Wilson's
1 or 2 Sections of repeated, similar Phrases and speed, sometimes quality can be very similar, **but** steady or falling pitch (Grace's almost always rising) and shorter, with fewer Phrases (avg. 10 vs. 15, some overlap but ID good starting point).

Elements simpler, higher, a bit brighter

Most songs fall in pitch toward end of 1-Section song, or between Sections

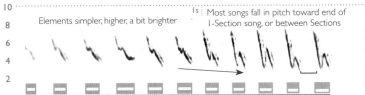

Overall quality very similar, but Wilson's a bit brighter, and, toward end, more emphatic, percussive due to simpler, Expanded, shorter Elements, longer Intervals

Wilson's B1
2-Section song, generally higher, brighter quality; pitch range more Expanded (Phrases span 3–8 kHz vs. 3–6.5 kHz).

1st Section Elements similar, but 2nd Section Phrases more Expanded, emphatic, brighter

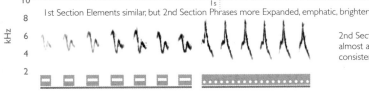

2nd Section dramatically lower than 1st; almost all Grace's rise in pitch with more consistent Phrases, smaller pitch changes

Orange-crowned B2
Separable by speed alone: all Sections faster Trills (avg. 16 Phrases/sec. vs. 8). Grace's rarely Trilled, and never in both Sections of 2-Section song. Orange-crowned also usually shorter (avg. 1.5 sec. vs. 1.9).

Simpler, shorter Phrases with longer Interval so sound less Complex, more emphatic

Usually obviously wavering pitches (vs. steady or slowly rising pitch)

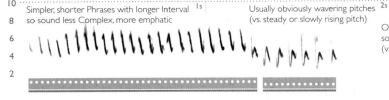

Overall pitch trend of all songs is falling or steady (vs. almost always rising)

Yellow-rumped (Audubon's) A2
Repeated, 2-Element Phrases usually without drastic changes in pitch or speed; noticeably slower (avg. 5 Phrases/sec. vs. 8); fewer Phrases in last Sections (avg. 2 vs. 6.5); never only 1 Section (common for Grace's).

Almost always 2-Element Phrases (never in Grace's)

More Complex, Compressed Phrases with short Intervals sound warbled, slurred; Grace's more emphatic

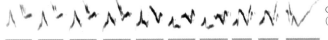

Often fades out toward end (vs. more emphatic as song progresses)

Grace's (cont.)

Virginia's A3 Similarly repetitive, **but** 2-Element Phrases, slower, always countable speed (avg. 5 Phrases/sec. vs. 8); minimum 2 diverse Sections, usually 3 or 4, vs. 1 or 2 similar Sections; often higher pitched; more Expanded, longer Phrases sound more slurred, less distinct/emphatic.

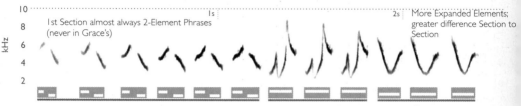

1st Section almost always 2-Element Phrases (never in Grace's)

More Expanded Elements; greater difference Section to Section

Lucy's A2 Range overlap **but** habitats differ; Elements usually more intricate, varied. Phrases change more drastically between Sections in speed and pitch; Grace's songs simpler, Phrases and Sections more similar.

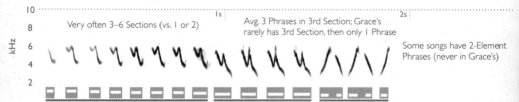

Very often 3–6 Sections (vs. 1 or 2)

Avg. 3 Phrases in 3rd Section; Grace's rarely has 3rd Section, then only 1 Phrase

Some songs have 2-Element Phrases (never in Grace's)

Dark-eyed Junco Steady, 1-Section song, often a faster Trill, without small changes in speed/pitch found in all Grace's; most Elements much more elaborate with short, Expanded Elements adding obvious brightness or bell-like tinkling (Grace's more Compressed). This version closer in speed, quality than most.

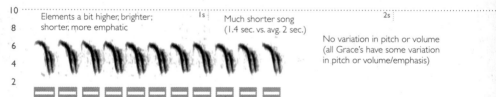

Elements a bit higher, brighter, shorter, more emphatic

Much shorter song (1.4 sec. vs. avg. 2 sec.)

No variation in pitch or volume (all Grace's have some variation in pitch or volume/emphasis)

Nashville Warbler C1 Usually much lower, faster 2nd Section so easily separable. Some western songs have shorter 2nd Section and could be confused. 1st-Section Phrases much slower, (avg. 4.3 Phrases/sec. vs. 8).

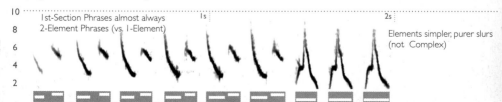

1st-Section Phrases almost always 2-Element Phrases (vs. 1-Element)

Elements simpler, purer slurs (not Complex)

HERMIT

Setophaga occidentalis   Male/Female - All Seasons

- ✓ Plain yellow face with prominent dark eye, variably black or gray nape
- Variably gray back
- White undersides
- No side streaking
- White wing bars
- Lores always yellow

- Variably black or pale throat
- White tail and undersides
- White UnTC
- No side streaking

- Variably black or pale throat
- All white below without streaking
- All-white tail and UnTC

Distinctive Views

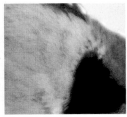

Additional Photos

Plainest of the *virens* superspecies, with black throat and blank yellow face, no streaking or yellow below

Prefers and breeds in conifers but will use all woodland habitat in migration

are vagrant to the East

Overlaps in breeding range with Townsend's, and they occasionally hybridize (hybrid shown here)

Often found in treetops, exploring out to the tips of branches; high feeding often makes them hard to see

ery clear white below, including long, l-white tail

Adult male's striking, plain yellow face with isolated black eye distinctive even in poor views

First year in fall has less yellow in face, bordered by gray/olive, so "moon face" effect is less obvious

rst-year birds show pale yellow fore-own contrasting with darker nape; ale lores

Black in throat is variable

Only adult males show all-black throat

Plain yellow face and lores
No yellow below throat
All white below, no streaking
Long, white tail
Throat usually black or mottled
Black or gray back

Comparison Species

Black-throated Green Rarely overlaps range; olive upperparts (vs. gray/black); olive auricular patch (vs. none or smudgy gray); dark lores (vs. always clear lores); olive forehead (vs. yellow); side streaking (vs. none); diagnostic yellow in vent (vs. white)

Golden-cheeked Extremely restricted range; black eyeline (vs. plain face); side streaking (vs. none)

Townsend's Olive back (vs. gray/black); contrasty black cheek patch (vs. none or smudgy gray); dark lores (vs. always clear lores); dark forehead (vs. yellow); side streaking (vs. none); yellow extends into breast (vs. white)

Olive Orangey or yellow face with auricular patch (vs. plain face); larger with longer bill; weaker wing bars; notched tail (vs. squarer); lacks black in throat

Hermit x Townsend's All ages often show head pattern of Hermit, olive-green upperparts with black streaks; yellowish breast below black throat; some show thin pencil-like streaks on sides and flanks

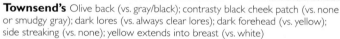

Aging and Sexing

Races: 1 Summary *Spring:* Sexable, first-year birds sometimes separable   *Fall:* AdM, extreme 1yF separable, 1y birds sometimes ageable   **What to Notice** *Spring:* Black in back, nape, throat, and chin, yellow on face, streaking on flanks and back   *Fall:* Black, olive, or brown in back, nape, throat, chin; presence of ear patch, flank streaks, black streaks in median coverts

AdM/1yM Sp *Diagnostic male:* nape and back of crown black, front of crown and face pure yellow, gray back with black streaking, throat entirely black; some 1yM have yellow chin, mottling on top of head, and are similar to AdF.

AdF/1yF Sp Throat not all black (mottled with yellow and yellow chin); *Diagnostic female:* crown and back dark olive with little or no streaking; ear patch outlined with olive (not clear yellow); *Diagnostic when present 1y:* dark streaks in median covert tips.

AdM Fa Similar to spring male, sometimes duller with mottling of ear and throat; solid white median covert tips.

AdF/1yM Fa Similar to spring female; dark streaks in median coverts indicate a 1y bird.

1yF Fa Extreme Browner, unstreaked back, ear patch olive-brown and indistinct surrounded by dark yellow; eyering more obvious, pale brown throat fading to whitish below; *Diagnostic when present:* triangular dark centered median covert tips.

Hermit/Townsend's Hybrid Zone in Washington and Oregon

Spring

| Early | Middle | Late |

Fall

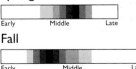

| Early | Middle | Late |

HOODED
Setophaga citrina   Male/Female - All Seasons

✓ Bright yellow face outlined by black hood and throat, or olive hood with varying black

- Plain olive-green back
- No wing bars
- Bright yellow underparts
- Often low, in shaded forest
- Dark or smudgy lores

- Black or yellow throat
- Unstreaked yellow underparts
- Long, all-white tail with yellow UnTC
- No wing bars

- Black or yellow throat
- Unstreaked yellow underparts
- Long, all-white tail with yellow UnTC

Distinctive Views

Additional Photos

Relatively low forager; requires dense shrubby understory habitat for breeding

Flashes white tail frequently, revealing bird's presence in deeply shaded habitats

Drab birds show contrast between face and uniform crown/back

ong, broad, all-white tail with yellow nTC

Bright birds show solid olive back without wing bars, contrasting with black hood

Drab birds have olive back and hooding that blend together; hood usually has some trace of black

right birds have striking black-and-yellow face and hood

Bright bird's hood is distinct even in flight

Deep-chested and heavyset but may look slim due to long, broad tail; note dark lores

ome older females have hoods similar adult males but never as extensive glossy

Olive, yellow, and black, with flashing white tail feathers

Requires large tracts of unbroken forest and is particularly susceptible to forest fragmentation, nest predation, and cowbird parasitism

Plain olive back
Plain yellow below
Long white tail, yellow UnTC
Plain yellow face, darkish lores
Black cowl, or varying
black in head

Bright

Drab

Comparison Species

Canada Gray upperparts (vs. olive); white eyering; more active; black necklace streaking in breast; white UnTC (vs. yellow); longer, dark tail (vs. white)

Yellow No dark hood so head lacks contrast; pale yellow edges to wings; male has red streaking in breast; yellow tail (vs. white); no black in throat

Wilson's Face, especially auriculars, blends more smoothly with nape (not hooded); lacks dark lores; smaller; paler olive upperparts; thinner, dark tail (vs. white) is wagged, not flashed; smaller bill with pale underside (vs. dark); usually some black cap; never black in throat; dusky cheek patch and crown emphasize lighter supercilium (vs. plain, more uniform face contrasting with crown or hood)

Kentucky Yellow throat; black in cheek, lores; strong yellow supercilium and half eyering; feeds more on ground; shorter, all-dark tail (vs. white)

Common Yellowthroat AdM Smaller; wren-like behavior; duller olive upperparts; black mask/yellow throat instead of yellow face/black hood; duller flanks; longer, dark tail (vs. white)

Common Yellowthroat Drab Smaller; wren-like behavior; cheek, crown, nape and lores same color (vs. hooded); faint eyering; contrasting yellow throat (never black); dull brown/buffy flanks (vs. yellow; note: Sonoran race may show more yellow); long, dark tail (vs. white); yellow UnTC contrast with paler belly (vs solid yellow undersides)

Aging and Sexing

Races: 1 Summary *Spring:* Sexable, 1yF, AdF may be separable   *Fall:* AdM separable, 1yF may be separable, others not   **What to Notice** *Spring/Fall:* Black hood, mottling in head and throat, olive ear patch and back

AdM/1yM Sp/Fa *Diagnostic male:* full black hood.

AdF Dull Sp/Fa Faint hood outline.

AdF Bright Sp/Fa Nearly full hood; *Diagnostic female:* black in crown always mottled yellow.

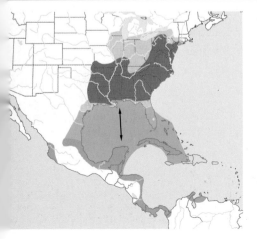

1yF Sp/Fa Olive back and head; *diagnostic when present:* no trace of black in head, faint olivey ear patch.

Spring

Early   Middle   Late

Fall

Early   Middle   Late

Hooded
Hooded monks at the monastery hurry, hurry, hurry to greet you

Summary *Slow, fairly low, rich* song. 3–6 Sections, first 2 or 3 Clear *Compressed Phrases, so not percussive or bright;* slowly slurred 1st Section followed by faster Sections with *only 1 Phrase each,* so song a bit rushed at end. **2 Types: A,** Ending accented, Clear downslur or up/downslur; **B,** Longer; ending usually truncated to short, higher note; less emphatic.

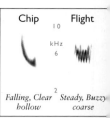

Chip   Flight

Falling, Clear   Steady, Buzzy
hollow   coarse

Type A1   All Sections have very Compressed, Clear, rich tone. More accented, slightly faster ending. All Sections after 1st only 1 Phrase. Rhythm very steady, slow.

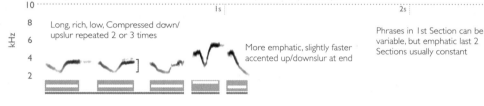

Long, rich, low, Compressed down/upslur repeated 2 or 3 times

More emphatic, slightly faster accented up/downslur at end

Phrases in 1st Section can be variable, but emphatic last 2 Sections usually constant

Type A2   Shorter version of standard song.

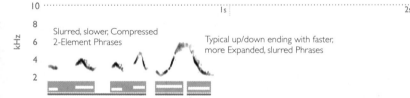

Slurred, slower, Compressed 2-Element Phrases

Typical up/down ending with faster, more Expanded, slurred Phrases

Type B   Shares the pace and low, rich, Clear quality of Type A.

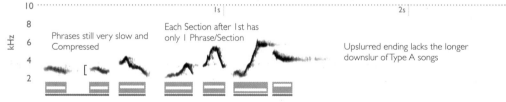

Phrases still very slow and Compressed

Each Section after 1st has only 1 Phrase/Section

Upslurred ending lacks the longer downslur of Type A songs

American Redstart A1   Am. Redstart B songs easily separable (1 Section vs. 3+), **but** Type A similar with repetitive 1st Section, accented up/down ending; differs by more Phrases in 1st Section (4–8 vs. 2 or 3), higher and thinner overall (avg. 3.5–8.5 kHz vs. 2.6–6.4 kHz).

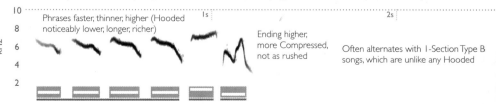

Phrases faster, thinner, higher (Hooded noticeably lower, longer, richer)

Ending higher, more Compressed, not as rushed

Often alternates with 1-Section Type B songs, which are unlike any Hooded

Magnolia A1
Very similar shape, **but** ending doesn't speed up; overall, higher, thinner, faster, and more even (vs. lower, slow, slurred song with faster, emphatic ending).

Phrases higher, more Expanded, brighter

Ending more similar speed and pitch range to prior Sections

Magnolia songs always 4 Sections or fewer (vs. Hooded Type B 6+)

Magnolia
Easier to separate 2-Section song (vs. 3+ Sections in all Hooded)

Higher, brighter, fairly **Expanded**; Hooded more Compressed

Ends with 1-Section upslur; type A Hooded ending always 2 Sections, last a downslur

Yellow
Elements higher, brighter, much more **Expanded**; 1st Section is 4 Expanded Elements at faster speed (vs. 2 or 3 slower, lower, more Compressed Elements).

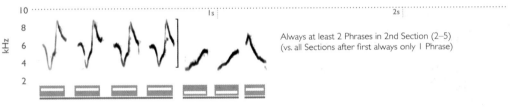

Always at least 2 Phrases in 2nd Section (2–5) (vs. all Sections after first always only 1 Phrase)

Chestnut-sided A1
Structure similar: repeated Phrases in 1st Section and accented up/downslurred ending, **but** brighter, faster, more emphatic, with most Elements much more Expanded.

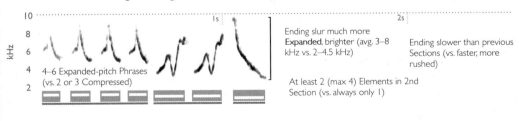

4–6 Expanded-pitch Phrases (vs. 2 or 3 Compressed)

Ending slur much more **Expanded**, brighter (avg. 3–8 kHz vs. 2–4.5 kHz)

At least 2 (max 4) Elements in 2nd Section (vs. always only 1)

Ending slower than previous Sections (vs. faster, more rushed)

KENTUCKY

Geothlypis formosa   Male/Female - All Seasons

- ✓ Bold yellow spectacles stand out against black crown and face
- Plain, dark-olive back
- No wing bars
- Bright yellow underside and throat
- Long legged
- Typically ground-dwelling

- Bright yellow underside and throat
- All-dark, short tail with long yellow UnTC
- Distinct black face and neck pattern
- Heavy and short tailed
- Yellow underparts

Distinctive Views

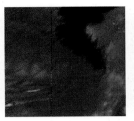

Additional Photos

Black crown with grayish-blue flecks

Generally a shy and well-hidden bird; lack of white in tail rules out otherwise similar Hooded Warbler

Prefers humid, swampy forest or rich, mature deciduous forest with dense undergrowth

Compact, short tailed, and heavy bodied

S.E. breeder, sometimes found as "overshoots" in spring migration north of breeding range

Sings from high spots in trees, partially hidden, and source of song may be difficult to pinpoint

Usually hops; rarely walks

Females are duller and have more restricted black in the head

Tosses leaves with body tilted forward and tail in the air

Usually skulking on or near ground

Bold yellow spectacles
Black auriculars, neck line
Plain bright yellow below
Short dark tail
Long yellow UnTC
Plain olive above
Large, often ground-dwelling

Comparison Species

Canada Blue-gray upperparts (vs. olive); necklace (vs. none); white, complete eyering (vs. yellow, incomplete); smaller; active in trees (vs. ground dwelling); white UnTC (vs. yellow); longer tail

Mourning Lacks yellow in face/black face patches; often grayish throat, so less uniform below; usually hooded

Common Yellowthroat Smaller; more active, wren-like behavior (vs. ground-dweller); duller, browner upperparts, dull brownish flanks (vs. olive/yellow); lacks yellow in face; whitish in belly (vs. yellow); longer tail

Hooded All-yellow face lacking black around and below eye; smaller and more active; longer, all-white tail; males have black throat (vs. yellow)

Aging and Sexing

Spring AdM 1yM AdF 1yF   **Fall** AdM 1yM AdF 1yF

Races: 1 Summary *Spring:* Sexable, some 1yM separable   *Fall:* AdM separable, but other plumages variable and not definitively separable   **What to Notice** *Spring/Fall:* Quantity and quality of black in mask and cap

AdM/1yM Sp *Diagnostic male:* dark black mask and cap; *Diagnostic when present 1yM:* some olive mottling in black areas.

AdF/1yF Sp *Diagnostic female:* black on face reduced versus males, black crown reduced to mottling or streaking.

AdM Fa Similar to spring male with gray fringes on black feathers.

AdF/1yM/1yF Fa Clinaly duller than AdM; 1yF dullest with dark olive replacing black areas and weaker spectacles.

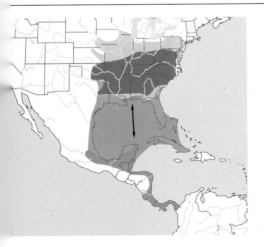

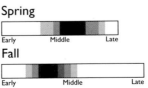

Spring

Early   Middle   Late

Fall

Early   Middle   Late

Kentucky
"Can-tucky" is state of doers: "will do, will do, will do"

Summary *Low, chanting, burry* and forceful, with no pitch changes or variations, ending abruptly. *1 Section of 2-Element Complex Phrases* (rarely 2-Section song with lower 2nd Section); 2nd Element usually higher, so Phrase has *strongly rising pitch profile*; long Intervals, so Phrases distinct; **I Type.**

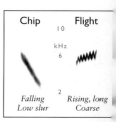

Chip	Flight
Falling	*Rising, long*
Low slur	*Coarse*

Type A1 Complex; slow, forceful, consistent, and mechanical, ending abruptly.

Typical 2-Element Phrases: longer 1st Element slurs into higher, short 2nd Element

Fairly long Interval so Phrases sound distinct, forceful

Complex Elements with articulated, fast, burry quality

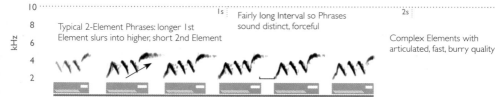

Type A2 Less-common variation. Elements more slurred, less burry, with a falling Phrase pitch profile; still 2-Element Phrases, forceful, distinct, and ending abruptly.

Downslurred Elements create falling pitch profile in Phrases

Elements slurred together and followed by long Intervals, typical for Kentucky

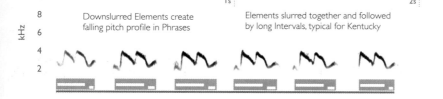

Type A3 A bit thinner than more common versions.

1st Element simpler slur but 2nd more Complex, so still some burry, Complex quality

2 Elements slurred together with short Interval, rising pitch profile

Slow speed and long Intervals between Phrases (sounds distinct, emphatic)

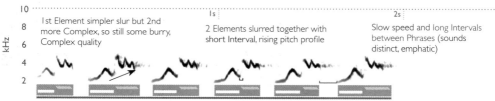

Mourning B1 Some 1-Section songs similar (most are 2+). Somewhat lower, richer, with more energy in lowest part of Phrase; more complex Phrase structure.

Elements more Complex, Expanded, with looser articulations; result is bubbly, richer sound

Down/flat/up Pitch profile adds to richness and Complexity

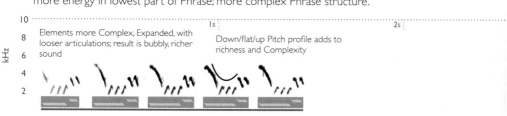

Carolina Wren Shared habitats, similar repeated, chanting Phrases (especially at a distance) **but** 1st Element almost always very Expanded, short, providing bright attack for each Phrase (Kentucky never Expanded or percussive).

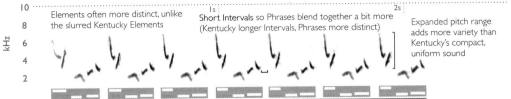

Elements often more distinct, unlike the slurred Kentucky Elements

Short Intervals so Phrases blend together a bit more (Kentucky longer Intervals, Phrases more distinct)

Expanded pitch range adds more variety than Kentucky's compact, uniform sound

Common Yellowthroat Similar habitats, 1-Section song, **but** usually 3 or 4 Phrases (vs. 5–8). Clear, slurred Elements (vs. burry, Complex Elements); noticeably slower Phrase speed (avg. 1.8 Phrases/sec. vs. 3.5).

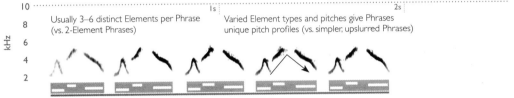

Usually 3–6 distinct Elements per Phrase (vs. 2-Element Phrases)

Varied Element types and pitches give Phrases unique pitch profiles (vs. simpler, upslurred Phrases)

Ovenbird A1 Similar habitats, ground dwelling, and 1 Section of 2-Element Phrases, **but** Phrases much more Expanded, including very high frequencies, thus higher, brighter, and usually fall in Pitch (Kentucky usually rises); 8–11 Phrases/song (vs. 5–8); longer song (avg. 2.7 sec. vs. 1.9).

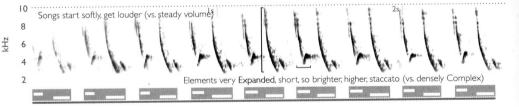

Songs start softly, get louder (vs. steady volume)

Elements very Expanded, short, so brighter, higher, staccato (vs. densely Complex)

Prothonotary A3 Similar breeding habitats, 1 Section of strongly upslurred Phrases; especially confusable at a distance **but** 1-Element Phrases, smoother, less Complex (vs. Compressed 2-Element Phrases), noticeably higher, brighter.

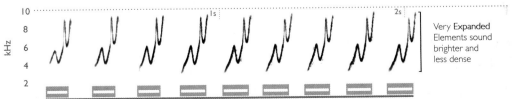

Very Expanded Elements sound brighter and less dense

KIRTLAND'S

Setophaga kirtlandii   Male/Female - All Seasons

- Large and large-billed
- Blue-gray above and yellow below
- Black streaking on back and sides
- White eye-arcs and black lores in males
- Pale edging on greater coverts
- Overall impression is of a rough, streaked texture above and on sides

- Blue-gray above and yellow below
- Black streaking on sides
- Large, white tail spots and white UnTC
- Frequently pumps tail
- Very rare, localized, and hardly ever seen in migration
- Often shows small throat specks

- Large-billed
- Lemon-yellow underside with white UnTC
- Fairly long tail
- White spots in tail corners
- Pumps tail frequently

Distinctive Views

Additional Photos

One of rarest breeding warblers in the U.S., nesting exclusively in young jack pines in Michigan and Wisconsin

Even from distance, large bill, white eye-arcs, and dark upperparts/yellow underparts distinctive

On males white eye crescents are obvious and contrast with black lores; note roughly streaked look

Females and immature males are duller, and eye crescents may be less obvious

Frequently pumps tail, flashing white spots in the tail corners

Males generally sing from the tops of small pines; note small throat spots (diagnostic)

Young fall females very dull with brown tones

Jack pine habitat is good for 5–15 years, and controlled burns help maintain suitable nesting habitat

Most activity is concentrated low in pines or on the ground

Females have less black in the face and more indistinct, finer streaking

Yellow below
Black flank streaking
Gray face, wide white eye-arcs
Fairly long tail, white tail spots
White UnTC
Faint wing bars
Regularly pumps tail

Comparison Species

Pine Unstreaked, paler upperparts; lacks white eye-arcs; no black side streaks; more distinct wing bars; yellow, unstreaked upper breast (vs. side streaks/throat spots); longer tail with larger white spots

Palm Also pumps tail; yellow UnTC (vs. white); supercilium; overall brownis often with rufous cap (vs. gray); square black base of tail; often in flocks

Prairie Smaller with smaller bill; unstreaked greenish upper parts; yellowish wing bars; more complex, different face pattern; also pumps tail but less consistently; less black in tail

Canada Plain upperparts (vs. streaked); complete eyering (vs. eye-arcs); yellow lores; black necklace (vs. side streaks); brighter yellow underpar dark tail (vs. some white)

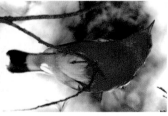

Magnolia Olive back (vs. gray); cleaner white wing bars; doesn't pump tail; smaller with smaller bill; all-white tail with wide black terminal band diagnostic; pale gray throat band (vs. throat spotting)

Aging and Sexing

Races: 1 Summary *Spring:* Sexable, not ageable   *Fall:* AdM separable, others variable and not safely separable   **What to Notice** *Spring:* Black in face and forehead, streaking in back and flanks, spotting in breast   *Fall:* Black in face (especially lores)

AdM/1yM Sp *Diagnostic male:* black lores and forehead, fine black streaking on head, bold black streaking on gray back, bold flank streaking, black spotting on upper breast.

AdF/1yF Sp Eye-arcs thinner, limited spotting in center of chest, weaker side streaks; *Diagnostic female:* little or no black in face, brownish cast in back streaking.

AdM Fa Similar to spring male, but duller; black in lores is diagnostic.

AdF/1yM/1yF Fa Similar to spring female, and not easily separable from each other.

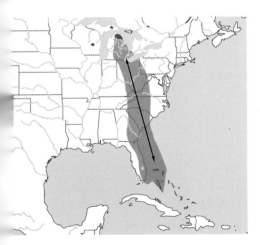

Migration Rarely seen in migration. Generally arrives on breeding grounds in mid-May, and departs breeding grounds by early October.

Kirtland's

So rare, you approach with slow steps, getting faster, then higher, happy reward

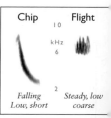

Chip   Flight

10

kHz

6

2

Falling   Steady, low
Low, short   coarse

Summary *Short, low, dense, Compressed Phrases;* loud, almost *explosively sung;* fast percussive notes separated by long enough Intervals to sound emphatic. **2 Types: A,** 3 Sections (rarely 2 or 4), accented, increasing in speed, volume, pitch, ending abruptly; **B,** 4 Sections (rarely 5), less emphatic, longer, more rambling.

Type A1 All Elements fairly similar shape, emphatic quality. Song becomes louder, higher, more slurred.

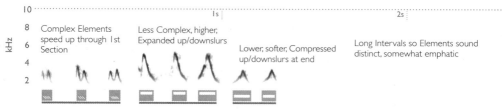

Complex Elements speed up through 1st Section

Less Complex, higher, Expanded up/downslurs

Lower, softer, Compressed up/downslurs at end

Long Intervals so Elements sound distinct, somewhat emphatic

Type A2 2-Section version of more common 3-Section song: lacks lower 3rd Section.

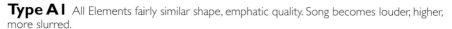

Gets louder, higher and speeds up

2nd-Section Phrases louder and higher but still Complex; ends abruptly

Type B Longer, less accented; retains some of same basic, percussive quality of A song, but has more variety, including some slower, slurred Phrases; still fairly short.

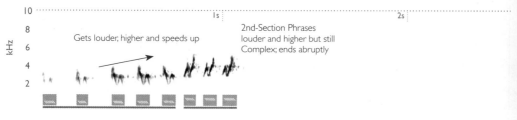

2 different Elements are repeated in twos or threes at fairly fast speed

Breaks rhythm with long Interval before last Sections: very unusual for a warbler song

Northern Waterthrush Superficially similar (emphatic and often grows in intensity and speed), **but** typically longer (avg. 1.9 sec. vs. 1.2); Expanded short slurs, so more accented, emphatic, rhythmic, and much brighter (vs. Compressed, lower, darker).

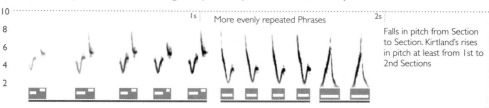

More evenly repeated Phrases

Falls in pitch from Section to Section. Kirtland's rises in pitch at least from 1st to 2nd Sections

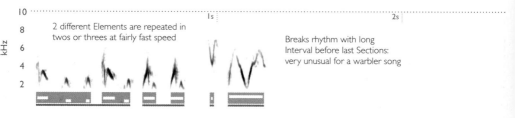

Connecticut A1 Percussive, accented Phrases with acceleration at beginning, **but** only 1 Section (vs. 2 or 3), 3- or 4-Element Phrases (vs. 1 or 2).

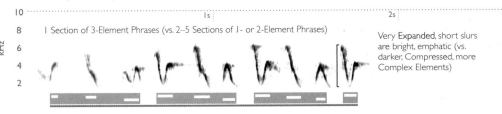

I Section of 3-Element Phrases (vs. 2–5 Sections of 1- or 2-Element Phrases)

Very Expanded, short slurs are bright, emphatic (vs. darker, Compressed, more Complex Elements)

Indigo Bunting (shown)/House Wren Repeated Elements and somewhat emphatic, sometimes harsh, quality, **but** both much longer songs, with many Sections and a much wider variety of Phrases; higher, more Expanded Phrases sound brighter, thinner.

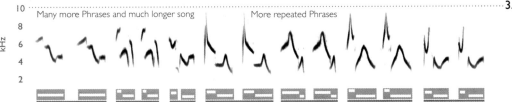

Many more Phrases and much longer song

More repeated Phrases

LOUISIANA WATERTHRUSH

Parkesia motacilla   Male/Female - All Seasons

- Plain brown above without streaking or wing bars
- Typically ground-dwelling, walking and bobbing tail usually in semicircular pattern
- Bright pink legs
- Wide streaking, sparser than Northern Waterthrush
- Bold white, flaring supercilium, sometimes buffy in front

- Large body and head, with long, heavy bill and short tail
- Unspotted/slightly spotted pale throat
- Bold white, flaring supercilium, sometimes buffy in front
- Often shows buffy tones on rear flanks

- Short, brown tail
- Long, pointed bill
- Buffy or whitish UnTC
- Wide streaking, sparser than Northern Waterthrush
- Bright pink legs

Distinctive Views

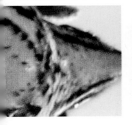

Additional Photos

onstant, semicircular tail bobbing, riginating from lower body; generally een on the ground

Long, "bubblegum pink" legs, usually brighter than Northern Waterthrush, especially in spring

Streaking in the breast is sparser than in Northern Waterthrush

hin buffy supraloral contrasts with ider and whiter post-ocular section of percilium

Bill is longer and heavier than in Northern Waterthrush; white supercilium striking at a distance

Supercilium wraps around back of head, tends to flare behind the eye; note: appearance changes with head posture

enerally prefers rushing streams and oving water (Northern Waterthrush ore likely to breed near still water)

Often shows a buffy wash at the rear of the flanks only

Throat is usually clear of any markings (although some birds show some throat speckling)

eds on a variety of stream life includ- small fish and amphibians

Shape is stockier than Northern: front heavy, with large head and bill

Buffy color isolated in rear flanks (vs. Northern Waterthrush more uniform white or buffy below)

Plain brown above
Wide, white, flared supercilium
Thick, sparse streaking below
Often buffy flanks
Short tail, large bill, front-heavy
Wags back 1/3 of body

Comparison Species

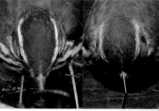

Northern Waterthrush Uniform buffy body/supercilium, sometimes white (vs. always white); narrower, unicolored supercilium doesn't wrap as far around head (vs. flaring, sometimes buffy in front, wraps around head: note that flaring may be more evident from some angles); denser, thinner, less-broken streaking, especially in upper breast; throat usually flecked or streaked (vs. usually clear); moves only tail up and down, not body (vs. often moves back 1/3 of body); legs average darker, especially in spring; smaller, more compact, with smaller bill, so more elongated (vs. stockier)

Northern Waterthrush (right) supercilium doesn't wrap as far around head and is often buffier and monocolored (vs. sometimes buffy at front)

Northern Waterthrush (right) shows more streaking in throat; often buffier color; denser, thinner, and less-broken streaking

Palm Buffy wing bar (vs. none); slimmer and smaller; finer bill; often in flocks; pumps tail but without moving lower body; often diffuse rufous breast streaking (vs. strong, brown); yellow UnTC (vs. paler); longer tail, with distinct black base (vs. all dark)

Ovenbird Plumper; white eyering; lacks supercilium; lighter, olive upperparts (vs. brown); orange crown; pronounced "chicken walk" — bobs head while walking; denser, black streaking focused more in upper chest

Thrushes (Hermit shown) La[rger]; wide supercilium; spotting in breast (v[s.] streaking); darting movements with pauses (vs. walking); smaller-billed, lon[ger]-tailed; often perch perfectly still

Aging and Sexing

Spring AdM 1yM AdF 1yF   **Fall** AdM 1yM AdF 1yF

aces: 1 **Summary** *Spring/Fall:* Generally not separable

Note Some first-year birds may show rusty fringing in tertials, which allows aging but not sexing. This mark is extremely subtle and may be only visible in the hand.

All Birds All plumages similar in all seasons.

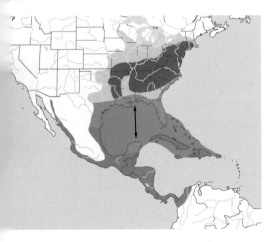

Spring

Early		Middle		Late

Fall

Early		Middle		Late

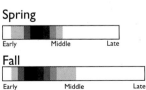

Louisiana Waterthrush

To get to LA, go slowly down south, where they slur words, chat endlessly

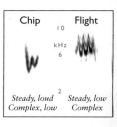

Chip	Flight
Steady, loud Complex, low	Steady, low Complex

Summary All songs start with *1 or 2 Sections of Compressed, long slurs* with long Intervals, *almost always falling in pitch from Phrase to Phrase*; *next few Sections diagnostic* combination of shorter slurs and Expanded, short chips; **2 Types: A,** 1.5–2 sec. long, 5–9 Sections; 1st Section: 2 or 3 slow, smooth long slurred Phrases that fall in pitch (simple downslurs, or up/downslurs); next 2–4 Sections: slightly variable but diagnostic; **B,** Longer, sometimes very long (1.8–11 sec.); begins as A, then unique, variable number of 1-Phrase Sections with a *variety of erratic fast chips and slurs, usually fading in volume.*

Type A1 Typical, shorter song.

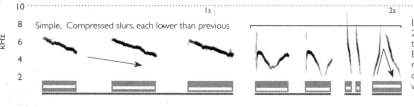

Simple, Compressed slurs, each lower than previous

Last Sections diagnostic: 2 intricate slurs, then two short, very Expanded, percussive notes, then long up/downslur, almost like a wheeze

Type A2 Similar to A1 but more elaborate up/downslurs and steadier pitch in 1st Section.

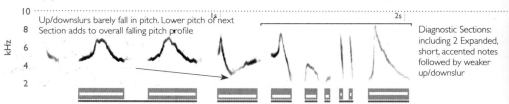

Up/downslurs barely fall in pitch. Lower pitch of next Section adds to overall falling pitch profile

Diagnostic Sections: including 2 Expanded, short, accented notes followed by weaker up/downslur

Type B Commonly sung on breeding grounds, sometimes in migration; often very extended ending; rambling song unlike any other warbler, can last as long as 11 seconds.

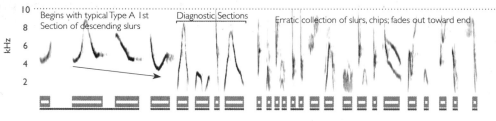

Begins with typical Type A 1st Section of descending slurs

Diagnostic Sections

Erratic collection of slurs, chips; fades out toward end

Swainson's A2 Very similar form, quality to Type A songs: 1st-Section Pitch falls from Element to Element, **but** ending Sections more slow, even, less varied.

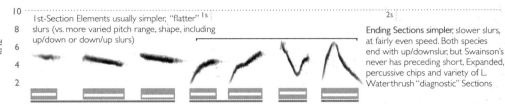

1st-Section Elements usually simpler, "flatter" slurs (vs. more varied pitch range, shape, including up/down or down/up slurs)

Ending Sections simpler, slower slurs, at fairly even speed. Both species end with up/downslur, but Swainson's never has preceding short, Expanded, percussive chips and variety of L. Waterthrush "diagnostic" Sections

Yellow-throated A1 1st Section superficially similar falling slurs, **but** many more Phrases in 1st Section (avg. 7 vs. 2.7), fewer Sections (avg. 2 or 3 vs. 5–9), and lacks number of variable Phrases of Type B songs.

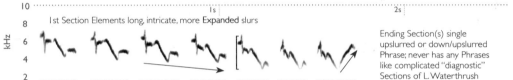

1st Section Elements long, intricate, more Expanded slurs

Ending Section(s) single upslurred or down/upslurred Phrase; never has any Phrases like complicated "diagnostic" Sections of L. Waterthrush

Northern Waterthrush Similar habitat, descending quality **but** 3, sometimes 4 Sections (vs. Type A 5–9 Sections, Type B many more); pitch descends Section to Section (vs. within Sections); overall song quality very consistent, rhythmic, with repeated similar, emphatic Phrases (vs. slurred, less rhythmic, more variable Phrases, especially at end); Expanded, short Elements sound emphatic, not slurred like L. Waterthrush.

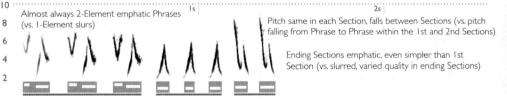

Almost always 2-Element emphatic Phrases (vs. 1-Element slurs)

Pitch same in each Section, falls between Sections (vs. pitch falling from Phrase to Phrase within the 1st and 2nd Sections)

Ending Sections emphatic, even simpler than 1st Section (vs. slurred, varied quality in ending Sections)

LUCY'S

Oreothlypis luciae   Male/Female - All Seasons

- Smallest warbler, with a tiny bill
- Gray above, pale gray below; drab
- ✓ Chestnut rump
- Chestnut crown patch (not always visible)
- Plain face with vague pale eyering and lores, and dark eye
- Frequents arid habitats, mesquite and riparian thickets

- White UnTC and underparts
- Medium-long pale tail
- Smallest warbler, with a tiny bill
- Often pumps tail

- Pale below
- Medium-long pale tail and UnTC
- Smallest warbler, with a tiny bill

Distinctive Views

Additional Photos

Range is limited to the Southwest; commonly found in mesquite

Only warbler with chestnut rump

A short-distance migrant, so wings are short and rounded

An active warbler, often seen probing from all angles for insects

The only warbler aside from Prothonotary to nest in a cavity

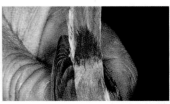

Young females often lack crown patch and have a paler, tawnier rump

Rufous crown patch is sometimes visible

Very fine bill; all white below, with medium-long white tail

Prefers more-arid habitats and lower elevations than Virginia's

May be confused with other drab birds of the Southwest, such as Verdin and Bell's Vireo

Juveniles show tawny fringing in wings

Smallest breeding warbler in the U.S./ Canada

Uniform plain gray above
Plain face with pale lores
Chestnut rump
Medium-long white tail
Plain grayish-white below
Tiny, with tiny bill

Comparison Species

Bell's Vireo Larger and stockier with a heavier, hooked bill; eye-arcs and eye-line create more complex facial pattern; lacks chestnut or tawny patches; often very vocal; yellow flank wash; longer tail

Colima Larger; brownish tones over-all (vs. gray); more contrasting eyering; yellow-orange rump (vs. rufous); heavier bill; yellow-orange UnTC (vs. pale); much longer tail

Verdin Juvenile Sharper, thicker-based bill with a pale yellow-pink base; browner above; much longer tail; gray rump (vs. rufous); adult has partly yellow head (vs. gray)

Virginia Usually yellow in breast (vs. gray); yellow-green rump (vs. rufous); darker above; thinner, more defined eyering, longer, darker tail; yellow UnTC (vs. pale); prefers higher elevations, less-arid habitats

Gnatcatcher Blue upperparts (vs. gray); stronger eyering; longer bill; very long tail; often black eyebrow

Yellow 1yF Sonoran Larger, with heavier bill; pale yellow edging on wing coverts; yellow-toned underparts (vs. gray); shorter, yellow tail (vs. gray); yellow UnTC (vs. pale)

Orange-crowned Drab More complex facial pattern with short supercilium and eye-arcs; overall yellowy olive, yellowish UnTC (vs. gray); longer, dark tail

Warbling Vireo Much larger; heavier bill; more complex face with supercilium and undereye arc; olive-toned upperparts (vs. gray); yellow-olive wash in flanks

Aging and Sexing

Races: 1 **Summary** *Spring/Fall:* Sometimes sexable, not ageable
What to Notice *Spring/Fall:* Rufous crown patch, quality of rump color

AdM/1yM Sp/Fa Rufous crown patch (not always visible) and deep rufous rump, fall birds slightly duller; *Diagnostic when present male*: any bird showing a large crown patch is male, but absence of that patch is not significant.

AdF/1yF Sp/Fa Usually more limited rufous crown patch than males (not always visible), rump more orange-washed than rufous; fall birds slightly duller.

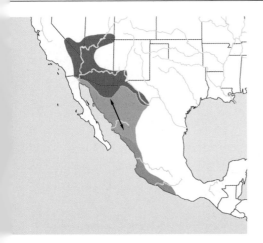

Migration Rarely seen in migration. Generally arrives on breeding grounds in mid-March, and departs breeding grounds by early September.

Lucy's

Let Lucy loose, she goes on and on, repeating one thing, then another, another

Summary Highly *variable*, simple, usually *Clear 1-Element Phrases*, moderate pitch range and speed; 2 or 3 (sometimes 4–6) Sections, usually separated by pitch/speed changes; Phrases of 1st Section almost always 1-Element, Compressed; *1 Section usually a Trill*; **Types:** variable.

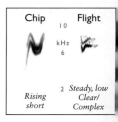

Chip   Flight

Rising short   Steady, low Clear/ Complex

Type A1 2 Sections; 2nd Section slower, higher.

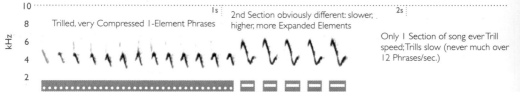

Trilled, very Compressed 1-Element Phrases

2nd Section obviously different: slower, higher, more Expanded Elements

Only 1 Section of song ever Trill speed; Trills slow (never much over 12 Phrases/sec.)

Type A2 Typical 3-Section song; Sections differentiated by obvious changes in speed and pitch.

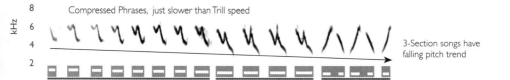

Compressed Phrases, just slower than Trill speed

3-Section songs have falling pitch trend

Type A3 Longest variation: 5-Section song; fairly simple, 1-Element Phrases with speed and pitch changes differentiating Sections.

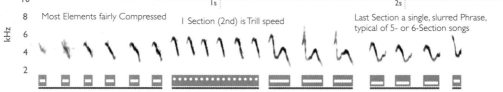

Most Elements fairly Compressed

1 Section (2nd) is Trill speed

Last Section a single, slurred Phrase, typical of 5- or 6-Section songs

Virginia's A3 Most similar, **but** never Trill speed (avg. 4–7 Phrases/sec.) while 75% of Lucy's songs have a Trilled Section; more likely to have upslurred Elements (most Lucy's Elements downslurs), fewer Phrases (avg. 11 vs. 16), usually less change in speed between Sections so rhythmically steadier, smoother.

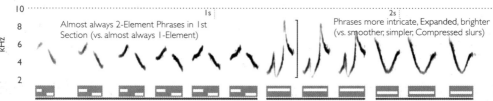

Almost always 2-Element Phrases in 1st Section (vs. almost always 1-Element)

Phrases more intricate, Expanded, brighter (vs. smoother, simpler, Compressed slurs)

Yellow-rumped (Audubon's) Repeated, similar Phrases with 2 or more Sections, **but** Phrase speed always countable (avg. 5.5 Phrases/sec. vs. 8) while 75% of Lucy's have a Trilled Section; little speed/quality change between Sections (Lucy's more dramatic changes).

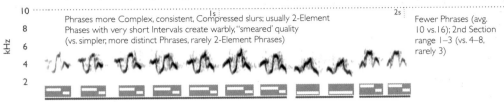

Phrases more Complex, consistent, Compressed slurs; usually 2-Element
Phases with very short Intervals create warbly, "smeared" quality
(vs. simpler, more distinct Phrases, rarely 2-Element Phrases)

Fewer Phrases (avg.
10 vs.16); 2nd Section
range 1–3 (vs. 4–8,
rarely 3)

Yellow B3 4- to 5-Section songs similar to longer Lucy's, **but** Sections shorter (2 or 3 Phrases) so Yellow has more active, changing quality (vs. repetitive Lucy's); Avg. 8 Phrases/song vs. 16; usually slower, 1st Section avg. 5.5 Phrase/sec. vs. 8.6; never Trilled 1st Section as in some Lucy's.

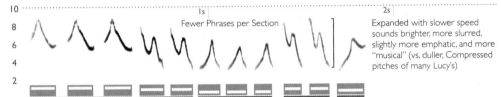

Fewer Phrases per Section

Expanded with slower speed
sounds brighter, more slurred,
slightly more emphatic, and more
"musical" (vs. duller, Compressed
pitches of many Lucy's)

Wilson's B2/B1 Often only 1 Section (Lucy's never); pitch always lower in 2nd Section (many 2-Section Lucy's rise in pitch); never more than 3 Sections (vs. often 4+); fewer Phrases (avg. 11 vs. 16); 2-Section songs avg. 5 Phrases in 1st Section (vs. 9); some overlap, **but** songs with long 1st Sections almost always Lucy's; usually very short, Expanded Phrases with long Intervals, sounding sharper, more emphatic, staccato (vs. Compressed, more slurred Phrases).

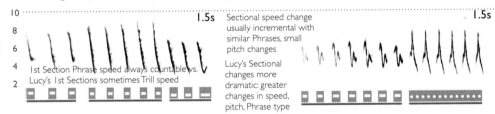

1st Section Phrase speed always countable vs.
Lucy's 1st Sections sometimes Trill speed

Sectional speed change
usually incremental with
similar Phrases, small
pitch changes

Lucy's Sectional
changes more
dramatic: greater
changes in speed,
pitch, Phrase type

Orange-crowned B1/Nashville Orange-crowned: 1 or 2 Sections (vs. usually 3–5, never 1); both Sections Trills (vs. Lucy's only 1 slower Trilled Section, sometimes no Trill); Expanded, short Elements so more emphatic, staccato (vs. slower, slurred, Compressed). Nashville: only 1 or 2 Sections, 2nd falls in pitch (Lucy's almost always rises).

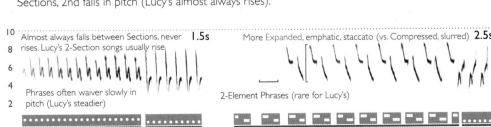

Almost always falls between Sections, never
rises. Lucy's 2-Section songs usually rise

Phrases often waiver slowly in
pitch (Lucy's steadier)

More Expanded, emphatic, staccato (vs. Compressed, slurred)

2-Element Phrases (rare for Lucy's)

MACGILLIVRAY'S

Geothlypis tolmiei   Bright Birds - All Seasons

- Thick, short, white eye-arcs in all plumages
- Often on or near ground
- Blue-gray hood contrasts with olive back
- Yellow belly and UnTC
- Wide black lores in adult male

- Thick, short, white eye-arcs
- Bright yellow belly and UnTC
- Slate to blue-gray hood
- Medium-long tail with short UnTC

Distinctive Views

Additional Photos

Note variation in brightness of hood and body (but always hooded); paler throats lack any yellow tones

Darker throat, but lacks concentrated black patches found in Mourning

Eye crescents are thick and broken

Adult spring female is similar to male, but hood uniformly pale gray without dark bib and lores

Tail is often twitched sideways

Black lores thick and connect across forehead in adult male (never connects in Mourning)

Skulky but easier to see than Mourning: more readily pished, and often migrates through more open habitat

Bright yellow and dark gray hood make a strong impression even with brief views

Similar to Mourning but found in West (no range overlap)

Generally low or on the ground

Compared to Mourning, head is slightly more rounded and tail is longer, with shorter UnTC

Tail is longer and UnTC are shorter than in Mourning, Connecticut, or Kentucky

Thick white eye-arcs
Plain, bright yellow belly/UnTC
Plain olive uppers
Contrasting blue-gray hood
Dark lores
Long tail, short UnTC
Large; often near ground

Comparison Species

Connecticut Rarely overlaps range; complete eyering in all plumages; walking behavior; shorter tail

Orange-crowned Overall, less contrast: paler yellow below, less dark olive above; usually diffuse streaking below; shorter legs and smaller, finer bill; more active and not terrestrial; stronger eyeline and supercilium; longer, thinner tail

Nashville Smaller, finer-billed; more active gleaner, flittier; complete eyering; yellow throat; white vent contrasts with yellow underparts

Mourning Rarely overlaps in range; usually no eyering in bright birds—if present, thin and faint (vs. thick eye-arcs); sometimes dark lores but never connecting across bill (vs. black lores, often connected); almost always more concentrated black in breast; shorter tail with longer UnTC; vocalizations, including chip calls, most reliable way to separate difficult birds

Aging and Sexing

Spring AdM 1yM AdF 1yF   **Fall** AdM 1yM AdF 1yF

Races: 1 Summary *Spring:* Sexable, some 1yM separable *Fall:* Some males separable, extreme 1yF may be separable **What to Notice** *Spring/Fall:* Quality of hood and throat, dark mottling in lower throat

AdM/1yM Sp *Diagnostic male:* blue-gray hood, black lores, variable dark mottling on lower throat, bold eye-arcs; *Diagnostic when present 1yM:* brownish tinge on upperparts.

AdF/1yF Sp Paler hood, chin and throat than males; *Diagnostic female:* no dark throat mottling.

AdM/1yM Fa Similar to spring male, but somewhat duller; dark mottling on lower throat.

AdF/1yM/1yF Fa Similar and variable plumages; 1yF may show more olive-brown hood and buffier throat, 1yM may show gray chest, grayer hood and less buffy throat than AdF; some 1yM show black feathers in breast, which overlaps AdM.

1yF Fa Extreme Olive-brown hood, buffier throat; only most extreme plumages should be separated.

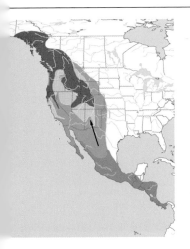

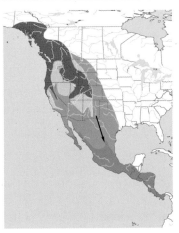

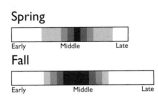

Spring

Early   Middle   Late

Fall

Early   Middle   Late

MacGillivray's

MacG's were a Complex Clan, often rising, then falling, but always burry

Summary *Low, Complex, burry Phrases in 2 or 3 Sections.* Song, Phrase forms variable; usually 2-Element Phrases rise in 1st Section, are lower, faster, and fall in 2nd; *Expanded Elements* with high frequencies *often sound harsh or shrill*; some versions Clearer-toned, but always some Complexity to Phrases; **3 Types: A**, 2-Sections, 2-Element Phrases rising in first Section and lower, faster falling in 2nd; **B**, 2 or 3 Sections, rising/variable pitch profiles, steady or accelerating speed; **C**, 1 Section of steady, Complex Phrases.

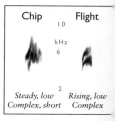

Chip   Flight

Steady, low   Rising, low
Complex, short   Complex

Type A 2 Sections of 2-Element Phrases that rise in 1st and are lower, faster, and falling in 2nd.

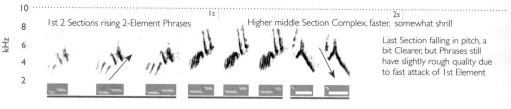

2-Element Phrases with rising pitch profile

Complex, Expanded 2nd Element creates harsh, shrill quality

Lower, faster, somewhat Clearer 2nd Section with falling pitch profile

Type B 2 or 3 Sections, variable (shown) or rising pitch profiles, and steady or accelerating speed.

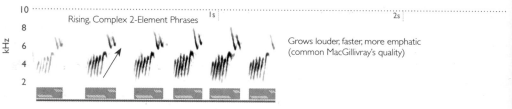

1st 2 Sections rising 2-Element Phrases

Higher middle Section Complex, faster; somewhat shrill

Last Section falling in pitch, a bit Clearer, but Phrases still have slightly rough quality due to fast attack of 1st Element

Type C Uncommon; 1 Section of Steady, Complex Phrases, sometimes sung with short 2nd Section.

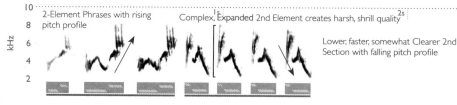

Rising, Complex 2-Element Phrases

Grows louder, faster, more emphatic (common MacGillivray's quality)

Mourning A1

Very similar form, quality, **but** usually slightly shorter, faster 2nd Sections with fewer Phrases; a bit lower, more Compressed, richer (vs. harsher, rapidly Complex, Expanded); songs in western part of range tend to be 1-Section (uncommon for MacGillivray's); MacGillivray's may sing less in migration.

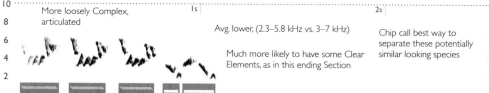

More loosely Complex, articulated

Avg. lower, (2.3–5.8 kHz vs. 3–7 kHz)

Much more likely to have some Clear Elements, as in this ending Section

Chip call best way to separate these potentially similar looking species

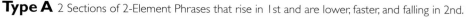

Mourning A2 Likely to have Clearer Elements (60% of 2- or 3-Section songs); MacGillivray's almost never has completely Clear Phrases.

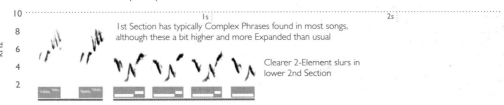

1st Section has typically Complex Phrases found in most songs, although these a bit higher and more Expanded than usual

Clearer 2-Element slurs in lower 2nd Section

Mourning (first 3), MacGillivray's (last 2) These waveform snapshots highlight the quality difference between many MacGillivray's and Mourning songs.

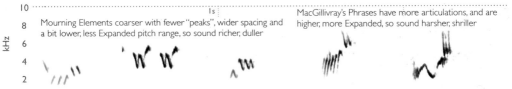

Mourning Elements coarser with fewer "peaks", wider spacing and a bit lower, less Expanded pitch range, so sound richer, duller

MacGillivray's Phrases have more articulations, and are higher, more Expanded, so sound harsher, shriller

Black-throated Gray A1 Buzzy Phrases, **but** shorter 2nd Sections (avg. 1 Phrase in 2nd and subsequent Sections vs. MacGillivray's avg. 2.5 Phrases for Sections 2 and 3).

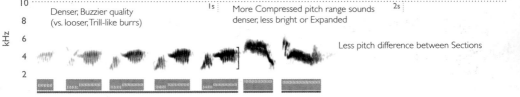

Denser, Buzzier quality (vs. looser, Trill-like burrs)

More Compressed pitch range sounds denser, less bright or Expanded

Less pitch difference between Sections

Townsend's A2 Burry/Buzzy mixed with Clear qualities, **but** most songs have Sections with mainly Clear Elements, unlike any MacGillivray's.

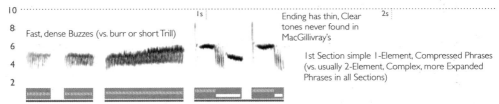

Fast, dense Buzzes (vs. burr or short Trill)

Ending has thin, Clear tones never found in MacGillivray's

1st Section simple 1-Element, Compressed Phrases (vs. usually 2-Element, Complex, more Expanded Phrases in all Sections)

MACGILLIVRAY'S

Geothlypis tolmiei   Drab Birds - All Seasons

- Broad, short, white eye-arcs in all plumages
- Gray to olive-brown hood
- Bright yellow belly and UnTC
- Long pale legs and base to bill

- Broad, short, white eye-arcs
- Bright yellow belly and UnTC
- Gray to olive-brown hood
- Medium-length dark tail

Distinctive Views

 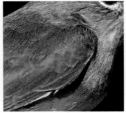  

Additional Photos

~ulky but easier to see than Mourn-
~g; more readily pished and often
~igrates through more open habitat

Generally low or on the ground

Throat may be pale but never has yellow tones found in Mourning; hood
always complete

~ead is slightly more rounded and tail
~onger than Mourning

Similar to Mourning but found in West (limited range overlap outside wintering
grounds)

~te variation in brightness of hood
~d body (but always hooded); paler
~oats lack any yellow tones

~abber plumages usually have pale
~raloral area; useful in separating
~m Connecticut

Eye-arcs always present; usually wider
than eyerings of Mourning

Mourning with eyerings resembling arcs
usually thinner and complete at least at
rear; note the yellowish tones in throat
of this Mourning; lighter lores also
more likely to be yellowish

Broad, white eye-arcs
Gray or brown-olive hood
Plain yellow below, UnTC
Long tail, short UnTC
Chip call good ID point
Large, often close to ground

Comparison Species

Common Yellowthroat Smaller; lacks hood; has yellow throat; faint eyering (vs. eye-arcs); pale belly/grayish flanks (vs. bright yellow); longer tail

Orange-crowned Overall, less contrast: paler yellow below, less dark olive above; usually diffuse streaking below; shorter legs and smaller, finer b more active and not terrestrial; stronge eyeline and supercilium; longer, thinner tail

Mourning 1yF Some very similar; may be impossible to separate without vocalizations, but in general: yellow tones in throat (vs. almost never); sometimes broken breast band (vs. always complete hood); sometimes complete eyering (vs. always eye-arcs); eye-arcs, when present, narrower and usually complete at rear of eye (vs. wide, broken); shorter tail projection beyond UnTC

Connecticut Rarely overlaps rang walks (vs. hops); complete or almost complete eyering (vs. eye-arcs); larger shorter tail, longer UnTC

MAGNOLIA

Setophaga magnolia   Bright Birds

- Bright yellow underparts and throat
- ✓ Strong black streaking attached to black neck band
- Black face mask with white supercilium and white under-eye arc
- Small bill
- Broad white wing patch
- Black in back with yellow rump

- ✓ Unique tail pattern—black tail with broad white base
- Contrasting white UnTC and lower belly
- ✓ Strong black streaking attached to black neck band

- ✓ Unique tail pattern—black tail with broad white base
- Contrasting white lower belly/ UnTC

Distinctive Views

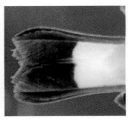

Additional Photos

Adult males have a black back and may show black flecking in the cap

One of three warblers that have a bright yellow rump (along with Yellow-rumped and Cape May)

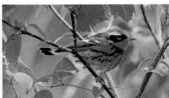

Heavy black necklace that extends down sides (unlike Canada)

Moderately active, usually in low to mid-story

Tail pattern is unique and diagnostic

Often spreads tail

Some birds show more limited black in back

Adult females and 1y males show less black in the back, more olive, fainter face pattern and less streaking

Very contrasty bird

Often spreads tail, showing white tail spots very high in tail, which is diagnostic

During migration it is versatile, foraging in many habitats

Bright yellow throat, underparts
White vent, UnTC
White tail/black terminal band
Black necklace/streaking
Black mask/white post-ocular
Wide white wing bars or panel

Comparison Species

Canada No side streaking; different facial pattern including full eyering and yellow lores; lacks supercilium/wing bars; black necklace is denser and doesn't extend as far down body; all-dark tail (vs. white with black tip)

Kirtland's Streaked back and flanks; no necklace or white wing patch; eye-arcs (vs. eyering); much larger overall including larger bill; frequently pumps tail (vs. never)

Prairie No black mask or white supercilium; orangier yellow overall; rufous back patch; neck band is broken in middle of breast; (vs. complete); yellow wing bars (vs. white); frequent tail pumper (vs. never); yellow may extend into UnTC; all-white tail (vs. black tip)

Townsend's No range overlap; mor[e] yellow, less black in face including behind eye; black throat (vs. yellow); olive above (vs. gray/black); more back/wing contrast; yellow below less extensive; all-white tail (vs. black terminal band)

Yellow-rumped White throat (vs. yellow); yellow shoulder patches; heavier bill; black "U" on white underparts (vs. yellow); lacks black tip to tail

Aging and Sexing

Spring AdM 1yM AdF 1yF   **Fall** AdM 1yM AdF 1yF

Races: 1 Summary *Spring/Fall:* One of the most complicated and challenging birds to age/sex, even for experienced banders; very drab and bright birds may be sexed, most should not be aged   **What to Notice** *Spring/Fall:* Black in back and uppertail coverts, extent of black in face, wing panel vs. bars, intensity of streaking

AdM/1yM Sp Extensive black in back, auriculars and forehead, white wing panel, gray crown, bold black side streaking, dark uppertail coverts; some 1yM show reduced black in back, others similar to AdM; *Diagnostic AdM:* solid black back combined with full wing panel and all black uppertail coverts.

1yM/AdF Sp AdF auriculars not solid black, and usually less black, more olive on back, average less black in uppertail coverts than most males; usually duller than male with duller side streaking; wing bars (vs. wing panel), but some AdF not separable from males.

1yF Sp Extreme Plain gray face, white eyering; *Diagnostic 1y:* brown/worn primary coverts and alula.

AdM Fa Extreme Similar to spring AdM but somewhat duller, strong side streaks, black spots on back, usually retains black in face; *Diagnostic when present:* all-black uppertail coverts combined with bold wing bars, black in face.

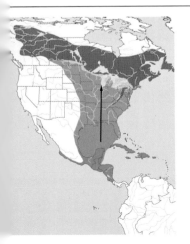

All Birds Fa Some flank streaking, dull with gray breast band, gray face.

1yF Fa Extreme Very dull, with little or no streaking on upperparts and flanks (extreme birds may be separated).

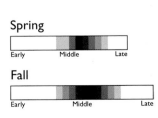

Spring

Early	Middle	Late

Fall

Early	Middle	Late

Magnolia

Magnolia flower sweet smelling, reaches peak after only 2 days, then falls

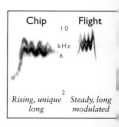

Chip   Flight

Rising, unique   Steady, long
long   modulated

Summary Usually *very short* (good ID point), with simple, Clear slurred Phrases. 1st Section 2 or 3 2-Element Phrases; *Sections 2–4 only 1 Phrase each.* **2 Types:** **A,** Last 2 Sections accented, higher; *accented, short up/down ending* at same speed or a bit slower than prior Phrases; **B,** Often longer; ending slurs usually a bit lower, simpler, less emphatic.

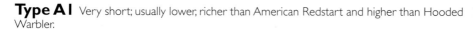

Type A1 Very short; usually lower, richer than American Redstart and higher than Hooded Warbler.

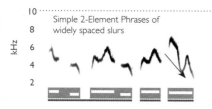

Simple 2-Element Phrases of widely spaced slurs

Last 2 Sections more accented single Phrases, upslur then downslur; speed not rushed, about same as previous Elements

Many similar species, like Yellow, Chestnut-sided, have contrasting 2nd Sections with 2 or more Phrases then accented ending Section; Magnolia 2nd and following Sections only 1 Phrase each

Type A2 A bit longer 1st Section; still very short.

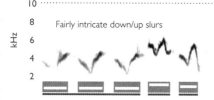

Fairly intricate down/up slurs

Ending Phrases Compressed and only 1 Phrase/Section; speed not rushed, about same as previous Elements

Type B Slightly longer, less-accented song; still very short; may be more difficult to recognize, **but** shortness and 1-Phrase Sections help separate from similar species. Most unaccented Chestnut-sided or Yellow songs much longer with many more Phrases.

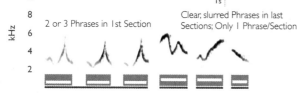

2 or 3 Phrases in 1st Section

Clear, slurred Phrases in last Sections; Only 1 Phrase/Section

All Phrases somewhat Compressed; relatively low

American Redstart A1
Most likely to be confused and sometimes difficult to separate. Never sings 4-Section songs (30% for Magnolia); usually higher, thinner (avg. 3.5–8.5 kHz vs. 3.1–5.6); often alternates with 1-Section songs (vs. never sings 1-Section songs).

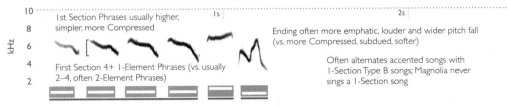

1st Section Phrases usually higher, simpler, more Compressed

Ending often more emphatic, louder and wider pitch fall (vs. more Compressed, subdued, softer)

First Section 4+ 1-Element Phrases (vs. usually 2–4, often 2-Element Phrases)

Often alternates accented songs with 1-Section Type B songs; Magnolia never sings a 1-Section song

Hooded A1
Similar shape, **but** all songs 3+, sometimes 5 or 6, Sections (many Magnolia have 2 Sections, never 5 or 6); lower with purer, stronger tone. Overall lower, slower, slurred song with faster emphatic ending (vs. higher, thinner, faster but more even overall).

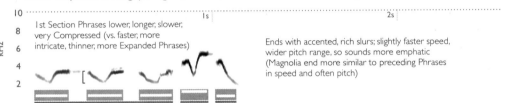

1st Section Phrases lower, longer, slower, very Compressed (vs. faster, more intricate, thinner, more Expanded Phrases)

Ends with accented, rich slurs; slightly faster speed, wider pitch range, so sounds more emphatic (Magnolia end more similar to preceding Phrases in speed and often pitch)

Chestnut-sided A1
Similar structure: repeated Phrases in 1st Section and downslurred, accented ending, **but** length noticeably longer (avg. 1.5 sec. vs. 0.9); always 2+ Phrases in 2nd Section and usually 2+ in subsequent Sections (vs. always only 1 Phrase each in 2nd, 3rd Sections).

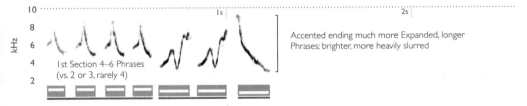

1st Section 4–6 Phrases (vs. 2 or 3, rarely 4)

Accented ending much more Expanded, longer Phrases; brighter, more heavily slurred

Yellow A1
Longer songs, with more Phrases; very Expanded, emphatic slurs; much wider pitch range between Sections.

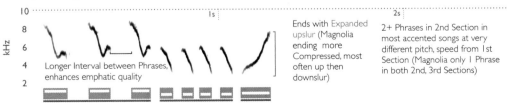

Longer Interval between Phrases, enhances emphatic quality

Ends with Expanded upslur (Magnolia ending more Compressed, most often up then downslur)

2+ Phrases in 2nd Section in most accented songs at very different pitch, speed from 1st Section (Magnolia only 1 Phrase in both 2nd, 3rd Sections)

MAGNOLIA
Setophaga magnolia   Drab Birds

- Yellow rump, underparts, and throat
- ✓ Pale gray neck band on bright yellow throat/breast
- Small-billed
- Eyering on gray face
- Variable diffuse flank streaking doesn't extend into throat
- Two wing bars rather than a patch
- Spreads tail but doesn't pump it

- Variable diffuse breast streaking doesn't extend into throat
- Yellow underparts with white lower belly and UnTC
- ✓ Unique tail pattern—black tail with broad white base

- ✓ Unique tail pattern—black tail with broad white base
- Small billed
- Yellow underside with white belly and UnTC

Distinctive Views

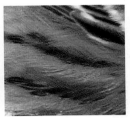

Additional Photos

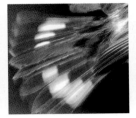

Bright yellow rump but different shape/tone than Yellow-rumped

Pale gray neck band is diagnostic

ail pattern is dramatic and diagnostic

Frequently fans dark tail: very high white tail spots diagnostic

Streaking may be indistinct and faint

ctive feeder, often at low and medium eight

Black tail with broad white base diagnostic

treaking can be very diffuse but is most always present

Widely variable plumage so difficult to age/sex

Streaking may be broken or more complete

Bright yellow throat, underparts
White vent, UnTC
Gray neck band
White tail/black terminal band
Variable, diffuse flank streaking
Contrasting white wing bars
Gray head, olive back

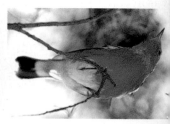

Comparison Species

Canada Lacks wing bars; lacks olive in back; yellow loral area; gray streaking in neck (vs. flanks); thicker bill; more extensive yellow in underparts; all-dark tail (vs. white with black tip)

Prairie Diffuse under-eye arc (vs. eyering); lacks yellow rump; yellow jaw stripe; wing bars yellowish and diffuse; lacks gray neck band; more extensive yellow in underparts; white tail lacks large black terminal band

Kirtland's Extremely restricted range and rarely seen in migration; larger size and bill; paler yellow in underparts; bobs tail habitually (vs. never); darker back without clear white wing bars; white tail spots without large black terminal band

Northern Parula Lacks side streaking; shorter white tail lacks black tail band; more limited yellow in breast; bicolored bill

Nashville Smaller and more active; lacks wing bars; greener back contrasts with blue-gray head; finer bill, pale vent contrasts with yellow underparts; yellow UnTC and all-dark tail (vs. white with black tip); lacks streaking

MOURNING

Geothlypis philadelphia   Bright Birds

- Large, skulking, ground-dwelling bird
- Lacks bold white eyering
- Bluish-gray hood
- Variable dark patch on breast and black in lores
- Plain olive uppers with bright yellow underparts

- Variable dark patch on breast
- Bright yellow undersides
- Short tail with long UnTC
- Pale legs and bill
- All-dark face with varying dark in lores; rarely thin white eyering

- Bright yellow underside
- Short tail with long UnTC
- Pale legs and bill

Distinctive Views

Additional Photos

This bird lacks dark lores, which is diagnostic vs. bright Macgillivray's

Mourning hops more than Connecticut, which walks

Found low or on the ground, often stalking through dense underbrush

Gray hood contrasts with olive back

A typical view of a Mourning warbler

Slightly smaller and slimmer-looking than Connecticut Warbler

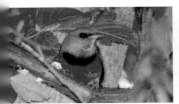

Adult males show variable strong black breast mark in the spring

Tail and UnTC length is a good separator from Macgillivray's

May show dusky lores

Calls fairly often; vocalizations are best way to distinguish from MacGillivray's

Males will often start singing from low in the vegetation and work their way higher before diving back into the undergrowth

In typical fast glimpse, they appear very bright, especially the yellow below

Bright yellow below
Bluish-gray hood
Often black breast band
Plain olive above
Short dark tail, long UnTC
Large, often near ground

Comparison Species

Connecticut Slightly bulkier and more thrush-like; walks, doesn't hop; bold eyering (vs. rarely has eyering but thinner, less distinct); less black in throat; shorter tail extension; somewhat duller yellow; generally less vocal

MacGillivray's Thick white eye-arcs (vs. none, or rarely thinner, less distinct, usually more complete); bolder black lores that join over bill (vs. usually thinner, never joined; sometimes no black, which is diagnostic for Mourning); longer tail extension; distinctive chip call; less concentrated black in breast

Nashville Smaller and more active in low canopy (vs. often on ground); distinct yellow throat (vs. hooded); complete, clear eyering (vs. rarely present, thinner); finer bill; pale vent contrasts with undersides (vs. uniform yellow); thinner, proportionally longer tail, often pumped

Aging and Sexing

Spring AdM 1yM AdF 1yF   **Fall** AdM 1yM AdF 1yF

Races: 1 Summary *Spring:* Sexable, some first-year birds ageable *Fall:* Adult male separable, others clinal and not easily separated **What to Notice** *Spring/Fall:* Overall contrast, black in chest, brown in upperparts, faint eyering

AdM/1yM Sp Generally no eyering; *Diagnostic male:* slate-gray hood, upper breast mottled black; *Diagnostic when present 1yM:* slightly duller/browner on upperparts and narrow, faint, broken eyering.

AdF/1yF Sp Duller than males, paler hood, some show narrow, broken, whitish eyering; *Diagnostic female:* no black feathering, throat may be pale; *Diagnostic when present 1yF:* near-complete narrow eyering.

AdM Fa Similar to spring male, sometimes with brownish wash.

AdF/1yM/1yF Fa All duller than AdM, hood brownish, throat paler at center, faint partial eyering; plumages generally clinal and not safely separated; *Diagnostic when present 1yM:* veiled black in throat.

1yM Fa *Diagnostic when present:* veiled black in throat.

1yF Fa Extreme Brownest and dullest plumage, with palest, yellowish throat; only drabbest birds should be separated.

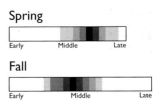

Spring

Early   Middle   Late

Fall

Early   Middle   Late

Mourning
When in mourning, you try to look up, but then you must look down—rough

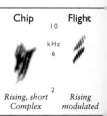

Chip   Flight

Rising, short Complex   Rising modulated

Summary *Rich, low, Complex (often burry) Phrases* in 1–3 Sections, 2nd or 3rd Section often has some or all Clear Elements; combination of *low, burry Phrases and Clearer Sections diagnostic in East*; **3 Types: A,** 1st Section Phrases always 2-Element, usually rise from Element to Element; 2nd Section usually lower, falling 2-Element Phrases; 2nd Section Phrases often Clearer, less Complex; **B,** Simple 1-Section; **C,** More variable, with variable pitch profiles; 2 or 3 Sections, 2nd Section higher.

Type A1   2 Sections, 2nd Section faster, lower.

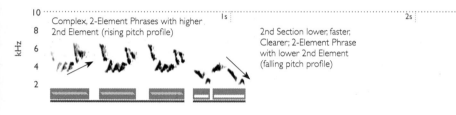

Complex, 2-Element Phrases with higher 2nd Element (rising pitch profile)

2nd Section lower, faster, Clearer; 2-Element Phrase with lower 2nd Element (falling pitch profile)

Type A2   Mourning Elements usually Complex but more likely to have Clear Section than MacGillivray's.

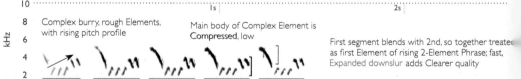

Rising 2-Element Phrases with only some burry quality

Lower, slightly faster 2nd Section, with Clear Phrases

Type B   1-Section song; may be more common in western part of range.

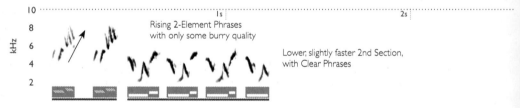

Complex burry, rough Elements, with rising pitch profile

Main body of Complex Element is **Compressed,** low

First segment blends with 2nd, so together treated as first Element of rising 2-Element Phrase; fast, Expanded downslur adds Clearer quality

Type C   3-Section song with variable pitch profile.

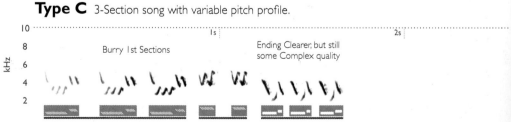

Burry 1st Sections

Ending Clearer, but still some Complex quality

Kentucky A1 1 Section (vs. most Mourning 2 or 3); 1-Section Mourning lower, richer, with Clear slurred "attack" and then more emphasis in lowest, Compressed part of Phrase.

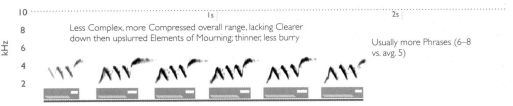

Less Complex, more Compressed overall range, lacking Clearer down then upslurred Elements of Mourning; thinner, less burry

Usually more Phrases (6–8 vs. avg. 5)

MacGillivray's B1 Very similar in form, quality, **but** tend to have longer, slower 2nd Sections with more Phrases; rarely sings 1-Section songs (may be common for Mourning in western part of range); usually lacks Clear Elements (vs. 60% of Mourning 2- or 3-Section songs Clear in 1 Section); higher, more Expanded (avg. 3–7 kHz vs. 2.3–5.8 kHz). Chip calls diagnostic and both species can be fairly vocal.

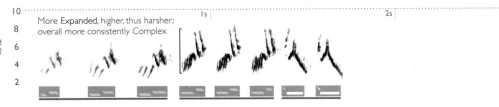

More Expanded, higher, thus harsher; overall more consistently Complex

Mourning (first 3) vs. MacGillivray's (last 2) These waveform snapshots help highlight the quality difference between many MacGillivray's and Mourning songs.

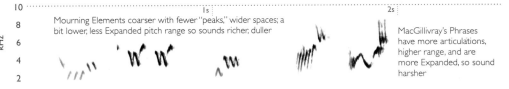

Mourning Elements coarser with fewer "peaks," wider spaces; a bit lower, less Expanded pitch range so sounds richer, duller

MacGillivray's Phrases have more articulations, higher range, and are more Expanded, so sound harsher

Carolina Wren / Common Yellowthroat Similar habitats, and repeated, usually 3-Element Phrases could be confused with 1-Section Mourning songs from a distance, **but** neither sings 2- or 3-Section songs (common for Mourning); both have simpler, Clear, slurred Elements (never Complex).

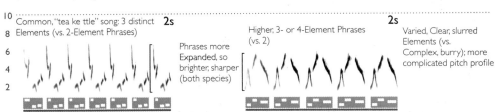

Common, "tea ke ttle" song: 3 distinct Elements (vs. 2-Element Phrases)

Phrases more Expanded, so brighter, sharper (both species)

Higher, 3- or 4-Element Phrases (vs. 2)

Varied, Clear, slurred Elements (vs. Complex, burry); more complicated pitch profile

MOURNING

Geothlypis philadelphia   Drab Birds

- Often thin, nearly complete eyering
- Drab olive above, bright yellow below
- Supraloral area paler or yellowish

- Bright yellow underside
- Medium tail projection past UnTC
- Hood varies from gray to almost blended with back in first-year females
- Thin eyering, usually complete at least at one end
- Yellow from breast sometimes continues into paler throat

Distinctive Views

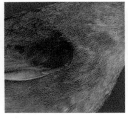

Additional Photos

ow ground feeders; Mournings hop
ather than walk/amble like a
Connecticut

Found low or on the ground, often
stalking through dense underbrush

A typical view of a Mourning warbler

lightly smaller and slimmer-looking
than Connecticut Warbler

Tail and UnTC length is a good separator from MacGillivray's

Skulky like Common Yellowthroat, but
note the bright yellow flanks and
underparts, larger size

omewhat flattened head shape

ompared to Common Yellowthroat,
ote larger size, bright yellow flanks

Blue-gray hood sometimes
broken in front
Thin, nearly complete eyering
Plain, fairly bright yellow below
Short tail
Large, often near ground

Comparison Species

Common Yellowthroat More active and not as ground-dwelling; not hooded, with contrasting, bright yellow throat; white belly and grayish flanks (vs. even yellow); longer tail

Nashville Smaller and more active; distinct yellow throat; finer bill; pale ven contrasts with undersides (vs. even yellow); proportionally longer, thinner tail often wagged; brighter eyering

MacGillivray's 1yF Some can be very similar and may be impossible to separate without using distinctive vocalizations; always have wide and short eye-arcs (vs. eyering); Mourning eyerings are thinner and usually complete at least at rear (can be hard to see, but width of MacGillivray's eye-arcs usually more obvious); always hooded (vs. sometimes broken throat band); throat usually whitish-gray with no yellow (vs. often yellow); longer tail extension past UnTC

Orange-crowned Smaller, more active, rarely on ground; overall drabbe smaller and finer-billed; faint eye-line (v eyering); shorter, thinner legs; proportionally longer, thinner tail; drabber underparts

MacGillivray's (left) Always show hood, while Mourning (right) may show yellow breast intruding into throat

Connecticut Bulkier and more thrush-like; walking gait; unbroken hoo throat not yellow; shorter tail extensio larger and longer-billed; paler yellow underparts; never pale supraloral (vs. sometimes)

NASHVILLE

Oreothlypis ruficapilla   Male/Female - All Seasons

- Small and compact with fine sharp bill
- Olive-green back contrasts with blue-gray head
- Bright white eyering
- Yellow throat
- May show chestnut crown patch
- No wing bars, yellow-olive edges to flight feathers

- Small and compact with fine, sharp bill
- Yellow UnTC, belly, and throat with contrasting pale vent
- Dark, thin tail
- Bright white eyering

- Small and compact with fine, sharp bill
- Yellow UnTC, belly, and throat with contrasting pale vent
- Dark, thin tail

Distinctive Views

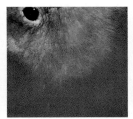

Additional Photos

small, with a large, rounded head and narrow tail, bright eyering

Notice pale area in vent/feet area; rufous crown patch

Often flips tail

some birds show a rufous crown patch, which is usually hidden

A small bird; compare with the Yellow-rumped behind it

In flight, note yellow body, hooded appearance, and eyering; also small size and fluttery flight style

active and quick foragers, they are often found in low to mid-level habitat

From behind may appear hooded, but throat is always yellow

Yellow continuous from throat onto body, not as sharply restricted as Common Yellowthroat; malar more blended, less contrasty

mount of white in the belly varies; ote the yellow UnTC and short, narrow, dark tail

Yellow in body and white in belly is variable; throat is often paler than upper breast; western birds average whiter in vent area/brighter in rump

Olive rump and back, with a gray or blue hood; rump a bit brighter, especially in Western birds

Small, fine bill
Striking eyering
Yellow throat, underparts
White in vent
Dark, thin tail
Gray head contrasts green back
Greenish-edged flight feathers

Comparison Species

Mourning, MacGillivray's, Connecticut 1yF Much larger with larger bill; usually no or much less yellow on throat; less flitty, active; pale legs (vs. darker); wider, proportionally shorter tail; lack white vent; only Connecticut has bright contrasty eyering

Yellow 1yF Larger, with heavier bill; pale yellow edging on wing coverts; uniform yellow to olive-toned upperparts (vs. head/back contrast); yellow in tail (vs. dark); shorter, wider tail; lacks white eyering

Orange-crowned Supercilium, eyeline, split eyering, so face usually more complex; lower contrast and duller tones overall; lacks bright eyering

Wilson's Yellow face (vs. blue-gray); most show black cap (vs. none); more uniform above; lacks greenish wing edgings, contrasting white vent; longer tail; lacks bright eyering

Common Yellowthroat Larger bill; more wren-like/skulking behavior; less pronounced eyering; browner above; lacks head/body contrast; lacks greenish flight feather edging; dull flanks (vs. yellow); yellow throat more isolated and contrasts more strongly with dark cheek; longer, wider tail

Virginia's Uniform, gray upperparts lacking head/back contrast; no green edging on flight feathers; less, more-restricted yellow below; longer tail

Aging and Sexing

Spring AdM 1yM AdF 1yF **Fall** AdM 1yM AdF 1yF

Races: 2 (*O.r. ruficapilla* in east, duller with less white in belly; *O.r. ridgwayi* in west) **Summary** *Spring/Fall:* Sex and age differences clinal; all but extremely bright and dull birds not separable **What to Notice** *Spring/Fall:* Overall contrast, brightness of underparts, extensive crown patch

AdM Sp Extreme High contrast between blue-gray head and green back, bright yellow underparts, extensive rufous crown patch (often hidden) may be AdM.

All Others Sp Lower contrast between head/back, duller yellow underneath, reduced crown patch (but often hidden).

1yF Sp Extreme Very dull, washed with brownish, with pale underparts and whitish throat may be 1yF.

O.r. ridgwayi (west) Averages brighter yellow-green rump, more white in vent; note that qualities are average and not necessarily separable from *O.r. ruficapilla.*

All Birds Fa Similar to spring; *Diagnostic when present male:* obvious crown patch is male, probably adult, but patch often hidden.

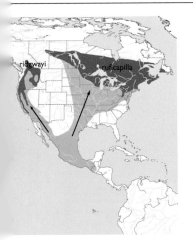

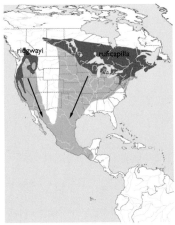

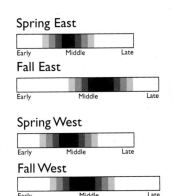

Spring East

Early · Middle · Late

Fall East

Early · Middle · Late

Spring West

Early · Middle · Late

Fall West

Early · Middle · Late

Nashville

Take 2 trains to Nash- ville, one elevated and slow, the second low and fast

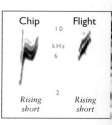

Chip   Flight

10
kHz
6

2

Rising   Rising
short   short

Summary Consistent, simple format; 6–9 *2-Element, Clear emphatic falling-pitch Phrases*, followed by *lower, faster Section*. Elements long enough to still sound like slurs, but long Intervals create emphatic, distinct quality. **3 Types: A**, Slurred 2-Element Phrases in 1st Section; 2nd Section lower, 1-Element Phrases, about twice as fast as 1st, often slow Trill; **B**, Western form: shorter ending, more slurred quality; **C**, Lacks 2nd Section.

Type A1 Most common Type with 2 Sections.

3.1

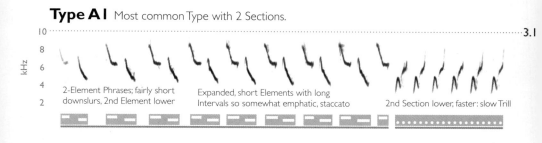

kHz 10 8 6 4 2

2-Element Phrases; fairly short downslurs, 2nd Element lower

Expanded, short Elements with long Intervals so somewhat emphatic, staccato

2nd Section lower, faster: slow Trill

Type A2 Simpler, less common version. 1-Element Phrases in 1st Section, rather than more common 2-Element Phrases.

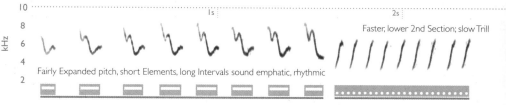

kHz 10 8 6 4 2

1s   2s

Faster, lower 2nd Section; slow Trill

Fairly Expanded pitch, short Elements, long Intervals sound emphatic, rhythmic

Type A3 Typical structure including 2-Element Phrases in 1st Section, and lower 2nd Section, but shorter, less contrastingly low ending; 1st section has uncommon rising-pitch Phrases.

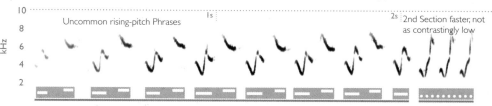

kHz 10 8 6 4 2

1s   2s

Uncommon rising-pitch Phrases

2nd Section faster, not as contrastingly low

Type B1 Western songs can be somewhat different from eastern songs, **but** same form (1st Section with 2-Element Phrases and lower, faster 2nd Section).

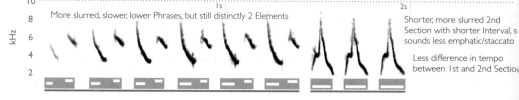

kHz 10 8 6 4 2

1s   2s

More slurred, slower, lower Phrases, but still distinctly 2 Elements

Shorter, more slurred 2nd Section with shorter Interval, s sounds less emphatic/staccato

Less difference in tempo between 1st and 2nd Sectio

Wilson's B3 Similar form of repeated Phrases in two Sections, the 2nd lower, faster, **but** often sings 1-Section songs (Nashville rarely sings isolated 1st Sections, but usually sings 2-Section song eventually).

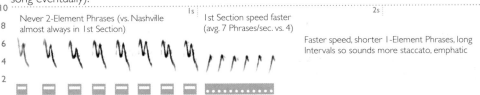

Never 2-Element Phrases (vs. Nashville almost always in 1st Section)

1st Section speed faster (avg. 7 Phrases/sec. vs. 4)

Faster speed, shorter 1-Element Phrases, long Intervals so sounds more staccato, emphatic

Virginia's A2 Virginia's usually more complicated with 3 or 4 Sections, **but** some songs very similar. Slower, slurred 1st Section Elements with shorter Intervals sound more smeared/ slurred together, making 2-Element quality harder to hear (vs. staccato, emphatic, rhythmic Nashville Elements); 2nd Section slower, never Trilled, similar to 1st Section (avg. 6 Phrases/sec. vs. 9).

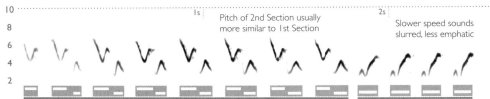

Pitch of 2nd Section usually more similar to 1st Section

Slower speed sounds slurred, less emphatic

Cape May B1/Black-and-white A1/American Redstart (excerpts) Most Nashville are 2 Sections with strong pitch, speed differences (easy to separate); sometimes sings only 1st Section which could be confused, **but** almost always eventually sings full song.

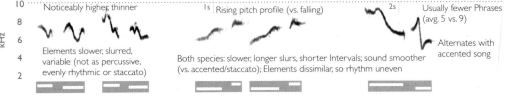

Noticeably higher, thinner

Rising pitch profile (vs. falling)

Usually fewer Phrases (avg. 5 vs. 9)

Elements slower, slurred, variable (not as percussive, evenly rhythmic or staccato)

Both species: slower, longer slurs, shorter Intervals; sound smoother (vs. accented/staccato); Elements dissimilar, so rhythm uneven

Alternates with accented song

Tennessee A1 Similar structure, **but** almost all songs 3 Sections (vs. 2 Sections); more Expanded, much shorter Elements with longer Intervals sound obviously brighter, more emphatic, percussive, staccato; little pitch change between Sections (vs. markedly lower 2nd Section).

3.7s

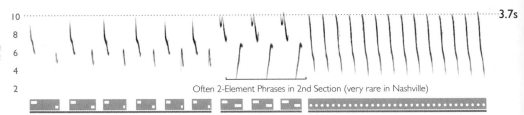

Often 2-Element Phrases in 2nd Section (very rare in Nashville)

NORTHERN PARULA

Setophaga americana   Male/Female - All Seasons

- Very small and active
- Blue back and yellow throat/breast
- ✓ Green back patch surrounded by blue
- Variable amount of orange and black in breast
- Broken eye-arcs, black lores
- White wing bars

- Appears short tailed from below
- Yellow throat/upper breast blends into bright yellow lower mandible
- Variable amount of orange and black in breast
- ✓ Black and orange breast band on yellow diagnostic when present

- Short tail with white tail spots and white UnTC
- Yellow throat/breast blending into yellow lower mandible
- Variable amount of orange and black in breast
- ✓ Black and orange breast band on yellow diagnostic when present

Distinctive Views

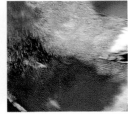

Additional Photos

emales have either a pure yellow
breast or yellow with some orangey
wash

Greenish-olive back patch surrounded
by blue diagnostic

Actobatic feeders, often hanging upside
down

rom below can look all white if yellow
pper breast is not visible; note short,
white tail

Wing bars often prominent

Male chest bands can be very striking
and are diagnostic

lay feed in mid- to high canopy, but in
igration often comes down to lower
vels

Breeding birds are often associated
with Old Man's Beard in the North
and with Spanish Moss in the South

Bill is brightly bicolored, unlike most
other warblers

east band varies from dark to non-
istent; note yellow is restricted to
ry high on breast

Bright yellow throat and breast blending with bright yellow lower bill diagnostic for parulas

Eye-arcs prominent on plain bluish face;
yellow lower mandible blends into
throat

Blue above/green mantle
Yellow throat/lower mandible
Often orange/dark breast band
White below including UnTC
Short white tail
White wing bars
White eye-arcs

Comparison Species

Canada Slate blue upperparts (vs. powder blue), lacking green back patch; complete eyering (vs. eye-arcs); yellow supraloral (vs. black); lacks wing bars; necklace (vs. colored breast bands); yellow much more extensive (vs. white belly, lower breast); longer, dark tail (vs. shorter, with white tail spots)

Tropical Parula Lacks eye-arcs; diffuse orange wash on breast (vs. ofter dark or orange-banded); more extensive yellow extends past wing bars (vs. ends before); straighter boundary to throat; more black below and behind eye

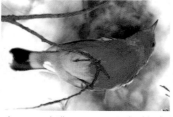

Magnolia Complete eyering (vs. eye-arcs); gray and olive upperparts (vs. blue); more yellow in underparts (vs. white belly/lower breast); black flank streaking (vs. none); longer, white tail with large black terminal band

Pine Much larger, larger bill; much longer tail; some diffuse streaking (vs. none)

Nashville Lacks wing bars; complete eyering (vs. eye-arcs); blue-gray hood contrasts with green back (vs. all blue); all-yellow underparts with contrasting pale vent; small, fine, dark bill; yellow UnTC (vs. white); longer, all-dark tail (vs. some white)

Aging and Sexing

Spring AdM 1yM AdF 1yF   **Fall** AdM 1yM AdF 1yF

Races: 1 Summary *Spring/Fall:* Sexable, some first-year birds, some fall AdF ageable using subtle marks   **What to Notice** *Spring/Fall:* Breast bands, lore color, overall contrast, green in hood, green edging on flight feathers

AdM/1yM Sp Contrasty blue upperparts, distinct green back patch, bright eye-arcs, black lores; *Diagnostic male:* variable chest band with chestnut and black; *Diagnostic when present 1yM:* brown alula and primary coverts, and green-edged flight feathers (vs. blue).

AdF/1yF Sp Duller than male, less contrasting back patch, gray lores, green-tinged crown; *Diagnostic female:* no breast bands (unless faint trace of chestnut); *Diagnostic when present 1yF:* brown alula and primary coverts, and green-edged flight feathers (vs. blue).

AdM Fa Similar to spring male, slightly duller with green wash on crown and neck, no black in lores, chest bands duller.

1yM Fa More green wash than AdM; *Diagnostic 1y:* Primaries, secondaries, alula, and primary coverts edged green (vs. blue in AdM).

AdF Fa Similar to spring female but duller, blue-edged flight feathers (vs. green in 1y); *Diagnostic when present adult:* orange wash in yellow throat.

1yF Fa *Diagnostic when combined:* strongly washed green on upperparts, with no hint of color bands in breast, green-edged wing bars and secondaries, and less distinct back patch.

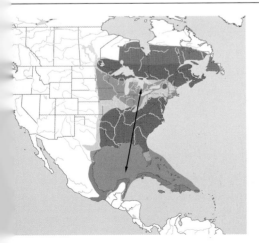

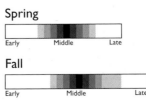

Spring

Early   Middle   Late

Fall

Early   Middle   Late

Northern Parula

Parula is a jeweler, her rough necklaces rise up and snap at the top

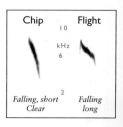

Chip	Flight
Falling, short Clear	Falling long

10 kHz 6 2

Summary Unique profile easy to ID: *long rising Trill ending in short, Clear up/down slur.* No other species sings such a *long, rising Buzz or Trill.* Trill can be pulsed or broken into 2 Sections with Trilled or less often Buzzy Phrases. Western birds can have different, short Buzzy rising ending, but still unique. **3 Types: A,** 2-Section, smooth rising Trill with fast up/down accented slur at end; **B,** 3-Section, Complex, modulated, broken Trill in 1st Section; **C,** Western with less emphatic Buzz at end.

Type A
Most common; 2-Sections, smooth rising Trill ending with fast, up/down accented slur; length and quality can vary: sometimes sounding Clearer (especially from distance) or looser.

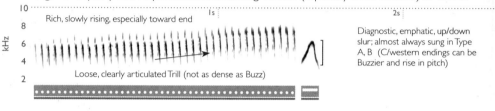

Rich, slowly rising, especially toward end

Loose, clearly articulated Trill (not as dense as Buzz)

Diagnostic, emphatic, up/down slur; almost always sung in Type A, B (C/western endings can be Buzzier and rise in pitch)

Type B1
3 Sections; broken or pulsating Trill in 1st Section; ending diagnostic.

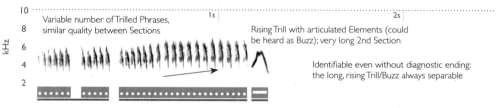

Pulsing, slurred, Complex Phrases

Diagnostic long collection of many fast, dense Buzzy Phrases, rising in pitch. No other warbler has Section like this within a multi-Section song

Typical, diagnostic fast up/down slur (occasionally omitted)

Type B2
Multiple Trilled Sections (unlike Type A 1-Section Trill); form is variable; sometimes alternated with Type A songs.

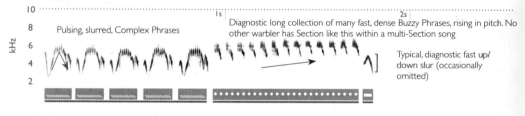

Variable number of Trilled Phrases, similar quality between Sections

Rising Trill with articulated Elements (could be heard as Buzz); very long 2nd Section

Identifiable even without diagnostic ending: the long, rising Trill/Buzz always separable

Type C
Sung by birds nesting in western part of range.

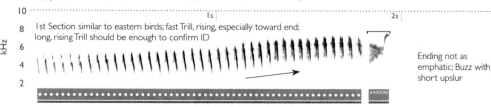

1st Section similar to eastern birds; fast Trill, rising, especially toward end; long, rising Trill should be enough to confirm ID

Ending not as emphatic; Buzz with short upslur

Cerulean A1 vs. B
N. Parula Type A songs easy to separate, Type B more similar; Cerulean has rising pitch between Sections **but** steady within Sections (vs. rising pitch profile within at least 2nd Section, often 1st and 2nd).

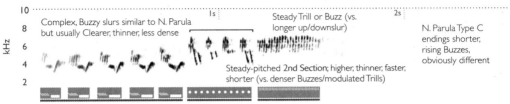

Complex, Buzzy slurs similar to N. Parula but usually Clearer, thinner, less dense

Steady Trill or Buzz (vs. longer up/downslur)

N. Parula Type C endings shorter, rising Buzzes, obviously different

Steady-pitched 2nd Section; higher, thinner, faster, shorter (vs. denser Buzzes/modulated Trills)

Blackburnian A1 vs. B
Pulsing Trills, **but** always lacks accented, up/down ending slur (usually in N. Parula), 1st Section Phrases shorter, more articulated with longer Intervals (7 or 8 Phrases vs. 2–5).

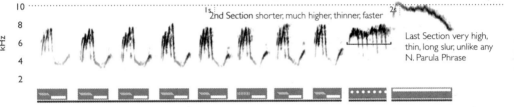

2nd Section shorter, much higher, thinner, faster

Last Section very high, thin, long slur, unlike any N. Parula Phrase

Black-throated Blue A3 vs. B
Buzzy quality, Phrases rise in pitch (vs. 1st and 2nd Sections much more Complex, faster, more intricate Phrases).

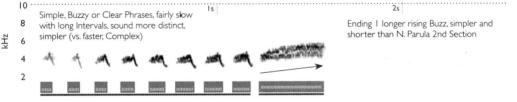

Simple, Buzzy or Clear Phrases, fairly slow with long Intervals, sound more distinct, simpler (vs. faster, Complex)

Ending 1 longer rising Buzz, simpler and shorter than N. Parula 2nd Section

Prairie A1 vs. B
Buzzy Phrases rise evenly and slowly throughout single Section (vs. more Complex Phrases, rhythmically uneven Sections); always lacks accented up/down N. Parula ending.

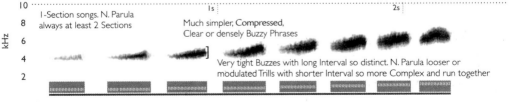

1-Section songs. N. Parula always at least 2 Sections

Much simpler, Compressed, Clear or densely Buzzy Phrases

Very tight Buzzes with long Interval so distinct. N. Parula looser or modulated Trills with shorter Interval so more Complex and run together

NORTHERN WATERTHRUSH

Parkesia noveboracensis   Male/Female - All Seasons

- Large, with large bill
- Uniform yellowish, buffy, or whitish below with dense brown streaking
- Chin usually finely streaked with dots
- Even buffy or white supercilium, usually narrowing behind eye
- Generally ground dwelling, walking slowly, moving tail up and down

- Yellowish, buffy, or whitish below with dense brown streaking
- Chin finely streaked with dots
- Even buffy or white supercilium
- Dull pink legs

- Well-defined brown streaking
- Streaking usually in lines and densest in upper breast
- Almost always some streaking or flecking on throat
- White or buffy UnTC with short brown tail
- Long bill, dull pink legs

Distinctive Views

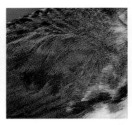

Additional Photos

Shorter bill and longer tail than Louisiana; color of supercilium even and same as that of underparts

Large, short tailed, and heavily streaked

Averages denser streaking than Louisiana, especially in the center of the breast, with streaks usually in the throat

supercilium always same tone as underparts

Usually shows overall yellow or buff wash, but some birds are white

Reading supercilium can be tricky—this one looks particularly long; use multiple ID points vs. Louisiana Waterthrush

often probes under leaves and branches

Eye stripe doesn't flare or wrap around back of head and is same color as breast; evenly colored throughout

Cline in plumage tone from gray-brown with white underparts to olive-brown with pale buff underparts

nds to prefer still waters

Usually walks on the ground but sometimes walks on tree branches

Up/down tail wagging walk is reminiscent of Spotted Sandpiper

Prominent. tapered supercilium
Densely streaked upper breast;
often extends into throat
Uniform white/buffy below
White or buffy supercilium
Short tail, long bill
Bobs tail up and down

Comparison Species

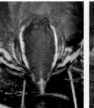

Louisiana Waterthrush Overall stouter shape, with larger bill/shorter tail; white supercilium (often buffy supraloral) flares behind eye and wraps more around head (vs. usually buffy, shorter); white underparts but often buffy on flanks (vs. more even tone); averages brighter pink legs; sparser, more broken side streaks, especially in center of breast; usually lacks streaking in throat (not diagnostic: some Northern show worn, unspotted throats; Louisiana can show limited throat spotting); averages less contrasty eyeline and streaking; prefers habitat with faster-moving water; tail movements tend to involve whole back end of body in slower, circular movements (not with Northern), but Louisiana can do up/down movements (similar to Northern)

Northern Waterthrush (right) Supercilium doesn't wrap as far around head and is often buffier and monocolored (vs. sometimes buffy at front)

Northern Waterthrush (right) shows more streaking in throat; often buffier color; denser, thinner, and less-broken streaking

Thrushes (Hermit shown) Spotting in breast (vs. streaking); eyering (vs. supercilium); quick, darting movements on ground with long, still pauses (vs. more leisurely walking); smaller billed; longer tailed

Ovenbird Rounder and fatter; white eyering (vs. supercilium); olive upperparts (vs. brown); orange crown stripe; distinctive "chicken walk": bobs head while walking; denser streaking, focused in upper chest; pure white throat (vs. usually streaks)

Palm Slimmer and smaller, smaller bi hopping (not walking); often in flocks; pumps tail but without moving lower body; rufous cap/breast streaking (vs. brown); yellow UnTC (vs. white); longe white tail/large black base

Aging and Sexing

Spring AdM 1yM AdF 1yF   **Fall** AdM 1yM AdF 1yF

Races: 2 (eastern *P.n. noveboracensis*; and western *P.n. notabilis*, which is grayer overall with whitish underparts and face)   **Summary** *Spring/Fall:* Not ageable or sexable

All Birds All plumages similar in all seasons.

White Adult Some birds are paler white with less buff; may be confused with Louisiana Waterthrush; white birds are not necessarily *notabilis* race.

P.n. notabilis Race Reportedly grayer overall, with whitish underparts and face; average differences, and not necessarily separable from *noveboracensis*.

Note Some first-year birds may show rusty fringing in tertials, which allows aging but not sexing. This mark is extremely subtle and may be only visible in the hand.

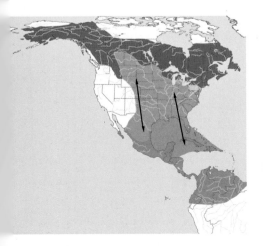

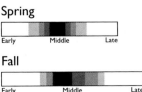

Spring

Early   Middle   Late

Fall

Early   Middle   Late

Northern Waterthrush

In the North, no slurring, just repetitive, energetic steps down to the water

Summary Very distinctive, *loud, strongly rhythmic Phrases*; 3 Sections (uncommonly 1-Phrase 4th Section); *speed increases, pitch steady within Sections but falls between Sections*; may begin softly, but by middle of 1st Section very emphatic until end; gives Chip call often; **I Type.**

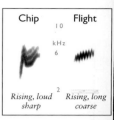

Chip   Flight

Rising, loud   Rising, long
sharp   coarse

Type A1 Speeds up and pitch falls between Sections; steady Pitch within Sections; almost always 2-Element Phrases in 1st Section.

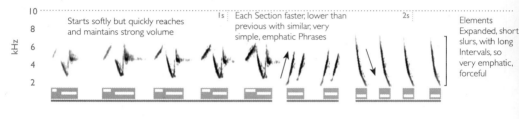

Starts softly but quickly reaches and maintains strong volume

Each Section faster, lower than previous with similar, very simple, emphatic Phrases

Elements Expanded, short slurs, with long Intervals, so very emphatic, forceful

Type A2 Pitch falls between 1st and 2nd Sections; steady Pitch within Sections; short, Expanded Elements with long Intervals sound emphatic, staccato.

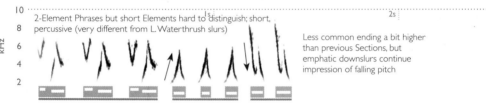

2-Element Phrases but short Elements hard to distinguish; short, percussive (very different from L. Waterthrush slurs)

Less common ending a bit higher than previous Sections, but emphatic downslurs continue impression of falling pitch

Type A3 The speed of most songs gets faster throughout song.

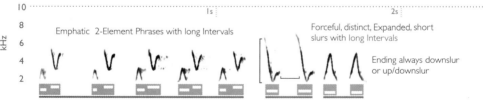

Emphatic 2-Element Phrases with long Intervals

Forceful, distinct, Expanded, short slurs with long Intervals

Ending always downslur or up/downslur

Louisiana Waterthrush A2 Similar habitat, overall falling pitch profile, **but** more Sections: Type A 5–9, B much longer; both usually end with fade-out (vs. 3 or 4 emphatic Sections).

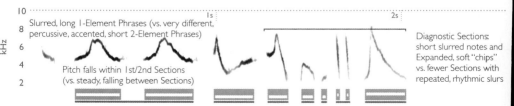

Slurred, long 1-Element Phrases (vs. very different, percussive, accented, short 2-Element Phrases)

Pitch falls within 1st/2nd Sections (vs. steady, falling between Sections)

Diagnostic Sections: short slurred notes and Expanded, soft "chips" vs. fewer Sections with repeated, rhythmic slurs

Connecticut A1 Similar habitat, walking; song emphatic, **but** 1 Section (vs. 3 or 4).

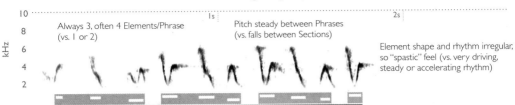

Always 3, often 4 Elements/Phrase (vs. 1 or 2)

Pitch steady between Phrases (vs. falls between Sections)

Element shape and rhythm irregular, so "spastic" feel (vs. very driving, steady or accelerating rhythm)

Kirtland's A1 Similar speed, emphatic feel and often 3 Sections, **but** usually shorter (avg. 1.2 sec. vs. 1.9); Element quality changes from Complex to more slurred as song progresses (vs. consistently Expanded, more emphatic Clear Elements, steadier rhythm).

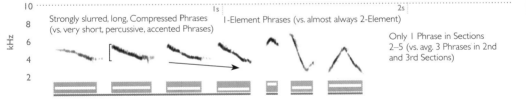

Elements Compressed, low, dark (vs. Expanded, more accented, emphatic, much brighter)

Rises in pitch from 1st to 2nd Section; overall more varied pitch profile (vs. falls in pitch over course of song)

Swainson's A1 Similar strong delivery, descending pitch profile, **but** somewhat higher, thinner, with 4 or 5 Sections, 1 or 2 Phrases in 2nd, the rest only 1 Phrase each (vs. never 5 Sections); Pitch falls between Phrases in 1st Section (vs. steady, falls between Sections).

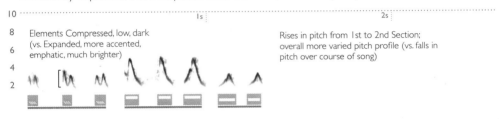

Strongly slurred, long, Compressed Phrases (vs. very short, percussive, accented Phrases)

1-Element Phrases (vs. almost always 2-Element)

Only 1 Phrase in Sections 2–5 (vs. avg. 3 Phrases in 2nd and 3rd Sections)

Yellow-throated A1 Falling pitch profile similar, **but** usually only 2 or 3 Sections (vs. always 3 or 4); steady speed throughout (vs. usually speeding up); obviously higher, thinner.

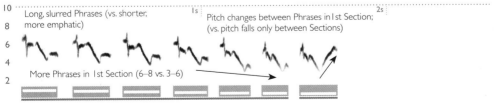

Long, slurred Phrases (vs. shorter, more emphatic)

Pitch changes between Phrases in 1st Section; (vs. pitch falls only between Sections)

More Phrases in 1st Section (6–8 vs. 3–6)

ORANGE-CROWNED

Oreothlypis celata   Male/Female - All Seasons

- Small with sharply pointed bill
- Low-contrast olive-yellow body or bright yellow body and grayish-olive or green back
- Subtle, blurry streaking below
- Pale yellowish or whitish supercilium, faint eyeline, split eyering
- Pale patch at bend in wing

- Olive underparts and yellowish UnTC
- Longish dark tail
- Faint streaking below, often very diffuse
- Pale patch at bend in wing

- Sharply pointed bill
- Olive to yellow underparts and yellowish UnTC
- Longish dark tail
- Faint streaking below

Distinctive Views

Additional Photos

Often in weedy, flowery, or seedy areas

Drab and very low contrast, which is a good ID point

Orange crown feathers are rarely seen

Birds vary in brightness, some quite drab and gray-headed, others brighter yellow-green

Often probes into dead leaf clusters, catkins, and flower heads

Relatively long, dark tail; short eyeline not contrasty but usually visible along with faint supercilium

Some birds show strong grayish hood

Split eyering, short, faint eyeline and supercilium

Eastern birds very late fall migrants, often into late October; western birds are quite early migrants

Note variation in yellow and sometimes paler ventral area

Fine, pointy, spike-like bill

Doesn't bob or wag tail

Low contrast, yellowish/olive
Always yellowish UnTC
Long, thin, dark tail
Eye-arcs, thin eyeline
Yellow/greenish below
Faint, diffuse streaking

Comparison Species

Tennessee Bright Greener back; more contrasty facial pattern; longer primary projection; more contrasting, bluer hood; white UnTC (vs. buffy/yellow); shorter, usually paler tail; no breast streaking (vs. often dull streaks)

Tennessee Drab More contrasty facial pattern: stronger eyeline and supercilium; white UnTC (vs. buffy/yellow); shorter, usually paler tail; no breast streaking (vs. sometimes dull streaks)

Black-throated Blue Higher contrast between upper and lower parts; dark cheek patch; white handkerchief; more contrasting supercilium; blue-green tones above; heavier bill

Philadelphia Vireo Much larger; thicker billed; more heavily marked face including brighter supercilium; more contrast between upper and lower parts; yellow concentrated in throat

Nashville 1yF Bright eyering (vs. eye-arcs); brighter contrast overall; bluer hood; stronger, unstreaked yellow below; contrasting yellow throat (vs. no contrast or hooded)

Wilson's Plainer; yellow face; usually has black cap; blunter bill with pale lower mandible; brighter yellow; longer tail; often wags tail

Yellow Yellow or pale edging on wing coverts; plainer face; pinkish legs (vs. dark); blunter bill; shorter, wider, yellow tail

Mourning (shown), MacGillivray's 1yF Much larger; often on ground (vs. rarely); long pale legs (vs. dark); wider, shorter tail

Aging and Sexing

Spring AdM 1yM AdF 1yF   **Fall** AdM 1yM AdF 1yF

Races: 4, *O.c. celata* (east), *O.c. oerestera* (central), *O.c. lutescens* (west), and *O.c. sordida* (Channel Islands and nearby mainland coast, CA)   **Summary** *Spring/Fall:* Not ageable or sexable

All Birds Sp/Fa Not easily ageable or sexable; bright orange crown patch in fall indicates a male.

Hooding Hood color is variable and may indicate race (*lutescens* never hooded), but does not indicate sex or age.

Races Not easily separable: breeding birds solidly in their ranges are probably the location-appropriate race; *lutescens* never shows gray hood, and breeding birds are brightest of all races, but many overlap with other races; other birds best left unidentified.

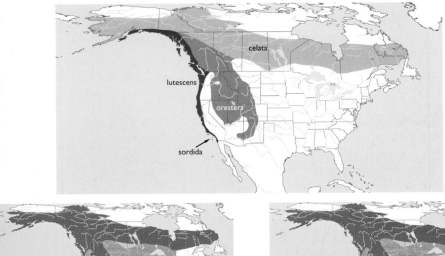

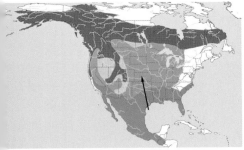

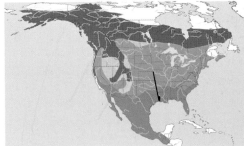

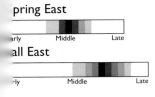

Spring East

Early   Middle   Late

Fall East

Early   Middle   Late

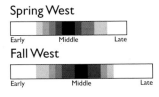

Spring West

Early   Middle   Late

Fall West

Early   Middle   Late

Orange-crowned

An orange, quickly bouncing on your crown, will eventually slow down and fall

Summary *1 or 2 Sections of Trilled,* Clear, short, usually emphatic Phrases; *pitch and speed often waver but usually fall* toward end; 2nd Section almost always lower, never higher; short slurs, long Intervals sound staccato, but *not strongly emphatic or bright.* **2 Types:** A, 1 Section, Trill speed, pitch wavers throughout; end often falls in pitch, volume, speed; **B,** 2 Sections, both Trills, 2nd almost always lower; either faster or slower.

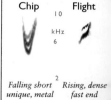

Chip	Flight
Falling short unique, metal	Rising, dense fast end

Type A 1 Section Trill; pitch wavers obviously throughout song.

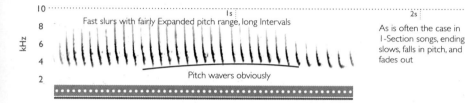

Fast slurs with fairly Expanded pitch range, long Intervals

Pitch wavers obviously

As is often the case in 1-Section songs, ending slows, falls in pitch, and fades out

Type B1 2 Sections, 2nd almost always lower, usually somewhat faster or slower.

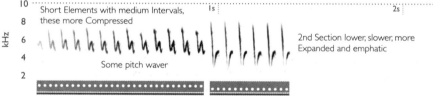

Short Elements with medium Intervals, these more Compressed

Some pitch waver

2nd Section lower, slower, more Expanded and emphatic

Type B2 2-Section song, 2nd Section lower, slower and softer.

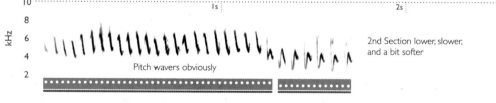

Pitch wavers obviously

2nd Section lower, slower, and a bit softer

Type B3 2-Section song with little pitch change from Section to Section.

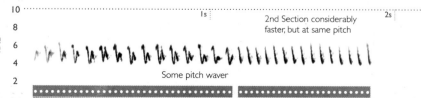

2nd Section considerably faster, but at same pitch

Some pitch waver

Colima A1
Only 1-Section songs similar; slow Trill overlaps slowest version of Orange-crowned, can sound very similar; 2-Section songs have 1–3 Phrases in 2nd Section vs. avg. 8; no breeding range overlap.

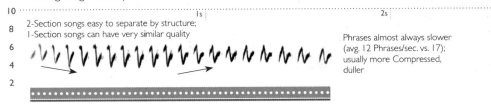

2-Section songs easy to separate by structure; 1-Section songs can have very similar quality

Phrases almost always slower (avg. 12 Phrases/sec. vs. 17); usually more Compressed, duller

Grace's B1
Similarly repeated Phrases in 1 or 2 Sections with small pitch changes, **but** slower (almost all Phrases countable and uncommon Trilled Sections mixed with slower Sections; avg. 8 Phrases/sec. vs. Orange-crowned always Trilled, avg. 17).

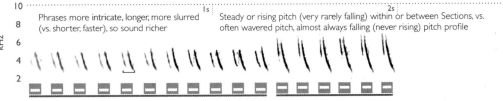

Phrases more intricate, longer, more slurred (vs. shorter, faster), so sound richer

Steady or rising pitch (very rarely falling) within or between Sections, vs. often wavered pitch, almost always falling (never rising) pitch profile

Wilson's B1
Similar repeated Phrases can speed up or fall in pitch toward end, **but** 1st Section Phrases slower, always countable (1st Section avg. 7 Phrases/sec. vs. 17).

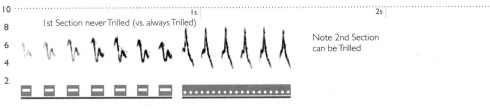

1st Section never Trilled (vs. always Trilled)

Note 2nd Section can be Trilled

Worm-eating A2/Pine B1/Chipping Sparrow
None sing 2-Section songs; little or no Pitch/speed waver; **Worm-eating/Chipping**: much more Expanded Elements, brighter, more emphatic; **Chipping** more Complex Elements, Buzzy low-frequency and/or tinkling quality; **Pine Type A** songs much slower (6–11 Phrases/sec.).

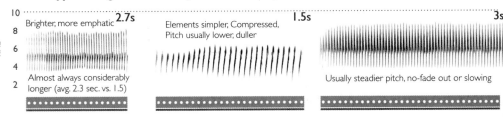

Brighter, more emphatic   2.7s

Almost always considerably longer (avg. 2.3 sec. vs. 1.5)

Elements simpler, Compressed, Pitch usually lower, duller   1.5s

Usually steadier pitch, no-fade out or slowing   3s

OVENBIRD

Seiurus aurocapilla   Male/Female - All Seasons

- Walks on ground with head-bobbing, chicken-like gait
- ✓ Orange crown patch bordered by black
- Large-eyed, with bold white eyering
- Plain brownish-olive above
- Malar stripe and heavy breast streaks in central breast and flanks
- Pinkish legs

- Black lateral throat stripe contrasts strongly with white malar stripe and unmarked white throat
- Heavy breast streaks
- Short, brown tail and white UnTC
- Large-eyed with bold white eyering

- Heavy streaking in breast, flanks
- Short, brown tail and white UnTC
- Plump body shape
- Legs and lower mandible pinkish

Distinctive Views

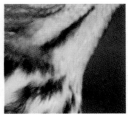

Additional Photos

Imost always walking on the ground

Very vocal; on breeding grounds, birds often sing from high perches, triggering neighbors to sing as well

"Chicken-walker": bobs head and struts through leaf litter; tail often cocked or flipped up

/hen walking, often flicks tail up; tail is cked more quickly when agitated

Combination of crown pattern and large eye with strong white eyering diagnostic

Sometimes looks thrush-like

enbird nests are distinctive, dome-ped structures with a side entrance, an oven

Relatively large; black lateral throat stripe contrasts with white malar stripe and unmarked white throat (diagnostic)

Tail is frequently cocked

te strong eyering and heavy streak-concentrated in upper breast

When agitated (often in response to pishing) will raise crest, conspicuously showing orangish color of median crown

Latin name *aurocapillla* means "golden hair"

Bobbing-head "chicken walk"
Contrasting white eyering
Heavy upper breast streaking
Black/orange crown stripes
Plain olive above
Thick malar stripe
Often on ground

Comparison Species

Louisiana Waterthrush More elongated shape with larger, heavier bill; bright supercilium (vs. eyering); lacks black/orange crown stripes; different walking style (vs. "chicken walk"); bobs tail instead (vs. cocking it up); brown upperparts (vs. olive); streaking less concentrated in breast and brown (vs. black)

Thrushes Darting movements with pauses (vs. "chicken walk"); lack black/orange crown stripes; weaker eyerings; spotting in breast (vs. streaking); larger and more elongated; longer tails

Northern Waterthrush More elongated shape with longer, heavier bill; bright supercilium (vs. eyering); lacks black/orange crown stripes; usually streaking in throat (vs. clear); different walking style (vs. "chicken walk"); bobs tail (vs. cocking it up); brown upperparts (vs. olive); streaking less concentrated in breast, brown (vs. black)

Aging and Sexing

Races: 3, *S.a. aurocapilla* (east), *S.a. furvior* (east) and *S.a. cinereus* (central/west), not generally separable in field   **Summary** *Spring/Fall:* Not sexable

All Birds Sp/Fa Not generally ...geable or sexable.

S.a. cinereus Race Breeds eastern slope of Rockies from southern Alberta to Colorado; may average grayer overall but not reliably separable.

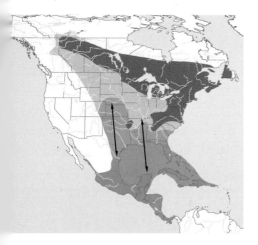

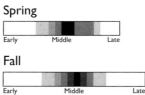

Spring

| Early | Middle | Late |

Fall

| Early | Middle | Late |

Ovenbird

Teacher, TEAcher, TEAcher; get the teacher out of the oven!

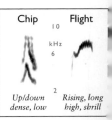

Chip	Flight
Up/down dense, low	Rising, long high, shrill

Summary Usually easy to ID: emphatic, *distinct 2-Element Phrases* ("TEA Cher"), 1st Element almost always higher than 2nd; *starts softly, increases in volume over at least first 1/4 of song;* very *long* song for warbler (avg. 2.7 sec.). Also sings longer, jumbled flight/display song, sometimes at night. **I Type.**

Type A1 Starts very softly, takes 5 or 6 Phrases to reach full, emphatic volume (good ID point); distinct, even 2-Element Phrases with long Intervals.

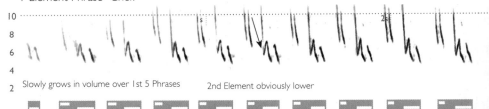

Type A2 Long; lower, louder, Complex 2nd Element; slightly less even rhythm; can sound like 1-Element Phrase "Cher."

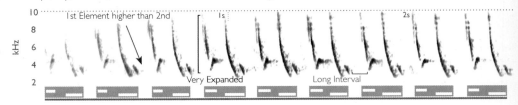

Type A3 3-Element Phrase (more like Carolina Wren or Common Yellowthroat); higher, more percussive than C. Wren, Elements less varied than C. Yellowthroat; neither fades in over long time.

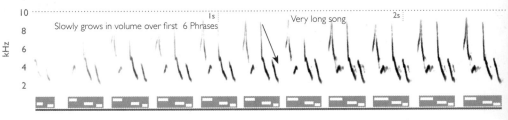

Type A4 Slurred 2nd Element so less percussive quality than most other variations; still has falling pitch profile.

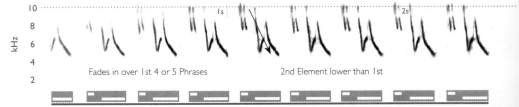

Carolina Wren Falling 2-Element quality could be confused, especially from distance, **but** accented short attack contrasts with much lower, duller Elements (vs. all higher, more Expanded Elements with brighter sound).

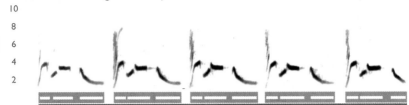

Mourning B1 Similar repeated, Complex Phrases, **but** much lower; most are 2 or 3 Sections (vs. 1 for all but night song); shorter songs (avg. 1.4 sec. vs. 2.7), volume steady throughout (vs. increasing).

Longer, more slurred, Complex, less accented Elements (vs. shorter)

Higher 2nd Element creates rising pitch profile in almost all 1-Section songs (vs. falling profile)

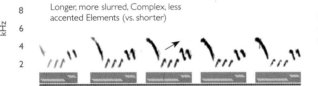

Kentucky A1 Similar habitat, repeats 2-Element Phrases in 1 Section, **but** fewer Phrases (5–8/song vs. 9–10), noticeably shorter (avg. 1.9 sec. vs. 2.7); Phrases almost always rising pitch (vs. falling).

Very steady in volume, intensity (vs. starts softly/slowly grows in volume)

Lower, **longer**, Complex Elements more Compressed, burry

Common Yellowthroat 1-Section songs, often 3-Element Phrases, **but** most Ovenbird songs 2-Element Phrases (very uncommon for C. Yellowthroat); shorter songs with fewer Phrases, (avg. 3 vs. 10), obviously slower (avg. 2 Phrases/sec. vs. 4).

Relatively long, slurred Elements of varying pitches, shapes (vs. short, accented, percussive Ovenbird Elements)

Overall Phrase pitch profile varied, usually up then down (vs. fast, falling pitch profile)

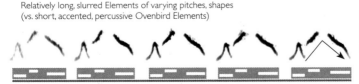

PAINTED REDSTART

Myioborus pictus   Male/Female - All Seasons

- ✓ Bright red breast and black upperparts
- • Bold white wing patch
- • White under-eye arc
- • Long tail
- • Very active, with frequent tail fanning, sallying, and wing drooping

- ✓ Bright red breast and black upperparts
- • Bold white wing patch
- • White under-eye arc
- • Long white tail

- ✓ Bright red breast and black chin
- • Long all-white tail
- • Distinctive, black bars on white UnTC
- • Gray lower belly and vent

Distinctive Views

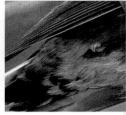

Additional Photos

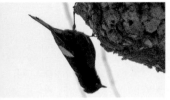

Often seen working on trunks and limbs alike.

Outer tail feathers all white; Slate-throated Redstart has black base to tail

Painted Redstarts often droop their wings

Very long tailed

Striking red, black, and white combination is unique

Tail fanning and wing drooping may be used to stir up insects

Juveniles retain their plumage later than most warblers (sometimes into August) and so are seen more often

Limited to the Southwest in higher altitudes

Many diagnostic views for this species!

Restricted range
Bright red breast
Black upperparts
Striking white wing panel
Long white tail often fanned
Black-barred UnTC
Under-eye arc

Comparison Species

American Redstart No range overlap; orange (vs. bright red) and limited to shoulders, wings, and tail (vs. lower breast/belly); lacks under-eye arc; shorter tail with distinctive black and orange pattern

Red-faced Red face and neck, with black "earmuffs" (vs. red belly); gray upperparts with thin wing bar (vs. black with white wing patch); white breast and belly (vs. red); red throat and chin (vs. black); longer dark tail (vs. white)

Aging and Sexing

Spring AdM 1yM AdF 1yF   **Fall** AdM 1yM AdF 1yF

Races: 1 Summary *Spring/Fall:* Not sexable but ageable   **What to Notice** *Spring/Fall:* Red in belly, color of secondaries

Adult Sp/Fa Not separable, though females may show slightly paler red in belly.

Juvenile May be seen more often than typical juvenal warblers in summer; *Diagnostic:* shows black in belly.

1y Sp/Fa *Diagnostic 1y:* flight feathers appear brownish, in contrast to black surrounding feathers.

Migration Rarely seen in migration. Generally arrives on breeding grounds in late March through late April, and departs breeding grounds by early September. A few birds may winter in southeastern Arizona.

Painted Redstart
Slow, uneven, erratic Painting isn't a good way to Start the job

Summary Variable; distinctive; *low, long, Compressed slurred Phrases* in 2–6 Sections; usually starts with long 2-Element Phrases; following Sections *similar pitch range and quality without abrupt changes*; overall rhythmic quality often *erratic* due to subtle changes in Phrase pitch profiles and types. **Types:** variable.

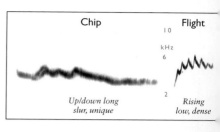

Chip   Flight

10

kHz
6

2

*Up/down long   Rising
slur, unique   low, dense*

Type A1 2-Section song of slow 2-Element Phrases speeding up in 2nd Section. Overall pitch range very Compressed and consistent.

Very **Compressed**   Very long Phrases

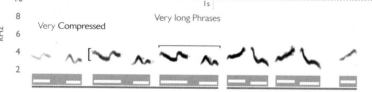

Type A2 6-Section song; Element pitch ranges all similar; changing Phrase profiles, (e.g., from rising to falling, long to short, and from 1- to 2-Element Phrases), create overall erratic rhythm.

Many songs fade in over   Changing pitch profiles and Phrase lengths
2 or 3 Phrases   and speeds create uneven rhythmic quality

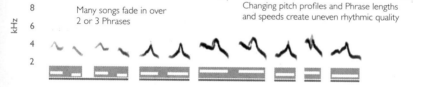

Type A3 3-Section song

3-Element Phrase fades in   2nd Section faster, 2-Element
a bit during 1st Section   Phrases; 3rd slower, creating
          uneven, awkward overall rhythm

Compressed pitch range
throughout song

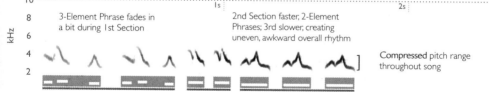

Type A4 Slightly more even, 3-Section variation

Phrases all similarly Compressed, with small changes in speed and pitch

Red-faced A2
Shares range, similar short, slurred Sections, **but** many more Sections (avg. 7 vs. 3) and rarely more than 2 Phrases/Section.

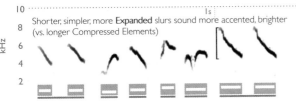

Shorter, simpler, more **Expanded** slurs sound more accented, brighter (vs. longer Compressed Elements)

Almost always 1-Element Phrases (vs. almost always 2 or 3)

More abrupt, wider pitch changes between Sections

Virginia's A1
Faster 1st Section, so hard to hear individual Elements in 2-Element Phrases (P. Redstart Elements always distinct); avg. 7 Phrases/sec. in 1st Section vs. 3; Element shapes and ranges change more drastically between Sections (vs. all very similar).

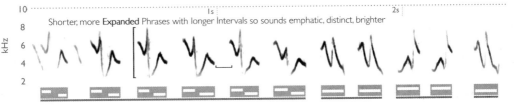

Shorter, more **Expanded** Phrases with longer Intervals so sounds emphatic, distinct, brighter

Yellow-rumped (Audubon's) A2
Can be very similar, **but** more Phrases in longer 1st Section (avg. 6.2 vs. 2.8, some overlap), songs faster (1st Section avg. 5 Phrases/sec. vs. 3.3), only 2 or 3 Sections (vs. often 4+).

Phrases more Complex with Expanded, shorter Elements and shorter Intervals so sounds rough, burry (vs. very simple slurs)

More repetitive, simple rhythm (vs. usually irregular, erratic)

Lucy's A2
More Phrases (avg. 16 /song vs. 7), faster speed (avg. 8 Phrases/sec. vs. 4); often 1 Trilled Section (vs. never Trilled); noticeably higher; changes in pitch, Element type between Sections more dramatic; rhythm more consistent, repetitive.

1st 2 Sections almost always 1-Element Phrases (vs. almost always 2-Element, often in 2nd Section as well)

Many Elements more **Expanded**, shorter, sounding brighter, more emphatic and staccato

PALM

Setophaga palmarum   Male/Female - All Seasons

- Constantly pumps tail
- Crown/breast streaking often rufous
- Brown tones on back with tan, low-contrast wing bars
- Wide, prominent supercilium
- Variable yellow below but always yellow UnTC
- Brown lateral throat stripe

- Often yellow or yellowish throat
- Yellowish rump and yellow UnTC
- Brown lateral throat stripe
- Often seen on ground in flocks

- ✓ Long tail with square, blocky black tail base and square white end
- Variable yellow underparts; always yellow UnTC
- Streaking in chest often rufous

Distinctive Views

Additional Photos

Tail pumping is an excellent ID point; note yellow UnTC and paler uppertail coverts

Often on or near ground in open country in flocks during migration

Strong yellow UnTC even in drab gray birds

Often not shy; note strong, wide supercilium, yellow wash

A long, slim warbler with long legs

Tail shows distinct white terminal band and black, squared base

Bright yellow UnTC and white tail spots

Rufous cap and streaking contrasts with yellow body

Tail spots, yellow body/UnTC, and striking supercilium conspicuous in flight

Uppertail coverts are yellow

Variable, sometimes patchy yellow wash; only UnTC are consistently yellow

Supercilium prominent but thinner in this individual

Long supercilium, dark cap
Constantly pumps tail
Yellow UnTC
Long white tail/wide black base
Brownish overall/buffy wing bars
Diffuse streaking below
Often rufous cap/streaking

Comparison Species

Cape May Smaller, more active; finer bill; shorter tail; no tail pumping; grayer upperparts/no rufous; white UnTC and almost all-white tail lacking broad black base; lacks long supercilium; green wing edging

Orange-crowned Plainer face lacks strong supercilium; smaller, with finer bill; more active; olive tones (vs. brown); doesn't pump tail; lacks pronounced streaking in breast; dark tail (vs. white)

Yellow-rumped Bright yellow rump (vs. dull yellow-green); different face pattern; grayer upperparts; more active feeder; yellow shoulder patches; white UnTC (vs. yellow); doesn't pump tail

Pine Lacks any rufous; plainer face lacks pronounced supercilium; strong white wing bars (vs. thin, buffy); darker, contrasting wings; diffuse, gray streaking (vs. fine, rufous); white UnTC (vs. yellow); longer, white tail, lacks wide black base; yellow (when present) mainly in upper breast

Kirtland's Pumps tail but no contrasting cap/supercilium; blue-gray back (vs. brown); dark lores and white eye-arcs; larger; more upright posture; white UnTC (vs. yellow); less contrasting tail pattern

Prairie Less frequent and pronounced tail pumping; no cap; wider, shorter supercilium when present; olive in back (vs. brown); smaller; plumper; black or gray side streaks (vs. rufous); lacks extensive black at base of tail; UnTC lighter yellow/contrasts less with body; yellow underparts even, never patchy

Waterthrushes Pump tail but larger with larger bill; darker brown upperparts; lack wing bars; buffy or white underside (no yellow); heavier streaking; shorter, dark tail, whitish UnTC (vs. yellow)

Aging and Sexing

Spring AdM 1yM AdF 1yF   **Fall** AdM 1yM AdF 1yF

Races: 2, *D.p. palmarum* (western) paler in breast and belly, yellow much patchier than in vent, *D.p. hypochrysea* (eastern); both races seen in eastern U.S. during migration   **Summary** *Spring/Fall:* Not sexable or ageable   **What to Notice** *Spring/Fall:* Yellow in underparts, especially lower breast and belly, to separate races

All Birds Sp/Fa Not sexable or ageable, although some 1y birds may be duller.

D.p. hypochrysea (eastern) Sp Uniformly yellow through body and some yellow in face.

D.p. hypochrysea (eastern) Fa Uniformly yellow through body and some yellow in face.

D.p. palmarum (western) Sp Paler in breast and belly, yellow much patchier than in vent.

D.p. palmarum (western) Fa Paler in breast and belly, solid yellow vent and patchy yellow elsewhere.

Note: Some birds may show unusual yellow patterning, which may indicate a hybrid or some other mechanism that is not fully understood.

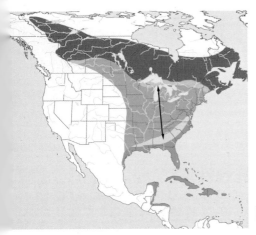

Spring East			
Early	Middle		Late

Fall East			
Early	Middle		Late

Spring West			
Early	Middle		Late

Fall West			
Early	Middle		Late

Palm

The wind blows the rough, burry palm frond up and down, back and forth, evenly

Summary 7–12 *1-Element Phrases in 1 Section*; distinctive *Buzzy, Complex quality* in *down/up slurs*; often soft (easier to confuse from distance); pitch, speed rarely vary. Calls regularly, doesn't sing as often or emphatically in migration as many species; **2 Types: A,** Slower, countable; **B,** Trill.

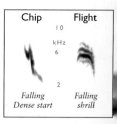

Chip	Flight
Falling Dense start	*Falling shrill*

Type A1 | Section of down/up slurred, Complex 1-Element Phrases; Intervals long enough so Phrases distinct.

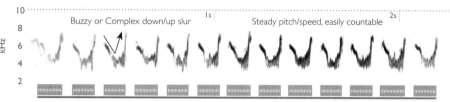

Buzzy or Complex down/up slur   Steady pitch/speed, easily countable

Type A2 More slurred version

Complex slur with Buzzy quality; down/up profile   Pitch and speed steady, at easily countable rate

Phrases distinct, separated by fairly long Intervals

Type A3 More Complex, less Buzzy version; steady, countable speed.

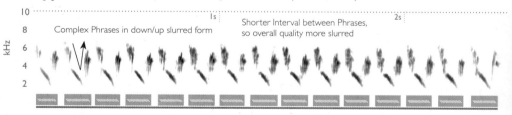

Complex Phrases in down/up slurred form   Shorter Interval between Phrases, so overall quality more slurred

Type B Less common version of song with Complex Elements repeated at Trill speed.

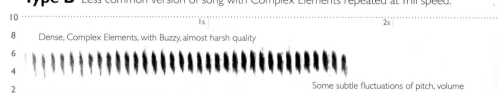

Dense, Complex Elements, with Buzzy, almost harsh quality

Some subtle fluctuations of pitch, volume

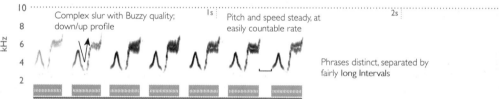

Pine A1
Slowest Trills can be confusing at a distance, **but** faster (avg. 9 Phrases/sec. in slowest songs vs. 5.5); lower, richer, simpler quality.

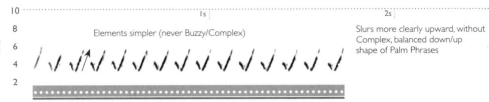

Elements simpler (never Buzzy/Complex)

Slurs more clearly upward, without Complex, balanced down/up shape of Palm Phrases

Yellow-rumped (Myrtle) A3
Almost all 2+ Sections (vs. 1) with changes in pitch, speed or Phrase type; simpler songs sung at a countable speed and often weakly delivered can be similar, especially during migration.

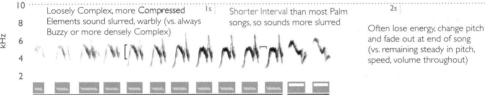

Loosely Complex, more Compressed Elements sound slurred, warbly (vs. always Buzzy or more densely Complex)

Shorter Interval than most Palm songs, so sounds more slurred

Often lose energy, change pitch and fade out at end of song (vs. remaining steady in pitch, speed, volume throughout)

Wilson's A2
Most easily separable: 2 or 3 Sections, and speed up and/or fall in pitch (vs. 1-Section steady in speed/pitch); 1-Section songs could be confusing, **but** Phrases always Clear slurred tones (vs. Buzzy); even simpler songs usually fall in pitch toward end (vs. steady).

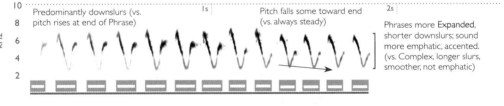

Predominantly downslurs (vs. pitch rises at end of Phrase)

Pitch falls some toward end (vs. always steady)

Phrases more Expanded, shorter downslurs; sound more emphatic, accented. (vs. Complex, longer slurs, smoother, not emphatic)

Chipping Sparrow/Dark-eyed Junco/Pine/Orange-crowned vs. B
Chipping variable; some low, Buzzy quality similar, **but** Buzzes lower, rougher, and combined with Expanded Phrase, so brighter too; **Junco** slur with very fast attack sounds doubled (vs. Complex **but** more Compressed, simpler Buzzes).

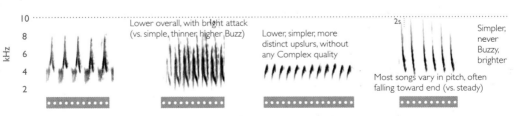

Lower overall, with bright attack (vs. simple, thinner, higher Buzz)

Lower, simpler, more distinct upslurs, without any Complex quality

Simpler, never Buzzy, brighter

Most songs vary in pitch, often falling toward end (vs. steady)

PINE

Setophaga pinus   Male/Female - All Seasons

- Large, with relatively large bill
- Head and breast variably yellow
- Unstreaked back
- Pale neck patch contrasts with dark cheek
- Wide wing bars, low-contrast wing, low contrast between wing bars
- Plain face with broken eyering, short eyeline, often pale supralorals

- Throat and breast variably yellow
- White tail and UnTC, with dark "V" outlining UnTC
- Short primary projection
- Variable, diffuse side streaking
- May wag tail periodically
- Long tail held loosely and so appears deeply notched

- Long white tail spots and long tail projection beyond UnTC
- White tail, belly, and UnTC, with dark "V" outlining UnTC
- Throat and breast variably yellow
- Relatively large bill
- Often creeps along branches
- Long tail often held loosely and so appears deeply notched

Distinctive Views

Additional Photos

Note "goggles" effect of eyering and bright supraloral area on bright birds

Faint, thin eyeline and eye-arcs, pale supraloral and smoky cheek patch create a recognizable facial pattern

Short-distance migrant: only warbler with main winter range within U.S.; difficult to differentiate migrants/residents

Frequently pumps tail, but not as strongly as Palm or Prairie Warblers; note very long tail

Can appear "bubble-headed": large round head, no neck and bulky body

Tends to forage less actively than other warblers: probes crevices for insects with large bill; prefers pines

Note pale neck patch and goggles

Birds vary from totally gray to washed with yellow; sometimes come to feeders for suet

Yellow in throat and upper breast variable, as is streaking

All birds have unstreaked backs and lower contrast tertial edging (vs. Blackpoll/Bay-breasted with streaked backs, white tertial edges)

Note pale supraloral area and dark cheek contrasting with pale neck patch

Contrast between yellow front and gray/white rear is distinctive for brighter plumages

Dark cheeks, pale neck patch
Large bill, pale supraloral
Variable streaking below
Variable yellow wash
Wide white wing bars
Long tail/large white tail spots

Comparison Species

Yellow-throated Vireo Thicker, hooked bill; stronger yellow spectacles; less extensive yellow in belly with sharper cutoff; no streaking; shorter, dark tail without large white tail spots; overall more contrasty (between bright yellow head/darker wings/white wing bars)

Prothonotary Brighter yellow face, body; plainer face; more contrasting blue wings/green back; lacks wing bars; more orangey-yellow color extends into belly; shorter tail

Prairie Chestnut back patch (vs. plain olive); more contrasty face pattern; smaller; smaller-billed; yellowish wing bars; always more extensive yellow throughout underparts (vs. variable); often yellow-suffused UnTC; heavier black streaking (vs. diffuse); more white in tail

Palm Constant tail wagging (vs. occasional); often rufous cap/breast streaks; pronounced supercilium (vs. faint); brownish tones on back (vs. olive); faint, low-contrast buffy wing bars (vs. broad, white); brown malar stripe; tail shows broad, square, black base (vs. black "V" around UnTC); yellow UnTC (vs. white)

Dark cheeks, pale neck patch
Large bill, pale supraloral
Variable streaking below
Variable yellow wash
Wide white wing bars
Long tail/large white tail spots

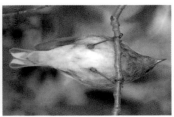

Blackpoll More contrasty facial pattern; longer eyeline; lacks isolated pale supraloral; cheek blends into throat and neck (vs. pale neck patch); longer primary extension; more contrasting white edges to tertials and primaries; shorter, lighter bill; streaked back (vs. plain); more contrasting wing bars; shorter tail with smaller white tail spots; more boat-shaped body; orange feet (at least soles) and often legs (vs. sometimes pale but never orange); more, finer streaking in throat

Bay-breasted Longer primary extension; contrasty tertial/primary edging; streaked, greener back; more contrasty wing bars; eyeline more pronounced; often shows rufous in flanks; shorter tail with smaller white tail spots; often shows buff in vent/undersides/UnTC

Yellow-rumped (Myrtle) Bright yellow rump; usually yellow shoulder patches, streaking on back and heavier streaking in breast (especially center); more active feeding; similarly contrasting cheek, but stronger supercilium; more prominent black borders to smaller, more rounded, white tail spots

Tennessee/Orange-crowned (Tenn. shown) Lack wing bars; smaller and more active; finer bill; more contrasty facial pattern; shorter tail

Blackburnian Orangey face and breast (vs. yellow); triangular cheek patch; striking supercilium; usually more defined streaking on flanks and back; somewhat shorter, all-white tail

American Redstart F Yellow shoulders/tail base; lacks pale neck patch and wing bars; more active, often tail-fanning; black-and-yellow tail diagnostic; greener back

Cape May Smaller, finer bill; yellow-green rump; lacks wide wing bars; usually more obvious eyeline, especially behind eye; fine, even breast streaking especially in upper breast/throat (vs. diffuse, on sides); shorter tail; often yellowy in vent; greenish wing edging

Aging and Sexing

Races: 1 **Summary** *Spring/Fall:* Only extreme bright or dull birds sexable/ageable   **What to Notice** *Spring/Fall:* Intensity/extent of yellow and side streaking

AdM Sp/Fa Extreme Bright, extensive yellow across back, head and breast, variably dense black or olive side streaking, pronounced yellow eyering.

All Others Sp/Fa Not reliably separated; variable color eyering, yellow in body and head, streaking.

1yF Sp/Fa Extreme Little or no yellow, white eyering, little or no breast streaking.

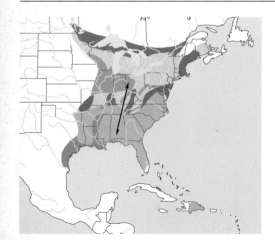

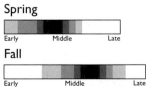

Spring

Early   Middle   Late

Fall

Early   Middle   Late

Pine
Low hanging pine needles can be quickly picked, one at a time

Summary 1 Section of *1-Element simple Phrases*; almost always *Trilled*; low, *Compressed simple upslurs* or down/upslurs; volume often fluctuates at beginning and end; pitch can also fluctuate subtly; any intricacies in Element structure subtle and in lower frequencies, unlike brighter Worm-eating; **2 Types:** A, Slowest Trills, Clear upslurs; B, Faster Trills.

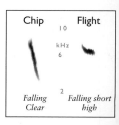

Chip | Flight

Falling Clear | *Falling short high*

Type A Slowest Trills (9–12 Phrases/sec.); Clear, simple upslurs.

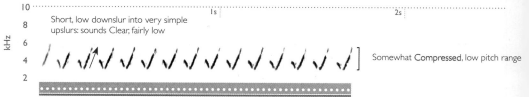

Short, low downslur into very simple upslurs: sounds Clear, fairly low

Somewhat **Compressed**, low pitch range

Type B1 Faster (17–25 Phrases/sec.), simple, upslurred Phrases; fairly low, mellow, without high frequencies or strongly accented quality.

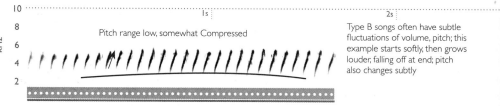

Pitch range low, somewhat Compressed

Type B songs often have subtle fluctuations of volume, pitch; this example starts softly, then grows louder, falling off at end; pitch also changes subtly

Type B2 Example of fastest Type B songs.

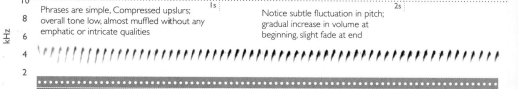

Phrases are simple, Compressed upslurs; overall tone low, almost muffled without any emphatic or intricate qualities

Notice subtle fluctuation in pitch; gradual increase in volume at beginning, slight fade at end

Palm A4 vs. A Similar at a distance **but** always slower (avg. 5.5 Elements/sec. vs. 9+).

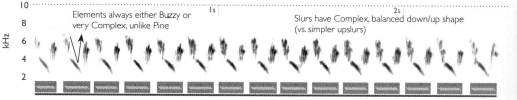

Elements always either Buzzy or very Complex, unlike Pine

Slurs have Complex, balanced down/up shape (vs. simpler upslurs)

Yellow-rumped (Myrtle) A3 vs. A

Almost as fast as slowest Pine songs, **but** almost all 2 or more Sections (vs. 1), fewer Phrases (avg. 10 vs. 15).

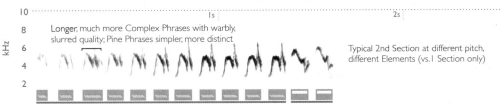

Longer, much more Complex Phrases with warbly, slurred quality; Pine Phrases simpler, more distinct

Typical 2nd Section at different pitch, different Elements (vs. 1 Section only)

Worm-eating (excerpts)

Similar, **but** most obviously faster than any Pine Type A; very Expanded, short downslurs are emphatic, bright (avg. pitch span 5 kHz vs. 2.8 kHz). Faster example (right) still more Expanded, brighter, shorter with longer Intervals, so more distinct, dry quality (vs. Compressed, dull).

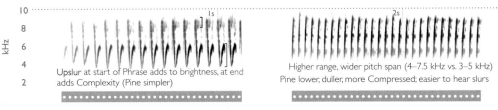

Upslur at start of Phrase adds to brightness, at end adds Complexity (Pine simpler)

Higher range, wider pitch span (4–7.5 kHz vs. 3–5 kHz)
Pine lower, duller, more Compressed; easier to hear slurs

Palm B1/Chipping Sparrow x3/Swamp Sparrow x3 Chipping

Variable, **but** all separable as brighter with higher, more Complex frequencies, "tinkling" (vs. duller Pine), abrupt endings; **Swamp** all audibly more Complex.

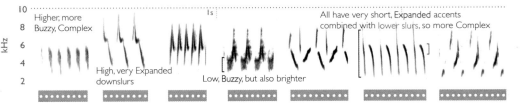

Higher, more Buzzy, Complex

High, very Expanded downslurs

Low, Buzzy, but also brighter

All have very short, Expanded accents combined with lower slurs, so more Complex

Orange-crowned x2

All noticeably higher; many songs 2 Sections (vs. 1) or obvious falling pitch at end (vs. subtler changes).

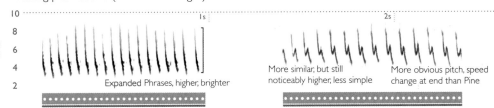

Expanded Phrases, higher, brighter

More similar, but still noticeably higher, less simple

More obvious pitch, speed change at end than Pine

PRAIRIE

Setophaga discolor   Male/Female - All Seasons

- Extensive yellow underparts
- ✓ Dark or gray semicircle under eye creates distinctive "tired" look
- Dark neck spots and side streaking
- Olive back; often shows chestnut patch
- Yellow wing bars in bright birds
- Often wags tail
- Rufous back patch

- ✓ Black or gray semicircle under eye
- Dark neck spots and side streaking
- Yellow fades past legs
- Pale UnTC, sometimes yellowish
- Long all-white tail
- Often wags tail

- Variably dark neck spots and side streaking
- Pale UnTC, sometimes yellowish
- Long all-white tail
- Often wags tail

Distinctive Views

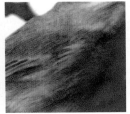

Additional Photos

Not actually found in prairies; prefers open brushy areas, short secondary growth, mangroves

Frequent tail wagger: tail is dipped and then slowly raised to horizontal

Feeds in low trees, but rarely on ground

Sings into midday; note dark breast streaking, long white tail

Yellowish wing bars

Side streaking can be blurry

Rufous back patch pronounced in bright birds; actually a group of spots

Dark line under eye always darkest part of the face

Note yellow fades out past legs and diffuses into whitish UnTC

Some females are bright but show little marking

Large white tail spots flash during flight; note rufous mantle

Dark neck spots and under-eye arcs; neck spots present in all plumages

Distinctive facial pattern
Yellow wing bars
Dark or black flank streaking
Long white tail
Rufous back patch
Often wags tail

Comparison Species

Palm Chestnut crown; yellow-green rump; longer supercilium; often on ground (vs. rarely); brown malar stripe; more consistent tail bobbing; brownish streaking (vs. black/gray); brighter yellow UnTC; yellow may fade in upper body (vs. fades toward tail); tail has contrasting, square, black base; browner above

Kirtland's Also wags tail but extremely restricted range, rarely seen in migration; larger; lacks yellow crescent under eye; grayer, darker back/head; finer streaking and throat spots; whiter UnTC and more black in base of tail

Pine Larger, heavier-bodied; pale eye-arcs; no black under eye or on neck; white wing bars (vs. yellow); lacks back patch; yellow ends higher up; white vent and UnTC (vs. yellowish); more diffuse streaking

Yellow Plainer yellow face; no chestnut in back; yellow edging to wings; red streaking in breast (vs. black side streaks); yellow tail (vs. white)

Nashville Complete eyering (vs. eye arc); plainer face; lacks side streaking, wing bars; smaller and more active; finer bill; shorter, dark tail (vs. white); pale vent (vs. yellow)

Prairie Drab for comparison

Magnolia Complete eyering, lacks eyeline; yellow rump (vs. olive); white wing bars (vs. yellow or none); gray neck band (vs. neck marks); streaking more focused in lower flanks; stronger contrast between yellow breast and white vent/UnTC; black tail band; no tail bobbing

Aging and Sexing

Spring AdM 1yM AdF 1yF   **Fall** AdM 1yM AdF 1yF

Races: 2 *D.d. discolor* and *D.d. paludicola* (Florida only, duller overall)   **Summary**
Spring: Sexable, not ageable; *Fall:* AdM, AdF separable, 1y separable from adults but not
each other   **What to Notice** *Spring/Fall:* Intensity of streaking, chestnut in back, overall
contrast, yellow or pale around eye

AdM/1yM Sp *Diagnostic male:* strong side streaking and facial marks, distinct chestnut back patch, yellowish wing bars.

AdF/1yF Sp Duller than males; *Diagnostic female:* streaking paler and more olive, usually little or no chestnut in back.

AdM Fa Similar to adult male spring, slightly duller.

AdF Fa Similar to spring female but duller; yellow undereye arc (versus 1y birds).

1yF/1yM Fa Female may be duller overall, but not generally separable; *Diagnostic 1y:* pale gray around eye.

D.d. paludicola Florida only, duller overall.

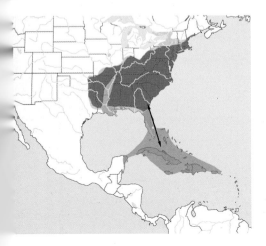

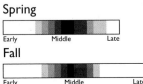

Spring

Early   Middle   Late

Fall

Early   Middle   Late

Prairie
Slowly stepping up yellow-flowered prairie, surrounded by buzzing bees

Summary *1 Section of Buzzy, Compressed, even, 1-Element Phrases rising* slowly in pitch; some start with Clearer Phrases, gradually becoming Buzzy by last half of song; most songs start softly, grow louder; long Intervals, Phrases distinct; fairly long song (1.9–2.7 sec.) **2 Types: A**, 1 Section, countable, long; **B**, Faster, uncountable. Rarely can have separated 2nd Section or more complicated form.

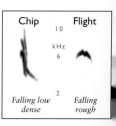

Chip	Flight
10
kHz
6
2
Falling low dense	*Falling rough*

Type A1 Countable, slowly rising, even, Buzzy Phrases; fairly long, at 2.2 sec.

Buzzy Phrases getting higher, louder as song progresses

Compressed Phrases of even length, speed

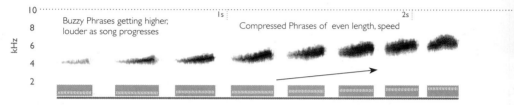

Type A2 Faster song (9 Phrases/sec.), still just countable; fairly long; Phrases very Compressed.

Constant speed with slow rise in pitch, slow increase in volume

Beginning tones fairly pure but by halfway through slowly become Buzzy

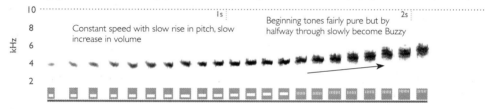

Type B Similar structure **but** uncountable, Trill speed; this example 15 Phrases/sec.

Simple, Compressed Phrases, increasing in pitch, volume (as Type A)

Starts fairly Clear and gradually becomes Buzzy

Black-throated Blue A3
Similar Buzzy quality, rising pitch trend, **but** always 2–3 Sections (vs. 1), 1st Section fewer Phrases (avg. 4 vs. 18).

1st-Section Phrases more intricate, often including short downslur (vs. very simple, 1-pitch Phrases)

Last Phrase markedly longer, slowly rises in pitch (vs. Phrases even length, speed)

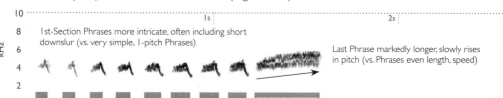

Palm A2 Buzzy Phrases at about same speed as slowest Prairie, **but** usually fewer Phrases (avg. 10 vs. 17), steady pitch/volume (vs. rising pitch trend).

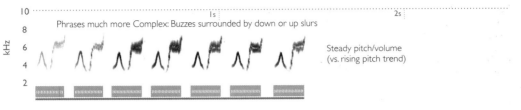

Phrases much more Complex: Buzzes surrounded by down or up slurs

Steady pitch/volume
(vs. rising pitch trend)

Northern Parula Variation with pulsed Trill could be confusing, **but** almost always 2- or 3-Section songs (vs. 1); speed faster than fastest Prairie, song shorter (avg. 1.6 sec. vs. 2.2); Elements more Complex, with pulsing quality and short Interval, so slurred together (vs. distinct).

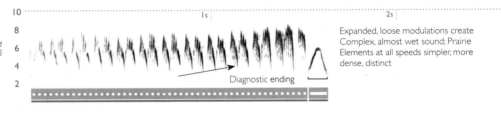

Expanded, loose modulations create Complex, almost wet sound; Prairie Elements at all speeds simpler, more dense, distinct

Diagnostic ending

Northern Parula B1 3 Sections (vs. 1); Prairie Phrases simpler, more Compressed, without any modulations or slurs.

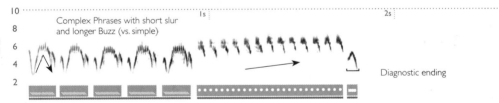

Complex Phrases with short slur and longer Buzz (vs. simple)

Diagnostic ending

PROTHONOTARY

Protonotaria citrea   Male/Female - All Seasons

- Bright golden-yellow face and underparts
- Plain face, large black bill (pale in fall)
- Unmarked blue wings
- Green back
- Strong contrast between back and head/breast
- Often in wet, forested habitats

- Golden yellow of variable amounts below
- Plain face
- Long black bill, pale in fall
- Long white UnTC
- Short, broad white tail with dark tips

- Golden yellow
- Long bill
- Long white UnTC
- Short, broad white tail with dark tips

Distinctive Views

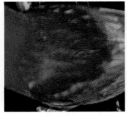
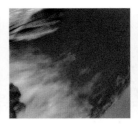

Additional Photos

This preening bird is puffed up, disguising its shape

Usually found near water; breeds in wet woods

White tail fringed with black; strong contrast between yellow body and white UnTC/tail

Blue/green/gold contrast is bright and striking

Female and immature birds show more olive in the crown

Bright males have strong yellow crown contrasting with olive back

Yellow in body is variable, from gold to more orangey gold; amount of white also variable

Usually forages at low levels, probing for insects

Note contrast between golden head, greenish mantle and bluish wings

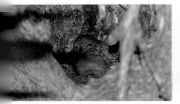

Prothonotary and Lucy's are the only cavity-nesting warblers

Some birds may show some orange in forehead

Their bright yellow is particularly striking in dim environs, hence their nickname: "Golden Swamp Warbler"

Bright golden head/underparts
Contrasting blue wings
Bright white UnTC
Short white tail
Large, with long, large bill
Plain face

Comparison Species

Blue-winged Usually in different, more open, dry habitats; smaller, more active; strong dark eyeline obscures eye (vs. plain face); wing bars (vs. none); smaller with finer bill; less orangey yellow; thinner tail often with white tapering to arrow shape (vs. uniformly wider white)

Wilson's Yellow UnTC (vs. white); smaller with smaller bill; longer gray tail (vs. white); lacks blue wings; often shows black cap

Hooded Face outlined by darker olive (vs. all yellow); often shows some black in head; olive wings (vs. blue); yellow UnTC (vs. white); longer tail; smaller bill

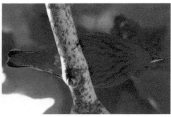

Yellow Less contrast between head/back; some show orange streaking; smaller with smaller bill; olive/yellow wings with yellow edging (vs. blue); yellow vent, tail, and UnTC (vs. white)

Aging and Sexing

Spring AdM 1yM AdF 1yF **Fall** AdM 1yM AdF 1yF

Races: 1 Summary *Spring/Fall:* Brightest birds are AdM, dullest 1yF, otherwise not definitively separable **What to Notice** *Spring/Fall:* Intensity of yellow, contrast of head with back, bill color

AdM Sp/Fa Bright yellow head contrasts green back; dark black bill; some birds show orange in breast and head; some overlap with 1yM.

1yM Sp/Fa Less contrasty than AdM between head and back, slight green wash to head; some overlap with AdM.

AdF Sp/Fa Greenish-yellow head, moderate contrast with back; base of bill may show brown; yellow overall less intense than males; some overlap with 1yF.

1yF Sp/Fa Dullest plumage, no contrast between head and back, wings dull and brownish, some overlap with AdF.

Stained Bird Staining caused by feeding in honeysuckle.

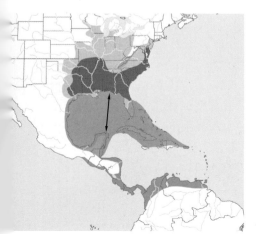

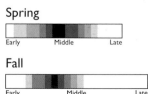

Spring

Early   Middle   Late

Fall

Early   Middle   Late

Prothonotary
Your local court notary repeatedly Tweets on Twitter

Summary 1-Section songs of 8–9 *Expanded, upslurred, rich, emphatic Phrases*; fairly slow, even, countable speed (slow enough to easily hear upslurred quality); Phrases' intricacies add brightness; long Intervals, so *distinct, rhythmic*. Only warbler that "Tweets." **I Type.**

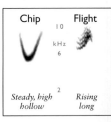

Chip | Flight

Steady, high hollow | Rising long

Type A1
I Section with even speed, pitch throughout; intricate slurs so sharper, brighter than simpler slurs, but always sound like upslurs.

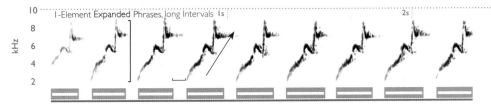

I-Element Expanded Phrases, long Intervals

Type A2
I Section; even, slow repetition of strongly rising upslurred Phrases; no change in pitch or quality.

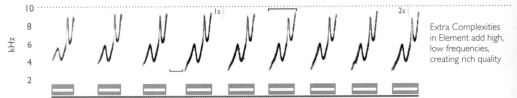

Downslurs at beginning of each Phrase adds to richness, but Phrases still sound predominantly like upslurs

Type A3
Expanded, fairly long upslurs; long and slow enough to hear the pitches, so sounds rich; short enough, long enough Intervals so somewhat emphatic.

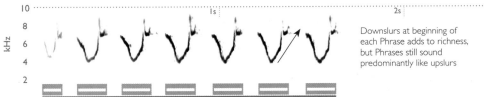

Extra Complexities in Element add high, low frequencies, creating rich quality

American Redstart B
Most songs 2+ Sections (vs. 1); or 2-Element Phrases (vs. 1). Almost always fewer Phrases (avg. 5 vs. 8); Phrases of most songs downslurs (vs. upslurs). This example more similar. Usually sings multi-Section Type A songs in same session.

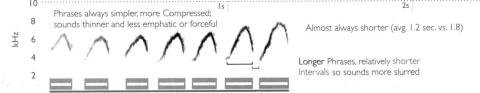

Phrases always simpler, more Compressed; sounds thinner and less emphatic or forceful

Almost always shorter (avg. 1.2 sec. vs. 1.8)

Longer Phrases, relatively shorter Intervals so sounds more slurred

Northern Cardinal
Similar habitat; variation with strong upslur could be confused, **but** upslur shape unique (Compressed, long, low beginning and very Expanded, short, accented ending), unlike even, longer, higher Prothonotary slur.

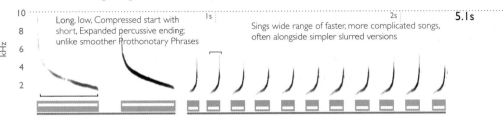

Long, low, Compressed start with short, Expanded percussive ending; unlike smoother Prothonotary Phrases

Sings wide range of faster, more complicated songs, often alongside simpler slurred versions

Swamp Sparrow
Usually fast, uncountable Trills (vs. much slower); some variations approach similar speed, **but** complicated, multi-Element Phrases (vs. simpler, smoother, more balanced upslurs).

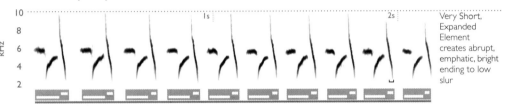

Very Short, Expanded Element creates abrupt, emphatic, bright ending to low slur

Kentucky Warbler A1
Similar breeding habitat; 1-Section songs, usually with upslurred Phrase, **but** lower, Compressed, burry Elements.

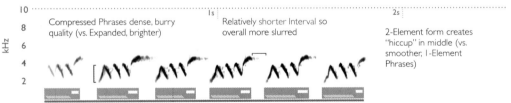

Compressed Phrases dense, burry quality (vs. Expanded, brighter)

Relatively shorter Interval so overall more slurred

2-Element form creates "hiccup" in middle (vs. smoother, 1-Element Phrases)

Cape May A1/Wilson's A1
Cape May: 1-Section songs much higher, thinner, fewer Phrases (avg. 5 vs. 8). **Wilson's**: often 2+ Sections, obvious pitch/speed changes (vs. 1 steady Section); always faster, usually obviously so (avg. 7 Phrases/sec. vs. 4.5); speed emphasizes emphatic, staccato quality of short, Expanded Phrases with very long Intervals; downslurs (vs. upslurs).

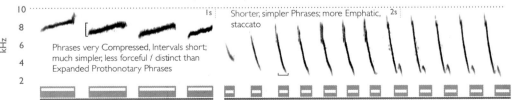

Shorter, simpler Phrases; more Emphatic, staccato

Phrases very Compressed, Intervals short; much simpler, less forceful / distinct than Expanded Prothonotary Phrases

RED-FACED

Cardellina rubrifrons   Male/Female - All Seasons

- Limited range/altitude
- ✓ Red face, throat, and upper breast
- ✓ Black cap that extends down sides of head creating "earflaps"
- ✓ Single white wing bar edged above with blackish base
- ✓ Pale white rump

- Whitish belly and UnTC
- ✓ Bright red throat, black earflaps
- Long gray tail, often flipped or wagged
- Short thick bill
- ✓ White rump

- Short thick bill
- ✓ Bright red throat
- Whitish belly and UnTC
- Long gray tail, often flipped or wagged

Distinctive Views

Additional Photos

Only in AZ/SW New Mexico; prefers mixed forests, steep terrain, usually above 2000 m

Long, slender shape; single white wing bar usually obvious

Only U.S. warbler with a bright red face

Note pale white rump, also visible in flight; distinctive red sides of head also visible from behind

Acrobatic when feeding

Long tail and gray body ending in bright red face

Restricted range
Bright red face/throat
Black cap/earflaps
Long gray tail, often flipped
Unstreaked white below
White UnTC, rump

Comparison Species

Painted Redstart All-black face and back (vs. red); red breast (vs. white); dark-barred UnTC (vs. white); long white tail (vs. dark)

Titmouse Larger, blunt conical bill; white throat (vs. red); more uniform gray overall

Olive Warbler Masked, including dark lores (vs. earflaps); orange or yellowy buff face (vs. red or pink); white tail (vs. dark)

Mountain Chickadee Black throat (vs. red); smaller with finer, thinner bill; longer tail

Aging and Sexing

Spring AdM 1yM AdF 1yF   **Fall** AdM 1yM AdF 1yF

Races: 1 Summary *Spring/Fall:* Not sexable or ageable, juvenal plumage may be retained into June or July   **What to Notice** *Spring/Fall:* see below

All Birds Not generally separable; 1yF may show duller head pattern with less glossy black and more orangey-red, but not reliable.

Migration Rarely seen in migration. Generally arrives on breeding grounds in early April, and departs breeding grounds by mid-September.

Red-faced
Singing so many different Sections in a row would make any Face Red

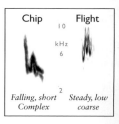

Chip | Flight

Falling, short Complex | Steady, low coarse

Summary *Many Sections of usually 1 (1–3) Clear slurred Phrases.* Elements long, but variable, Clear slurs, some Expanded, others Compressed; thus songs don't have repetitive or strongly rhythmic quality. Ending almost always 1 or 2 downslurs or up/down slurs, Expanded, accented. **Types:** variable.

Type A1 5 Sections of only 1–3, Clear, 1-Element Phrases.

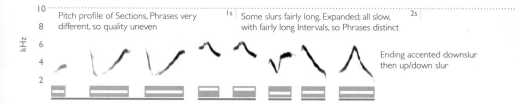

Pitch profile of Sections, Phrases very different, so quality uneven

Some slurs fairly long, Expanded; all slow, with fairly long Intervals, so Phrases distinct

Ending accented downslur then up/down slur

Type A2 6 Sections, most with only 1 Phrase each; Phrases simple, well separated slurs.

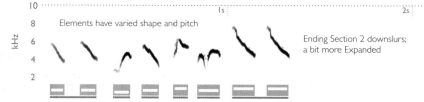

Elements have varied shape and pitch

Ending Section 2 downslurs; a bit more Expanded

Type A3 Longer variation, many Sections with only 1 Phrase/Section. No other western warbler has so many short Sections.

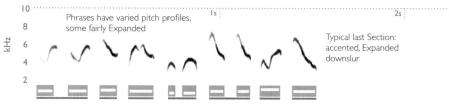

Phrases have varied pitch profiles, some fairly Expanded

Typical last Section: accented, Expanded downslur

Type A4 11 Sections, many with only 1 Phrase.

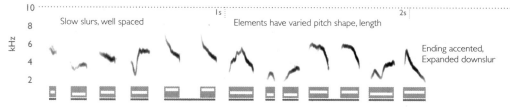

Slow slurs, well spaced

Elements have varied pitch shape, length

Ending accented, Expanded downslur

Painted Redstart A3
Similarly slurred Phrases, very even pace, **but** fewer Sections, often 2+ Phrases each; Phrases consistently much more Compressed, thus sound lower, duller.

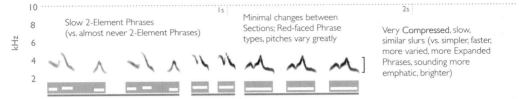

Slow 2-Element Phrases (vs. almost never 2-Element Phrases)

Minimal changes between Sections; Red-faced Phrase types, pitches vary greatly

Very Compressed, slow, similar slurs (vs. simpler, faster, more varied, more Expanded Phrases, sounding more emphatic, brighter)

Yellow B3
Slurred Phrases **but** accented wider slurs at song's end; much steadier, repetitive pace (vs. more variable Phrase speeds, shapes); 1st Section almost always at least 3 Phrases (vs. rarely more than 2); fewer Sections (2–5 vs. 4–12); does not commonly share same habitat.

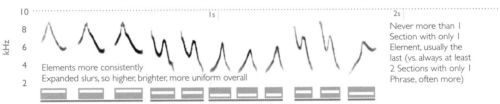

Elements more consistently Expanded slurs, so higher, brighter, more uniform overall

Never more than 1 Section with only 1 Element, usually the last (vs. always at least 2 Sections with only 1 Phrase, often more)

Virginia's A3
Slurred Phrases somewhat similar, **but** usually only 2 or 3 Sections (max. 4) vs. usually 6+, min. 4; 1st Section many more Phrases (avg. 6. vs. 2); pitch, speed changes between Sections less varied, more regular (vs. more dramatic pitch changes, often erratic speed changes).

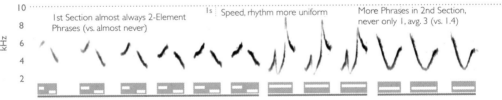

1st Section almost always 2-Element Phrases (vs. almost never)

Speed, rhythm more uniform

More Phrases in 2nd Section, never only 1, avg. 3 (vs. 1.4)

Yellow-rumped (Audubon's) A2
More Phrases in 1st Section (avg. 6, range 4–8, vs. avg. 2, range 1–3), only 2 or 3 Sections (vs. 4–12).

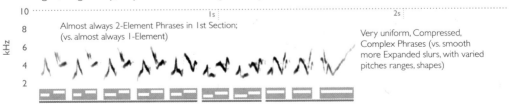

Almost always 2-Element Phrases in 1st Section; (vs. almost always 1-Element)

Very uniform, Compressed, Complex Phrases (vs. smooth more Expanded slurs, with varied pitches ranges, shapes)

SWAINSON'S

Limnothlypis swainsonii   Male/Female - All Seasons

- Brown crown, pale supercilium, and thick eyeline
- Brown-olive above, buffy below
- Large, spiky, pale bill
- No streaking

- Pink legs, large feet
- Grayish buffy below
- No streaking
- Large, spiky, pale bill
- Short, wide, brown tail
- Fairly long, buffy UnTC

Distinctive Views

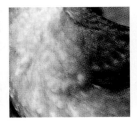

Additional Photos

Similar coloration to waterthrushes but unstreaked below and pointier billed

Large, brown and ground dwelling like waterthrushes but unstreaked and doesn't tail-bob

Short wide tail

Turns over dead leaves, and the resulting noise can be one of best ways of finding this skulker

Skulking and difficult to observe

Rare vagrants to the NE overshoot breeding grounds in spring migration

Long buffy/white UnTC, usually paler than Worm-eating and lacks gray spots

Unique behavior for U.S. warblers: shivers or shakes wings while feeding on ground

Breeds in two different habitats: canebrakes in SE U.S., and rhododendron thickets in S. Appalachia

Large bill, sloping forehead
Long supercilium/brown eyeline
Plain brown above/buffy below
Short, wide, dark tail
Plain buffy UnTC
Skulking, often near ground

Comparison Species

Carolina Wren Brighter rufous tones; more contrasty face, including flared, white supercilium; barring in wings and tail (vs. plain); long, thin tail; very vocal with different song and calls

Ovenbird Rounder and fatter; shorter, thinner bill; white eyering and lacks supercilium; olive upperparts (vs. brown); orange crown; streaking; head-bobbing "chicken walk"

Black-throated Blue Blue-green upperparts (vs. brown); white handkerchief; white under-eye arc and thinner supercilium; smaller with smaller bill; longer, dark tail; more active and easy to see

Louisiana Waterthrush Song similar; heavily streaked (vs. not); browner face, malar stripe, and brighter supercilium; chronic tail pumper; usually in open (vs. skulking)

Worm-eating Bold head stripes including buffy crown stripe; shorter bill; olive upperparts (vs. brown); contrasting head and back; richer, buffier underparts; gray-spotted UnTC (vs. plain buff); rarely forages on ground (vs. often)

Aging and Sexing

Spring AdM 1yM AdF 1yF   **Fall** AdM 1yM AdF 1yF

Races: 1 Summary *Spring/Fall:* Not generally ageable or sexable

All Birds All plumages similar in all seasons.

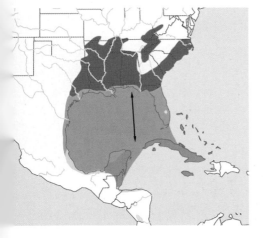

Spring

| Early | Middle | Late |

Fall

| Early | Middle | Late |

Swainson's
Professor Swainson started classes with "well, well, well, I'll teach you well"

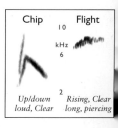

Chip	Flight
Up/down loud, Clear	Rising, Clear long, piercing

Summary Distinctive, starting with 2-4 strong, simple, Compressed downslurs; *pitch usually falls in 1st Section*; ending several long, loud, mostly Expanded slurs in several Sections with 1 Phrase each, the last almost always an up/downslur; **I Type.**

Type A1 Typical; pitch usually falls in 1st Section (sometimes only subtly).

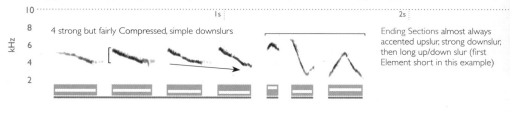

4 strong but fairly Compressed, simple downslurs

Ending Sections almost always accented upslur, strong downslur, then long up/down slur (first Element short in this example)

Type A2 1st Section falls from 1st to 2nd Phrase; simple, Compressed slurs.

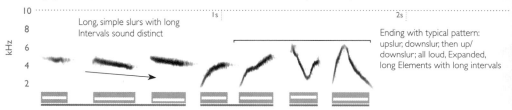

Long, simple slurs with long Intervals sound distinct

Ending with typical pattern: upslur, downslur, then up/downslur; all loud, Expanded, long Elements with long intervals

Louisiana Waterthrush A2 Very similar in form, quality, found in similar habitats
but 1st Section slurs more intricate, slower, longer, more Expanded than Compressed Swainson's Phrases; only 2 or 3 Phrases in 1st Section (vs. often 4, never 2); Swainson's ending slower, more even speed, more emphatic, and never has chip-like Expanded Elements.

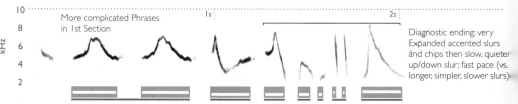

More complicated Phrases in 1st Section

Diagnostic ending: very Expanded accented slurs and chips then slow, quieter up/down slur; fast pace (vs. longer, simpler, slower slurs)

Yellow-throated A1 Repeated slurs that fall in pitch, accented slurred ending similar,
but 1st Section much longer, more Phrases (range 6–8 vs. 3–5).

Brighter due to more intricate, Expanded downslurs (vs. simpler, more Compressed)

Much greater drop in pitch over 1st Section

More regular song, with more repeated Phrases, simpler ending

Northern Waterthrush A2 Similarly strong delivery, falling pitch, **but** usually only 3 Sections, never more than one 1-Phrase Section (vs. 4 Sections, last few only 1 Phrase each); somewhat lower, richer. Overall more repetitive and strongly rhythmic.

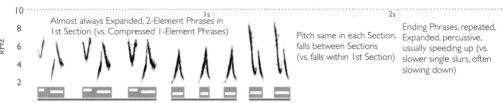

Almost always Expanded, 2-Element Phrases in 1st Section (vs. Compressed 1-Element Phrases)

Pitch same in each Section, falls between Sections (vs. falls within 1st Section)

Ending Phrases, repeated, Expanded, percussive, usually speeding up (vs. slower single slurs, often slowing down)

Hooded A1 Loud song with opening slurs, accented ending, **but** lower, richer Phrases; shorter (avg. 1.2 sec. vs. 1.7). 1st Section slurs usually more complicated form.

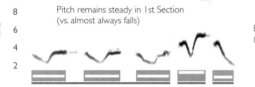

Pitch remains steady in 1st Section (vs. almost always falls)

Ending simpler, Elements more Compressed (vs. more Sections, more varied Phrases)

TENNESSEE
Oreothlypis peregrina   Male/Female - Spring/Fall

- Small, short-tailed, fine-billed
- Long wings with long primary projection
- Faint wing bars (often very faint)
- Bright green above, contrasting gray head in spring males
- Short supercilium and dark eyestripe, with eye-arcs

- UnTC can be yellow-tinged but always whiter than breast
- Plain gray underside with varying amounts of yellowish wash
- Fine, pointy bill
- Contrast in the face created by eyestripe, faint supercilium and broken eye-arcs

- Unstreaked
- Small, sharp bill
- Very short-tailed, long-winged
- UnTC white or in some plumages yellow-tinged, but always whiter than breast
- Tail light or dark gray

Distinctive Views

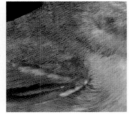

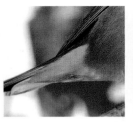

Additional Photos

Sharp, pointy bill for gleaning insects

Long primary projection, especially compared with Orange-crowned

White UnTC and more conspicuous supercilium than Orange-crowned

Plain, unstreaked breast

Plain, unstreaked, smooth underparts cleaner looking than Orange-crowned

Nonbreeding birds show an olive head that blends into back

Amount of yellow in breast can be limited or extend to UnTC; note very short tail

Often forages high and acrobatically, but can be seen at any level during migration

Short but prominent supercilium

Quick, active feeder

Very short tail, pointy bill

Breeding males show a contrasting blue-gray hood

Short tail, dark or grayish spots
Short supercilium/thin eyeline
Whitish UnTC
Very thin, short bill

Comparison Species

Orange-crowned More subdued facial pattern, less distinct eyeline and supercilium; eye-arcs more prominent; pale patch at the bend of the wing; sometimes diffuse breast streaking; yellowish UnTC (vs. white); longer, dark, unspotted tail; very different call

Pine Plainer face; larger, heavier-billed; wide wing bars; much longer, white tail; often diffuse breast streaking

Chestnut-sided Complete eyering (vs. arcs); bright green upperparts/head; yellowish wing bars; all white below; much longer, all-white tail

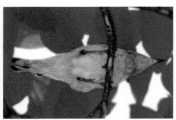

Bay-breasted More complex, contrasty head with pale neck patch, darker cheek; wide, contrasty wing bars; back streaking; boat-shaped; longer, wider tail; uneven buff below usually including UnTC

Cape May Fine streaking in upper breast/throat; greenish-yellow rump; longer, whiter tail; varying amount of yellow wash below; grayer overall

Blackburnian Triangular cheek patch; wider supercilium; pale back braces; orange wash in head/breast, streaking; longer, whiter tail

Cerulean Usually some blue-toned streaking; tail spots larger with darker border and unique shape; blue upperparts; heavier bill

Philadelphia/Warbling/Red-eyed Vireos Larger; heavier, hooked bill; stouter legs; whiter supercilium; contrasty under-eye patch; slower behavior; yellowish UnTC (vs. white); longer tail (esp. Warbling Vireo)

Aging and Sexing

Races: 1 Summary *Spring:* AdM and 1yF may be separable, others not; *Fall:* Some AdM may be separable, all others not   **What to Notice** *Spring/Fall:* Contrast of head and body, green/gray in head, overall contrast

All Birds Sp Contrasting blue-gray head with green back and whitish underparts; females average slightly duller than males, but overlap.

AdM Sp No trace of green in head, high contrast overall probably AdM, but not always definitive.

1yF Sp Lacks any gray in crown; duller overall.

All Birds Fa Little or no contrast between head and back, and average buffier underparts; white in belly and undertail coverts variable.

AdM Fa *Diagnostic:* blue or gray in crown indicates AdM.

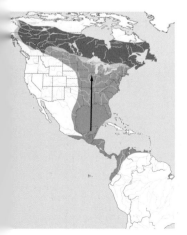

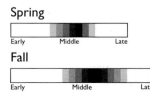

Spring

| Early | Middle | Late |

Fall

| Early | Middle | Late |

Tennessee

Ten-ness-see: it takes a long time to say this three-section word

Summary *3 Sections* of fast, emphatic Phrases; *one of longest warbler songs,* avg. 3.2 sec.; all Elements very short, extremely Expanded with long Intervals so sounds *emphatic, staccato, percussive* (amongst most emphatic of all warblers); **I Type:** 1st, 2nd Sections often 2-Element Phrases, 3rd Section 1-Element Phrases; Section 2 or 3 can be Trills; little pitch change between Sections.

Chip   Flight

10

kHz
6

Falling short   Rising long
Clear   Complex

2

Type A1 2-Element Phrases in first Sections, I-Element Phrases in last; overall very bright, staccato, emphatic; I st Section slowest; pitch lowest in 3rd Section.

3.7

Very Expanded, short Phrases, long Intervals

Type A2 All Elements very Expanded with long Intervals, so very staccato, forceful; last Section just below Trill speed; little pitch change between Sections; last Section highest.

3.7

Type A3 Typical: pitch rises to short 2nd Section, then falls in 3rd; last Section usually fastest; 2nd, 3rd Section Elements usually similar speed.

3.

Very short, Expanded Elements with long Intervals

Type A4 Less common form with 2-Element Phrases in 3rd Section; Phrase speed fairly consistent; last Section sounds faster due to transition to 2-Element Phrases.

3.

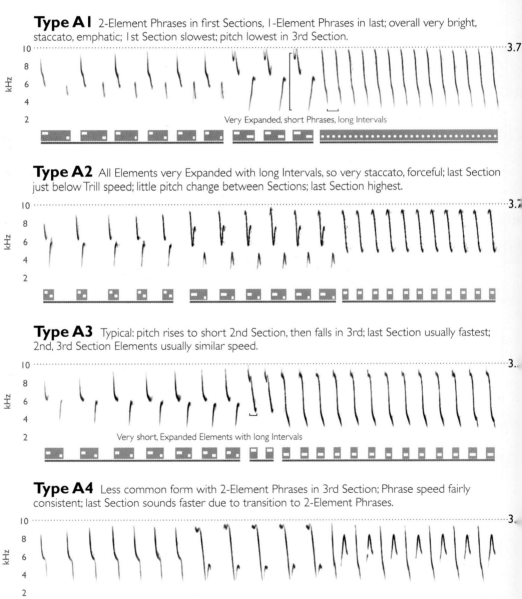

Nashville
Similar structure with emphatic Elements **but** 2-Section Songs (vs. 3 Sections); almost always 1-Element Phrases in 2nd Section (vs. 2-Element Phrases). Longer Elements, so more slurred, less strongly emphatic.

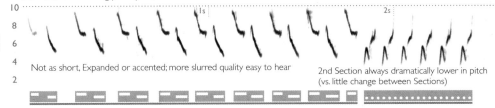

Not as short, Expanded or accented; more slurred quality easy to hear

2nd Section always dramatically lower in pitch
(vs. little change between Sections)

Wilson's B1
Similar emphatic Phrases, **but** 1 or 2 Sections (vs. almost always 3, never 1); generally much shorter (range 1–1.9 sec. vs. 2–4 sec.).

All Phrases longer, more Compressed intricate slurs
(vs. noticeably more percussive, accented, brighter)

2nd Section dramatically lower in pitch (vs. similar
pitches and rarely overall falling profile)

Cerulean A1
Similar structure (3 Sections, the last a Trill), **but** length much shorter (avg. 1.4 sec. vs. 3.2), large pitch change between Sections (vs. usually steady, never strongly rising), last Section higher, thinner, faster Trill.

All Phrases Compressed, Complex, slurred and/or Buzzy
Elements (vs. Expanded, staccato, emphatic, bright Phrases)

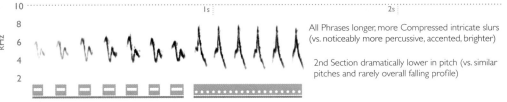

Ends with Buzz or very
fast Trill, faster than any
Tennessee Phrases

TOWNSEND'S

Setophaga townsendi   Male/Female - All Seasons

- High-contrast yellow face with dark ear patch and yellow undereye arc
- Variably black throat bordered by yellow; dark streaking
- Dark olive-green back
- White wing bars
- Dark flight feathers contrast with body

- Variably black throat bordered by yellow
- Side streaking
- White belly, UnTC, and tail
- Sometimes shows dark lines in UnTC

- Variably black throat bordered by yellow
- Yellow breast with dark streaking
- White belly
- White vent, UnTC, long, all-white tail
- Sometimes shows dark lines in UnTC

Distinctive Views

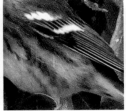

Additional Photos

Breeding range overlaps with Hermit Warbler's and hybrids (as in this photo) are found annually

Breeds in conifers; during migration can use range of habitats, but often found in pines when available

Bright birds very high-contrast; note extensive yellow in breast

Note three different "sections": yellow head/breast, white belly and black wings

Distinctive, contrasty facial pattern

Long white tail with white UnTC; note the few black streaks on the UnTC

Black in the throat varies by age, sex, and individuals

Spotted, dark-olive back blends into a black or olive cap; note black back streaking

Black throat bordered by yellow is striking from below

Sometimes shows dark lines in UnTC

Although there is a range of yellow on the breast, there is always much more than is ever found on Black-throated Greens

Even pale birds have darker auricular patches than Black-throated Green, and lack the paler center

Solid dark ear patch
Wide supercilium
Black streaking below
Contrasty yellow face/breast
Long all-white tail/UnTC
White wing bars, olive back
Variable black in throat

Comparison Species

Black-throated Gray Gray back (vs. olive); lacks yellow in throat/breast; high-contrast black-and-white face with yellow supraloral mark

Black-throated Green No range overlap; lower-contrast face, with olive cheek patches that have lighter centers; little or no yellow in breast; paler olive back with fainter black streaking; yellow tint at base of legs (vs. white) diagnostic

Blackburnian No range overlap; triangular face pattern; streaking finer; lacks black in throat; orange throat (vs. yellow); black back (vs. olive) with pale braces; shorter tail

Hermit Plain face or smudgy auricular; gray back (vs. olive); lacks side streaking and yellow in breast

Golden-cheeked No range overlap; yellow face with black eyeline (vs. cheek patch); much darker back; no yellow underparts (vs. extensive)

Hermit x Townsend's Combines features of both species; usually plain yellow face without dark ear patch, all or partial black throat, side streaking below on yellow breast; some may show paler facial characteristics of Townsend's but without yellow below

Aging and Sexing

Spring AdM 1yM AdF 1yF   **Fall** AdM 1yM AdF 1yF

Races: 1 Summary *Spring:* Some AdM, AdF, and 1yF separable *Fall:* AdM and some 1yF separable **What to Notice** *Spring/Fall:* Black in throat and face, overall contrast

AdM Sp Black throat and mask, yellow breast, dark olive upperparts streaked with black; some 1yM may have entirely black throats, so only most contrasty birds should be considered AdM.

AdF/1yM Sp Yellow chin with mottled black throat, overall duller than AdM; 1yM may show yellow or mottling in throat, or have all-dark throat; *Diagnostic when present AdF:* no black shaft streaking in white covert tips, combined with yellow chin.

1yF Sp *Diagnostic when extreme:* totally yellow throat, very dull overall.

AdM Fa Similar to AdM Sp but slightly duller in black areas; back feathers fringed green.

AdF/1yM Fa Chin yellow, with variable black mottling in throat, more green overtones in back than AdM.

1yF Fa Indistinct black smudging on flanks, no black in back or sides of throat; overall paler and yellower than AdF/1yM; combined characteristics indicate 1yF.

Hermit/Townsend's Intergrade Zone in Washington and Oregon

Spring

Early   Middle   Late

Fall

Early   Middle   Late

Townsend's
You can Buzz right through, but at town's end, put on your squeaky brakes fast

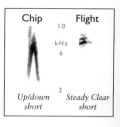

Chip   Flight

10

kHz

6

2

Up/down short   Steady Clear short

Summary Variable, but always *some combination of pure and Buzzy Elements* (similar to other *virens*); often begins with 3–9 repeated 1-Element Phrases; last Section usually 2 Buzzy Phrases starting higher than 1st Section, ending with Clear, fast, lower slur. **Types:** variable.

Type A1 Typical: starts with several Clear to Buzzy, simple Phrases, ends with 2 higher, accented, Buzzy downslurs.

Clear Elements at steady pitch; sometimes can be Buzzier and rise in pitch

Buzzy Phrases with Clearer downslurs (typical hybrid-quality of Townsend's Phrases)

Type A2 Buzzier variation; simple dense Buzzes rarely found in other western *virens* species.

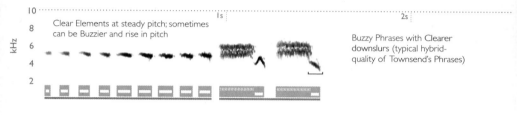

Simple, Buzzy, 1-Element Phrases (more likely than in Hermit)

Last Section has typical intricate, hybrid Buzzy/Clear Elements

Type A3 Structure similar to Black-throated Green Warbler (normally no range overlap).

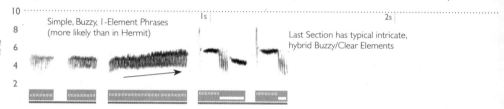

Elements Clear but with slight Buzzy quality, typical of *virens* species

Less regular rhythm

More intricately modulated than Black-throated Green Elements

Hermit A3 Often very similar, sometimes inseparable; small overlap in breeding ranges, much overlap during migration. Townsend's reportedly tends to sing more during migration.

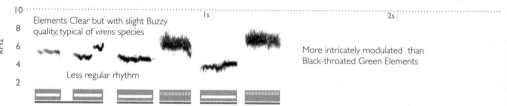

2-Element Phrases in 1st Section, found in many songs (vs. always 1-Element Phrases in 1st Section)

2nd Section Buzzes somewhat high, thin, with Expanded downslur; almost never simple, dense (vs. usually simpler, denser Buzzes)

Intricate Phrase ending in upslur (vs. usually ends in downslur but some overlap)

Hermit A2
Can have Buzzy Phrases, **but** Buzzes usually have Clear 2nd Element (vs. Buzzes tending to be denser, lower, simpler); very active burry/Clear Phrases in 1st 2 Sections (vs. usually simpler, without swings of pitch, Element types).

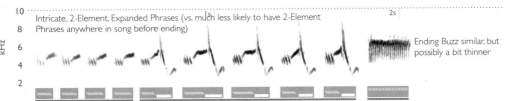

Intricate, 2-Element, Expanded Phrases (vs. much less likely to have 2-Element Phrases anywhere in song before ending)

Ending Buzz similar, but possibly a bit thinner

Black-throated Gray A1
Usually all or almost all Buzzy Phrases (vs. almost always some Clear Phrases); denser Buzzes; overall lower song (vs. thinner, less dense Elements).

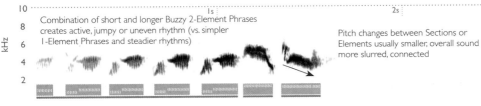

Combination of short and longer Buzzy 2-Element Phrases creates active, jumpy or uneven rhythm (vs. simpler 1-Element Phrases and steadier rhythms)

Pitch changes between Sections or Elements usually smaller, overall sound more slurred, connected

MacGillivray's A1
Similar combination of burry/Buzzy qualities, **but** never Sections with only simple, Clear Phrases (vs. sometimes); Complex burry Elements but never denser Buzzes like some Townsend's; almost always 2-Element Phrases in 1st Section (vs. 1-Element Phrases).

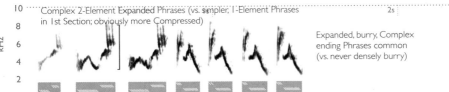

Complex 2-Element Expanded Phrases (vs. simpler, 1-Element Phrases in 1st Section; obviously more Compressed)

Expanded, burry, Complex ending Phrases common (vs. never densely burry)

Black-throated Green B1/Golden-cheeked B1
No range overlap; **Golden-cheeked** Type A easily separable: several 1-Phrase Sections (vs. 2 or 3 Sections, 4+ Phrases in 1st); Type B lower, richer, denser buzzes; simpler endings; overall Townsend's 1st Sections Clearer, all Buzzes a bit higher, less rich, dense; endings more complicated.

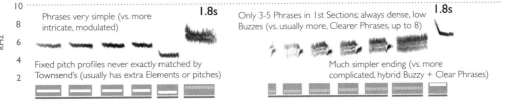

Phrases very simple (vs. more intricate, modulated)

Only 3-5 Phrases in 1st Sections; always dense, low Buzzes (vs. usually more, Clearer Phrases, up to 8)

Fixed pitch profiles never exactly matched by Townsend's (usually has extra Elements or pitches)

Much simpler ending (vs. more complicated, hybrid Buzzy + Clear Phrases)

VIRGINIA'S

Oreothlypis virginiae   Male/Female - All Seasons

- Limited range and habitat
- Grayish back and head
- White eyering
- ✓ Variable yellow patch on breast
- Yellow rump and UnTC
- Chestnut crown patch, often hidden

- White eyering contrasting with gray head and back
- Long, thin, gray tail
- ✓ Yellow UnTC and chest patch contrasts with gray tail and body
- Wings grayish, without any brighter edging
- ✓ Variable yellow patch on breast

- ✓ Yellow UnTC and chest patch contrasts with gray tail and body
- Long, thin, gray tail

Distinctive Views

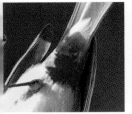 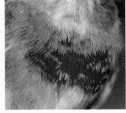  

Additional Photos

Chestnut crown sometimes seen

Gray overall with strongly contrasting yellow rump and UnTC diagnostic

Noticeably longer-tailed than Nashville; often wags its tail

Yellow on breast varies from almost none to extending from throat to mid-breast

No contrast between gray head and back, unlike Nashville

In migration found in brushy areas; on breeding grounds prefers steep slopes adjacent to higher trees above 1500 m

Yellow patches bright and stand out on overall gray body

Extensive yellow usually still appears patchy with some gray on sides of throat or breast

Flight feathers same gray tones as back and lack any brighter greenish edgings found in Nashville

Grayish head and back
White contrasting eyering
Restricted yellow patch on
upper breast
Yellow rump/UnTC
Long, dark tail often flipped

Comparison Species

Lucy's Chestnut rump (vs. yellow); pale around eye (vs. stronger eyering); more contrast between gray back and pale underparts; whitish UnTC (vs. yellow); shorter, paler tail (vs. dark); lacks any yellow on underparts

Verdin Juvenile Lacks eyering; sharper, deeper-based bill; adults show yellow in head; gray rump (vs. yellow); longer, lighter tail; white UnTC (vs. yellow)

American Redstart F Yellow shoulders/tail base (vs. breast, rump, UnTC); eye-arcs (vs. eyering); olive back (vs. gray); black-and-yellow tail diagnostic

Common Yellowthroat More olive above; eyering thinner, paler, not as contrasting; stouter shape; heavier bill; lacks yellow rump; browner/buffier underparts

Colima Larger; brownish tones overall including back and flanks (vs. gray); lacks yellow on breast; more orangey UnTC; rarely pumps tail

Nashville Olive back contrasts with gray head (vs. all gray); yellow throat/underparts (vs. restricted in breast); shorter tail; rump slightly duller; bright green edgings to flight feathers (vs. gray)

Aging and Sexing

Spring AdM 1yM AdF 1yF   **Fall** AdM 1yM AdF 1yF

Races: 1 Summary *Spring/Fall:* Extreme AdM and 1yF may be separable, others not   **What to Notice** *Spring/Fall:* Crown patch, extent of yellow breast patch, brown in back

AdM Sp/Fa Extreme Extensive yellow patch spanning breast, sometimes extending to chin/flanks; rufous crown patch (often concealed); *Diagnostic:* in fall, any bird with a pronounced crown patch is AdM.

All Others Sp/Fa Slightly duller than male, yellow does not reach flanks, crown patch paler and smaller (but often concealed).

1yF Sp/Fa Extreme Little or no yellow on breast, faint brown tone on upperparts.

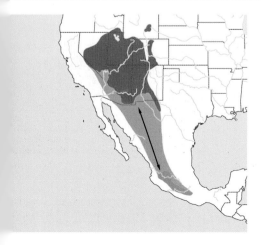

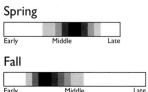

Spring

Early   Middle   Late

Fall

Early   Middle   Late

Virginia's
Virginia is more abrupt, emphatic, and shorter than her friend loquacious Lucy

Summary 2–4 *Sections of Clear Phrases*, 1st Section always 3–8 downslurred, fairly percussive, usually 2-Element Phrases; next Sections less emphatic, slower slurs; 2nd Section almost always 3 or 4 1-Element lower Phrases at about same speed; mostly downslurred Elements but often 1 Section with contrasting upslurs; speed, pitch don't change dramatically; *speed always relaxed, countable, never Trilled*; **I Type.**

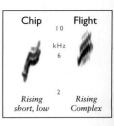

Chip | Flight

Rising short, low | *Rising Complex*

Type A1 Longer, 4-Section song; 1st Section almost always 2-Element Phrases, **but** speed can make them sound like complicated 1-Element Phrases.

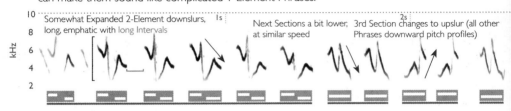

Somewhat Expanded 2-Element downslurs, long, emphatic with long Intervals • Next Sections a bit lower, at similar speed • 3rd Section changes to upslur (all other Phrases downward pitch profiles)

Type A2 2-Section song; as always, 1st Section 2-Element Phrases, 2nd Element lower; Phrase speed, pitch change fast enough to create somewhat percussive, accented quality.

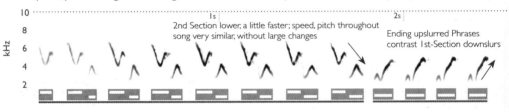

2nd Section lower, a little faster; speed, pitch throughout song very similar, without large changes • Ending upslurred Phrases contrast 1st-Section downslurs

Type A3 Typical 3-Section song; 1st Section 2-Element emphatic Phrases with falling pitch trend, fast enough so hard to hear 2-Elements clearly.

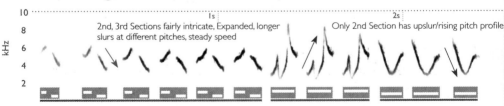

2nd, 3rd Sections fairly intricate, Expanded, longer slurs at different pitches, steady speed • Only 2nd Section has upslur/rising pitch profile

Nashville A4 Almost always 2 Sections (vs. most 3 or 4 Sections); 2nd Section usually much faster than 1st, often Trill speed, avg. 9 Phrases/sec. (vs. more even pitch/speed between Sections, never Trill speed, avg. 6 Phrases/sec.).

Sometimes rising pitch profile; more obviously separated 2-Element Phrases (vs. less separated; always falling pitch profile) • 2nd Section Elements usually shorter, more Expanded, longer Interval so more emphatic, staccato (vs. 2nd, subsequent Sections usually longer slurs, less emphatic)

Lucy's A3
Similar quality, structure, **but** faster, almost always 1 Trilled Section (vs. never Trilled); usually more Phrases (avg. 16 vs. 11); more change in speed, Element type between Sections: sounds more varied, less rhythmically consistent.

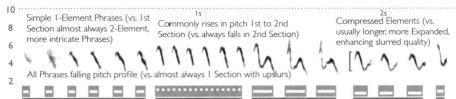

Simple 1-Element Phrases (vs. 1st Section almost always 2-Element, more intricate Phrases)

Commonly rises in pitch 1st to 2nd Section (vs. always falls in 2nd Section)

Compressed Elements (vs. usually longer, more Expanded, enhancing slurred quality)

All Phrases falling pitch profile (vs. almost always 1 Section with upslurs)

Wilson's B1
Often sings 1-Section songs (vs. never); 2nd Section almost always Trill (vs. never close to Trill speeds); 1st Section usually faster (avg. 7 Phrases/sec. vs. 5); rarely 3rd Section, emphatic when present (vs. often 3rd, 4th Sections with slower slurs).

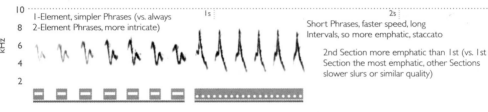

1-Element, simpler Phrases (vs. always 2-Element Phrases, more intricate)

Short Phrases, faster speed, long Intervals, so more emphatic, staccato

2nd Section more emphatic than 1st (vs. 1st Section the most emphatic, other Sections slower slurs or similar quality)

Yellow/Red-faced A3
Yellow: 1st Section key: Usually fewer Phrases (avg. 3.4 vs. 6); 1-Element, long, Expanded Phrases (vs. more percussive 2-Element Phrases); higher, brighter. **Red-faced**: usually 6+ Sections, never under 4 (vs. usually 2 or 3, sometimes 4); 1st Section avg. 2 Phrases, most Sections 1 or 2 (vs. avg. 6 Phrases 1st Section).

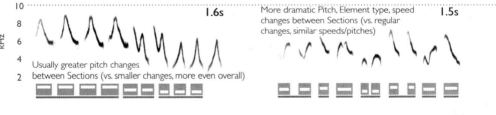

More dramatic Pitch, Element type, speed changes between Sections (vs. regular changes, similar speeds/pitches)

Usually greater pitch changes between Sections (vs. smaller changes, more even overall)

Yellow-rumped (Audubon's) A3/Painted Redstart A4
Painted Redstart: Generally slower, 1st Section avg. 3.3 Phrases/sec. vs. 7; lower-pitched. Overall more consistent speed, rhythm uneven, less regular.

Phrases more Complex, Compressed: subdued, "warbly" quality (vs. simpler, more Expanded slurs, longer Intervals: more distinct, emphatic, brighter)

Much more Compressed with shorter Intervals (vs. more emphatic, brighter)

All Sections similarly Compressed (vs. often even more Expanded 2nd Section)

WILSON'S
Cardellina pusilla   Male/Female - All Seasons

- Small overall
- Tiny bill that is black above and pale below
- Yellow underparts and olive back
- ✓ Often shows at least a partial black cap; otherwise, low contrast
- Plain face with faint olive cheek patch

- Yellow underparts and UnTC
- Long dark tail
- Small-billed
- Darker cheek/crown creates yellow supercilium

- Yellow underparts and UnTC
- Long dark tail
- Small-billed
- Pink legs

Distinctive Views

Additional Photos

Black cap is more extensive in males; females may show some black cap, but usually dull and blended with olive

Females may not show a cap but always show a plain yellow face with dusky cheek patch

Large area of yellow on forehead contrasting with black on crown

Very active, with frequent hover-gleaning and flitting or cocking tail

Female with some limited black in head; note yellow supercilium contrasting with dark cheek, crown

Always uniform yellow below; yellow tone may be brighter (in West) or duskier and somewhat duller (in East)

Wilson's are widespread in U.S. during migration; very common in the West

Yellow from bill to UnTC and lacking pale or yellow tail spots

Small, plump, with no white or yellow in the tail; frequently found in dense understory

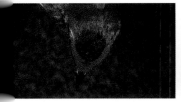

Females of the two western races may show more complete black caps

Broad yellow supercilium contrasts with darker cheek/crown in dull plumages

Don't just look for a black cap! Long dark tail with yellow body and UnTC are good ID points

Very yellow below and above
Contrasting bluish wings
Small, with small, bicolored bill
Long dark tail
Darker cheek/crown creates
yellow supercilium

Comparison Species

Hooded Larger, with larger black bill; dusky lores (vs. pale); plain yellow face with contrasting olive or black hood (vs. dusky cheek patch and crown emphasizing faint supercilium); white tail, frequently flashed (vs. dark)

Canada More complex face: striking eyering, supraloral; gray back (vs. olive); wings blend with back (vs. contrast); necklace (vs. none); thicker bill; white UnTC (vs. yellow)

Yellow Larger and more compact; extensive pale yellow edging in wings; some show red breast streaking; larger bill; yellow tail (vs. dark); shorter tail with longer UnTC; doesn't wag or cock tail as actively

Nashville Contrasting white eyering (vs. none); gray hood contrasts olive back (vs. all olive); fine, pointy bill, shorter tail; white in vent (vs. yellow)

Orange-crowned (shown)/Tennessee Duller olive above; finer, pointy bill; more complex face with dark eyeline and pale eye-arcs; Orange-crowned may show diffuse streaking below; duller buff or yellowish underparts; shorter tail not flipped or cocked

Aging and Sexing

Spring AdM 1yM AdF 1yF **Fall** AdM 1yM AdF 1yF

Races: 3: C.p. *pusilla* (east), C.p. *pileolata* (AK through west), and C.p. *chryseola* (Pacific Coast) **Summary** *Spring/Fall:* Not ageable; eastern race sexable **What to Notice** *Spring:* Check for presence/extent/shape of black cap, overall contrast *Fall:* Presence/extent/shape of black cap, contrast in face

AdM/1yM Sp/Fa (*pusilla*) *Diagnostic male:* complete, shiny black cap with clearly defined edges; Fall 1yM may show more olive in cap (variable).

AdF/1yF Sp/Fa, 1yF Sp (*pusilla*) Duller; *Diagnostic female:* no female *pusilla* shows any black cap.

1yF Fa (*pusilla*) No cap, averages low contrast, yellow-olive forehead.

AdM Sp/Fa *chryseola* Pacific Coast; more golden color than *pileolata*, auriculars and upperparts brighter and more yellow or orangey.

1yF Fa *chryseola* Pacific Coast; more golden color than *pileolata*, cheeks yellowish, often some orangey tones in forehead, lores.

AdM Sp/Fa *pileolata* Alaska through West; slightly brighter than *pusilla*.

1yF Fa *pileolata* Alaska through West; slightly brighter than *pusilla*.

Note Almost all *chryseola* and *pileolata* adult females show a partial black cap (usually much more limited than males); a very small percentage have extensive black or no black in the cap, which makes them difficult to separate from males and 1yF in the field, but most can be separated to a high level of probability.

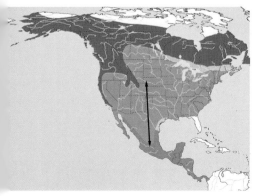

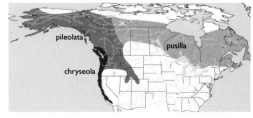

Spring East

| Early | Middle | Late |

Fall East

| Early | Middle | Late |

Spring West

| Early | Middle | Late |

Fall West

| Early | Middle | Late |

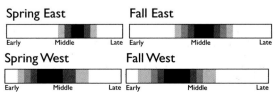

Wilson's

Pres. Wilson started out strong but fell, gradually, due to repetitive policies

Summary *1 or 2 Sections* of fairly simple, short, distinct repeated Phrases; *usually speeds up, falls in pitch gradually or in 2nd Section*; often louder, more emphatic toward end; *1st Section always slow, countable*, usually simple, slurred Phrases; 2nd Section of 1-Element Phrases, usually Trilled; always long Intervals; **2 Types: A**, 1 Section; **B**, 2 or 3 Sections.

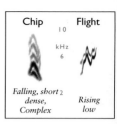

Chip Flight

Falling, short dense, Complex

Rising low

Type A1 1-Section; this example very emphatic, remaining steady in pitch, tempo.

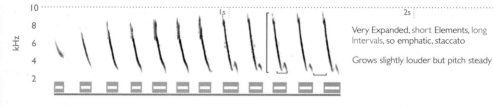

Very Expanded, short Elements, long Intervals, so emphatic, staccato

Grows slightly louder but pitch steady

Type A2 Less common; more slurred, slightly less emphatic.

Fast, Expanded downslur dominates sound in these Phrases; weak upslurred component, so less emphatic, but still percussive

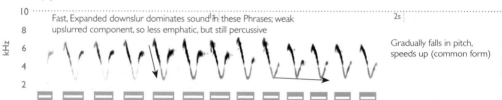

Gradually falls in pitch, speeds up (common form)

Type B1 2 Sections, the 2nd Trilled; in this example 2nd Section short.

Compressed, somewhat intricate 1-Element Phrases

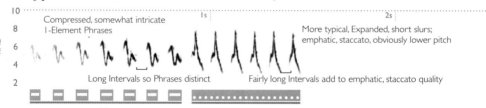

More typical, Expanded, short slurs; emphatic, staccato, obviously lower pitch

Long Intervals so Phrases distinct   Fairly long Intervals add to emphatic, staccato quality

Type B2 Uncommon, 3-Section song; speed increases and pitch falls throughout; 1-Element Expanded Phrases with very long Intervals so sounds emphatic, quickly slurred.

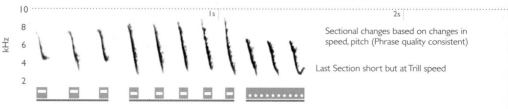

Sectional changes based on changes in speed, pitch (Phrase quality consistent)

Last Section short but at Trill speed

Type B3 2-Section song, 2nd Section faster (Trilled) and lower.

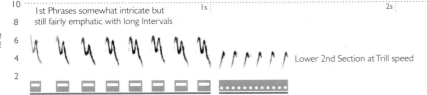

1st Phrases somewhat intricate but still fairly emphatic with long Intervals

Lower 2nd Section at Trill speed

Nashville A1 Similar form (repeated Phrases in 2 Sections, 2nd lower, faster), **but** rarely sings 1-Section song (vs. often 1-Section songs); almost always percussive, 2-Element Phrases, with sharply separated Elements (vs. never 2-Element Phrases).

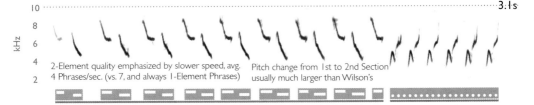

2-Element quality emphasized by slower speed, avg. 4 Phrases/sec. (vs. 7, and always 1-Element Phrases)

Pitch change from 1st to 2nd Section usually much larger than Wilson's

Virginia's A3 Always 2–4 Sections (never 1); 1st Section usually slower (avg. 5 Phrases/sec. vs. 7); 2nd Section avg. 6 Phrases/sec and no Trilled Sections (vs. 2nd Section normally Trilled); 3rd/4th Section usually slower slurs (vs. rarely has 3rd Section; if so it's faster than any Virginia's).

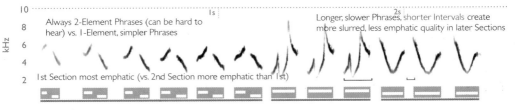

Always 2-Element Phrases (can be hard to hear) vs. 1-Element, simpler Phrases

Longer, slower Phrases, shorter Intervals create more slurred, less emphatic quality in later Sections

1st Section most emphatic (vs. 2nd Section more emphatic than 1st)

Lucy's Never sings 1-Section songs, often 4+ (vs. 1 or 2, rarely 3), more Phrases (avg. 16 vs.11), usually more Phrases in 1st Section (avg. 9 vs. 5).

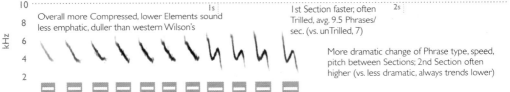

Overall more Compressed, lower Elements sound less emphatic, duller than western Wilson's

1st Section faster, often Trilled, avg. 9.5 Phrases/sec. (vs. unTrilled, 7)

More dramatic change of Phrase type, speed, pitch between Sections; 2nd Section often higher (vs. less dramatic, always trends lower)

WORM-EATING

Helmitheros vermivorum   Male/Female - All Seasons

- ✓ Mustard-colored head with four bold black stripes
- Long, pale, decurved bill
- Plain, dusky-olive back and wings

- Buffy pale undersides
- Short tail
- ✓ Gray spots in buffy UnTC
- Black eyestripe

- Buffy pale undersides
- Long pale bill
- ✓ Gray smudgy spots in buffy UnTC
- Short dark tail

Distinctive Views

Additional Photos

Male and female look the same in all seasons

Four-stripe head pattern is unique for North American warblers

Contrasting dark head stripes usually easy to see

Deliberate and acrobatic in its explorations of the understory

Long, pointy, slightly curved bill

Faint beige/gray spotting in UnTC is diagnostic

Specializes in picking insects from hanging dead leaves

Unique buffy/mustard color
Contrasting black head stripes
Plain olive back/wings
Long pale bill
Short tail
Dark spots on UnTC

Comparison Species

Swainson's Plain rusty/brown crown (vs. striped); larger; longer-billed; brown above (vs. olive); pale supercilium (vs. mustard); pale/buffy UnTC (vs. buff with gray spots)

Waterthrushes Brown above (vs. olive); whiter below; heavily streaked (vs. none); larger; usually forage on ground (vs. rarely); pumps tail (vs. never)

Black-throated Blue Blue-green above (vs. olive); dark cheek, thin pale eyebrow and under-eye arc (vs. striped head); often shows white handkerchief; plumper shape; buffy color below more yellowy; UnTC lack darker smudgy spots

Aging and Sexing

Races: 1 Summary *Spring/Fall:* Not sexable or ageable

All Birds All plumages similar in all seasons.

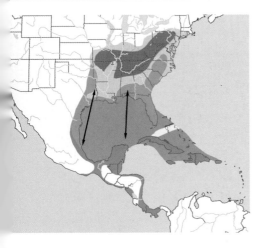

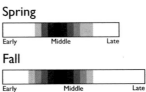

Spring

Early	Middle	Late

Fall

Early	Middle	Late

Worm-eating

It's hard to eat all of the worms when so many are popping up so fast

Summary *Long songs; 1 Section, fast Trill;* very Expanded, short slurs, long Intervals, sung very fast: *percussive, staccato, bright*; often does not end as abruptly as Chipping Sparrow. **2 Types:** Slow song (A) and fast song (B) but no intermediate speeds; A, Slower; Phrases more intricate (often short slurs adjacent to main slur add extra low, high frequencies unlike some similar species); B, Fastest, simpler Phrases, less Complex, "drier."

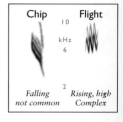

Chip   **Flight**

Falling not common   *Rising, high Complex*

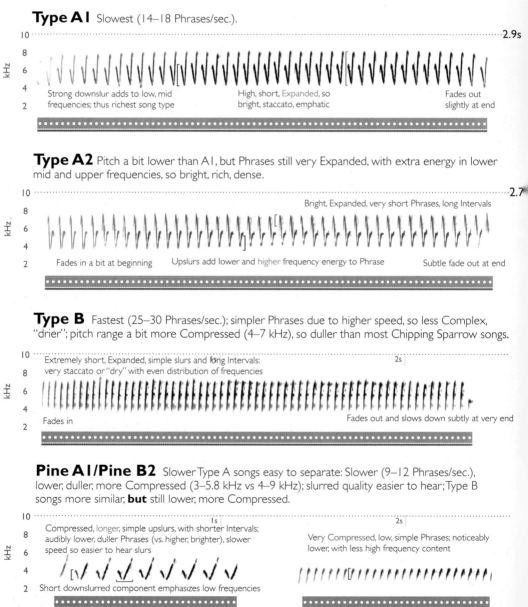

Type A1 Slowest (14–18 Phrases/sec.).

2.9s

Strong downslur adds to low, mid frequencies; thus richest song type

High, short, Expanded, so bright, staccato, emphatic

Fades out slightly at end

Type A2 Pitch a bit lower than A1, but Phrases still very Expanded, with extra energy in lower mid and upper frequencies, so bright, rich, dense.

2.7

Bright, Expanded, very short Phrases, long Intervals

Fades in a bit at beginning   Upslurs add lower and higher frequency energy to Phrase

Subtle fade out at end

Type B Fastest (25–30 Phrases/sec.); simpler Phrases due to higher speed, so less Complex, "drier"; pitch range a bit more Compressed (4–7 kHz), so duller than most Chipping Sparrow songs.

Extremely short, Expanded, simple slurs and long Intervals: very staccato or "dry" with even distribution of frequencies

2s

Fades in   Fades out and slows down subtly at very end

Pine A1/Pine B2 Slower Type A songs easy to separate: Slower (9–12 Phrases/sec.), lower, duller, more Compressed (3–5.8 kHz vs 4–9 kHz); slurred quality easier to hear; Type B songs more similar, **but** still lower, more Compressed.

1s

Compressed, longer, simple upslurs, with shorter Intervals; audibly lower, duller Phrases (vs. higher, brighter), slower speed so easier to hear slurs

Short downslurred component emphasizes low frequencies

2s

Very Compressed, low, simple Phrases; noticeably lower, with less high frequency content

Chipping Sparrow x2
Many variations, some easy to separate, some very similar, especially from distance; often fade in quickly, end very abruptly (possible ID points); usually more intricate Phrases, with both very high and very low complexities that add "tinkling" and lower Buzzy qualities (vs. never as high/low); more often in open, treed areas, not forests (overlap during migration).

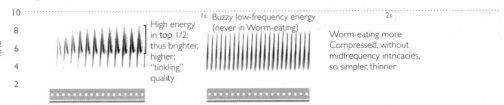

High energy in top 1/2; thus brighter, higher; "tinkling" quality

Buzzy low-frequency energy (never in Worm-eating)

Worm-eating more Compressed, without midfrequency intricacies, so simpler, thinner

Chipping Sparrow
Very similar variation in right sonogram; same speed as Type B, but ends very abruptly, with even more emphatic, higher final Phrase (vs. slightly lower and softer last few Phrases); Phrases much more Complex with more low- and high-frequency components, so sounds deeper and "tinkling" simultaneously (vs. more Compressed, simpler).

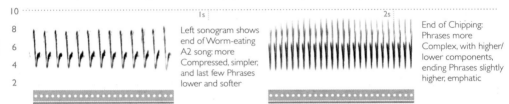

Left sonogram shows end of Worm-eating A2 song: more Compressed, simpler, and last few Phrases lower and softer

End of Chipping: Phrases more Complex, with higher/ lower components, ending Phrases slightly higher, emphatic

Dark-eyed Junco/Swamp Sparrow
Trills vary in speed/quality, some similar, **but Junco** noticeably lower; shorter Intervals so more slurred; shorter song. **Swamp:** Intricate, 2-Element Phrases (Elements are very short, Expanded accent plus louder, lower downslur); so more complicated, with doubled or stuttered quality; lowest portion below range of Worm-eating.

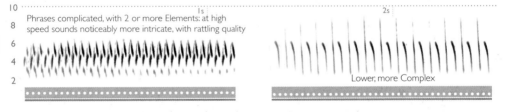

Phrases complicated, with 2 or more Elements: at high speed sounds noticeably more intricate, with rattling quality

Lower, more Complex

Blackpoll B1/Orange-crowned A1
Blackpoll: Uncommon, Type B songs similar in speed to fastest songs, **but** fades in for 1/3 or 1/2 of the song. **Orange-crowned:** almost all songs separable by 2nd Section/changes in speed/pitch; considerably shorter (avg. 1.5 sec. vs. 2.3).

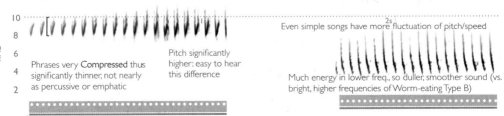

Phrases very Compressed thus significantly thinner, not nearly as percussive or emphatic

Pitch significantly higher: easy to hear this difference

Even simple songs have more fluctuation of pitch/speed

Much energy in lower freq., so duller, smoother sound (vs. bright, higher frequencies of Worm-eating Type B)

YELLOW

Setophaga petechia   Male/Female - All Seasons

- Plain face with round, black eye and pale eyering
- Stout black bill stands out against yellow face
- Yellow edging on wing feathers
- Some show red streaking in breast
- Compact shape
- Overall low contrast

- ✓ Yellow underparts, UnTC, and tail
- Some show red streaking in breast
- Compact shape and stout bill

- Yellow underparts, UnTC, and tail
- Compact shape and stout bill
- Relatively short tailed

Distinctive Views

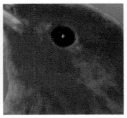

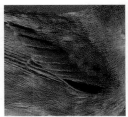

Additional Photos

A very widespread species, found in low trees and woodland edges, often in willows or wet areas

The amount of red breast streaking is variable, usually dull or lacking in females

Some birds, especially in SW, can be very pale and lack yellow covert and wing edgings

Frequently pumps tail, but movement not as exaggerated or active as Prairie, Palm, or Wilson's

Even drab, brownish young birds show contrasting yellow UnTC and tail; note pale wing covert edgings

Yellow tail with yellow UnTC is unique among U.S. warblers

Completely yellow underneath

Note yellow wing edgings, yellow UnTC, yellow tail

This bird is darker olive in the upperparts; note the pale lores and pronounced eyering

Yellow wing edging is good mark for separating from Wilson's or Hooded

Always very low overall contrast, in this case pale olive upperparts fading into head and face

Streaking in breast variable

Plain yellow or yellowish face
Pale eyering, stout bill
Low contrast
Yellow edging on wings
Short yellow tail and UnTC
Sometimes red breast streaks

Comparison Species

Prothonotary Larger and higher contrast; plain blue wings and green back (vs. olive); lacks eyering; white UnTC and tail (vs. yellow); larger, longer bill; orangier

Blue-winged Blue-gray wings; white wing bars (vs. yellow); strong black eyeline; finer pointy bill; white UnTC and tail (vs. yellow); smaller and finer-bodied

Wilson's Blue-toned wings; often shows at least some black cap; yellow supercilium contrasts with duller cap and cheek; longer, dark tail; smaller bill

Hooded Lacks pale edging in wings; black or olive hood contrasting with the paler face; longer, white tail (vs. yellow), often flashed

Orange-crowned More contrasting facial pattern: faint eyeline, pale eye-arcs, faint supercilium; finer pointy bill; darker olive above, no pale wing edging; longer, dark, thin tail (vs. yellow)

Common Yellowthroat F Stouter; heavier bill; darker olive above; dark cheek contrasts with yellow throat; skulkier; longer, dark tail (not yellow); yellow UnTC contrast body; typically browner flanks

Goldfinch Smaller with small, conical bill; black wings/pronounced wing bar; often in flocks; strongly notched, pale tail

Lucy's Gray (no yellow); rufous in rump; smaller; finer bill; flitty; thinner, pale tail without any yellow tones

Tennessee Smaller, with thinner bill; olive/green above contrasts more with wings; more complex face: short, strong eyeline, eye-arcs, supercilium; shorter, pale tail (vs. yellow); paler UnTC

Aging and Sexing

Races: Many, in 3 Complexes: Aestiva, Erithachorides (Mangrove) and Petechia (Golden); 9 races in Aestiva Complex, *D.p. aestiva* (east of Rockies), *D.p. rubiginosa* (coastal Northwest, BC to southern AK), *D.p. morcomi* (BC to Baja, AZ, NM, TX), *D.p. sonorana* (Baja, southern AZ, NM, western TX), *D.p. dugesi* (Mexico), *D.p. brewsteri* (coastal WA to CA), *D.p. banksi* (central AK), *D.p. parkesi* (northern Canada) **Summary** *Spring/Fall:* Extreme birds sexable/ageable, others not **What to Notice** *Spring/Fall:* Streaking in breast, overall brightness/contrast, extent of yellow edging in flight feathers, primary covert color

AdM/1yM Sp (*aestiva*) *Diagnostic when present male:* bright yellow/olive upperparts and yellow underparts, red streaks in breast, strong yellow edging in flight feathers; *Diagnostic when present 1yM:* shows brown primary coverts (subtle) and less red streaking.

AdF/1yF Sp (*aestiva*) Less or no red streaking, lower contrast (versus males); greenish crown; *Diagnostic when present 1yF:* brown primary coverts (subtle) and no red streaking.

AdM Fa (*aestiva*) Similar to spring males, slightly duller with reduced streaking.

AdF/1yF/1yM Fa (*aestiva*) Similar to spring females, little to no streaking; *Diagnostic AdF:* black primary coverts (subtle); *Diagnostic 1y:* brown primary coverts (subtle).

1yF Fa Extreme (*aestiva*) Dullest plumage, no streaking, buffy underparts, grayish upperparts, relative little yellow overall and very low contrast; duller primary coverts (subtle).

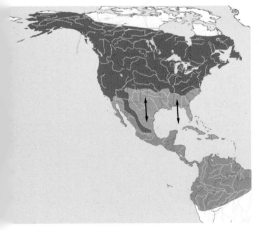

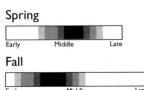

Spring

Early   Middle   Late

Fall

Early   Middle   Late

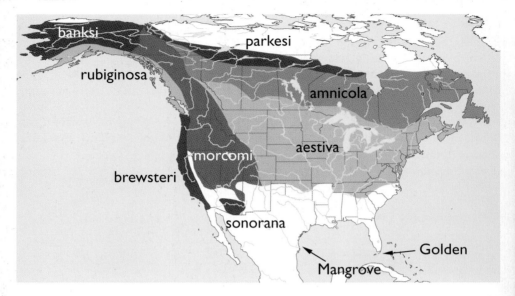

AdM Sp *rubiginosa* Some races often show greenish tone

AdM Sp *sonorana* Baja, southern AZ, NM, and western TX

Golden (petechia complex) *gundlachi*

AdM

AdF

1yM

Mangrove (erithachorides complex) *oraria*

AdM

AdF

1yM

1yF

Yellow

Bright yellow lemon meringue pie is "sweet, sweet, oh so sweet"

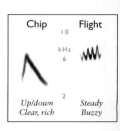

	Chip	Flight
	Up/down Clear, rich	Steady Buzzy

Summary *Expanded, long Clear slurs in usually 3–5 Sections.* Many variations beyond typical "I'm so sweet"; always starts with 3 or 4 (rarely 5) long, slurred, 1-Element Phrases; *Phrases usually 1-Element*, fairly Expanded with long enough Intervals to sound emphatic, distinct; usually *large pitch/ Phrase shape changes between Sections*; usually gets faster between Sections as song progresses; **2 Types: A**, shorter, usually 3-Section songs with emphatic, accented ending (usually Expanded upslur); **B**, longer songs with more Phrases, less emphatic ending.

Type A1 Familiar, accented, "Sweet Sweet Sweet I am so so Sweet" easily recognized; speeds up throughout song.

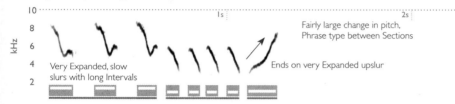

Very Expanded, slow slurs with long Intervals

Fairly large change in pitch, Phrase type between Sections

Ends on very Expanded upslur

Type A2 3 Sections without traditional "Sweet" upslurred ending; 1st Section only 3 Phrases, (common) unlike most Chestnut-sided 4+ Phrases.

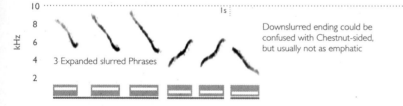

3 Expanded slurred Phrases

Downslurred ending could be confused with Chestnut-sided, but usually not as emphatic

Type B1 Less accented ending, usually longer; this version short.

3 intricate, very slow slurs; unusually Complex

2nd Section Expanded slurs

Ending Compressed, unaccented

Type B2 Uncommon form; unaccented, 2nd Section of 2-Element Phrases.

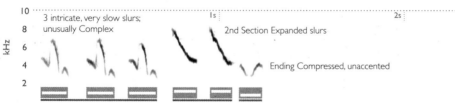
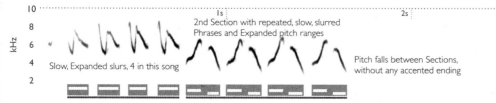

Slow, Expanded slurs, 4 in this song

2nd Section with repeated, slow, slurred Phrases and Expanded pitch ranges

Pitch falls between Sections, without any accented ending

Type B3
Good example of variability of this species; long like Type B, but ending like Type A; many Sections with long, slurred Phrases repeated 2 or 3 times.

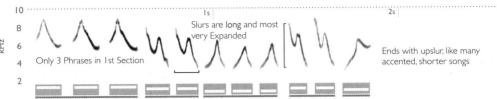

Only 3 Phrases in 1st Section

Slurs are long and most very Expanded

Ends with upslur, like many accented, shorter songs

Type B4
Long; Phrases somewhat more Compressed than other examples and thus can be tougher to ID.

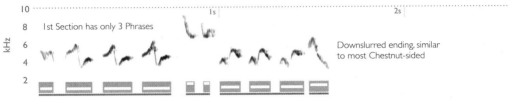

1st Section has only 3 Phrases

Downslurred ending, similar to most Chestnut-sided

Chestnut-sided A1
Accented Chestnut-sided generally easily separable, **but** some Yellow songs have similar form, same downslurred ending; Chestnut-sided usually 4+ Phrases in 1st Section (vs. only 3) and ending more emphatic.

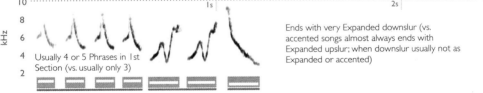

Usually 4 or 5 Phrases in 1st Section (vs. usually only 3)

Ends with very Expanded downslur (vs. accented songs almost always ends with Expanded upslur; when downslur usually not as Expanded or accented)

Chestnut-sided B1
Unaccented songs very similar, sometimes hard to separate, **but** longer, unaccented songs often have accented Section in middle; 2-Element Phrase in last Section not uncommon in Chestnut-sided but very rare in Yellow (almost never 2-Element Phrases).

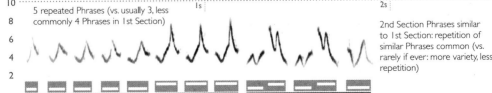

5 repeated Phrases (vs. usually 3, less commonly 4 Phrases in 1st Section)

2nd Section Phrases similar to 1st Section: repetition of similar Phrases common (vs. rarely if ever: more variety, less repetition)

Yellow (cont.)

Red-faced A2 vs. B Slurred Phrases, Expanded slurs at end, **but** rarely overlap
habitats; more variable Phrase speeds, shapes, overall rhythm (vs. much steadier, repetitive, even pace); always at least two 1-Phrase Sections (vs. almost never has 1-Phrase Sections other than last); more Sections, avg. 7 (range 4–12) vs. avg. 3 (range 2–5).

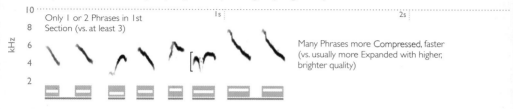

Only 1 or 2 Phrases in 1st Section (vs. at least 3)

Many Phrases more Compressed, faster (vs. usually more Expanded with higher, brighter quality)

Hooded A1 Noticeably lower, Phrases slower, much more Compressed.

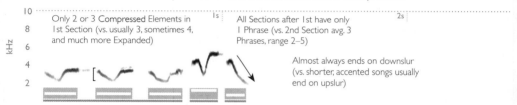

Only 2 or 3 Compressed Elements in 1st Section (vs. usually 3, sometimes 4, and much more Expanded)

All Sections after 1st have only 1 Phrase (vs. 2nd Section avg. 3 Phrases, range 2–5)

Almost always ends on downslur (vs. shorter, accented songs usually end on upslur)

Magnolia B1 Common accented songs usually obviously shorter with fewer Phrases; lower, richer with more slurred, less emphatic quality (avg. peak 5.6 kHz vs. 7.8 kHz); only 1 Phrase in both 2nd, 3rd Sections (vs. at least 2 Phrases, avg. 3 in 2nd Section).

Generally more Compressed pitch range (vs. more Expanded, brighter, more emphatic)

Ending Compressed (vs. usually much more Expanded slur)

American Redstart A1 Accented song easy to distinguish; never more than 3 Sections (vs. almost always at least 3 Sections, often 4 or 5).

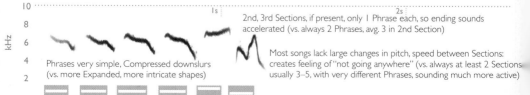

2nd, 3rd Sections, if present, only 1 Phrase each, so ending sounds accelerated (vs. always 2 Phrases, avg. 3 in 2nd Section)

Phrases very simple, Compressed downslurs (vs. more Expanded, more intricate shapes)

Most songs lack large changes in pitch, speed between Sections: creates feeling of "not going anywhere" (vs. always at least 2 Sections, usually 3–5, with very different Phrases, sounding much more active)

American Redstart C2

American Redstart C2 More uncommon, longer songs can be more difficult to separate; often alternated with 1-Section Type B song (vs. never sings 1-Section songs). Usually only 2 Sections; higher, thinner; 2nd Section always higher (vs. in rare Yellow 2-Section songs 2nd Section always lower).

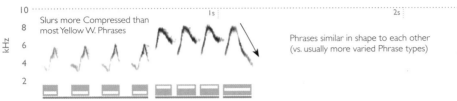

Slurs more Compressed than most Yellow W. Phrases

Phrases similar in shape to each other (vs. usually more varied Phrase types)

Lucy's A1

Lucy's A1 Repeated slurs and several Sections of longer songs could be confusing, **but** more Phrases per song, avg. 16 (vs. 8); and more in 1st Section, avg. 8 (vs. 3); song faster, avg. 9 Phrases/sec. (vs. 6), 1st Section sometimes Trill (vs. never Trill); Elements more Compressed and shorter (vs. longer, more Expanded, brighter).

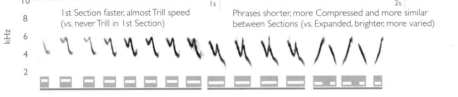

1st Section faster, almost Trill speed (vs. never Trill in 1st Section)

Phrases shorter, more Compressed and more similar between Sections (vs. Expanded, brighter, more varied)

YELLOW-RUMPED

Setophaga coronata   Bright Birds

Myrtle (eastern)

Audubon's (western)

- Streaked on breast, flanks, back
- Under-eye arc
- ✓ Yellow crown patch, rump, and shoulders; yellow throat on Audubon's
- White throat and sides of neck, contrasting cheek patch
- Blue-gray above and white undersides
- Wing bars or wing panel (male Audubon's)

- ✓ Yellow shoulder patches with black breast streaking
- Streaking on breast and flanks in inverted "U" pattern
- White (Myrtle) or yellow (Audubon's) throat
- Large tail with distinctive pattern: large white spots, black tail edges, and black base
- Frequent chip calls

- ✓ Yellow shoulder patches with black breast streaking
- Audubon's shows white in 4 or more outer tail feathers, Myrtle in 3 or fewer
- Large tail with distinctive pattern: large white spots, black tail edges, and black base

Distinctive Views

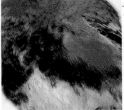

Additional Photos

Bright yellow rump is prominent and often exposed by drooped wings

More contrasty head of Myrtle has white throat, supercilium, and black mask

Tails spots and yellow rump are conspicuous in flight

Yellow crown patch usually visible and distinctive

Gray-and-black-streaked back with contrasting crown stripe

A versatile feeder, utilizes many habitats and can eat waxy berries in winter

Highly visible, active warbler, often perching on exposed branches and sallying for insects

Audubon's overall plainly patterned head has straighter throat edge and lacks supercilium of Myrtle

Usually the only warbler seen in winter in NE U.S., often in flocks; chip calls frequently

Conspicuous white tail spots with large black border distinctive

Shoulder patches usually very obvious in bright birds

Yellow patches bordered by black and blue-gray make this Audubon's unmistakable

Black streaks/blobs breast/sides
Long tail with large white
spots/black borders
Bright yellow rump
Bright yellow shoulders
White wing panel or wing bars

Comparison Species

Races of Yellow-rumped:

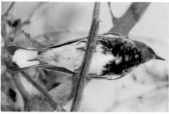

Audubon's (western) Yellow in throat; throat border more limited; doesn't extend into cheek; plainer face with no supercilium.

Myrtle (eastern) White throat extends past cheeks; white supercilium and supraloral spot; wing bars rather than wing patch

Magnolia Yellow underparts (vs. white); black necklace of finer streaks (vs. heavy black streaks); black mask and white supercilium (vs. none in Audubon's); black back (vs. gray streaked black); black terminal band on white tail diagnostic

Townsend's Yellow extends to breast; varying black throat; different shape to face patch

YELLOW-RUMPED
Setophaga coronata   Drab Birds

Myrtle (eastern)

Audubon's (western)

- Bright yellow rump
- Variably yellow shoulder patches
- Variably streaked breast, flank, back
- Eye-arcs
- White throat and sides of neck, wrapping around contrasting cheek patch (Myrtle)
- Wing bars
- Audubon's variably yellow in throat

- Variably yellow shoulder patches
- Variably streaked breast and flanks
- Large white tail spots bordered with black

- Variably yellow shoulder
- Variably streaked breast and flanks
- Long tail with large white spots surrounded by large black border
- Audubon's variably yellow in throat
- Audubon's shows white in 4 or more outer tail feathers, Myrtle in 3 or fewer

Distinctive Views

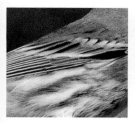

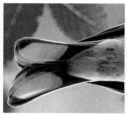

Additional Photos

Young birds may show little or no yellow in shoulders but considerable brown in back and flanks

Tails spots, yellow rump are conspicuous in flight; rump brighter, better defined than Cape May, Magnolia

Bright yellow rump, even in drabbest birds

Conspicuous white tail spots with strong black border are distinctive

Some Audubon's show almost no yellow in the throat or shoulders

A versatile feeder: can eat waxy berries in winter

Body streaking is faint in some birds

Audubon's tail averages less white and can show distinct stepped pattern of white bordered by black when fanned

Highly visible, active warbler, often perching on exposed branches and sallying for insects

This warbler has lost its tail

Yellow-rumps are very adaptable and will take advantage of many food sources

Often the only warbler seen in winter in the NE; usually in flocks, calling often

Bright yellow rump
Varying yellow shoulders
Some streaking below
White or buffy wing bars
Often active feeder

Comparison Species

Audubon's Race Grayer upperparts; plain face lacks supercilium; variable yellow in squared, narrower throat, which doesn't wrap around ear patch; less contrasting cheek blends with face

Myrtle Race Browner upperparts; wider white throat extends past and wraps around cheeks; always some supercilium and lighter loral spot; darker, more contrasting cheek

Cape May Smaller with finer bill; finer streaking more uniform, often extending into throat; duller greenish-yellow rump; shorter, white tail; usually shows some yellow in middle of breast

American Redstart F Yellow shoulders/tail; eye-arcs, no supercilium; unstreaked; more active, tail flashing; black-and-yellow tail diagnostic; olive in back (vs. none)

Palm Yellow UnTC (vs. white); larger; squarer black at tail base; brown or rufous cap/streaking; duller yellow uppertail coverts; constant, exaggerated tail-pumping; browner back; larger supercilium

Pine Bigger, more sluggish bird; gray rump (vs. yellow); often stronger wing bars; plainer face than Myrtle; often yellow in throat or center of upper breast; long white tail with less black border

Blackpoll More contrasty face with distinct eyeline; yellow to yellow-olive wash on sides and flanks; contrast between yellow underparts and white UnTC; often orange legs/feet; shorter tail

Lucy's More uniform pale gray; no yellow; pale lores (vs. dark); chestnut uppertail coverts (vs. yellow); shorter, white tail; smaller with finer bill

Virginia's Yellow breast/UnTC (vs. shoulders/throat); eyering (vs. eye-arcs lighter lores; gray back and underparts rufous crown patch (not always visible long gray tail (vs. white); fine bill

Aging and Sexing (Myrtle) Spring AdM 1yM AdF 1yF Fall AdM 1yM AdF 1yF

Races: 4, 2 in U.S./Canada *S.c. coronata* (east, "Myrtle"), *S.c. auduboni* (west, "Audubon's") **Summary** *Spring:* Sexable, some first-year birds ageable *Fall:* Extreme AdM and 1yF separable, others not **What to Notice** *Spring/Fall:* Black mask, intensity of side streaking, brightness of yellow shoulder patches, overall contrast, brownish back cast, buffy or white undersides

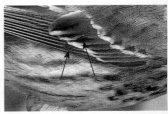

AdM/1yM Sp Black mask, white supercilium and throat, bright yellow shoulder patches, black on chest and sides; *Diagnostic when present 1yM:* may show browner primary coverts and flight feathers.

AdF/1yF Sp Duller than males, less streaking on head and back, lores paler and less flank streaking, more brown in underparts, mask is gray-brown, yellow patches duller, less black on underparts.

1y Sp *Diagnostic when present 1y:* may show browner primary coverts and flight feathers; note contrast of these feathers with blackish greater coverts.

AdM Fa Extreme similar to spring female, but strong yellow shoulder patches, distinct brown mask and bold black streaking; *Diagnostic:* distinct black lores.

All Other Fa Duller than AdM extreme, fainter streaking, more brown overall, variable yellow shoulder patch.

1yF Fa Extreme Dullest plumage faint, diffuse streaking, brown back, buffy underneath, no yellow in shoulder patches, reduced streaking below.

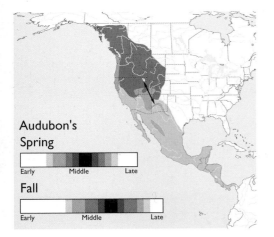

Audubon's
Spring

Early Middle Late

Fall

Early Middle Late

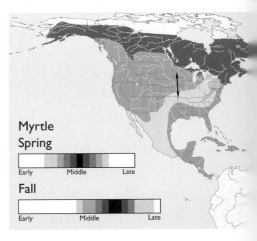

Myrtle
Spring

Early Middle Late

Fall

Early Middle Late

Aging and Sexing (Audubon's) Spring AdM 1yM AdF 1yF **Fall** AdM 1yM AdF 1yF

Races: 4, 2 in U.S./Canada *S.c. coronata* (east, "Myrtle"), *S.c. auduboni* (west, "Audubon's) **Summary** *Spring:* AdM and 1yM sometimes separable, all others separable *Fall:* Extreme AdM and 1yF separable, others generally not **What to Notice** *Spring/Fall:* Back color, quality of black in breast, shoulder/throat color, overall contrast, amount of white in tail, presence of two ages of feathers in greater coverts (black with white tips vs. brown with buff tip)

AdM Sp Gray back, bright and contrasty, sharply defined yellow throat contrasting with dark head; black blotches in breast; *Diagnostic when present:* complete wing panel.

1yM Sp Usually less white in tail than AdM (more black in tail base and between tail halves); *Overlap AdM:* black in head and breast (may approach AdM); *Diagnostic from AdM:* black blotching in breast combined with incomplete wing panel.

AdF Sp Less yellow in throat and shoulders than males; *Diagnostic from male:* more brown in back than males and less black in breast (streaks, not blotches), wing bars, not wing panel.

1yF Sp Browner back, paler yellow or whitish shoulders and throat than AdF; *Diagnostic when present:* no yellow in shoulders

AdM Fa Extreme Gray and black in back; black lores; black streaks in breast (not blotches); overlap with AdF so only contrasty birds with extensive black reliably aged/sexed.

AdF/1yM Fa Averages lighter/thinner breast streaking, more brownish back than AdM, but some overlap.

1yF Fa Extreme Very dull, with white or slightly yellow-tinted throat, very light breast streaking; some overlap with AdF, so only extreme birds should be aged/sexed.

Diagnostic when present: fall 1y birds may show two feather ages in greater coverts (black with white tips vs. brown with buff tip).

Intergrade Zone Audubon's and Myrtle overlap breeding range in western Canada, where they interbreed.

Note the variation in drab fall Audubon's, especially in throat and shoulder color, back tone and streaking

Yellow-rumped (Audubon's)

Sitting on your rump, mumbling the same Phrases, never makes a strong point

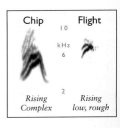

Chip   Flight

Rising   Rising
Complex   low, rough

Summary *Loosely Complex, Compressed Phrases in 2 or 3 Sections* with only small pitch variations; short Intervals and Complex Phrases create *warbly, slurred quality*; Sections usually similar pitches; short Intervals add to general overall slurred, indistinct quality; *last Section often fades out*, as if losing energy; 1st Section 4–8 almost always 2-Element Phrases; 2nd, 3rd Sections usually only 2 Phrases each. **Types:** variable.

Type A1 Typical song with 8 Phrases in first Section.

Complex, slow, long
2-Element Phrases

Pitch gradually rises over 1st Section

Compressed pitch, relatively short
Intervals so overall slurred, warbly quality

Last Section short downslur

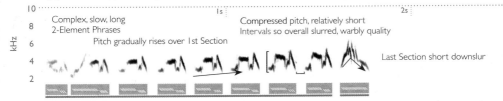

Type A2 3 Sections; Phrases very similar in quality, pitch, speed between Sections.

Loosely Complex,
2-Element Phrases

Only small pitch change in 2nd Section

Last Section fades out, as if
song runs out of energy

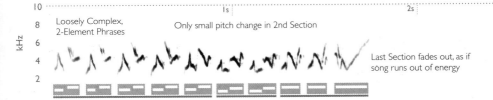

Type A3 Slightly more Expanded and emphatic version.

Complex, long, Compressed, warbly
2-Element Phrases with short Intervals

2nd Section short, and
falls off in pitch, volume

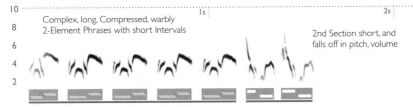

Virginia's A2 Structurally similar, **but** much more likely to have 4th Section (vs. very rare), shorter, more Expanded Elements with longer Intervals, so distinct, more emphatic. More variety between Sections.

Expanded 2-Element Phrases more emphatic,
percussive (vs. Compressed, slurred, warbly)

Simple, Clear upslurs, long Intervals;
obviously different from 1st Section in
pitch, quality; not warbly or Compressed

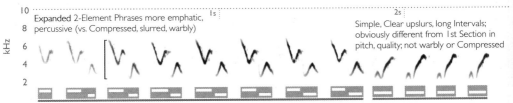

MacGillivray's A1
Complex 2-Element Phrases, **but** usually fewer Phrases in 1st Section (avg. 4 vs. 6); transition between Sections much more drastic.

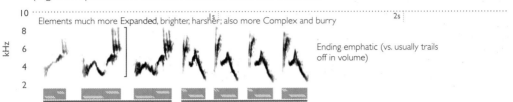

Elements much more Expanded, brighter, harsher; also more Complex and burry

Ending emphatic (vs. usually trails off in volume)

Painted Redstart A2
Sometimes very similar, **but** almost always fewer Phrases in 1st Section (avg. 3 vs. 6); commonly has 4–6 Sections (vs. 2 or 3); erratic changes in speed, Phrase shape, create unsteady, almost spastic rhythm (vs. fewer Sections/more repetition in 1st Section creating steady rhythmic quality).

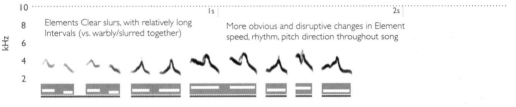

Elements Clear slurs, with relatively long Intervals (vs. warbly/slurred together)

More obvious and disruptive changes in Element speed, rhythm, pitch direction throughout song

Red-faced A2
Fewer Phrases in 1st Section (avg. 2 vs. 6), many Sections (avg. 7 vs. 2 or 3); very simple, Expanded, smooth slurs, lacking all Complexity, distinct with long Intervals (vs. Complex, Compressed slurred Phrases with short Intervals).

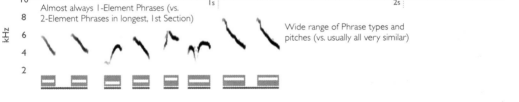

Almost always 1-Element Phrases (vs. 2-Element Phrases in longest, 1st Section)

Wide range of Phrase types and pitches (vs. usually all very similar)

Grace's B1/Lucy's A1/Dark-eyed Junco
Grace's: Noticeably faster (avg. 8 Phrases/sec. vs. 5), 1-Element Phrases (vs. 2-Element in 1st Section). **Lucy's:** Often 4–6 Sections (vs. 2 or 3), many more Phrases (avg. 16 vs. 10); short simpler slurs with longer Intervals so more distinct, emphatic; more dramatic changes between Sections.

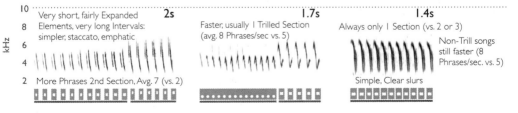

Very short, fairly Expanded Elements, very long Intervals: simpler, staccato, emphatic

More Phrases 2nd Section, Avg. 7 (vs. 2)

Faster, usually 1 Trilled Section (avg. 8 Phrases/sec vs. 5)

Always only 1 Section (vs. 2 or 3)

Non-Trill songs still faster (8 Phrases/sec. vs. 5)

Simple, Clear slurs

Yellow-rumped (Myrtle)

Sitting on your rump, mumbling the same Phrases, never makes a strong point

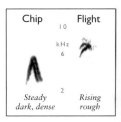

Chip	Flight
Steady dark, dense	Rising rough

Summary Variable. 1 or 2 Sections of loosely Complex, Compressed, usually 1-Element Phrases with *slurred, warbly quality*; *1st Section 6–12 Phrases*, countable; *2nd slightly different pitch, faster* (sometimes Trilled); *often fades out*; usually very Compressed; short Intervals so slurred, indistinct quality; song *often weakly delivered* during migration; **Types:** variable.

Type A1 1st Section has many Complex Phrases, speed blurs 2-Element Phrases to sound like Complex 1-Element slurs.

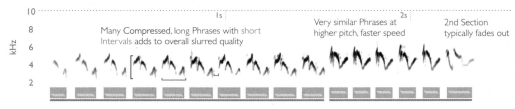

Many Compressed, long Phrases with short Intervals adds to overall slurred quality

Very similar Phrases at higher pitch, faster speed

2nd Section typically fades out

Type A2 Myrtle more likely to have 1-Section songs than Audubon's; fairly weak, warbly delivery.

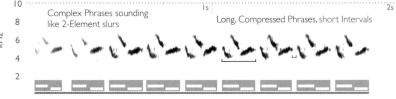

Complex Phrases sounding like 2-Element slurs

Long, Compressed Phrases, short Intervals

Type A3 Typically long 1st Section with many Phrases, followed by a short, higher ending.

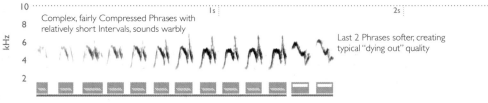

Complex, fairly Compressed Phrases with relatively short Intervals, sounds warbly

Last 2 Phrases softer, creating typical "dying out" quality

Type A4 Speed/Phrase quality remain similar throughout; many Phrases in 1st Section.

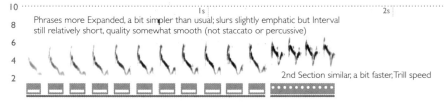

Phrases more Expanded, a bit simpler than usual; slurs slightly emphatic but Interval still relatively short, quality somewhat smooth (not staccato or percussive)

2nd Section similar, a bit faster, Trill speed

Type A5 9 simpler, slurred Phrases that gradually increase in pitch and volume.

Pitch range fairly Compressed, Intervals short, so smooth, overall slurred quality

Ending Phrases similar, lower, fading or dying out, without emphatic ending found in many warbler songs; often useful ID point

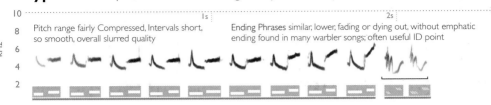

Chestnut-sided B2 (shown)/Yellow Some unaccented songs could be confusing, **but** more Sections (3–5; vs. 1 or 2), fewer Phrases in 1st Section (3–6 vs. avg. 10).

Slurs more Expanded, longer Interval so sound Clearer, less warbly

Larger pitch, Element type changes between Sections, so song overall sounds more varied, active

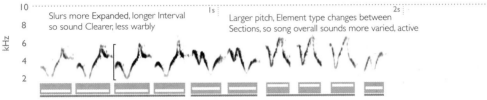

Palm A2 Possibly confusing at a distance during migration, when song is delivered with less energy; Complex Elements, often weakly delivered; always only 1 Section (vs. usually 2); always Buzzy or densely Complex Elements (vs. warbly, never Buzzy).

More Expanded with longer Intervals, thus Phrases sound more distinct and less slurred together

Usually even volume throughout (vs. often losing energy, fades out at end)

Always Buzzier quality

Pine A1 Possibly confusing at a distance during migration, when song is delivered with less energy; slowest songs almost same speed as fastest Yellow-rumped, **but** only one section (vs. usually 2), many more Phrases (avg. 15 vs. 10).

Elements of slower songs very simple upslurs with long Intervals, sound distinct, percussive (vs. warbly, more intricate)

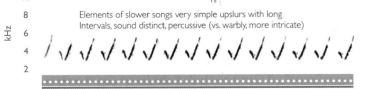

Yellow-rumped (Myrtle, cont.)

Wilson's B1 Never sings 2-Element Phrases in 1st Section (vs. sometimes); never rises in pitch (vs. often in 2nd Section); almost always more Phrases in 2nd Section (4–10 vs. avg. 3.6).

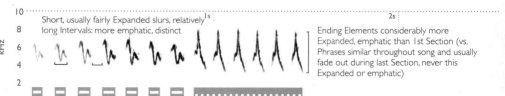

Short, usually fairly Expanded slurs, relatively long Intervals: more emphatic, distinct

Ending Elements considerably more Expanded, emphatic than 1st Section (vs. Phrases similar throughout song and usually fade out during last Section, never this Expanded or emphatic)

Orange-crowned B1 All Sections Trilled (vs. never in 1st Section, uncommonly in 2nd), 1st Section avg. 16 Phrases/sec. (vs. 5); short, Expanded slurs with relatively long Intervals, creating much more emphatic, articulated sound.

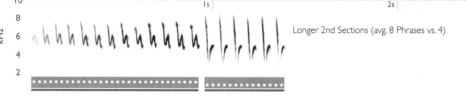

Longer 2nd Sections (avg. 8 Phrases vs. 4)

Audubon's vs. Myrtle
The vocalizations of these two races are very similar, **but** certain average differences can be noted. These generalizations should be used with caution, especially in areas where the two normally overlap.

Chip Calls With experience the chip calls should be separable: Myrtle flat, dense without overall rising or falling profile vs. Audubon's breathier, more loosely Complex, more rising quality.
Flight Calls Identical; note: often gives chip call in conjunction with flight call during migration.
Songs and Statistics: There is overlap in most of these characteristics, but they can serve as focal points for study.
Audubon's (vs. Myrtle):
1st Section almost always 2-Element Phrases (vs. usually 1-Element)
Slower, emphasizing 2-Element Phrases in 1st Section (avg. 4.9 Phrases/sec. vs. 5.6)
Never Trilled (vs. often Trilled in 2nd Section)
More Sections (2 or 3, never 1, vs. sometimes 1, never 3)
Shorter song, fewer Phrases per Section, especially 1st Section (avg. 6 vs. 10)
2nd, 3rd Sections usually only 2 Phrases each (vs. avg. 4 in 2nd, almost never 3rd)
Avg. lower pitch.

	Audubon's	Myrtle
Pitch Range	3.0–5.1 kHz	3.7–5.7 kHz
Total Sections	2 or 3	1 or 2
Song Length	1.2 sec. avg. (0.7–1.5)	1.8 sec. avg. (1.5–2.2)
Speed (Phrases/sec.)	5.4 avg.	6.7 avg.
1st Section	5.2 avg.	6.6 avg.
2nd Section	6.8	9.4 avg.
Phrase counts	9.6 avg.	12.2 avg.
1st Section	6.3 avg. (4–8)	9.7 avg. (9–12)
2nd Section	2.2 avg. (1–3)	3.6 avg. (2–6)
3rd Section	2.2 avg. (1–3)	n/a

YELLOW-THROATED

Setophaga dominica   Male/Female - All Seasons

- Large, high-contrast warbler with an elongated profile and long bill
- Bright yellow chin, throat, and breast
- Strongly contrasting black cheek patch, lores, with white under-eye arc, strong supercilium
- White wing bars contrast strongly with intervening black
- White neck stripe

- Black cheek patch and foreneck lead into extensive black side stripes
- Bright yellow throat more striking due to black border
- Bright white underparts and tail
- Often creeps along branches

- Bright white underparts with black side streaking
- Bright yellow throat, bordered by black
- Long all-white tail
- Overall long profile, with long black bill and tail

Distinctive Views

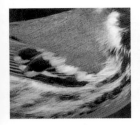

Additional Photos

Often creeps along branches like a nuthatch or Black-and-white Warbler

One of the longest-billed warblers, which contributes to its elongated profile

Some birds may come to feeders, especially in winter; note strong white supercilium, neck patch

Strong black face pattern and side streaking

Extensive white in tail creates a mostly white undertail pattern

Yellow throat almost always a quick ID point; note it's more lemony yellow than Blackburnian Warbler

Large, slow-moving, and deliberate

The *albilora* race (west of the Appalachians) has white supraloral, sometimes with tinge of yellow; southeastern *dominica* has yellow supraloral

Striking yellow throat bordered by black obvious from long distance

Even when high in canopy, bright yellow throat and black flank streaking on white underparts good ID points

Gray back creates strong contrast with yellow throat and black cheek/neck patch and streaking

High contrast black/white
Strong, isolated yellow throat
Long bill, broad supercilium
White neck patch
Long, all-white tail
Black cheek/throat border
Black flank streaking

Comparison Species

Grace's Ranges don't overlap; wider, all-yellow supraloral; yellow throat extends into face and neck (vs. wider black border); less black in the face overall; no white mark on neck; smaller bill

Northern Parula Smaller, plumper, and more active; powder-blue upperparts (vs. gray); olive back patch; lacks black on face/neck; no streaking; shorter tail; smaller bill with all-yellow lower mandible

Pine Bright Olive back (vs. gray); no strong black on face/neck; overall yellowish face and breast; less, more diffuse side streaking; overall lower contrast

Kirtland's Breeding ranges don't overlap; lacks white supercilium/neck patch; more extensive dull yellow throat fades lower into body; pumps tail; forages lower in denser vegetation

Blackburnian Bright Throat/face orange (no yellow), blends into breast (vs. sharply delineated); side streaking more limited, thinner; white back braces; black back (vs. gray); more black in tail

Blackburnian Dull Overall lower contrast, orangier; more diffuse orange throat; buff supercilium (vs. white); pale back braces; no bright white patch on side of neck; shorter bill and tail

Black-and-white Black and white, with no yellow; bolder wing bars; white tertial edging and white streaking on black back; black marks in UnTC; shorter tail

Aging and Sexing

Spring AdM 1yM AdF 1yF   **Fall** AdM 1yM AdF 1yF

Races: 4, 3 in the U.S./Canada, *S.d. dominica* (east of Appalachians), *S.d. albilora* (west of Appalachians), *S.d. stoddardi* (northwest Florida and coastal Alabama resident)
Summary *Spring/Fall:* Not generally ageable or sexable: see note

All Birds Most birds not easily separated (see note)

AdM *albilora* Mostly migrates west of Appalachians, but also seen in East in migration; shorter bill than *dominica*, white supraloral (vs. yellow in *dominica*); note some birds have partial yellow in supraloral.

AdM *stoddardi* Northwest Florida and coastal Alabama resident; more slender, longer bill than *dominica*.

Note Separating Yellow-throated warblers is difficult. Females may be duller than males, and may show less black in the crown as well as lighter side streaking. First-year birds may show subtly dull or brownish primary coverts and flight feathers. In addition, first-year females may show a buff wash on the flanks and a less-distinct cheek patch. All marks are subtle and difficult to use in the field, and most birds are not separable.

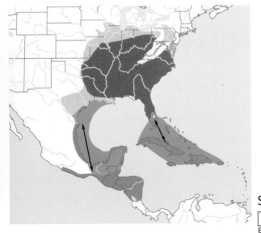

Spring

Early   Middle   Late

Fall

Early   Middle   Late

Yellow-throated

Yellow scarf flows down the front, covering the throat; but curls up at the end

Summary 2–4 Sections of Clear Phrases with *overall falling pitch profile*; long *1st Section* and *short, usually upslurred ending*; 1st Section 6–8 slow, intricate, downslurred Phrases, strongly falling pitch profile; ending variable, most often upslur, sometimes fading in volume; *no other warbler has so many similar, descending slurs anywhere in song*; leisurely speed, long Intervals so Phrases distinct; **I Type.**

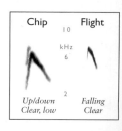

Type A1 Typical: 6 descending Phrases followed by ending upslur; Phrases complicated but slurred and sound like 1-Element Phrases.

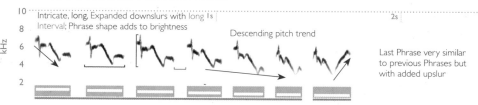

Intricate, long, Expanded downslurs with long Is Interval; Phrase shape adds to brightness

Descending pitch trend

Last Phrase very similar to previous Phrases but with added upslur

Type A2 6 descending Phrases and slightly more complicated, 2-Section ending; endings variable, **but** 1st Section's many intricate, descending downslurs unique.

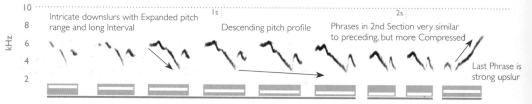

Intricate downslurs with Expanded pitch range and long Interval

Descending pitch profile

Phrases in 2nd Section very similar to preceding, but more Compressed

Last Phrase is strong upslur

Type A3 Songs usually end in accented upslurs, but this example ends with downslurs; some songs lack accented ending Section completely.

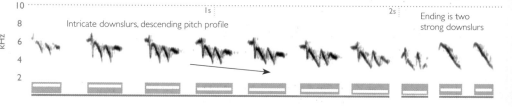

Intricate downslurs, descending pitch profile

Ending is two strong downslurs

Louisiana Waterthrush A1 Similarly starts with falling slurs, **but** many fewer Phrases in 1st Section (2 or 3 vs. 6–8), more Sections (5–9+ vs. 2 or 3).

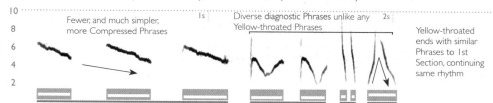

Fewer, and much simpler, more Compressed Phrases

Diverse diagnostic Phrases unlike any Yellow-throated Phrases

Yellow-throated ends with similar Phrases to 1st Section, continuing same rhythm

Swainson's A1 Similar repeated slurs that fall in pitch and accented slurred ending, **but** 1st Section many fewer Phrases (3–5 vs. 6–8); less regular, with fewer repeated Phrases and more complicated ending.

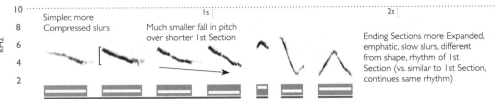

Simpler, more Compressed slurs

Much smaller fall in pitch over shorter 1st Section

Ending Sections more Expanded, emphatic, slow slurs, different from shape, rhythm of 1st Section (vs. similar to 1st Section, continues same rhythm)

Indigo Bunting Similar tone and sometimes has descending pitch profile, **but** speed, rhythm changes between Sections, including changes from 1-Element to 2-Element Phrases (vs. always 1-Element Phrases that remain similar most or all of song).

3.3s

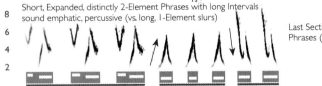

Many Sections with slightly or obviously different Elements (vs. only 1 long Section for bulk of song)

Northern Waterthrush A2 Repeated Phrases falling in pitch, **but** pitch falls between, not within, Sections; always 3 or 4 fairly balanced Sections (vs.1 main Section with 1 or 2 very short ending Sections); usually speeds up (vs. steady); 1st Section fewer Phrases (3–6 vs. 6–8); lower, richer, more emphatic and rhythmic.

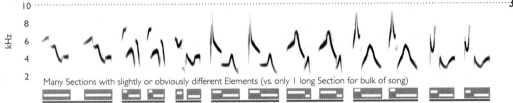

Short, Expanded, distinctly 2-Element Phrases with long Intervals sound emphatic, percussive (vs. long, 1-Element slurs)

Last Sections Expanded, short, emphatic Phrases (vs. usually ends on longer upslur)

Yellow Some songs similar: this version has descending pitch profile, ending with simple slurs; faster speed (avg. 7 Phrases/sec. vs. 4).

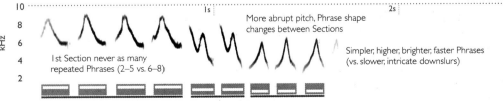

More abrupt pitch, Phrase shape changes between Sections

1st Section never as many repeated Phrases (2–5 vs. 6–8)

Simpler, higher, brighter, faster Phrases (vs. slower, intricate downslurs)

CRESCENT-CHESTED

Oreothlypis superciliosa   Male/Female - All Seasons

- Rare vagrant to southwestern U.S.
- Small, patterned like Parulas but not closely related
- No wing bars
- Plain upperparts with green patch
- Flaring white supercilium
- Bright yellow throat, upper breast
- ✓ Chestnut crescent on breast in bright adult plumages, but not all birds

- Bright yellow throat and upper breast
- ✓ Chestnut crescent on breast in bright adult plumages, but not all birds
- Long gray tail

Pronounced supercilium

Pronounced chestnut crescent diagnostic when present; may be faint or absent in some plumages

Normally found in mid-level montane habitat, but as vagrant could also occur in other areas

Comparison Species

Northern Parula Similar shape but has shorter tail, wing bars; lacks white supercilium; more limited yellow in breast

Tropical Parula Similar shape but has shorter tail; wing bars; lacks supercilium; lacks eye-arcs

Rufous-capped Rarity in U.S.; longer, cocked tail; extensive chestnut in head; longer tail

Range Map

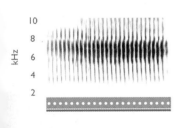

When Year-round

Where Most U.S. records are from southeastern Arizona with unconfirmed records for southern Texas, which is also a likely spot for them to occur; normally found in mid-level montane habitat, but as vagrant could also occur in other areas

Vocalizations

Songs Fast Trill of very Expanded but Complex Phrases; variable length and speed (24–46 Phrases/sec.); no pitch change (vs. Parulas); closest in quality to Chipping Sparrow but usually different pitch or speed.
Call high, short, a little like Northern Parula but steadier, higher, shorter

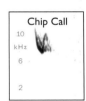

Chip Call

0.7 Sec.

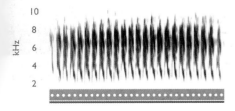

0.9 Sec.

FAN-TAILED

Basileuterus lachrymosus   Male/Female - All Seasons

- Large warbler
- Stays on or near ground flashing and fanning tail, often walks
- ✓ White eye-arcs and supraloral mark (face may appear spotted)
- Yellow crown patch
- No wing bars
- Yellow underparts mottled with orange

- ✓ Distinct white tail tips
- Stays on or near ground flashing and fanning tail
- Yellow underparts mottled with orange
- White vent/UnTC

Distinct white tail tips

Yellow crown and blue back unique in U.S. warblers

Often in rocky areas such as streambeds or canyons, flashing and fanning tail on or near the ground

Comparison Species

Northern Parula Shorter tail, wing bars, no white supraloral, more limited yellow in breast

Canada Rarely in known range for Fan-tailed vagrancy; black necklace; lacks orange mottling in breast; smaller; no tail fanning/walking; lacks yellow crown; yellow supraloral (vs. white)

Yellow-breasted Chat Much larger bill; olive back (not blue); goggled (vs. "spotted" face); white malar (vs. none); rarely on ground, never walks

Range Map

When Historically late spring/early summer and fall

Where U.S. records are from southeastern Arizona, New Mexico and Big Bend area of Texas; often in rocky areas such as stream beds surrounded by trees, and canyons or steeper terrain

Vocalizations

Songs Fairly long; low, Compressed slurs; similar to Golden-crowned but longer, more varied; Phrases build in volume and intensity, ending with long slur (similar to Swainson's Warbler but lower, different ending form). **Call** Compressed, long slur; higher, thinner than Olive Warbler

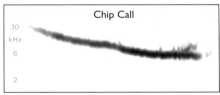

Chip Call

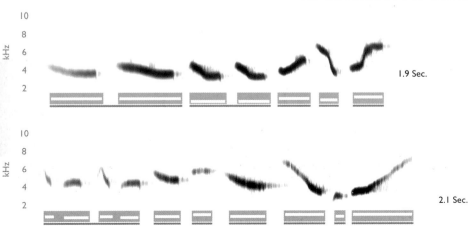

1.9 Sec.

2.1 Sec.

GOLDEN-CROWNED

Basileuterus culicivorus   Male/Female - All Seasons

- Overall drab

- Dark upperparts, no wing bars

- Black crown stripes with a yellow/orange median stripe (often hard to see)

- Yellowish supercilium/eye-arcs

- Long tail

- Yellow underparts (including UnTC)

- Long tail

- Orange/yellow legs

- Often active, flicking wings and cocking tail

Orange crown stripe not always conspicuous

Often found in feeding flocks; typically prominent in flocks in normal range

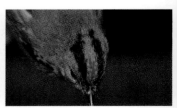

Prefers low/mid-level vegetation

Comparison Species

Worm-eating More pronounced head stripes; longer bill; shorter tail and buffy underparts (not yellow)

Wilson's Less contrast between upper and lower parts; lacks crown stripes; lacks contrasty supercilium/ eye-arcs

Orange-crowned Overall more uniform color; lacks head stripes; dark legs (vs. orangey); less yellow below

Canada Prominent eyering; yellow supraloral; dark head (vs. striped); black necklace

Range Map

When Historically late fall to early spring

Where U.S. records are from southern Texas (Rio Grande Valley) and New Mexico in winter; often in mixed flocks in wooded areas; prefers low or mid-level vegetation

Vocalizations

Songs Not often given in U.S.; short songs, very Compressed slurs with clear quality; low; often ends on double upslur; similar to Hooded but much slower, more even; also slower than Compressed Phrases of Painted Redstart with more even rhythm; vocal flock leader at least in Central American range. **Call** Very short, low, dense; quality similar to Common Yellowthroat; often doubled or in rattling string

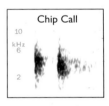

Chip Call

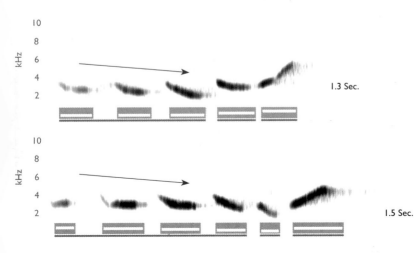

1.3 Sec.

1.5 Sec.

GRAY-CROWNED YELLOWTHROAT

Geothlypis poliocephala   Male/Female - All Seasons

- Heavy, bicolored bill
- ✓ Song and calls different from Common Yellowthroat
- Males show black loral area and blue-gray crown
- Tail long and graduated
- Wide eye-arcs in all plumages
- Usually in dry grassy scrub, not wet marshes

- Fall birds and first-year birds: crown may be browner and lack black lores
- Young birds may have yellow restricted to upper throat and UnTC
- Wide eye-arcs/heavy, bicolored bill in all plumages

Prefers dry, brushy habitat

Historically a resident of southeastern Texas (until early 20th century)

Hybrid Gray-crowned and Common Yellowthroat: note amount of black masking behind the eye, presence of a pale forehead band, thickness and color of the bill, width of eye-arcs (when present), and vocalizations.

Comparison Species

Common Yellowthroat 1yM Young males can be similar but smaller bill, not bicolored or decurved; black areas on face more diffuse, extend behind eye (vs. concentrated in lores); thin eyering (vs. wider eye-arcs); shorter tail that isn't wagged as much; different call and song; hybrids possible; **AdM** Same as 1yM, also much more extensive black in face, bordered by white/yellow

Yellow-breasted Chat Much larger; brighter yellow breast contrasting with lower white (vs. gray) belly; white UnTC (vs. yellow); more contrasty face with goggles, heavier bill

Range Map

When Historically very early spring to summer

Where U.S. records are from southern Texas (Rio Grande Valley, Brownsville area); prefers open, dry grassy scrub (not wet areas like Common Yellowthroat)

Vocalizations

Songs Good separator from Common Yellowthroat; fast series of low, varied Phrases of fairly Compressed pitch ranges; lacks regular rhythm of Common Yellowthroat and also more likely to have Buzzy or Complex Elements; cadence and quality a bit like Blue Grosbeak/Painted Bunting; can be very long. **Call** very raspy, much longer than Common Yellowthroat; often 2 or 3 Sections.

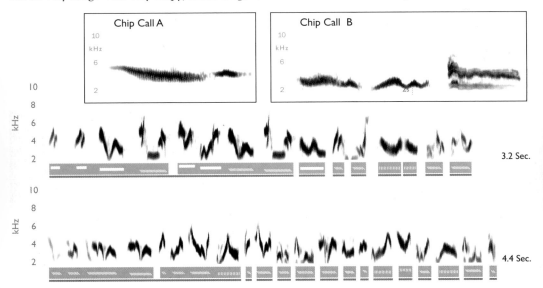

RUFOUS-CAPPED

Basileuterus rufifrons   Male/Female - All Seasons

- Large warbler, sparrow-like shape
- Very long, cocked tail
- ✓ Strong, long, white supercilium and rufous cap and cheeks
- Variably extensive bright yellow throat and upper breast
- Plain dark olive-and-gray body and upperparts
- Often skulking

- Bright yellow throat and upper breast
- White malar
- Very long, cocked tail
- Pale UnTC

Rufous cap distinctive and diagnostic

Extremely long tail with strong head/body contrast

Often skulking; may respond to pishing

Comparison Species

Common Yellowthroat Lacks very long tail, tail wagging; lacks any rufous

Yellow Lacks very long tail, tail wagging; yellowish upperparts; lower contrast (especially head/body)

Range Map

When Historically March–August

Where U.S. records are from southeastern Arizona (Chiricahua Mountains), South Texas from Big Bend to Falcon Dam; prefers scrubby, brushy areas in ravines, canyons and hillsides

Vocalizations

Songs Very fast, Expanded short Phrases; emphatic; different Phrase shape and speed between Sections gives odd, varied skipping rhythm; unlike any U.S. warbler. **Call** Complex, long with up/down pitch profile; often run together in scolding stream.

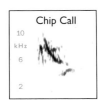

Chip Call

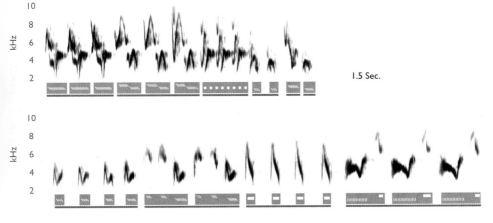

1.5 Sec.

2.3 Sec.

SLATE-THROATED
Myioborus miniatus   Male/Female - All Seasons

- Dark gray/black upperparts and bright red breast
- No eye-arcs or wing bars
- Long tail with large white spots, often fanned
- ✓ Underside pattern: red belly, white UnTC with black banding and large white tail spots
- Sometimes shows red crown

- Long tail with large white spots, often fanned
- ✓ Underside pattern: red belly, white UnTC with black banding, and large white tail spots

Distinctive pattern should be easy to identify; red crown may be hard to see depending on light/angle

Frequently fans tail

Prefers montane forest (conifers)

Comparison Species

Painted Redstart White wing patch (vs. none); white under-eye arc (vs. none); more white in tail (vs. large white spots), red in breast less extensive

Red-faced Lacks red in breast; lighter upper and underparts; black earflaps; red face/throat (vs. black)

Range Map

When Historically spring only

Where U.S. records are from southeastern Arizona, southwestern New Mexico and western Texas; prefers montane forests from 1,000 to 3,000 m

Vocalizations

Songs Fairly Expanded Clear slurs with long Intervals and uneven form, length; often downslurs; lower than Red-faced; similar to Painted Redstart but higher, brighter, more Expanded and more distinct due to longer Intervals. **Call** Falling, short, high, Clear.

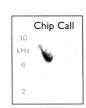

Chip Call

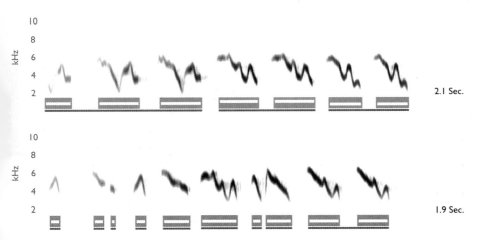

2.1 Sec.

1.9 Sec.

TROPICAL PARULA

Setophaga pitiayumi Male/Female - All Seasons

- Blue above, yellow below
- Variably diffuse orange in breast
- Dark around eye, no eye-arcs
- Green back patch
- Straight-edged throat border
- Bicolored bill

- Short white tail
- Variably diffuse orange in breast
- Yellow extends to legs
- Bicolored bill

Some birds show less black around eye, less orange in breast

Similar to Northern Parula: note more extensive yellow in breast, no eye-arcs

Note straight border between throat and head/shoulder

Comparison Species

Northern Parula White eye-arcs (vs. none); less black around eye; more limited yellow in underside; chestnut/black marking in breast (vs. more diffuse orange wash without band); blue shoulder intrudes into yellow throat (vs. straighter edge to throat)

Nashville No white in wings (vs. wing bars); complete eyering (vs. none); lacks white in tail; yellow undertail coverts (vs. white)

Range Map

When Summer in Arizona, year-round in South Texas, Fall/Winter records from North Coastal Texas and Louisiana, one spring record from Northern Colorado

Where U.S. records are from southeastern Arizona, South and Coastal Texas, with other reports from Lousiana and Colorado

Vocalizations

Songs Similar to Northern Parula with similar forms; often sounds higher, with tighter Buzzes; endings usually Buzzy, more similar to western Northern Parula populations. **Call** very similar to Northern Parula

Chip Call

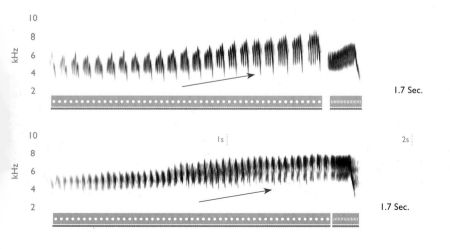

SIMILAR NON-WARBLER SPECIES

There are some non-warbler species that can look very much like warblers and can cause ID problems in the field. Often they share color and size characteristics, but their structure and shape are usually reliable ways to differentiate them from warblers. Bill and tail shape, and size and proportion, as well as tail proportions relative to the body, are among these important separating characteristics.

Kinglets Kinglets often flock with warblers and feed actively in a similar fashion. Only the very smallest warbler, Lucy's, is as small as a kinglet, though size is often very difficult to judge in the field. Note that both kinglet species have very short bills and thin, notched tails, which are important characteristics for separating them from warblers.

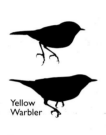

Yellow
Warbler

Lucy's

- Actively flicks wings, much more often than any North American warbler species
- Very short, thin, sharp-looking bills that are much shorter and finer than the bill of any warbler
- Strong yellow edgings on tertials and tail feathers, unlike on any similar warbler species
- Overall drab olive color differentiates from most warblers
- Broken eyering and wing bars easily separate from Lucy's, drab Orange-crowned, or other dull warblers
- Dark bar below lower wing bar differentiates kinglets from all warblers
- Strongly notched tail

Golden-crowned Kinglet

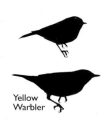

Yellow
Warbler

- Bill a bit thicker than Ruby-crowned, but still very short and fine
- Striking, contrasty cheek patch, supercilium, and dark crown edge; yellow or yellow-and-orange median crown patch distinctive
- Yellowish tertial edgings
- Dark bar below lower wing bar differentiates kinglets from all warblers
- Strongly notched tail

Bushtits Found in western United States, these birds are very small and highly social. Their active feeding and constant chatter are unlike any warbler species.

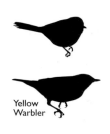

Yellow
Warbler

- Extremely long tail and short, stubby bill, unlike any warbler species
- Unique black or brown face-patch

Verdins Young Verdins can be easily confused with Lucy's Warblers, and are found in similar dry western scrub habitats. The yellow head and throat of adults should separate them easily from any warbler species.

Yellow Warbler

Juvenile   Adult

Lucy's

- Pointy, conical bills, similar to a Lucy's bill, but shorter, bulkier, especially at base
- Sometimes browner on the back than gray-toned Lucy's; lacking any rufous on rump or crown
- Little or no eyering, unlike Lucy's

Gnatcatchers Gnatcatchers are often found with warblers, exhibiting some of their same active feeding habits.

Yellow Warbler

Blue-gray Gnatcatcher

- Long, thin tail and longish, thin bill make diagnostic profile from any angle
- Moves tails very actively, often cocking, tilting, and flashing the long white outer tail feathers, unlike the behavior of any warbler species
- "Clean" look, lacking any streaking or contrasting marks other than an obvious eyering

Chickadees
The black throat and gray coloration of a chickadee can be confused for those of a warbler, especially from below.

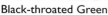

Yellow Warbler

Black-throated Green

Black-capped Chickadee

- Longer and thinner tails than any warbler species
- Short and stubby bill
- Uniquely colored, buffy-brownish flanks

Vireos
Vireos are sometimes found with warblers and some species can be very confusing. In general, vireos have large bodies and thick, often wide, hooked bills. Their tails are proportionally thinner and shorter, giving them a front-heavy appearance overhead. They are usually slow moving and more sluggish than most warblers, although some small species are quite active. Vireos are also very vocal, singing well into the day, when most warblers are often silent. Knowing their vocalizations is helpful in separating them from warblers.

Blue-headed, Plumbeous, and Cassin's Vireo

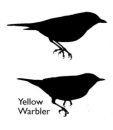

Yellow Warbler

American Redstart

- Shape different from warblers: large body, big bill, and thin, short tail
- Blue-headed: distinctive yellowish flanks on overall white undersides; bluish head contrasts with back-and-white goggles (a strong eyering with white supraloral area) diagnostic
- Plumbeous and Cassin's: less contrasty than Blue-headed, but bright white goggles and wing bars are diagnostic

Yellow-throated Vireo

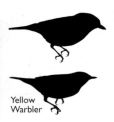

Yellow
Warbler

Pine

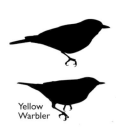

Pine

- Easily mistaken for bright Pine Warbler, which can also have a goggled look
- Broad, hooked bill larger than that of Pine
- Shorter, darker tail than Pine
- Yellow breast and throat brighter, more orangey than Pine Warbler's, and yellow only in the throat and upper breast with sharper cut off
- Lacks any streaking on breast, which accentuates yellow; Pine Warbler streaking or mottling on breast makes chest appear more muted in color

Red-eyed Vireo

Especially from below, Red-eyed Vireo can be confusing, as its all-white underparts are similar to the coloration of Tennessee and other warbler species. This can be even more problematic as Tennessee and Red-eyed Vireos often frequent the canopy, and a brief look at a tilted head may reveal a white supercilium on both species.

Yellow
Warbler

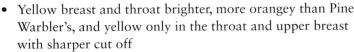

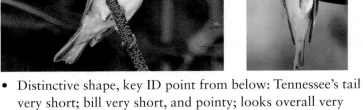

Tennessee

- Distinctive shape, key ID point from below: Tennessee's tail very short; bill very short, and pointy; looks overall very compact; vireo has longer, thin, narrow, dark tail; thick, long bill; and larger, bulkier body
- Overall shape and dark tail with buffy UnTC also separates from other warblers with white underparts (e.g. female Chestnut-sided Warbler with long all-white tail)
- In fall, yellowish vent versus whiter vent of Tennessee Warbler

Warbling and Philadelphia Vireo

These vireos are slightly more petite than the ones above. Their bills are larger and thicker than those of all warblers, and their shape is still vireo-like. Since they are whitish from below, they could also be confused with Tennessee Warbler.

Yellow Warbler

Tennessee

- Larger overall, thicker bill than short-tailed, compact Tennessee, which has a very pointy bill
- Eyelines more contrasty and generally overall bolder facial quality, including bill, supercilium, and eyeline

Bell's Vireo

Western Bell's Vireo can be confused with Lucy's Warbler.

Yellow Warbler

Lucy's

- Thicker, rounder bills, unlike pointed bill on Lucy's
- Lacks rufous in rump and crown
- Even drab birds have partial eyelines and supercilium, especially in the lores, unlike plain face, pale lores, and white eye ring of Lucy's
- Tail much longer and overall larger than Lucy's

Sparrows Some sparrows can be found feeding in the middle story and even canopy of trees, sometimes causing ID problems. Usually, once you have found the source of the movement, it is easy to separate these species from warblers by noting the shapes of their tails and bills. Likewise, some warbler species, such as Palm and Yellow-rumped, are often found foraging on the ground—sometimes with sparrows and towhees—and are similarly brown- or dark-colored.

House Sparrow

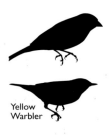

Yellow Warbler

Yellow-rumped

- Normally low and on the ground, but sometimes found feeding very high in trees
- Females brown, unlike most warblers
- Large, conical bills, different from that of any warbler
- Males are colorful; there are no warblers with a similarly colored chestnut head

Chipping Sparrow

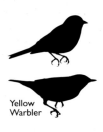

Yellow Warbler

- Often found in middle and top levels of trees
- Tails obviously longer, thinner
- Compact, short bills, much more conical and bulky than warbler bills

Small Sparrows Including American Tree, Field, Brewer's, Rufous-winged

Am. Tree
Sparrow

Yellow
Warbler

- Often move between the ground and smaller trees and bushes
- All have shorter, stubbier bills, bulkier, with more conical bases, unlike warblers' thinner, longer bills
- Relatively long, thin, notched tails are unlike any warbler tails
- Considerably larger; foraging habits differ: usually less prone to actively flitting about from branch to branch

Towhees

Yellow
Warbler

- Ground feeders that could be confused with Palm Warbler; western species more similar but don't normally overlap in range
- Foraging habits much more deliberate, including tossing leaves and moving twigs
- Much larger
- Lack broad supercilium
- Don't actively wag tail

YELLOW-BREASTED CHAT

Icteria virens   Male/Female All Seasons

- Large, heavy bill
- Extensive, sharply delineated yellow in breast and throat
- White goggles, black lores
- Larger than any warbler
- Previously categorized as a warbler, but very likely belongs elsewhere taxonomically

- Extensive, sharply delineated yellow in breast and throat
- Long gray tail with white UnTC
- Large, heavy bill

Additional Photos

Larger with a larger bill than any warbler

White undertail coverts with long, dark tail

Often skulky and found in dense, brushy habitats, although may perch high when singing

Comparison Species

Common Yellowthroat
Smaller; thin, non-decurved bill; not goggled; less yellow in body

Canada Yellow more extensive in breast and not sharply delineated; smaller; different face pattern

Yellow-throated Vireo Not a scrub specialist; yellow in face; different quality yellow; less extensive and not as sharply delineated yellow

Range Map

Races 2: *l.v. virens* (East) and *l.v. auricollis* in the West shown above (averages grayer upperparts, brighter, orangier breast, longer-tailed with more distinct white malar, but many are intermediate)

Vocalizations

Songs Widely-spaced, widely varying Sections, usually a repetition of one harsh Element, and sometimes a single wider slur or other sound. Lower than any warbler song, with a wide range of tones and gutteral calls including mimickry of other species. **Calls** Makes a wide range of single vocalizations; often harsh; longer than most warbler calls.

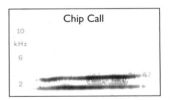

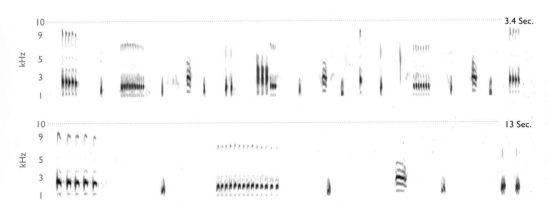

OLIVE WARBLER (Once considered a warbler, but now in totally separate taxonomic group)

Peucedramus taeniatus   Male/Female All Seasons

- Orange or yellow head and upper breast
- Variable dark mask
- White wing bars
- Long, thin bill
- Olive crown on females
- Small white patch at the base of the primaries

- Orange or yellow head and upper breast
- Variable dark mask
- Unstreaked below
- White undertail coverts; extensive white on underside of tail
- Long, thin bill
- Deeply notched tail

Additional Photos

Often forages slowly and deliberately in tops of pines, flicking wings in a kinglet-like manner

Female shows broad white wing bars and unstreaked yellow breast, unlike any warbler

Frequent loud, descending, whistled call

Comparison Species

1yF Hermit Warbler More yellow in face and auriculars, no white base to flight feathers, shorter bill, less-notched tail, browner, less-uniform upperparts

1yF Townsend's Green upperparts, streaked below

Drab Pine Larger, heavier bill; dull breast streaks; back more yellow-olive; lacks white at base of primaries; yellow less orangey; rarely shares range

Range Map

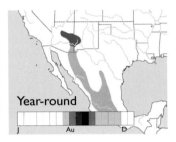

Year-round

When Generally July through September: most birds in the U.S. migrate to Mexico in winter, but some birds may reside year-round

Where Arizona and New Mexico; found above 7,000 ft. (2100 m)

Aging/Sexing: AdM orange hood, highest contrast. **1yM** averages more orange in head than AdF/1yF, may show hood with darker flecks; not always separable; may take two years to reach adult plumage. **AdF/1yF** may show more yellow in head than 1yM, with 1yF averaging drabber and brownish in upper back than AdF; not easily separable from each other

Vocalizations

Songs Fairly short 1- or 2-Section slow songs consisting of usually dissimilar Elements. The songs often have a fairly wide pitch jump from Phrase to Phrase, and can combine a Buzzy or Complex Phrase with a more slurred Phrase. **Calls** A: Very slow, unique, mournful call; B: Dense, short, rising, rough call.

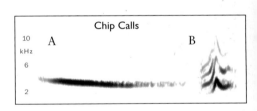

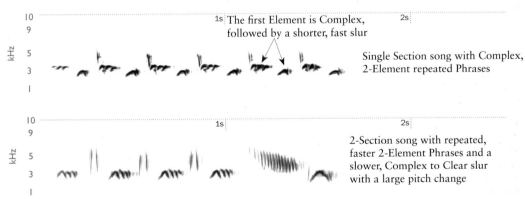

The first Element is Complex, followed by a shorter, fast slur

Single Section song with Complex, 2-Element repeated Phrases

2-Section song with repeated, faster 2-Element Phrases and a slower, Complex to Clear slur with a large pitch change

Juniper Titmouse has similar quality, however, no Olive Warbler songs have so many repeated Elements in such a long section. Also, Olive Phrases have much smaller pitch range, usually more Complex, 2-Element form.

HYBRID WARBLERS

Hybrid warblers are generally rare. The most common hybrids occur due to well-known hybridization zones between species where breeding ranges overlap. For example, *Brewster's* and *Lawrence's* are hybrids between *Golden-winged* and *Blue-winged*, who often share breeding habitats. *Townsend's* and *Hermit* also share a breeding range in Oregon and Washington, and the two races of *Yellow-rumped* (*Myrtle* and *Audubon's*) overlap ranges in western Canada and Alaska. Other hybrids are rarer, from *Sutton's Warbler* (*Northern Parula* x *Yellow-throated*) to a number of warblers whose parentage may never be fully known.

Brewster's A common hybrid between Golden-winged and Blue-winged, Brewster's generally shows a yellow cap, white face, eyeline, and some yellow in the breast, although there are a number of variations on this plumage.

Lawrence's A rarer hybrid between Golden-winged and Blue-winged than Brewster's, Lawrence's generally shows a yellow body with a black throat and mask, although many variations are possible.

Black and white x ? Banded in Michingan in 2004, this bird clearly shows Black-and-white warbler parentage. The other parent may be Chestnut-sided, Golden-winged, or some other species that contributes yellow wingbars and a gray back.

Hermit x Townsend's Townsend's and Hermit overlap in breeding range in Washington and Oregon and sometimes interbreed. This bird shows the plain face and black throat of a Hermit, with fine side streaks, greenish back, and yellow in the breast that indicate Townsend's parentage.

Possible Cape May x Yellow-rumped?
Photograped in Belize, February 2010, this bird shows clear Cape May characteristics (orangey breast with strong black side streaks), but also has a bolder yellow rump, supercilium, yellow crown stripe, and other qualities that indicate a possible Yellow-rumped warbler, although other parents are possible.

Northern Parula x Yellow-throated (Sutton's Warbler) Banded in Pennsylvania in May of 2008, this bird shows the large bill and clear yellow throat of a Yellow-throated and the blue back, clean white undersides and other characteristics of a Northern Parula.

Yellow-rumped Audubon's x Myrtle
A known intergrade zone in a band from southeastern Alaska through central British Columbia to southern Alberta results in interbreeding between the two races of Yellow-rumped Warbler. This bird looks largely like an adult male Audubon's, but the pale throat and supercilium indicate some Myrtle heritage.

QUIZ AND REVIEW

Where & When Crane Creek State Park, Ohio, mid-May

The Big Picture Peak migration in the East, so there are lots of choices. Largish size; twenty feet up in a mid-sized tree, feeding methodically, wags tail once. The underside view doesn't seem to give us much, or does it? The bird is large and "boat-shaped," it has a very short tail, bright orange legs, and what's with the weird, fine, spotty streaking in the malar and upper flanks?

Why It's Tricky The angle seems difficult to work with. How can we ID this bird without seeing the back or face?

The Rundown This bird presents a couple of interesting features at the outset. First, it has a very short tail. Second, there is some limited side streaking that seems somewhat broken up, including some spots or speckles, which continue strongly in the malar area. The bird also seems a bit "boat-shaped".

One bird that might have similar streaking is *Cape May*, but there is no yellow on the undersides, the streaking ends very high, and the tail is too short. The bird is also too big. *Yellow-rumped* is streaked and largish, but more densely so in the breast, and while there is a yellow wash on the shoulder of this bird, it's not a strongly concentrated shoulder patch. *Black-throated Green* would show yellow in the face and have a longer tail, as well as a yellow wash in the vent; a vagrant *Black-throated Gray* would have a longer tail, as well as thicker side streaks. *Black-and-white* would show more streaking overall, and it would have diagnostic black spots in the undertail coverts. Note that all of the previously mentioned birds have longer tails.

Waterthrushes and *Ovenbird* have short tails, but the streaking is also more extensive, their tails are dark and frequently pumped, and these birds are rarely high up in a tree. So the short tail, distinctive, limited spotted streaking (especially in the malar), and boat shape, plus the bright orange legs, all point to a female *Blackpoll*. Note that in spring, *Bay-breasted* is identically shaped, but it would show obvious chestnut stripes and no streaking.

Where & When Cape May, New Jersey, late September

The Big Picture A drab warbler in the fall. That doesn't help much! Low vegetation, no remarkable behaviors, no tail wagging. That it is unstreaked and with a greenish back contrasting with some buff on the undersides might help. The face also has some contrast, showing a short eyeline.

Why It's Tricky Drab birds are daunting because they don't have any screaming ID points, but if you look a little closer this bird is actually quite distinct. We'll go through the possibilities which include *Orange-crowned* and *Tennessee*. If it turns out to be one of these two, we may have a problem because the undertail coverts aren't bright white, but they're not yellow either, ID points that are usually critical in separating these similar species.

The Rundown This is a drab, unstreaked bird, so drab, streaked birds are ruled out. That includes *Cape May*, *Blackburnian*, and *Yellow-rumped*. Those birds all have white tail spots, which this does not. Our bird also lacks any yellow, which excludes *Wilson's*, *Canada*, and *Hooded*. *Yellow* can be very drab, but it never has any eyeline and supercilium (which this bird has) and almost always shows some yellow.

Two unstreaked, non-yellow birds are *Bay-breasted* and *Pine*, but both of these are fairly large birds, and *Pine's* tail is very obviously longer and whiter. *Bay-breasted* has wings with strong wing bars, and the tail also has more striking and well-defined white tail spots. Some fall *Bay-breasted* don't show any chestnut in the flanks, but the majority do, which is a supporting point in ruling them out. The underside tone looks similar to a *Black-throated Blue* female, which can be drab and can lack the "handkerchief," but their facial pattern, including the long thin supercilium, under-eye arc, and dark cheek patch is very different. The tail also projects farther past the undertail coverts.

Tennessee and *Orange-crowned* seem like a very likely fit, but which one? The undertail coverts are not pure white, but they are still lighter than the rest of the underparts. *Tennessee* has more contrast than *Orange-crowned* in three ways: the back contrasts more with the underparts, the face shows more contrast in the eyeline/eye-arcs, and the undertail coverts are always paler than the body, even if they're not white. *Orange-crowned* always has undertail coverts that are the same tone or darker than the body, and are usually more yellow. Some other features that support *Tennessee* are thin, but clear, wing bars; smooth, unstreaked underparts; shorter tail; longer wings; and a lack of a pale edge on the shoulder.

Where & When Mesquite and brushy area near water, Arizona, August

The Big Picture Average warbler size; skulky, actively hopping through dense brush, flicking wings and gleaning insects, which can make it hard to see well. Long tail is both bobbed and flipped. Plain gray without a lot of marks, large bill.

Why It's Tricky Drab gray birds can be daunting, since they lack any bright field marks. The plumage seems similar to *Lucy's* or maybe *Virginia's*, but it doesn't seem to quite fit.

The Rundown What western warbler (or vagrants) could be this drab? *Yellow Warbler* can be very gray (rarely), but it never has such a pronounced white supraloral area with faint eyeline, and its tail is much shorter with yellow spots and edgings, usually along with yellow edgings on the flight feathers. *Orange-crowned* is much yellower, has a shorter tail, and is darker, yellowish, and vaguely streaked below. It also lacks such prominent facial contrast, especially in the prominent supraloral area. *Lucy's* is fairly gray, so could be a good candidate. *Lucy's*, however, is tiny and has a fine, pointy bill, and the lores and supraloral area are always plain in *Lucy's*. It also lacks the wing bar this bird is showing. Most importantly, the tail isn't nearly as long. *Virginia's* has a striking eyering and yellow undertail coverts, and usually yellow on the breast. We're out of warblers and must turn to vireos, which the thick bill and rather large, rounded head fit. The facial pattern does not match *Warbling*—that one has a more contrasty face and a wider, longer supercilium, and it is larger but with a shorter, less active tail. We're left with *Bell's Vireo*, which fits in every aspect—small, skulky, plain gray. It's important to use size and shape to determine the type of bird early on in the ID process and to be ready to challenge basic assumptions—is this bird really a warbler?—if the ID process is foundering. As a postscript, this bird suddenly calls out in a very unwarbler-like way. *Bell's Vireos* are often quite vocal.

Where & When Mid-level in a juniper tree, New Jersey, early October

The Big Picture Smallish size, actively feeding, but no standout behaviors. Drab gray, low-contrast, and streaked.

Why It's Tricky Another drab fall warbler! This bird seems average in size, shape, and behavior, so we'll focus on plumage. Streaking is one quality. What other marks can we use?

The Rundown The pronounced streaking rules out *Tennessee*, *Orange-crowned*, and *Bay-breasted*, all of which also have shorter tails. One notable thing about this bird is its relatively pure gray tone, not brownish or greenish, which would eliminate birds like *Blackpoll* and drab *Yellow-rumped*. *Blackburnians* can be very gray, and they have some streaking, but their wing bars have much more contrasting white, and the streaking is restricted to the sides and is never in the upper chest and throat. *Blackburnian* also always has a diffuse orangey-yellow wash in the throat and upper breast, and the faint yellow color in this bird seems patchy. Finally, *Blackburnian* has a clear, wide supercilium and triangular cheek patch, unlike our bird.

Drab *Yellow-rumps* are streaked below, but the streaking is more restricted to the sides (never in the throat), and there is almost always a trace of a yellow shoulder patch. They also tend to be browner in the upperparts, as we mentioned. *Palm* is streaked but has strikingly yellow undertail coverts and conspicuously pumps its much longer tail. *Pine* can be streaked below, but the streaking is more diffuse and, again, restricted to the sides, never clumping in the upper middle of the breast and throat. It has contrasting white wing bars as well and an obviously longer tail. Some separating points for *Blackpoll* (in addition to the yellowish-gray color) are streaking restricted to the sides, shorter tail, very contrasting white wing bars, and streaking on the back. That leaves us with *Cape May*: the pure gray tones with some faint yellow mottling in the underparts, greenish-yellow rump (just visible), greenish flight feather edging, and fine streaking extending into the throat all help confirm the ID.

Where & When Mixed deciduous trees, California, October

The Big Picture Medium size, average feeding behavior. The yellow face and white underparts indicates this must be one of the Black-throated (*virens*) group, but which one?

Why It's Tricky The usual western species don't entirely fit. Could this be a vagrant?

The Rundown We have a lot to work with here. The contrasting dark wings, white wing bars, and overall strongly yellow/greenish head and upper back eliminate a lot of birds including *Wilson's*, *Orange-crowned*, *Yellow*, *Yellow-rumped* and *Black-throated Gray*. In the West our remaining regularly occurring birds are *Hermit*, *Townsend's*, and *Golden-cheeked*. *Hermit* never has streaking below, and its face is generally plainer. First-year females are also not as contrasty above, with paler wing bars and a grayer or darker olive back.

Golden-cheeked is way out of range and has a darker, more contrasting crown and back and lacks the olive cheek patch. *Townsend's* is our closest fit, but there's something off about it. *Townsend's* always has strong yellow from the throat through the breast, which is definitely lacking on this bird. And the facial pattern should be more contrasty, with solid auriculars even on a young bird. This bird's auriculars seem paler in the center.

Could it be a *Hermit* x *Townsend's* hybrid, which is possible in the West? They have a yellow face and streaking below. However, at least the most common forms usually have a much cleaner, all-yellow face (similar to *Hermit*) and much more yellow on the breast (like *Townsend's*). They also lack the yellow wash in the vent, and, although a bit hard to see here, would have a darker back, with less yellow-olive tones.

We're out of birds, and starting to suspect something unusual here. Note the vent: there's a yellow wash! For a yellow-faced warbler, this is diagnostic for *Black-throated Green Warbler*, a regular vagrant to the West. Note that the lack of much black in the throat indicates a young bird. Vagrants are often first-year birds and lack bright adult plumage.

Where & When A small pond, Pennsylvania, late April

The Big Picture A big, brown-backed, streaked bird feeding on the water's edge. Up/down tail pumping is continuous.

Why It's Tricky OK, it's a *waterthrush*—but which one?

The Rundown The size, location, coloration, and behavior all limit this bird to a few choices. The other large, ground-dwelling warblers are *Swainson's*, *Ovenbird*, and *Connecticut*. *Swainson's* would be way out of range, and it wouldn't be streaked. *Ovenbird* is olive above, with orange and black head stripes, lacks a supercilium, and "chicken-walks." *Connecticut* is bright yellow below, unstreaked, and a forest dweller. So we're dealing with a waterthrush.

The ground color of this bird is white, not a buffy yellow, so that means it's a *Louisiana*, right? Let's go over some marks: Overall, the bird looks a bit elongated, with a slightly long tail, and the bill doesn't seem noticeably large for a *waterthrush*. This sense of shape takes some experience to cultivate, but once learned it can give a quick start to an ID. The streaking is relatively narrow, dense, and linear, with some spotting in the throat, not a clincher, since some *Louisianas* can have a little spotting in the throat (though not normally this much).

The supercilium has a few important qualities: it seems to be fairly evenly wide from the front to just past the eye, and then quickly tapers off. *Louisiana's* supercilium usually starts fairly thin and often buffy in front of the eye and expands so that it's wider behind the eye and doesn't taper off so abruptly. Of course, the position of the head can change these impressions, but the characteristics are important to notice.

The tail bobbing is up and down, which *Louisiana* can also do; *Louisiana* does, however, often move the entire lower 1/3 of its body, which this bird is not doing. Finally, the legs are dullish pink, not the bright pink a *Louisiana* should have in the spring (only a supporting characteristic, but useful). All these points lead us to a white *Northern Waterthrush*, and if we hear a call note or song that will just confirm what we already know.

Where & When Wooded area, Virginia, late September

The Big Picture A largish warbler, unstreaked, feeding in the trees. Some green in the head and back, and some buffy color in the neck. Short tail that is wagged occasionally.

Why It's Tricky The classic drab-fall-bird question—*Blackpoll* or *Bay-breasted*?

The Rundown The size and shape seem to indicate a member of the famous *Pine/Blackpoll/Bay-breasted* group, but first we should rule out anything else. The contrasting wing bars immediately eliminate many species. Drab *Cape May* could vaguely resemble this color combination and also has pale neck sides, but it always shows more streaking below, especially in the throat, and never has strongly contrasting wing bars like this bird. *Blackburnian* should be considered, but it always has a very orangey-yellow cast to the head that is different, and the supercilium is always very wide. The cheek patch is also distinctively triangular, so this bird is definitely not a *Blackburnian*.

Palms can be very drab and, from certain angles, their long supercilium could seem thin. However, they always have very strongly yellow undertail coverts and a longer, more patterned tail. *Pine* has a much longer tail and an unstreaked back. Its wing bars also don't contrast as much with the darker section between them, which, in the case of our target bird, are very dark. *Pine*, especially in this view, would also show an obviously shorter primary extension due to its shorter wings.

Let's try *Blackpoll* next. Structurally, *Blackpoll* and *Bay-breasted* are very similar, so we have to use plumage characteristics. This bird lacks the usual features that makes separating *Blackpoll* from *Bay-breasted* easy: obvious streaking on the breast (*Blackpoll*) or a bay wash to the flanks or undertail area (*Bay-breasted*), so we have to go with subtler features.

First, the color on the face and back has some bright green tones; *Blackpoll* tends to be a duller, more yellowy green. *Blackpoll* also lacks the light collar found on this bird. The wing bars are very wide, which is good for *Bay-breasted*, and also the black area between the wing bars is very black. This is somewhat subtle, but high contrast between the white wing bars and the area between them is a very strong indicator for *Bay-breasted*. *Blackpolls* usually show a yellowish wash to the front part of the bird, contrasting with whiter lower belly and undertail coverts; this bird seems to have some buff in the breast and flanks, but otherwise is fairly even underneath. Finally, the facial pattern is muted: the eyeline barely protrudes behind the eye, and the supercilium is limited and short. These features all point to *Bay-breasted*, as *Blackpoll* almost always has a longer eyeline and supercilium. Our final answer is *Bay-breasted*.

Where & When Low scrubby brush and short trees in a migrant trap, California, September

The Big Picture Large, blocky headed and large-billed, with a shortish tail; skulky, moving through low vegetation. Conspicuous eyering, all yellow below.

Why It's Tricky The likely local choice for a skulking bird that is drab above and very yellow below is *MacGillivray's*, and we start from there. But something does not fit exactly. This warrants careful study!

The Rundown It's not a *Common Yellowthroat*, because it is too big, has bright yellow throughout the body (vs. buffy or brownish flanks and middle section contrasting with a yellow throat and undertail coverts), and the tail is a bit short. The eyering is striking. Can *MacGillivray's* have a complete eyering? Not really. They should show blunt, thick eye-arcs in all plumages. Although the dark lores seem to break the ring in the front, the back of the eyering looks complete.

Also, the yellow in the throat is coming straight up from the breast; *MacGillivray's* have white/grayish throats, never yellow. Even drab *MacGillivray's* should also seem more "hooded," with a definite color difference between the throat and upper breast and the breast and belly. Also, the supraloral seems a bit yellow and is obvious (not muted and whitish)—a useful supporting characteristic for *Mourning*.

We can just make out the ends of the undertail coverts, something that is often hard to see. It appears that the undertail coverts are covering at least half of the tail. This is a very good mark for *Mourning*; on a *MacGillivray's*, the tail would extend much farther past these coverts. But could it be a *Connecticut*, another rare vagrant? The complete eyering suggests *Connecticut*, but *Connecticuts* are always strongly hooded, are larger/fatter, and walk on the ground or limbs (vs. hopping through low brush). Also, although their throats can be pale or even buffy, they never have the clear yellow tones we see in this bird.

So we cautiously say this is a young *Mourning* with a bright eyering! Most *Mournings* would show a thinner eyering, but this one is not out of the range of possibility, and combined with our other field marks, *Mourning* seems to be the best choice. A short call note confirms the ID... very different from that of *MacGillivray's*, *Connecticut*, and *Common Yellowthroat*.

WARBLERS IN FLIGHT

The first time that one sees a warbler identified in flight, it seems like magic. How can anyone possibly identify a tiny flitting bird that darts away into the woods, or overhead to parts unknown? As with most things, the answer is "practice!" Daunting as it seems, learning to look more carefully at birds in flight can improve not only flight-ID skills, but also the ability to ID perched birds; and it creates a better understanding of the important combination of warbler identification points.

One critical component in successfully identifying flying warblers is learning their flight calls. Even if a bird cannot be identified immediately to species because certain distinguishing features are not observed, the combination of a call and a few visual cues can often lead to a confident ID. We present, below, a number of photos of warblers in flight, with notes on each species. Note that some of these ID points are subtle; flight style is especially tricky and is easily influenced by wind conditions, so it should be considered with caution.

Blackpoll

Black-throated Green

Bay-breasted

Blackburnian

Myrtle Drab

Pine

Lucy's

Cape May Drab

Worm-eating

Ovenbird

Northern Waterthrush

Louisiana Waterthrush

American Redstart AdM

Black-throated Blue
Male

Myrtle Bright

Audubon's Bright

American Redstart
1yM/F

Black-and-white

Cape May Bright

Connecticut

Yellow-throated

Townsend's

Canada

Common Yellowthroat

Blue-winged

Chestnut-sided

Palm

Northern Parula

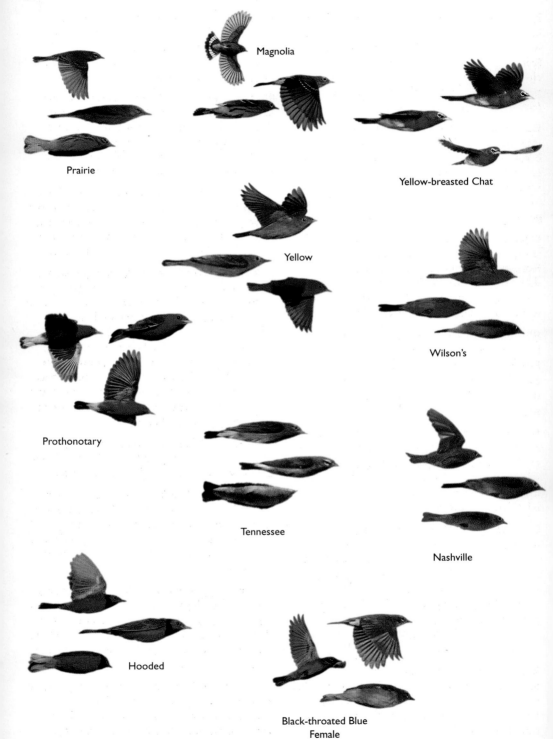

Magnolia

Prairie

Yellow-breasted Chat

Yellow

Wilson's

Prothonotary

Tennessee

Nashville

Hooded

Black-throated Blue
Female

American Redstart *Flight:* Tacking; rarely flies in a straight line; sputtery, with quick bursts of wingbeats mixed with short close-winged glides. *Features:* Slender with long, dark-tipped, and club-tipped tail; rounded wings; yellow/orange patches often visible; males' orange/black pattern conspicuous.

Bay-breasted *Flight:* Fast, direct, slightly swirling; slightly shallower and more flexed wingbeats than Blackpoll. *Features:* Deep belly and chest; big head; long, pointed, dark wings with white wing bars (bolder than Blackpoll); even or patchy buffy tone across lower body, brighter green above than Blackpoll.

Black-and-white *Flight:* Strong but bouncy and jerky, with deep downstroked, flexible wingbeats. *Features:* Long, pointed face with bill pointed downward; squarish tail; very contrasty streaking and wing bars; white undertail spots; blending of white/black in flight may appear blue.

Blackburnian *Flight:* Fast, direct, slightly bouncy; more flexed wingbeats than Blackpoll. *Features:* Longer neck and shorter wings than Blackpoll; white tail; streaked back; orange throat in males unique; triangular face patch sometimes visible.

Blackpoll *Flight:* Fast, strong, direct, slightly swirling; stiff, even-depth wingbeats with little gliding. *Features:* Deep chest; long, pointed wings; distinct contrast between yellower chest/head and whiter belly/UnTC; narrower wing bars than Bay-breasted.

Black-throated Blue *Flight:* Bouncy, direct, rocking; frequent, distinctive flight call; wingbeats fast, deep with short closed-winged glides. *Features:* Wide-bodied; football-shaped belly; straight-cut tail; holds head up; male very contrasty white underparts and dark head/upperparts, white handkerchief creates flash; female low contrast, slightly paler yellow below, dark cheek, handkerchief sometimes visible.

Black-throated Gray *Flight:* Fast, bouncy, tacking; sputtery wingbeats; sometimes flashes white tail feathers. *Features:* Stocky; rounded head; long tail; bold, black and white pattern in face, throat, and sides.

Black-throated Green *Flight:* Fast, direct, slightly swirling, undulating; stiff, sputtery wingbeats. *Features:* Tapered body; long, all-white tail; yellow head contrasts with white body; often black throat.

Blue-winged *Flight:* Direct, slightly swirling; steady wingbeats with short glides. *Features:* Solid chest but slim, tapered belly; contrast between white UnTC and lemon-yellow body; bold white wing bars; sharp black eyeline on yellow face diagnostic when visible.

Canada *Flight:* Strong, bouncy. *Features:* Long tail; plain, blue-gray upperparts contrast yellow underparts/white UnTC; eyering conspicuous; necklace diagnostic when visible; may appear similar to Magnolia when upperparts not seen.

Cape May *Flight:* Slow, level, slightly tacking; not bouncy; often high and in pairs; piercing call; shallow wingbeats. *Features:* Stout; angular in chest; wings very pointed with bulging secondaries; short, sharply cut tail; pointed face; yellow-green rump. Bright Plumage: yellow chest/belly and white UnTC/tail; orange face with eyeline, yellow neck; streaked underparts; olive above with white wing patch. Drab Plumage: Overall gray; pale neck patches; streaks; upperwing panel dull gray.

Cerulean *Flight:* Fast, strong, direct, slightly jerky; wingbeats deep and still. *Features:* Front-heavy with very short tail; pointed wings.

Chestnut-sided *Flight:* Direct, slightly bouncy and twisting; stiff wingbeats. *Features:* Slender; long tail; rounded head; gray face may appear hooded; lime-green upperparts sharply divided with clean whitish underparts; distinct eyering; yellow wing bars.

Common Yellowthroat *Flight:* Slow, darting, weak; sputtery, weak wingbeats; droops tail in flight; rarely seen flying long distances in the daylight. *Features:* Short, rounded wings; long tail; olive upperparts; paler yellow throat contrasts underparts.

Connecticut *Flight:* Fast, strong, and direct but more twisting and jerkier than Blackpoll; wingbeats shallower than Blackpoll, with shorter breaks than waterthrushes. *Features:* Large;

football-shaped belly; long neck; long, pointed wings; usually stongly hooded, with bright yellow underparts; some may appear to have a breastband with pale throat; eyering.

Golden-winged *Flight:* Direct, slightly swirling; steady wingbeats with short glides. *Features:* Solid chest but slim, tapered belly; light gray and white body with yellow flashes in wings and head.

Grace's *Flight:* Direct, strong, undulating. *Features:* Small, chesty; short tail; yellow face/throat contrasts white underparts.

Hermit *Flight:* Direct, fast. *Features:* Plump body, long tail; yellow face contrasts all-white underparts.

Hooded *Flight:* Moderately weak but direct. *Features:* Slender; round-winged; black hood on yellow body distinct when present; may flash white in long tail.

Kirtland's *Flight:* Strong, direct; slightly undulating. *Features:* Large, long tail; gray upperparts contrast yellow underparts; may flash white in tail.

Louisiana Waterthrush *Flight:* Strong, bounding or undulating; smoother, less tacking than most; slow wingbeats with long closed-winged glides, brief open-winged glides. *Features:* Large; more front-heavy than Northern (bigger head, bill, and chest); dark upperparts contrast with pale, streaked underparts; streaking on underparts sparser than Northern; strong white supercilium.

Lucy's *Flight:* Slow, bouncy; sputtery wingbeats. *Features:* Very small; pointy bill; pale gray, paler underneath; rufous in rump.

MacGillivray's *Flight:* Fast, direct, bouncy, often low. *Features:* Long tail; bright yellow underparts striking; hooded.

Magnolia *Flight:* Tacking, undulating; sputtery wingbeats. *Features:* Big, round head; long tail (less tapered at base than American Redstart); yellow chest, white belly/UnTC and obvious black tail tip; white base of tail may make tail appear detached from body; yellow rump.

Mourning *Flight:* Fast, bouncy, often low; rarely seen in extended flight. *Features:* Large head, long bill, long body; long winged, short tailed; bright yellow underparts.

Nashville *Flight:* Undulating, tacking; sputtery wingbeats. *Features:* Small; plump; rounded forehead with sharp bill; short wings; olive back with lighter rump; bright yellow underparts and UnTC; white eyering.

Northern Parula *Flight:* Slow, bouncy; body seems to rise with each flap; calls incessantly; sputtery wingbeats. *Features:* Very small; plump body; short tail; white UnTC and belly contrast yellow or dark throat (may appear hooded); strong, white double wing bar with blue-and-green back distinctive (compare Tennessee and Nashville).

Northern Waterthrush *Flight:* Very strong, bounding or undulating; smoother, less tacking than most; slow wingbeats with long closed-winged glides, brief open-winged glides. *Features:* Large, stout; pointy head; broad wings; dark upperparts and underwing coverts contrast pale, streaked underparts; overall dark impression; underparts usually yellowish; strong supercilium.

Orange-crowned *Flight:* Fast, direct, slightly undulating; steady wingbeats with short glides. *Features:* Overall lower contrast between upper- and underparts than Tennessee; longer tail than Tennessee; UnTC yellowish and don't contrast strongly with body.

Ovenbird *Flight:* Fast, less bounding, bouncier than waterthrushes; relatively slow wingbeats; relatively long closed-winged glides. *Features:* Large; round head; hunchback; pot belly; often points bill down; eyering often conspicuous; black streaking contrasts white lower breast/belly; brownish/olive upperparts.

Painted Redstart *Flight:* Fast, direct, bouncy with sputtery wingbeats. *Features:* Red belly/black upperparts, with large amounts of white in tail.

Palm *Flight:* Direct flier, slightly bouncy; shallow, steady wingbeats with little gliding. *Features: Slender; somewhat hunchbacked; distinct long tail and lower body pattern (often brightest yellow in UnTC, paler in body; large white tail spots); eye-arcs.

Pine *Flight:* Strong, rowing with irregular wingbeats, slightly undulating. *Features:* Large; very long, notched tail; long body.

Prairie *Flight:* Fast, direct with uneven undulations. *Features:* Small, thin, slight; long tail often flashes white; overall yellowy with olive back; side streaks and facial marks.

Prothonotary *Flight:* Strong, fast, undulating and bounding; infrequent, heavy, slow wingbeats with long, close-winged glides. *Features:* Large; long bill; big head; broad chest; bright yellow head and belly contrast white UnTC/dark back.

Red-faced *Flight:* Direct, bouncy, light with sputtery wingbeats. *Features:* Thin; long tail; white rump and neck patches evident; gray upperparts/white underparts; red head diagnostic.

Swainson's *Flight:* Direct, fast; steady wingbeats. *Features:* Similar to waterthrushes, but paler; long bill apparent.

Tennessee *Flight:* Fast, direct with slight undulations; steady wingbeats with short glides. *Features:* Small, angular body; long-winged; short tail; rounder wings, shorter neck than Blackpoll; green upperparts contrast white/yellowish underparts (but not white like Chestnut-sided); paler UnTC contrast with lower body.

Townsend's *Flight:* Fast, bouncy, tacking; sputtery wingbeats. *Features:* Stout; thin tail; yellow head/breast contrasts white belly/UnTC.

Wilson's *Flight:* Slow, bouncy, often low; sputtery wingbeats. *Features:* Slimmer, longer tailed than Yellow; rounded wings; dark, long tail; plain-looking and low contrast; somewhat darker upperparts.

Worm-eating *Flight:* Direct, slightly swirling; steady, fast wingbeats. *Features:* Pointy face; big head and bill; broad chest; short, broad tail; head stripes often evident; mustard underparts/olive upperparts (unusual for a warbler).

Yellow *Flight:* Direct, strong, with slight jerks; strong, even wingbeats. *Features:* Long, stout body, strongly contoured; short, yellow tail; yellow overall; thick-billed; overall low contrast; drab birds may appear dingy.

Yellow-breasted Chat *Flight:* Direct, low. *Display Flight:* Ascends high, fluttering while singing, then drops again. *Features:* Large, heavy body; long tail; projecting head with stout bill. Yellow breast sharply contrasting white belly/olive back; goggled.

Yellow-rumped *Flight:* Bouncy and strongly tacking; wingbeats irregular, mostly below body; short glides, both open- and closed-winged, often mixes flight and chip calls. *Features:* Large, stocky; hunchbacked; long, blunt wings; overall gray/dingy with yellow shoulders; wing bars; variable streaking, yellow rump.

Yellow-throated *Flight:* Tacking; sputtery wingbeats. *Features:* Hunchbacked, with evenly curved upper- and lowerparts; thin tail pinched at base; long bill; bold facial pattern; yellow throat and black streaking contrasts white body; wing bars and eye-arcs.

Virginia's *Flight:* Slightly undulating. *Features:* Small, thin; low contrast gray; yellow breast/UnTC.

NORTH AMERICAN WARBLER TAXONOMY

Bird taxonomy is a complicated business, and over the years the classification of different species (and even families) of birds has shifted, and it will inevitably continue to shift. This chart, developed through DNA research by Dr. Irby Lovette, describes the most up-to-date thinking on the historical evolution of the warblers, and hence illuminates which

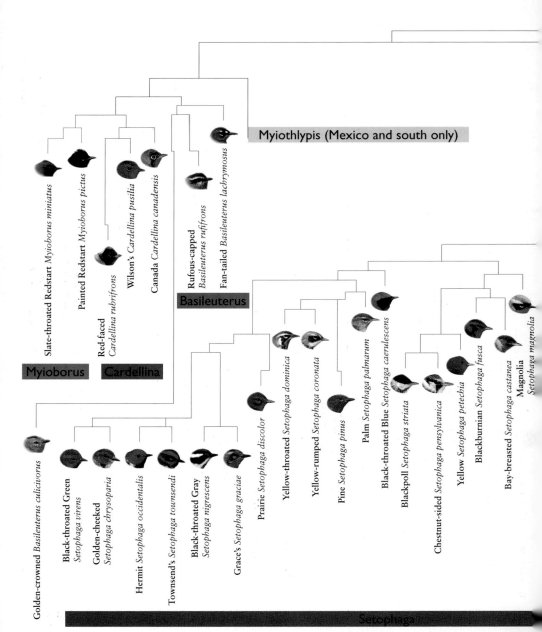

Myiothlypis (Mexico and south only)

Slate-throated Redstart *Myioborus miniatus*

Painted Redstart *Myioborus pictus*

Red-faced *Cardellina rubrifrons*

Wilson's *Cardellina pusilla*

Canada *Cardellina canadensis*

Rufous-capped *Basileuterus rufifrons*

Fan-tailed *Basileuterus lachrymosus*

Basileuterus

Myioborus

Cardellina

Golden-crowned *Basileuterus culicivorus*

Black-throated Green *Setophaga virens*

Golden-cheeked *Setophaga chrysoparia*

Hermit *Setophaga occidentalis*

Townsend's *Setophaga townsendi*

Black-throated Gray *Setophaga nigrescens*

Grace's *Setophaga graciae*

Prairie *Setophaga discolor*

Yellow-throated *Setophaga dominica*

Yellow-rumped *Setophaga coronata*

Pine *Setophaga pinus*

Palm *Setophaga palmarum*

Black-throated Blue *Setophaga caerulescens*

Blackpoll *Setophaga striata*

Chestnut-sided *Setophaga pensylvanica*

Yellow *Setophaga petechia*

Blackburnian *Setophaga fusca*

Bay-breasted *Setophaga castanea*

Magnolia *Setophaga magnolia*

Setophaga

birds are most (and least) closely related. The evolutionary time line starts at the top with Ovenbird, our "oldest" warbler, and branches into more recent species toward the bottom. Note that this chart includes only the warblers described in this book.

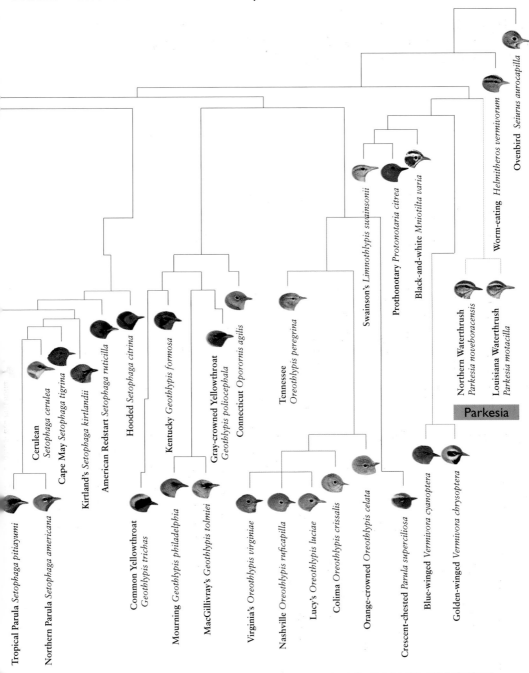

Tropical Parula *Setophaga pitiayumi*

Northern Parula *Setophaga americana*

Cerulean *Setophaga cerulea*

Cape May *Setophaga tigrina*

Kirtland's *Setophaga kirtlandii*

American Redstart *Setophaga ruticilla*

Hooded *Setophaga citrina*

Common Yellowthroat *Geothlypis trichas*

Kentucky *Geothlypis formosa*

Mourning *Geothlypis philadelphia*

MacGillivray's *Geothlypis tolmiei*

Gray-crowned Yellowthroat *Geothlypis poliocephala*

Connecticut *Oporornis agilis*

Virginia's *Oreothlypis virginiae*

Nashville *Oreothlypis ruficapilla*

Lucy's *Oreothlypis luciae*

Colima *Oreothlypis crissalis*

Orange-crowned *Oreothlypis celata*

Tennessee *Oreothlypis peregrina*

Crescent-chested *Parula superciliosa*

Blue-winged *Vermivora cyanoptera*

Golden-winged *Vermivora chrysoptera*

Swainson's *Limnothlypis swainsonii*

Prothonotary *Protonotaria citrea*

Black-and-white *Mniotilta varia*

Parkesia

Northern Waterthrush *Parkesia noveboracensis*

Louisiana Waterthrush *Parkesia motacilla*

Worm-eating *Helmitheros vermivorum*

Ovenbird *Seiurus aurocapilla*

Vermivora

MEASUREMENTS

	Length		Wingspan		Weight	[Range]	
	in	(cm)	in	(cm)	oz	[oz]	(gm)
American Redstart	5.10	(13.0)	8.06	(20.48)	0.34	[0.22–0.41]	(9.75)
Bay-breasted	5.45	(13.8)	8.75	(22.23)	0.45	[0.38–0.53]	(12.80)
Black-and-white	5.10	(13.0)	8.50	(21.59)	0.40	[0.31–0.52]	(11.40)
Blackburnian	5.00	(12.7)	8.25	(20.96)	0.35	[0.33–0.38]	(10.00)
Blackpoll	5.50	(14.0)	8.75	(22.23)	0.50	[0.35–0.69]	(14.10)
Black-throated Blue	5.20	(13.2)	7.50	(19.05)	0.37	[0.29–0.43]	(10.50)
Black-throated Green	5.00	(12.7)	7.75	(19.69)	0.33	[0.28–0.39]	(9.45)
Black-throated Gray	5.00	(12.7)	7.75	(19.69)	0.31	[0.25–0.36]	(8.90)
Blue-winged	4.70	(11.9)	7.35	(18.67)	0.33	[0.27–0.39]	(9.40)
Canada	5.30	(13.5)	8.06	(20.48)	0.38	[0.29–0.50]	(10.70)
Cape May	5.00	(12.7)	7.63	(19.37)	0.41	[0.32–0.53]	(11.70)
Cerulean	4.70	(11.9)	7.50	(19.05)	0.33	[0.29–0.36]	(9.40)
Chestnut-sided	5.00	(12.7)	7.81	(19.84)	0.36	[0.27–0.46]	(10.00)
Colima	5.70	(14.5)	8.13	(20.64)	0.35	[0.28–0.41]	(9.85)
Common Yellowthroat	5.00	(12.7)	7.38	(18.73)	0.42	[0.28–0.71]	(12.00)
Connecticut	5.70	(14.5)	8.88	(22.54)	0.57	[0.42–0.83]	(16.10)
Crescent-chested	4.30	(10.9)	6.30	(16.00)	0.32	[0.32–0.32]	(9.00)
Fan-tailed	5.90	(15.0)	7.88	(20.00)	0.54	[0.50–0.58]	(15.40)
Golden-cheeked	5.10	(13.0)	7.75	(19.69)	0.35	[0.29–0.43]	(10.00)
Golden-crowned	5.00	(12.7)	7.50	(19.05)	0.37	[0.34–0.42]	(10.60)
Golden-winged	4.75	(12.1)	7.70	(19.56)	0.33	[0.27–0.40]	(9.45)
Grace's	5.00	(12.7)	8.00	(20.32)	0.30	[0.26–0.32]	(8.60)
Gray-cr. Yellowthroat	5.50	(14.0)	8.00	(20.32)	0.52	[0.47–0.57]	(14.70)
Hermit	5.10	(13.0)	7.88	(20.00)	0.34	[0.28–0.39]	(9.50)
Hooded	5.25	(13.3)	7.50	(19.05)	0.38	[0.30–0.46]	(10.85)
Kentucky	5.20	(13.2)	8.38	(21.27)	0.53	[0.41–0.70]	(14.90)
Kirtland's	5.75	(14.6)	8.63	(21.91)	0.49	[0.43–0.56]	(14.00)
Louisiana Waterthrush	6.00	(15.2)	9.50	(24.13)	0.74	[0.62–0.90]	(20.90)
Lucy's	4.30	(10.9)	7.00	(17.78)	0.23	[0.18–0.26]	(6.50)
MacGillivray's	5.20	(13.2)	7.88	(20.00)	0.38	[0.31–0.43]	(10.75)
Magnolia	5.00	(12.7)	7.63	(19.37)	0.32	[0.22–0.43]	(8.95)
Mourning	5.20	(13.2)	7.88	(20.00)	0.45	[0.35–0.54]	(12.65)
Nashville	4.75	(12.1)	7.50	(19.05)	0.33	[0.24–0.47]	(9.40)
Northern Parula	4.40	(11.2)	7.00	(17.78)	0.31	[0.25–0.36]	(8.90)
Northern Waterthrush	5.80	(14.7)	9.13	(23.18)	0.65	[0.49–0.84]	(18.50)
Olive	5.20	(13.0)	9.25	(23.50)	0.39	[0.18–0.43]	(11.20)
Orange-crowned	5.00	(12.7)	7.38	(18.73)	0.33	[0.25–0.40]	(9.35)
Ovenbird	6.00	(15.2)	9.25	(23.50)	0.71	[0.51–0.95]	(20.20)
Painted Redstart	5.60	(14.2)	8.63	(21.91)	0.29	[0.21–0.33]	(8.30)
Palm	5.30	(13.5)	8.25	(20.96)	0.35	[0.25–0.46]	(10.00)
Pine	5.45	(13.8)	8.63	(21.91)	0.42	[0.32–0.53]	(11.90)
Prairie	4.75	(12.1)	7.25	(18.42)	0.28	[0.21–0.35]	(8.00)
Prothonotary	5.45	(13.8)	8.63	(21.91)	0.58	[0.49–0.67]	(16.45)
Red-faced	5.35	(13.6)	8.13	(20.64)	0.43	[0.29–0.39]	(12.20)
Rufous-capped	5.20	(13.0)	7.67	(19.47)	0.39	[0.19–0.38]	(10.95)
Slate-throated Redstart	5.20	(13.2)	8.66	(22.00)	0.34	[0.34–0.34]	(9.50)
Swainson's	5.45	(13.8)	8.63	(21.91)	0.55	[0.46–0.71]	(15.60)
Tennessee	4.75	(12.1)	7.75	(19.69)	0.40	[0.27–0.62]	(11.30)
Townsend's	5.00	(12.7)	7.88	(20.00)	0.32	[0.25–0.38]	(9.20)
Tropical Parula	4.50	(11.4)	6.63	(16.83)	0.25	[0.25–0.24]	(7.00)
Virginia's	4.65	(11.8)	7.50	(19.05)	0.29	[0.25–0.34]	(8.20)
Wilson's	4.70	(11.9)	7.25	(18.42)	0.27	[0.20–0.34]	(7.50)
Worm-eating	5.20	(13.2)	8.50	(21.59)	0.48	[0.44–0.53]	(13.50)
Yellow	5.00	(12.7)	7.88	(20.00)	0.37	[0.27–0.53]	(10.50)
Yellow-breasted Chat	7.50	(19.1)	9.63	(24.45)	0.91	[0.36–1.19]	(25.90)
Yellow-rumped	5.40	(13.7)	8.88	(22.54)	0.46	[0.35–0.59]	(13.00)
Yellow-throated	5.40	(13.7)	8.25	(20.96)	0.34	[0.30–0.37]	(9.55)

	Length in	Wingspan in	Weight oz		Length in	Wingspan in	Weight oz
Ruby-crowned Kinglet	4.20	7.20	0.30	Kentucky	5.20	8.38	0.53
Lucy's Warbler	4.30	7.00	0.23	MacGillivray's	5.20	7.88	0.38
Crescent-chested	4.30	6.30	0.32	Mourning	5.20	7.88	0.45
Northern Parula	4.40	7.00	0.31	Worm-eating	5.20	8.50	0.48
Blue-gray Gnatcatcher	4.40	6.00	0.20	Slate-throated Redstart	5.20	8.66	0.34
Tropical Parula	4.50	6.63	0.25	Hooded	5.25	7.50	0.38
Bushtit	4.50	6.00	0.20	*Least Flycatcher*	5.30	7.80	0.40
Verdin	4.50	6.50	0.20	Canada	5.30	8.06	0.38
Virginia's	4.65	7.50	0.29	Palm	5.30	8.25	0.35
Blue-winged	4.70	7.35	0.33	Red-faced	5.35	8.13	0.43
Cerulean	4.70	7.50	0.33	Yellow-rumped	5.40	8.88	0.46
Wilson's	4.70	7.25	0.27	Yellow-throated	5.40	8.25	0.34
Prairie	4.75	7.25	0.28	Bay-breasted	5.45	8.75	0.45
Golden-winged	4.75	7.70	0.33	Pine Warbler	5.45	8.63	0.42
Tennessee Warbler	4.75	7.75	0.40	Prothonotary	5.45	8.63	0.58
Nashville Warbler	4.75	7.50	0.33	Swainson's	5.45	8.63	0.55
Bell's Vireo	4.80	7.00	0.30	Blackpoll	5.50	8.75	0.50
American Goldfinch	4.90	8.70	0.50	Gray-cr Yellowthroat	5.50	8.00	0.52
Blackburnian	5.00	8.25	0.35	*Blue-headed Vireo*	5.50	9.50	0.60
Black-throated Green	5.00	7.75	0.33	*Chipping Sparrow*	5.50	8.50	0.40
Black-throated Gray	5.00	7.75	0.31	*Warbling Vireo*	5.50	8.50	0.40
Cape May	5.00	7.63	0.41	*Yellow-throated Vireo*	5.50	9.50	0.60
Chestnut-sided	5.00	7.81	0.36	Painted Redstart	5.60	8.63	0.29
Common Yellowthroat	5.00	7.38	0.42	Colima	5.70	8.13	0.35
Grace's	5.00	8.00	0.30	Connecticut	5.70	8.88	0.57
Magnolia	5.00	7.63	0.32	Kirtland's	5.75	8.63	0.49
Orange-crowned	5.00	7.38	0.33	Northern Waterthrush	5.80	9.13	0.65
Townsend's	5.00	7.88	0.32	Fan-tailed Warbler	5.90	7.88	0.54
Yellow	5.00	7.88	0.37	Louisiana Waterthrush	6.00	9.50	0.74
Golden-crowned	5.00	7.50	0.37	Ovenbird	6.00	9.25	0.71
Hutton's Vireo	5.00	8.00	0.40	*Red-eyed Vireo*	6.00	10.00	0.60
White-eyed Vireo	5.00	7.50	0.40	*Eastern Wood-pewee*	6.20	9.80	0.50
American Redstart	5.10	8.06	0.34	*House Sparrow*	6.20	9.50	1.00
Black-and-white	5.10	8.50	0.40	*Scarlet Tanager*	7.00	11.50	1.00
Golden-cheeked	5.10	7.75	0.35	*Swainson's Thrush*	7.00	11.90	1.20
Hermit	5.10	7.88	0.34	*Orchard Oriole*	7.30	9.30	0.70
Olive	5.20	9.25	0.39	Yellow-breasted Chat	7.50	9.63	0.91
Rufous-capped	5.20	7.67	0.39	*Baltimore Oriole*	8.80	11.30	1.20
Black-throated Blue	5.20	7.50	0.37				

Eastern Warblers

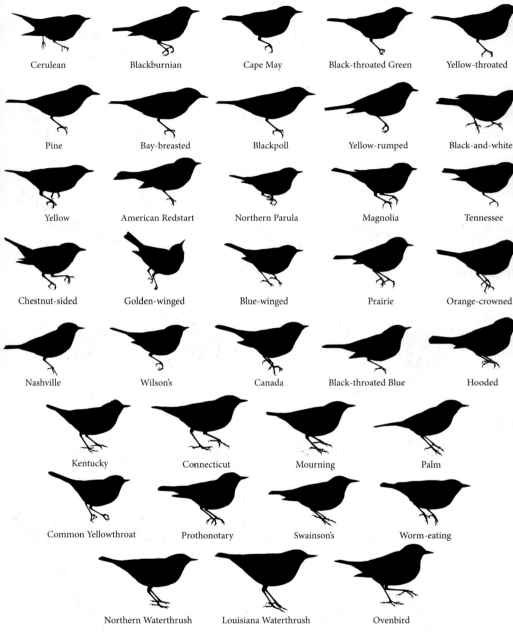

Cerulean

Blackburnian

Cape May

Black-throated Green

Yellow-throated

Pine

Bay-breasted

Blackpoll

Yellow-rumped

Black-and-white

Yellow

American Redstart

Northern Parula

Magnolia

Tennessee

Chestnut-sided

Golden-winged

Blue-winged

Prairie

Orange-crowned

Nashville

Wilson's

Canada

Black-throated Blue

Hooded

Kentucky

Connecticut

Mourning

Palm

Common Yellowthroat

Prothonotary

Swainson's

Worm-eating

Northern Waterthrush

Louisiana Waterthrush

Ovenbird

Limited Range

Colima

Kirtland's

Golden-cheeked

Eastern Non-Warblers

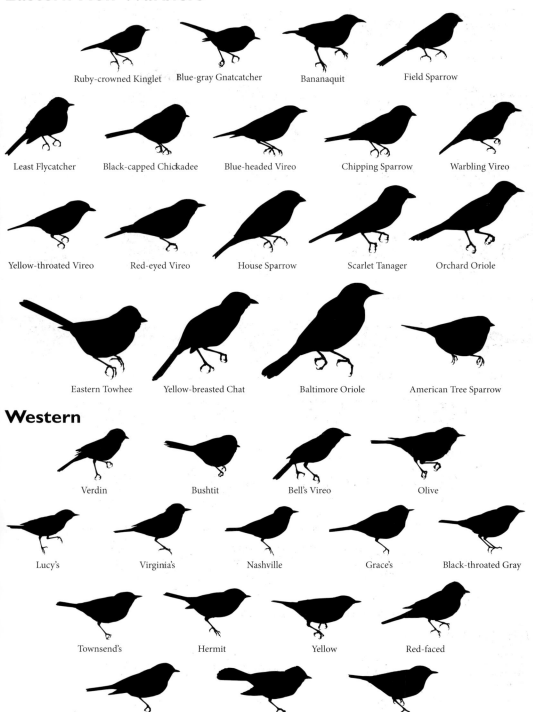

Ruby-crowned Kinglet

Blue-gray Gnatcatcher

Bananaquit

Field Sparrow

Least Flycatcher

Black-capped Chickadee

Blue-headed Vireo

Chipping Sparrow

Warbling Vireo

Yellow-throated Vireo

Red-eyed Vireo

House Sparrow

Scarlet Tanager

Orchard Oriole

Eastern Towhee

Yellow-breasted Chat

Baltimore Oriole

American Tree Sparrow

Western

Verdin

Bushtit

Bell's Vireo

Olive

Lucy's

Virginia's

Nashville

Grace's

Black-throated Gray

Townsend's

Hermit

Yellow

Red-faced

Yellow-rumped

Painted Redstart

MacGillivray's

HABITAT AND BEHAVIOR

	Foraging Behavior	Foraging Location	General Breeding Habitat	Vagrancy
Am. Red-start	Very active; sallies, hover-gleans; fans, tail, droops wings	Low to mid-level; can be higher	Open deciduous and mixed woods; edges; often near water; river bottoms, swampy woods, riparian areas	Regular to West Coast in fall; may winter AZ, S CA
Bay-breasted	Deliberate, sluggish, gleans; pumps tail irregularly	Mid-level to canopy; interior	Boreal coniferous, spruce forests; dense or with bogs or clearings; sometimes mixed forest; a summer specialist on spruce budworm; migrants often attracted to conifers	Rare vagrant in West
Black-and-white	Creeps along trunks, large branches; often circles limbs	Mid-level; interior	Deciduous and mixed forests with large trees; riparian areas	Regular in West
Black burnian	Fairly deliberate, can sally; droops wings, raises tail	High canopy	Spruce, hemlock, coniferous forests or mixed; can breed in deciduous forest with just one large conifer; favors spruce budworm; requires tall trees	Fairly regular to West in fall
Blackpoll	Usually deliberate, sluggish; pumps tail irregularly	Mid-level to canopy; interior	Spruce, hemlock, coniferous forests or mixed; bogs; favors spruce budworm; breeds farther north than Bay-breasted; in stunted forests	Regular in West in fall, esp. CA, CO
Black-thr Blue	Deliberate; sometimes sallies; can feed on trunks	Low to mid-level; open branches	Inside mature deciduous or mixed forests with good understory shrubs, rhododendron-type thickets, and young trees	Fairly regular to West in fall
Black-thr Green	Sometimes hover-gleans, sallies; fairly active	Mid-level, interior	Wide range of coniferous, mixed, sometimes all deciduous; all with developed, varied understory; deciduous swamps in southern part of range	Regular vagrant in West
Black-thr Gray	Sometimes hover-gleans, sallies; methodical	Low to mid-level	Dry mixed oak, coniferous woodlands with denser, brushy understory; usually up to about 6,000 ft., lower than other local *virens*	Rare vagrant in East
Blue-winged	Acrobatic but deliberate; hangs, hover-gleans	Low to mid-level	Brushy secondary growth, power-line cuts, edges of woods, thickets; possibly wider range of habitats, later, denser successional growth than Golden-winged	Rare vagrant in West
Canada	Active; sallies; flips, wags, cocks tail; droops wings	Low to mid-level; understory	Wet deciduous and mixed forests with dense, tall understory; swamps, ravines, bogs	Fall vagrant to West
Cape May	Somewhat acrobatic; aggressive; hangs; sometimes sallies	High canopy; exterior, tips	Boreal spruce forests or spruce bogs; as Bay-breasted, greatly prefers (and population fluctuates with) spruce budworm	Vagrant in West
Cerulean	Fairly methodical; hover-gleans; sometimes sallies	High canopy; interior	Mature deciduous woods with tall trees (often oaks), dense canopies, lower understory; often by streams or wet areas	Very rare vagrant in West
Chestnut-sided	Methodical; not acrobatic; cocks tail, droops wings	Low to mid-level	Young, deciduous second growth, forest edges; cut areas in process of regrowing; thickets with young deciduous trees	Regular in West
Colima	Deliberate, sluggish; holds tail still	Mid-level to higher	Oak, mixed oak, pinyon-juniper w/dense low cover; usually 5,500–8,500 ft.; U.S. only Chisos Mts., Big Bend, TX	No records of vagrants
Common Yellow-throat	Very active; often skulking; cocks, flips tail	Low, ground; in dense vegetation	Always dense underbrush; marshes, wet fields, grassy fields, hedgerows, pond edges; SE subspecies in coastal mangroves; SW in riparian areas	
Connec-ticut	Walks on ground, logs; shy; can remain motionless for long time; bobs head, tail	On ground or low branches; sings from higher perch	Mixed forests and tamarack and spruce bogs; jack pine forests	Rare vagrant in West
Golden-cheeked	Deliberate; gleans; somewhat acrobatic	Mid-level to canopy	Mature Ashe Juniper (with loose bark for nest building) and oaks; low forests only to 30 ft.; Edwards Plateau, TX	Rarely ever seen in migration
Golden-winged	Often hangs; deliberate; can fly far to next singing perch	Low to mid-level; higher tree	Early successional open fields with saplings, brush, and thickets; power-line cuts, old pastures; reported to require less advanced succession than Blue-winged	Rare vagrant in West
Grace's	Gleans, sallies	High canopy; exterior	Mixed montane pines or pine/oak forests 5,500–7,500 ft.	Rarely seen during migration

	Foraging Behavior	Foraging Location	General Breeding Habitat	Vagrancy
Hermit	Hangs; sometimes sallies, hover-gleans	High canopy	Montane, tall coniferous forests, especially firs, pines	Rare vagrant in East
Hooded	Active; sallies, can hover-glean; often flashes white tail	Low to ground; sings higher, interior	Mature deciduous woods with dense understory; often by streams or wet or swampy areas	Regular vagrant to West
Kentucky	Turns over leaves, reaches up; skulking, shy; often cocks tail	Ground or low; fallen branches; sings higher, interior	Mature deciduous forests with dense understory, often in wet areas	Rare in West; more often spring
Kirtland's	Deliberate, reaches, sallies; pumps tail almost continuously	Very low to mid-level; sings higher, exterior	Young jack pines, less than about 20 ft. tall with dense low branches and understory; endangered species, nearly restricted to northern part of Michigan's lower peninsula; expanding some to other nearby areas	Rarely seen in migration, no records outside migrant corridor
Louisiana Water-thrush	Turns over leaves, picks from water; bobs tail usually with circular motion involving back 1/3 of body	Ground, low logs near water; sings from mid-level interior	Forested running streams, often in ravines; also lower wet or swampy areas with preference for moving water; possibly more open understory than Northern	Very rare vagrant in West
Lucy's	Active and acrobatic; hangs; bobs, flips tail very regularly	Low to mid-level	Mesquite in dry areas, riparian strips in drier scrub and desert; often near water; mixed deciduous at higher elevations; nests in cavities	Rare vagrant; migrants not often seen
MacGilli-vray's	Reaches up; skulking; moves to higher interior to sing	Ground, fallen logs, low foliage	Dense, dark understory, brush, scrub, tangles; surrounding trees and other aspects vary throughout range; also higher thickets in wet areas	Rare vagrant in East
Magnolia	Active; hover-gleans, sallies; fans tail with high, white spots	Low to mid-level; interior and tips	Coniferous forests, especially spruce, usually with dense understory; also mixed coniferous/deciduous woodlands or regrowing areas with dense undergrowth	Regular vagrant to West
Mourning	Gleans, reaches; very skulking; sings from higher interior perch	Ground, fallen logs, low foliage	Dense understory, brambles, thickets of edges, second growth, fields, power-line cuts; also swampy areas, wet woods with open canopy	Rare vagrant to West
Nashville	Acrobatic; gleans; pumps or wags tail	Low, mid-level, sometimes high; exterior	Open deciduous or mixed woodlands w/ dense understory; successional fields, edges of open woods, bogs	
N. Parula	Active; hangs, hover-gleans	Mid-level to high; often ext; lower in fall	Deciduous and mixed forests, but stays more on edge; wet bottomland forests, swamps; uses Old Man's Beard and Spanish moss but not required	Regular vagrant to West
N. Water-thrush	Turns over leaves, twigs, picks from water; continuously bobs tail up and down	Ground or low logs near water	Wet woods, thickets, swamps, bogs, usually with standing or slow-moving water rather than fast-running water preferred by Louisiana; more densely wooded areas than Louisiana; sings from mid-level interior	Regular in West
Olive	Deliberate; gleans, sometimes creeps	High, often tips	Conifers, mixed forests at high elevations, 8,000 ft. and higher	Rarely seen in U.S. outside nesting
Orange-crowned	Deliberate; reaches; acrobatic poses	Low to mid-level	Brush, thickets in variety of habitats: secondary growth, riparian areas, chaparral, woodland edges	
Oven-bird	Walks on ground slowly; bobs head, flips tail up	Ground; sings from mid-level interior perch	Large areas of mature deciduous or mixed forest with somewhat open understory and leaf litter; swamp bottomlands	Regular vagrant to West
Painted Redstart	Very active, flashes wings, tail; acrobatic; sallies, jerks, jumps	Ground to mid-level; logs, branches	Mixed pine/oak forests with understory on steep slopes or ravines; 5,000–7,000 ft; usually with some water nearby	Rare vagrant
Palm	Active; constantly pumps tail	Often on ground, low; all heights	Open bogs; other open areas with some trees	Regular vagrant in West
Pine	Deliberate; creeps along branches; can pump tail	Mid-level to high; on ground in fall	Pine forests usually with at least some tall mature trees	Rare vagrant to West

	Foraging Behavior	Foraging Location	General Breeding Habitat	Vagrancy
Prairie	Active; pumps tail, hover-gleans, sallies	Low to mid-level, ground	Power-line cuts, successional fields, dry scrub, forest edges; mixed secondary growth; dunes, coastal mangroves	Vagrant to West
Prothon-otary	Deliberate; creeps on trunks; not acrobatic	Low to mid; often flashes white in tail	Mature deciduous woodlands in swamps, flooded areas; wooded streams; usually near water even in migration; nests in cavities	Vagrant to West
Red-faced	Active, acrobatic; sallies; wags, flips tail	Mid-level; exterior	Coniferous and mixed forests 6,000+ ft.; often in ravines and canyons	Rare vagrant
Swainson's	Shy; methodical, tosses leaf litter; can "shiver" rear, shuffle feet; sound of leaves moving clue	On ground or very low; sings higher; often sits motionless	Two separate areas: SE coastal in lowland swamps, dense thickets near water, canebrakes; Appalachian Mts. up to 3,000 ft., wooded with understory of rhododendron, similar shrubs; often open areas in dense understory	Rare vagrant
Tennessee	Active; gleans, hangs	High canopy; low in fall	Coniferous, mixed, deciduous forests; bogs w/ open mossy ground layer, some brush; a spruce budworm specialist	Regular vagrant to West, esp. CA, CO
Townsend's	Hangs, hover-gleans, sometimes sallies	High; interior to tips	Mature coniferous forests usually with dense canopy	Rare vagrant to East
Virginia's	Active; sallies	Mid-level; interior	Dry areas with brush, often ravines and steep areas with juniper, conifers; usually 5,000+ ft.	Rare vagrant to Midwest, East; regular to S CA
Wilson's	Active; hover-gleans, sallies, fans wings/tail	Low to mid-level	Understory in variety of habitats incl. open mixed and coniferous woods, bogs, willows; often near wet areas	
Worm-eating	Deliberate, acrobatic; hangs, reaches; often in clusters of dead leaves	Low to mid-level; can be higher	Large areas of deciduous and mixed woodlands with understory; often on slopes but also other areas including wet bottomlands	Vagrant to West
Yellow	Gleans, sallies, hover-gleans	Low to mid-level; can be higher; exterior	Thickets, saplings, power-line cuts, brush in open areas; often near water; riparian strips; wide range of elevations, open habitats; wider breeding range than any other New World warbler; strictly deciduous habitats	
Yellow-breasted Chat	Deliberate; gleans; skulky, shy; but often sings in open, high	Low, interior	Dense tangles, thickets in open areas, power-line cuts, old fields, forest edges; or dense brush and thickets in riparian areas	
Yellow-rumped	Very active; gleans, aerial feeding: awkward sallying, hover-gleaning; flips tail, droops wings to reveal yellow rump	Low to high; often on open interior branches; also ground	Coniferous or mixed woodlands	Audubon's is a rare vagrant in East
Yellow-throated	Deliberate; creeps along branches, trunks; probes bark, cones; hangs	High	Varies with range and subspecies; tall trees, deciduous, pines or mixed; swampy bottomlands; deciduous trees along streams	Vagrant in West

NOTE All warblers can exhibit almost any behavior. Even a normally deliberate feeder may pursue prey or hover-glean. The behaviors listed above are general tendencies that may help with preliminary IDs.

The foraging locations apply to birds on their breeding territories, where often several species sharing the same habitat will engage in niche partitioning to avoid conflict, with some species tending to feed in interior and others in the exterior (closer to tips of branches) at different heights. During migration warblers may occupy any available location, but the preferences above can still be helpful clues. This is especially true for skulkers or species found usually on or near the ground.

GLOSSARY

accelerating describes Elements or Phrases gradually speeding up (increasing number of units per time)

adult older than one year; in late summer, when first-year birds become one year old, they molt all of their feathers (prebasic molt) and attain full adult plumage

aging and sexing determining age and sex of bird using plumage characteristics

allopatric occurring in separate geographic ranges

alternate plumage see **breeding plumage**

alula (pl. alulae) small feathered projection just in front of primary coverts; usually not molted by first-year birds

attack fast, accented, possibly harsh beginning of call or Element; usually caused by very Expanded, short sound; especially important characteristic for differentiating chip calls

audio spectrogram see **sonogram**

auriculars facial feathers on side of head, behind and below eye and covering ear

back feathers of upper part of warbler from nape to rump

basic plumage pattern and color of feathers produced by molt or replacement of all feathers in warblers more than one year old, usually after breeding and before migrating to wintering grounds

belly middle of warbler's lower body from breast to legs or vent

braces pair of pale, contrasting back streaks found in all plumages of Blackburnian Warbler

breast front of warbler's lower body from throat to belly

breathy describes Element with some hissing or sibilant thinness; often useful for separating warbler chip calls

breeding plumage pattern and color of feathers found on warblers in spring migration and on breeding grounds; usually a worn fall plumage (see **basic plumage**) but may contain some fresh body feathers acquired during late-winter molt (see **prealternate molt**); flight feathers always worn

Buzz Element consisting of sounds repeated so rapidly it is heard as one dense sound; can sound like noise, but pitch usually discernable

call short vocalization given by both males and females; for warblers usually shorter than 60 ms; two main types: chip and flight; chip calls generally used during day and flight calls during nocturnal migration (presumably to keep flocks together and to maintain distances between birds), but both types can occur during day or night; flight calls usually higher, thinner, and more modulated than chip calls

cap contrasting, usually dark, patch on top of head

cheek patch see **auriculars**

chin area just under bill; very top portion of throat

Clear describes smoothly sung Element; may be slurred or steady in pitch; not Buzzy, Complex, or Trilled; easy to imitate by whistling; Clear song has only Clear Elements

Complex describes rapidly modulated Element with burry or rough quality; not as dense or fast as Buzz; similar to Trill, but shorter, less than 0.3 seconds; Complex song has at least some Complex Elements

Compressed describes Element or Phrase with small pitch span, for example, 3 kHz to 4 kHz (or a 1 kHz pitch span); usually darker, duller sound and less bright than Expanded Element, which has much wider pitch span

chip call see **call**

contrast color standing out from others nearby; an area that is much lighter or darker than those of nearby areas

countable speeds Phrases repeated slowly enough to be easily counted; speeds up to 9 Phrases/sec.

crown top of bird's head, above supercilium (if present)

culmen top edge of upper mandible

dimorphic species with very different-looking males and females or spring and fall plumages

downslur smoothly sung Clear Element that falls in pitch; usually easy to imitate by whistling

Element each separate "event" or sound heard in a song

emphatic describes forceful, distinct effect of short, Expanded Elements with relatively long Intervals

Expanded describes Element with large pitch span; for example, ranging from 3.5 kHz to 8 kHz (a span of 4.5 kHz); often used as a relative term to compare two vocalizations; usually sounds bright and energetic, due to the presence of both high and low frequencies; overall quality affected by speed of the Element, with Short Expanded Elements sounding very harsh and percussive, and Long Expanded Elements sounding rich and pleasing

eye-arcs (eye crescent) contrastingly pale arcs occurring above and below the eye; basically an eyering that is broken both in front of and behind eye

eyeline dark line passing through the eye, varying from long (reaching from the bill to the back of the head) to short (just barely showing on both sides of the eye); when only behind the eye, called a post-ocular line; when just in front, called dark lores

eyering contrastingly pale circle surrounding the eye

fallout migrating birds, exhausted by extreme weather or other environmental and geographic factors, lands in large numbers in a small area; rare event

feather edgings contrastingly pale outer edges of feathers; often describes color found on the edge of the feathers of the folded wing, including the tertials, secondaries, and, sometimes the primaries; also can apply to the margins of the greater secondary coverts, which can blend into the lighter tips on birds with wing bars, creating a wing panel

first-year less than one year old; in late summer of their first year warblers replace some but not all of their feathers (preformative molt); they replace all of their body feathers but retain their primaries, secondaries, tertials, tail feathers, primary coverts and sometimes a few greater or median coverts and a variable number of tertials; adults at this time of year replace all of their feathers (prebasic molt); the retained juvenal feathers of first-year birds are older and become worn and faded; the difference between these feathers and the surrounding, fresher replaced feathers can be an important way of aging these birds

flank side of the bird, extending along the belly to the legs

flaring supercilium narrow supercilium in front of eye that gradually and evenly expands in width as it approaches and passes eye; widest behind eye; often narrows as it ends, sometimes wrapping partly around the head; found in Louisiana Waterthrush

flight call see **call**

flight feathers longest feathers of the wing; include primaries, secondaries (former and latter providing lift and power), and tail feathers (providing lift and steering)

flight song often long, complex songs given while the bird is in display flight (e.g., by Common Yellowthroat)

formative plumage pattern and color of feathers into which juveniles molt shortly after leaving nest (see **preformative molt**); consists of new body feathers and old flight feathers, retaining juvenal primaries, secondaries, alula, tail feathers, primary coverts and sometimes a few greater or median coverts and tertials; usually retained from bird's first fall until the following summer, when complete prebasic molt into adult plumage occurs

greater coverts (technically, greater secondary coverts) feathers that cover bases of secondaries; when tips contrast with feather bases, the tips form the bottom line of wing bars; sometimes the edges of these feathers are also pale and the combination creates a wing panel

goggles eyering combined with a similarly colored supraloral area (e.g., in Canada Warbler)

hertz (Hz) frequency of sound (i.e., speed of its vibrations) in cycles per second; low sounds have slow speeds, e.g. 60 cycles per second (60 Hz), as is a note from a cello; warblers usually sing between 2,500 Hz and 8,000 Hz; 1,000 Hz is usually abbreviated as 1.0 kHz ("k" for *kilo*, meaning "thousand")

hood contrasting, usually darker color on head; usually contrasts with the rest of the bird's body

hotspot location at which migrating birds are often found in relatively large numbers during migration; often created by geographic features such as large bodies of water

hover-gleaning feeding activity in which bird feeds while flying or hovering in the air, picking prey off foliage or other surface; sometimes a good ID point for species like Nashville and Cerulean warblers; different from sally feeding

hybrid (or cross) offspring of two different species that breed together; e.g., Brewster's Warbler is a cross between Golden-winged and Blue-winged warblers; these hybrids can then mate with pure species or other hybrids, creating multigenerational hybrids; Hermit and Townsend's warblers also regularly hybridize in a narrow overlapping range; there are a number of records of less common warbler hybrids, e.g., "Sutton's Warbler," a cross between Northern Parula and Yellow-throated Warbler

immature any warbler less than one year old; any warbler that is not in adult plumage

intergrade offspring of two races of a particular species, not the offspring of two different species (cf. **hybrid**); usually found where the nesting areas of the two races overlap (intergrade zone); young produced are intergrades rather than hybrids; intergrades of Audubon's and Myrtle subspecies of Yellow-rumped Warbler are frequently found during migration in the interior West

Interval space between Elements; length of Interval relative to Element determines whether Phrases sound slurred or more distinct and emphatic

juvenal pattern and color of feathers attained by recently hatched warblers (usually in the nest) replacing natal down; replaced shortly thereafter during the preformative molt; usually very drab and unlike the adult plumage of species; often includes streaked underparts; warblers in juvenal plumage are almost always attended by adults and are usually seen only on breeding grounds.

juvenile bird wearing juvenal plumage; after initiating preformative molt, juveniles are referred to as first-year

kilohertz (kHz) 1,000 Hertz (cycles per second); 5 kHz is 5,000 cycles per second

lateral crown stripe wide, dark stripe on side of crown above the supercilium (if present), e.g., on Worm-eating Warbler

lesser coverts (technically, lesser secondary coverts) small feathers just above the alula and median coverts; part of shoulder; not well differentiated in warblers

long describes Element or Phrase usually lasting more than 150 ms; Clear, Expanded Elements, with a wide Pitch range, sound pleasing to the ear when the Element is long because we have time to hear all of the frequencies clearly

lores area between the bill and the eye

lower mandible lower half of the bill; also known as "mandible"

malar narrow region of feathers extending from base of lower mandible toward or to shoulder, bordering throat

mantle feathers of upper back

median coverts feathers covering base of greater coverts; when pale feather tips contrast with dark bases, form top line of wing bar

median crown stripe usually pale, contrasting stripe in center of crown (e.g., on Yellow-rumped Warbler)

metallic describes harsh sound created by many high frequencies in short period; found in Expanded but very short Elements (usually less than 100 ms)

millisecond (ms) 1/1000 of a second; 1/10th of a second is 100 ms

mnemonic aid to memory; for example, images that link name of bird to general first impression of its song

modulated describes very fast changes in pitch that create roughness, harshness, or burry quality in sound; often useful for describing or differentiating Complex calls

molt; molting process in which some or all of bird's feathers are replaced; warblers undergo several molts, complete or partial feather replacements, during their life. The first plumage is the natal down, which is soon molted (prejuvenal molt) to the juvenal plumage. After a short period of time, usually only a couple of weeks, the bird undergoes its preformative molt, replacing all of its body feathers but retaining all of the flight feathers, tail feathers, primary coverts, alula, and sometimes a few greater or median covert and/or tertials; on the wintering grounds or on the way to the breeding grounds some warbler species replace a few of their body feathers in a prealternate molt. Finally, all warblers more than a year old, in late summer, replace all of their feathers in their prebasic molt.

molt limit in first-year birds, boundary between older feathers and newer feathers; usually applies to area of retained juvenal greater or median coverts next to a few new coverts replaced in the preformative molt; older feathers often look duller or browner

monotypic species with only one plumage type, such as Louisiana Waterthrush, in which all ages and sexes look very similar

neck general area between shoulder and face; used in warbler descriptions primarily when referencing light contrasting spots on the side of the neck (e.g., on Bay-breasted and Cape May warblers)

necklace narrow band of contrasting dark markings across upper breast (e.g., on Magnolia or Canada Warblers)

night songs extended vocalizations sung after dark by some warblers (e.g., Ovenbird)

notched describes tail with V-shaped gap at end; whereas many warblers show this, depending on the position of the tail, some species, like Pine Warbler and various sparrows, have a more uniquely shaped notch that deserves more attention, as noted in the text.

percussive describes rhythmic effect created by Phrases with short, Expanded Elements and long Intervals; generally, emphatic effect of many frequencies assaulting our ears in a short period of time

Phrase single, isolated Element, or grouping of one, two, three, or more repeated Elements

Phrases per second (P/sec.) speed of Section or song; sonograms make it easy to calculate Sectional speeds, which can sometimes be used to differentiate similar species. For example, the first Section of Orange-crowned Warblers' songs average 16 P/sec., Trill speed; Wilson's first Sections are always obviously slower, averaging 7 P/sec.

pitch frequency of an Element, usually given in kHz (see **kilohertz**); most warblers sing at pitches from 2.5 kHz to 8.5 kHz

pitch profile overall direction of the frequencies of an Element, Phrase, Section or song; can be rising, falling, steady, or variable; an upslur would have a rising pitch profile; a 2-Element Phrase that starts with a high Element and ends with a low Element would have a falling pitch profile; a Section with each Phrase lower than the previous would have a falling pitch profile

pitch span range of frequencies in an Element or song; an Element that starts at 3.5 kHz and ends at 8 kHz would have an Expanded pitch span of 4.5 kHz

plumage pattern and color of feathers; warblers can change their plumage by undergoing a molt that could include some or all body feathers, or a complete molt of all feathers

post-ocular line partial eyeline that does not include the lores but extends backward from the eye

prealternate molt process of replacing feathers on the wintering grounds or during spring migration resulting in breeding plumage; never includes any flight feathers; many warblers do not have a prealternate molt, and those that do generally replace few feathers; most common in species that have a drastic change from fall to spring plumage, e.g. Bay-breasted Warbler

prebasic molt in warblers, process of replacing all feathers after breeding season, generally before fall migration, by adults, not juveniles (who undergo preformative molt)

preformative molt process of replacing juvenal plumage by recently fledged warblers; replaces all body feathers but retains flight feathers, tail feathers, primary coverts and sometimes a few greater or median coverts and variable number of tertials; resulting plumage is formative plumage and is generally retained until following summer

primaries for warblers, nine outer and longest flight feathers of wing; provide power for forward movement through air; bottom layer of the stacked feathers on a folded wing

primary coverts (technically, **greater primary coverts**) small feathers covering base of primaries; retained by first-year birds; wear, and therefore color, compared with adjacent, fresher greater coverts, can help age some birds

primary projection on folded wing, extension of primaries past tip of longest tertial

race (see also **subspecies**) distinct populations of a species generally separated geographically. Some races are populations diverent enough to be formally named and accepted as a different subspecies. In other cases, separate populations are divergent enough to be designated as races but may be too similar to be accepted as a formal subspecies.

rectrices (sing. **rectrix**) tail feathers; six on each side in warblers; tips of adult rectrices more rounded than the more pointed tips of first-year birds in some species, aiding in aging and sexing; can be very worn in spring and early summer birds of all ages, especially so in first-year birds

remiges (sing. **remex**) long feathers of wing (primaries and secondaries); generate power and lift in flight

rhythm patterns formed by repetition of Elements and Phrases throughout a song; may be steady, irregular, or can speed up or slow down

rictal bristles longish, stiff, hair-like bristles extending from base of bill in nearly all warbler species; presumed to assist in capturing flying prey; particularly evident on highly aerial species (e.g., American Redstart); Common Yellowthroat nearly unique among warblers in lacking them

rump feathers above uppertail coverts and below back; several warbler species have contrasting yellow rumps (e.g., Yellow-rumped and Cape May warblers) which can aid in identification

sally feeding method in which a warbler flies from perch to catch prey then flies to the same or nearby perch; American Redstart a particularly good example

scapulars body feathers on the upper parts covering base of wing; part of shoulder

secondaries inner flight feathers providing lift for flight; on folded wing, the middle layer of stacked feathers between primaries and tertials

Sections groups of similar, repeated Phrases, differentiated by abrupt change in Phrase pitch, speed, and/or type

shaft streaks black streaks along feather shafts; contrast with paler webbing; important aging and sexing character when in coverts of some species but difficult to see without having bird in hand

short describes Elements lasting for very brief period; for songs, usually less than 50 ms; for calls, often less than 20 ms; Expanded Elements that last a short time assault the ear with many frequencies, too fast to hear separately, creating emphatic, percussive quality

shoulder area around and above bend of folded wing; consists of lesser coverts and scapulars; not well defined in warblers

side stripe wide contrasting band, usually black or chestnut, extending along sides of breast and flanks; can be short, ending before the belly, or longer, extending past the legs.

slurred describes Phrases separated by very short Intervals and thus run together, sounding almost smeared or joined one to the next

songs vocalizations sung by males to attract mates and defend territories; many warbler genera (e.g., *Setophaga*) have at least two types: accented, used to attract mates and sung more often during day; unaccented, used to defend territories, most often heard at dawn and dusk; other genera (e.g., *Geothlypis*) have one main song form and one less-common extended song given in display flight; rarely, females have been documented singing songs in some species

sonogram analysis of audio file presented in graphical form; vertical, or Y, axis represents frequency; horizontal, or X, axis represents time; density (darkness) of graphic represents volume

sotto voce very soft (referring to all or part of a song, often more rushed); can be given by young birds or sometimes during fall migration when full songs are not given as often

staccato short, Compressed Element with relatively long Interval; sounds distinct and very short

streaking contrasting or colored lines; found on crowns, backs, flanks, and breasts; thinner than side stripes; can be fairly wide (Magnolia) or very fine (Blackpoll spring female); density, especially in center of upper breast and throat, can be important ID point, as in separating Northern and Louisiana waterthrushes

stripe; striping wide, contrasting dark or colored bands; usually found as median crown stripes (e.g., Worm-eating Warbler) or side stripes (e.g., Chestnut-sided Warbler)

subspecies (see **races**) taxonomic category below species; generally separated geographically; not always distinguishable morphologically but sometimes by other characteristics; because of ability to interbreed with other birds of same species and other characteristics, not considered a separate species. These divisions may change over time, e.g., Yellow-rumped Warblers were once thought of as two species, Audubon's and Myrtle, but are now considered two races of the same species. The subspecies is indicated by a third word in the Latin name, e.g., the two races of Northern Waterthrush are called *Parkesia noveboracensis noveboracencis* (the "nominate"; abbreviated *P.n. noveboracencis*) and *Parkesia noveboracensis notabilis* (abbreviated *P.n. notabilis*)

supercilium contrasting lighter area over eye from the supraloral area to behind eye (may include supraloral); can be very long and wide, very thin, or very short without much contrast; usually but not always associated with a dark contrasting eyeline; sometimes created by a contrasting dark crown and cheek patch, as in Northern Waterthrush or Wilson's Warbler

superspecies group of closely related species with common ancestor; often similar in appearance; the best warbler example is *virens* group (Black-throated Green, Townsend's, Hermit, Golden-cheeked and, by some accounts, Black-throated Gray Warblers); presumed to have arisen due to relatively recent geological event(s) that separated ancestor species into various separate ranges where resulting species differentiated in isolation

supraloral area region between crown and lores; usually pale and contrasting with darker lores; can connect to an eyering, forming goggles, or merge with supercilium

sympatric describes two species that share at least some part of their geographical ranges

tail projection from underside, length of tail visible beyond undertail coverts; from above, length of tail visible beyond uppertail coverts; note that tail projection may appear different from above and below; can be important in differentiating similar species, such as MacGillivray's from Mourning, and Blackpoll from Pine

tail spot white or pale area surrounded by dark near end of outer tail feathers

tertials three innermost and widest wing feathers on trailing edge of wing; adjacent to secondaries; cover junction of body and wing, smoothing wing shape for more efficient flight; on closed wing, compose top layer of stacked feathers, protecting secondaries and primaries, which are folded under them; contrasting white or light edging can be good ID point (e.g., for Blackpoll Warbler)

throat area below bill and chin and above breast; bordered on the sides by malar region

transocular line see **eyeline**

Trill Phrases repeated too quickly to count—faster than nine Elements per second; unlike Buzzes, individual Elements can be heard; Trills last longer than 300 ms; Complex Elements similar but shorter (less than 300 ms)

uncountable speed Phrases occurring at rate too fast to count; more than nine Elements per second; see also **Trill**

under-eye arc contrasting semicircle under eye, as in female Black-throated Blue Warbler

undertail coverts (UnTC) feathers covering base of underside of tail; extend from vent to partway under tail; see also **tail projection**

up/down slur smoothly sung Element that first rises in pitch and then, without a break, falls in pitch; important form found in some warbler chip calls

upper mandible upper half of bill (also known as maxilla)

uppertail coverts feathers extending from rump and covering base of upper tail; extend partway over tail; color and/or pattern sometimes important aging and sexing point

upslur smoothly sung Clear Element obviously rising in pitch; easily imitated by whistling; quality determined by how long or short it lasts and by degree to which pitch span is Expanded or Compressed

vent area between legs in front of the undertail coverts and below belly; feathers of area often appear fluffier than surrounding feathers

virens group see **superspecies**

warblers more correctly, wood-warblers, which distinguishes New World species of the 9-primaried *Parulidae* family from Old World species; small, usually insectivorous birds, most highly migratory; successful and prolific; during breeding season density in northeastern United States reported to exceed that of all other birds combined

wing bars formed by contrasting white or paler tips on greater and median coverts

wing panel formed by pale contrasting tips of median coverts and tips and edgings of greater coverts blending together to form single contrasting area

RESOURCES

There are many great resources available for anyone interested in expanding their knowledge of warblers beyond the information we have been able to fit into these pages. Below are just a few of these resources.

www. press.princeton.edu/titles/9968.html This is our website, and it contains a host of additional information on identification, upcoming events, and other bird-related topics, as well links to warbler and birding-related sites. You can also find us on Facebook as TheWarblerGuide.

Books

American Warblers by Douglass Morse. Cambridge, MA, 1989: a classic text that compiles and expands on a wide range of research on the evolution and behavior of warblers in the U.S.

Bird Song by C. K. Catchpole and P.J.B. Slater. Cambridge, UK, 2008: an overview of research on how birds develop and use song

A Field Guide to Warblers of North America by Jon Dunn and Kimball Garrett. Boston, 1997: an immensely interesting and valuable compendium of information on all aspects of warbler identification, behavior and life histories

Identification Guide to North American Birds, Parts I and II by Peter Pyle. Bolinas, CA, 1987: technical information geared towards banders but has much interesting data on aging and sexing warblers

Pete Dunne's Essential Field Guide Companion by Pete Dunne. Boston, 2006: a good resource by a very experienced birder; especially useful information on behavior and flight characteristics

The Singing Life of Birds by Donald Kroodsma. Boston, 2005: an entertaining account of many aspects of bird song by an author with a long history of bird-song research

Stokes Field Guide to Warblers by Donald and Lillian Stokes. Boston, 2004

Warblers of the Americas by Jon Curson, David Quinn, and David Beadle. Boston, 1994: the only comprehensive guide to New World warblers, with many illustrations and other valuable information

Warblers of the Great Lakes Region and Eastern North America by Chris G. Earley. Toronto, 2003

Some other classic texts include *Life Histories of North American Wood Warblers* by Arthur C. Bent, Washington, DC, 1953; *The Warblers of North America* by Frank Chapman, NY, 1968; *The Warblers of America* by Ludlow Griscom and Alexander Sprunt, Jr., Garden City, NY, 1979; *Ornithology* by Frank Gill, NY, 2007

Audio

Songs of the Warblers of North America by Donald Borror and William Gunn: extensive collection available from Cornell University as a download

Stokes Field Guide to Bird Songs by D. and L. Stokes, Lang Elliott, and Kevin Colver

Research Papers

There are many research papers on warbler life histories, vocalizations, and all aspects of warbler life. Most large public libraries provide databases, such as the EBSCO host research database, that can be searched for topics of personal interest. Finding articles on common breeding birds in one's local area can be particularly interesting. Below are a few samples of available research papers.

Acoustic and Physical Models of Bird Sounds by S. Fagerlund, thesis, 2004

Acoustical Monitoring in Terrestrial Environments Using Microphone Arrays by D. Blumstein et al., *Journal of Applied Ecology* 48

Can Song Discriminate between MacGillivray's and Mourning Warblers in a Narrow Hybrid Zone? by Kenyon Haley et al., *The Condor* 113.3

Detecting Tropical Nocturnal Birds Using Automated Audio Recordings by J. Goyette et al., *Journal of Field Ornithology* 82.3

Female Song in the Hooded Warbler by L. J. Evans Ogden et al., *Northeastern Naturalist* 10.4

The Flight Songs of Common Yellowthroat by Gary Ritchison, *The Condor* 93

Food Supplementation, Territory Establishment, and Song in the Prothonotary Warbler by Charles E. Clarkson, *Wilson Journal of Ornithology* 119.3

Geographic Variation in Type I Songs of Black-Throated Gray Warblers by S.W. Janes et al., *Wilson Journal of Ornithology* 123.2

Independent Cultural Evolution of Two Song Traditions in the Chestnut-Sided Warbler by B. E. Byers et al., *American Naturalist* 176.4

Interspecific Song Imitation by a Cerulean Warbler by T. J. Boves et al., *Wilson Journal of Ornithology* 122.3

Test of Two Alarm Calls Given By Yellow Warbler during Nest Defence by S. Gill and S. Sealey, *Canadian Journal of Zoology* 81

Three Hybrid Zones between Hermit and Townsend's Warblers in Washington and Oregon by S. Rohwer and C. Wood, *The Auk*, 115.2

Variation in Vocal Performance in the Song of a Wood-warbler by M. Beebee, *Ethology* 110

Vocalization Attributes Of Cerulean Warbler Song and Pairing Status by S. R. McKillip et al., *Wilson Journal of Ornithology* 121.2

Wood-warbler Song Systems by David A. Spector, *Current Ornithology* 9: a valuable summary of research on warbler song types

Web Resources

There is a vast amount of information about birds and warblers on the internet, some very valuable, some less so. Due to the transient nature of the web in general, we here list only a few sites. Using a search engine can reveal the latest information on an ID problem or photos of a favorite warbler.

eBird *www.ebird.org* This site, a joint project by Cornell University's Lab of Ornithology and the Audubon Society, is a very valuable resource for current and some historical sightings of any warbler or other bird species. And by using it to post personal sighting records, one is increasing the status and distribution data available on the site, which serves a wide range of birders and researchers.

Surfbirds *www.surfbirds.com* A good example of a birder-run site that features trip reports, photo galleries, articles on identification and technology, and user forums.

Cornell University's All About Birds *www.allaboutbirds.org* Videos, photos and vocalizations of U.S. birds along with articles on identification and skill-building.

Frontiers of ID *birdingonthe.net/mailinglists/FRID.html* A user-driven forum on advanced bird identification

BirdCast *www.birdcast.info* An exciting site that is working on bird migration forecasting in real time

Birding Festivals

Birding festivals occur seasonally across the U.S., especially in hot spots. There are many great festivals, and here we list just a few. Search the web for festivals hosted in areas with species of personal interest.

Rio Grande Birding Festival *www.rgvbf.org*
Space Coast Birding and Wildlife Festival *www.spacecoastbirdingandwildlifefestival.org*
Crane Creek/Magee Marsh *cranecreekbirding.blogspot.com*
Cape May Birding Festival *www.birdcapemay.org*

Apps

There are many useful sources of bird ID information for the portable iPhone, iPad and Android platforms. Check the internet for the latest apps.

Sibley Birds App Convenient, digital version of one of the best field guides to U.S. birds

BirdTunes App Good collection of several song and call variations for most U.S. bird species; well-recorded by Lang Elliott

BirdsEye App Portal to Cornell's eBird that lists all of the birds seen near your location in the last few days, it can be used to find reports of specific rarities and also for keeping your own trip lists

Other Resources

The American Birding Association provides a magazine, *Birding*, which features articles on identification, photo quizzes, and other valuable information such as technical reviews. It also runs birding festivals, events for young birders, and guided bird tours in the U.S. and other countries. **Local Audubon Societies** run guided bird walks and can be a great way of learning more about local birding spots and resident and migrant species.

ACKNOWLEDGMENTS

We would like to thank the following people in the creation of this book:

Russ Galen and Robert Kirk for sharing our vision and shepherding it to reality; Tony Leukering for his invaluable knowledge and advice; Leslie Flis, Ellen Foos, and the Princeton team for their tireless efforts in design and production; Michael O'Brien, Kevin Karlson, Mike Lanzone, Sam Galick, Tom Johnson, and all the photographers who so graciously allowed us to use their images and audio files; Andrew Farnsworth, Glen Davis, Andrew Vallely, and Dale Dyer; Josh Engel, John Bates, Dave Willard, Ben Marks, and everyone at the Field Museum; Cameron Rutt for his valuable notes on warblers in flight; Dr. Irby Lovette for his research on warbler taxonomy and for allowing us to reproduce it in this book; Mark Stephenson, Mabel Thompson, and Dorothy McIlroy for getting TS started; Arthur Allen and Peter Paul Kellogg for their mentoring (TS); Greg Budney, Karl Fitzke, William McQuay, Tammy Bishop, Mary Guthrie, and everyone at the Cornell Lab of Ornithology; Chris Wood, Jessie Barry, and the eBird team; Larry Allen, Kimball Garrett, and the LA County Museum; Paul Sweet, John Ascher, and the American Museum of Natural History; Nick and Mary Freeman; Peter Dorosh, Rob Bate, Steve and Heidi Nanz, and the Brooklyn Bird Club; Jeff Nulle, Alice Deutsch, Gil Schrank, and The Linnaean Society of NY; Liz and Jeff Gordon, and everyone at the ABA ; Keith Barnes, Andrew Spenser; Stephen Ingraham, Rich Moncrief, and everyone at Zeiss; John Askildsen, Tom Burke; Glenn Phillips, and NYC Audubon; Molly Pollock; Amy Mintzer; Cin-Ty Lee, Andy Birch, and everyone at Surfbirds; Rob Jett; Brendan Wenzel and Keith and Virginia DuQuette for help with the icons; Kevin McDonnell; all the members of our focus group including Adam Welz, Michael Yuan, Matthew Rymkiewicz, Dennis Hrehowsik, Keir Randall, Dolores Brandon, Janet Schumacher, Matt Beck, Roberta Manian, Randolph Schutz, Stanley Greenberg, Phil Malek, Lynne Hertzog, Ed Crowne, Monica Berger, and Lenore Swenson; Scott Wegner; and especially TS's lovely wife Wendy, for all of her support and patience.

PHOTO CREDITS

For photos that appear multiple times, only the primary occurence is listed; letters designate page position, from left to right, top to bottom

Linda Alley Mourning p.353F

Michele Amyot Blackburnian p.166B Mourning p.350C Yellow p.466D

Kurt Anderson Townsend's p.443C

Danny Bales Golden-winged p.280C Grace's p.289C

Tony Battiste HermitxTownsend's p.524D

David D. Beadle Prairie p.410F

Giff Beaton N. Parula p.369F

Matt Brady Black-th. Gray p.196C Canada p.219E Connecticutx4 p.265E,H,I p.271H Golden-winged p.281I Palm p.399E Townsend's p.443F

Daniel Lee Brown Colima p.248C

Steve Brown Chestnut-sided p.241C Connecticutx3 p.265G,L p.270A MacGillivray's p.337G,H Mourning p. 353B Ovenbird p. 387B Virginia's p.449C

Michael H. Bruce Red-faced p.422C

Jim Burns Golden-crowned p.502A Olive p.522D Virginia'sx2 p.446B p.447E

John Cahill Crescent-chested p.498E Golden-crowned p.502C

Scott Cartier Connecticut p.270B

Allen T. Chartier Black-and-whitex? p.524C

Jon Cross Connecticut p.267B

Jeff Davis Swainson's p.429J

Don Delaney Canada p.216B

Gerard R. Dewaghe Black-and-white p.160B Connecticut p.264B Yellow p.467G

Robin Diaz Cerulean p.235D Golden-winged p.283C Kentucky p.309C Prothonotary p.419D

Kevin Doxstater Grace's p.289B

Rachel Echols Magnolia p.343E

Gil Eckrich Golden-cheekedx7 p.275J,K p.277A,B,D,E,F

Mary Carmona Freeman Hermit p.294D Yellow-br. Chat p.501C

Don Freiday Bay-breasted p.153G

Sam Galick Bay-breasted p.157J Canadax2 p. 535A,C

Doug Gochfeld L. Waterthrush p.000A Palm p.399F Ovenbird p.385K Yellow p.470A

Tony Godfrey Golden-crowned p.502B

Rob Gofreed Golden-winged p.280D

Manuel Grosslet and Georgita Ruiz S-t. Redstartx2 p.508A,B Golden-crowned p.502D G-c. Yellowthroatx2 p.504A,B

Marcel Holyoak S-t. Redstart p.508D

Frode Jacobsen Brewster's p.215A Hooded p.300D L. Waterthrush p.318B Nashville p.363C

Phil Jeffrey Chestnut-sided p.244A Hermit p.294B

Tom Johnson Audubon's p.535A Black-th. Gray p.196B Connecticutx4 p.271J p.535A,B,C Lucy'sx3 p.325N p.534A,B MacGillivray'sx3 p.331K p.337F Orange-crowned p.378A Prairie p.413C Wilson'sx2 p.455F,G Worm-eatingx2 p.534A,B Yellow p.470C Yellow-br. Chat p.536A

Kevin Karlson Hooded p.303C Lucy's p.325O Palm p.399C Prairie p.000A Swainson'sx5 p.429F,H,I,K,L Wilson's p.452B

David Kenyon/Michigan DNR Kirtland'sx2 p.313H,M

Tiffany L. Kersten Bay-breasted p.153F

Michael Kolakowski Ovenbird p.384C

Apiradee Lahrungsikul Fan-tailed p.500E

Michael J. Lanzone Black-th. Gray p.199B Cape May p.225E Cerulean p.235E Connecticutx4 p.267D,E p.271I p.50C Crescent-chestedx2 p.498C,D Fan-tailedx2 p.500C,D Golden-crowned p.502E Golden-winged p.283D Grace'sx2 p.289D,E Hermit p.297E Kentucky p.309D Lawrence's p.215E Lucy's p.325J MacGillivray'sx3 p.333J p.337K,L Mourningx5 p.353C,D p.357H,I p.50D Nashville p.363E P. Redstart p.390C Palm p.399B Rufous-capped p.506C S-t. Redstart p.508C Sutton's p.525D T. Parula p.510C Virginia'sx3 p.447F,L p.449A Wilson'sx2 p.453N p.455B Yellow-throated p.493L

Greg Lasley Colima p.249F Golden-cheekedx2 p.274A,B G-c. Yellowthroat p.504C Orange-crowned p.378B Yellow p.470F Yellow-throated p.495B

Peter LaTourrette Lucy's p.324A

Greg Lavaty Blackpoll p.179A Colima p.248B Red-faced p.422C T. Parula p.510B

Tony Leukering MyrtlexAudubon's p.525E Cape May p.535B

Matt Levanowitz Blackburnian p.172C

William Lynch Prairie p.410B

W.H. Majoros Palm p.396D Prairie p.410C

William McHale Brewster's p.214A Mourning p.350B

Ryan Merrill MacGillivray's p.333E

Bruce Miller Kirtland'sx2 p.312B,C

Steve Mlodinow Yellowx4 p.470D,E,G,I

Jeffery S. Moore Myrtle p.476C, T. Parula 510E

Steve Nanz Black-and-white p.163E Cape May p.222A Hermit p.294C Lucy's p.325K Wilson's p.455C Yellow p.469D

Alex Navarro Crescent-chested p.498A

John Norton G-c. Yellowthroat p.504D

Michael O'Brien A. Redstartx2 p.535A,C Black-and-white p.535B Bay-breastedx2 p.534C Blackburnianx3 p.534A,B,C Blackpollx2 p.534A,B Black-th. Bluex4 p.189C p.535A p.536A,C Black-th. Green p.534C Blue-wingedx2 p.535A,B Canada p.535B Cape Mayx3 p.534A,B,C G-c. Yellowthroat p.504E L. Waterthrush p.534B Magnoliax3 p.536A,B,C Myrtlex3 p.534A,B,C Nashville p.536C N. Parulax2 p.535A,C N. Waterthrush p.534C Ovenbirdx2 p.534A,B Palmx3 p.535A,C Pinex3 p.534A,B,C Prairiex2 p.536A Prothonotaryx3 p.536A,B,C Tennesseex2 p.536B,C Townsend's p.535A Wilson's p.536B Yellowx2 p.536A Yellow-throated p.535C

Joel B. Paige C. Yellowthroat p.256B

Lora L. Render Golden-cheeked p.274C

Robert Royse Audubon's p.485F Blackpoll p.179C Cerulean p.232A Chestnut-backed Chickadee p. 198E Connecticutx2 p.264A p.273 C. Yellowthroatx2 p.254A,B Golden-winged p.280A Grace's p.286A Hermit p.294A Lucy'sx2 p.325P p.327A MacGillivray's p.330A Mourning p.350A N. Waterthrushx2 p.372A p.375C Olive p.522A P. Redstart p.390A Pine p.402A Prairiex2 p.410A p.413D Prothonotary p.419E Swainson's p.428A Virginia's p.446A Yellow-br. Chat p.520A

Alan Schmierer Hermitx2 p.294A,F MacGillivray'sx2 p.336B p.337E Rufous-cappedx2 p.506B,D Townsend's p.443D Yellow p.470B

Bill Schmoker Bay-breasted p.153C MacGillivray's p.333D

Dominic Sherony S-t. Redstart p.508E

Brian Small Audubon'sx3 p.485C,D,E Bell's Vireo p.517D Black-th. Gray p.199A Cerulean p.232B Hermit p.297B Lucy's p.324B MacGillivray'sx2 p.336A p.337J Myrtle p.476A Nashville p.363D Olive p.522B Verdin p.514A

Allen Smith Nashville p.360B

Bryan Smith Fan-tailedx2 p.500A,B

David Speiser Black-and-white p.160A Black-th. Gray p.196A Colimax4 p.248A, 249E,G,H Kirtland's p.313M

Lloyd Spitalnik Brewster's p.215C Black-th. Blue p.187N,O Black-th. Green p.205B Blue-wingedx2 p.280B Hooded p.303D Mourning p.353E N. Parula p.369F Orange-crowned p.381C

Mary Beth Stowe Mourning p.356A

Scott Surner N. Waterthrush p.372C

Christopher Taylor Audubon'sx2 p.480D p.485G Black-th. Green p.205C Black-th. Gray p.199E Canada p. 219B Hermit p.297D Kirtland's p.312A Magnolia p.346A Prairie p.413C Rufous-capped p.506A Townsend's p.443B Wilson's p.455D Yellow p.466B Yellow-throated Vireo p.516B

Glen Tepke MacGillivray's p.330B Virginia's p.446C

Jeremiah Trimble Kentucky p.306B

J.-Maurice Turgeon N. Waterthrush p.372B

Peter "U" Usayto Blackpoll p.179B Black-th. Blue p.186A Blackburnian p.166A Canada p.216C

A. Richard Vial T. Parula p.510A

Glenn Walbek Virginia's p.447M

Chris West Crescent-chested p.498B

Richard T. Williams Bay-breasted p.156B Magnolia p.346B Mourning p.356B

Christopher Wood Bay-breasted p.156A Connecticut p.264C Lawrence's p.214B Rufous-capped p.506E

Joseph Wunderle Kirtland'sx4 p.313K,L p.315C,D

Roger Zachary Golden-cheeked p.274D

All other photos copyright Scott Whittle and Tom Stephenson. All museum skin photos by Tom Stephenson and courtesy the Field Museum of Natural History, Chicago, IL